A CENTURY TURNS

A CENTURY TURNS

New Hopes, New Fears

William J. Bennett

THOMAS NELSON
Since 1798

NASHVILLE   DALLAS   MEXICO CITY   RIO DE JANEIRO

Published in Nashville, Tennessee, by Thomas Nelson. Thomas Nelson is a registered trademark of Thomas Nelson, Inc.

Thomas Nelson, Inc., titles may be purchased in bulk for educational, business, fund-raising, or sales promotional use. For information, please e-mail SpecialMarkets@ ThomasNelson.com.

Library of Congress Cataloging-in-Publication Data

Bennett, William J. (William John), 1943–
    A century turns : new hopes, new fears / William J. Bennett.
      p. cm.
    Includes bibliographical references and index.
    ISBN 978-1-59555-169-6
    1. United States—Politics and government—1989– 2. United States—Social conditions—1980– 3. Political culture—United States—History. 4. Social change—United States—History. 5. United States—Foreign relations—1989– I. Title.
E881.B46 2009
973.92—dc22   2009042916

Printed in the United States of America

10 11 12 13 14 WC 5 4 3 2 1

To all the men and women—in uniform and out—who sacrifice to keep us safe, as embodied in the life and heroism of Rick Rescorla.

Contents

Introduction

I was not going to write this book—at least not right now. I concluded *America: The Last Best Hope*, volume II, with 1989, the last full year of the presidency of Ronald Wilson Reagan. In the epilogue, among other things, I wrote the following:

> I cannot find the right words yet to dispassionately describe the relevant history of what we have gone through since his [Ronald Reagan's] presidency ended. This is not because of my partisan or ideological convictions. Rather, it is because I believe more time needs to pass for us to fully and completely digest the history of the past two decades. Many of the players and actors of the past twenty years are still alive, and I wish to be fair to the times and root out any possible prejudice occasioned by my own association with the actors in this drama.

This was my position in 2006. But supply, as economists like to say, provides its own demand; just as demand can create its own supply. And since volume II's publication, a particular demand has arisen that I never expected: teachers across the country have taken volumes I and II and turned them into a vast American history curriculum, both in print and online (see RoadmapToLastBestHope.com), and several state and city school districts have put the books and supplemental materials on their official adoption lists for the classrooms in their states and cities. Student and teacher editions have been created, and I have received many letters, telephone calls, and e-mails asking for a third volume, a volume that brings us up to date over the past twenty years. History courses ought to be able to take us as close to the present as possible.

While I raised all my objections to a third volume, my correspondents and callers remained persistent and unconvinced. I kept an open mind, and noticing the demand from students and teachers alike, I changed it. John Maynard Keynes famously said, "When the facts change, I change my mind," and so, upon reflection, did I.

In thinking about volume III—the last twenty years—I realized how long such a span can, in fact, be. Take some examples: twenty years before Ronald Reagan was nominated as the Republican candidate for president of the United States in 1980, he was still a Democrat. Twenty years after Ronald Reagan was elected president in 1980, his vice president's son was elected president of the United States.

Almost twenty years after his resignation from the presidency in 1974, Richard M. Nixon was eulogized by President Bill Clinton, who, in 1974, was a law professor at the University of Arkansas running for a seat in Congress. At the same time, Bill Clinton's girlfriend, Hillary Rodham, had just finished service on the House Judiciary Committee staff investigating the possible impeachment of Richard M. Nixon. And one year before that, Monica Lewinsky (whose affair with President Clinton would lead to his actual impeachment) was born. Twenty years before this writing, few people in America knew who Hillary Clinton was, and Bill Clinton was a governor from Arkansas whose only national reputation—to the degree he had one at all—was for having delivered a long-winded speech at the 1988 Democratic National Convention. Margaret Thatcher was the prime minister of Great Britain twenty years ago; John McCain was serving his third year in the Senate; and Colin Powell had just been promoted to chairman of the Joint Chiefs of Staff.

Twenty years ago in our political and popular culture, there was no Fox News Channel; there was no *Tonight Show with Jay Leno*, no *Daily Show with Jon Stewart*, no *American Idol*, no Jonas Brothers, no Taylor Swift, no *Hannah Montana*. Chris Matthews was a reporter for the *San Francisco Chronicle*. Sean Hannity was just beginning his career in local talk radio. Most of the country had not heard of Anchorage sportscaster Sarah Palin.

And nobody but their families and friends had heard of Britney Spears, Jessica Simpson, Jennifer Lopez, Toby Keith, Tim McGraw, Justin Timberlake, Reese Witherspoon, Angelina Jolie, Jennifer Aniston, or Leonardo DiCaprio. The world did know of tyrants Saddam Hussein and the Ayatollah Ruholla Khomeini of Iraq and Iran, respectively. To the degree George W. Bush was known, it was as the fairly unnoticeable son of the then president and as the owner of a Texas baseball team.

Twenty years is a long time. Twenty years ago, if you had asked someone to "e-mail me" or said, "check out my Web site (or blog)," or began a phrase with "www" or asked if an article was "available online" or tried to tell someone what was on your "iPod playlist," you would have received a blank stare. "Amazon" was known simply as a forest in South America, "blackberry" was a fruit, and "google" meant nothing.*

Twenty years before this writing, a young man named Barack Obama— a second-year law student—was just elected the first black president of the *Harvard Law Review*.

A Note on the Sourcing

Finally, a note on the use of the first person and sources in this volume. I lived through almost all of the history written about here—and was involved in much of it, from the important to the ancillary. For this and other reasons, I relied less on other history books and documents and more on my own memories and contemporary notes than usual. In an effort to reveal conflicts of interest as well as to show the younger reader where some of my insights come from, a good number of personal anecdotes and self-reference is made: not for vainglory but—intentionally—for context.

---

* It certainly wasn't a verb. The search engine and software development company apparently took its name from something only mathematicians would recognize, the word *googol*, a noun signifying the value of ten raised to the hundredth power.

One

Enemies Abroad, Challenges at Home

Two things about George H. W. Bush: he was the kindest boss I ever had. A man of great decency, concerned for others' personal well-being and family, he said yes to any meeting requested and returned every phone call I ever placed to him. His handwritten and typed notes were models of decorum and goodwill, always with an inquiry or wish for a family member or family event he knew about. He was also tremendously athletic—an avid jogger and tennis player, a fine line-drive hitter, to say nothing of skydiving in his retirement. But when spending time with George H. W. Bush, one could not help picking up one overarching sense and theme of the man: a deep, abiding love of country—a quiet patriotism that stirred constantly within. Nowhere did I see this more pronounced than in a 1990 trip to Portland, Oregon, with him. We were looking out a hotel window, predawn, when I had agreed to go jogging with him, and he saw protestors outside burning a pile of items, protesting any number of things. One thing they burned was the American flag. President Bush turned to me and said, "I understand these young people and their protests—but what really gets to me is when they burn the American flag. Nothing gets me like that. Can anything be more disrespectful? Do they have any idea of what people have done to keep that flag held high?" I remember thinking, If only the rest of the world could hear this man and the weight he puts in his deeply reflective moments like that—if only they could see his sense of

America. He would be more loved. *But that was not the public President Bush; he was always more comfortable keeping his deepest feelings private. To my mind, he was a very emotional man who cared about more people and things than the public record, or he, would ever show.*

The years 1988 to 1992 were momentous—in the world and at home we would see CDs outsell vinyl records for the first time and the debut of such famous television shows as Seinfeld *and* The Simpsons; *the Ayatollah Ruholla Khomeini would call for an international death threat on a British author popular in America and would (himself) die of natural causes in 1989; terrorism would become more pronounced as a violent means of political expression with more Americans being targeted; an Egyptian cleric named Omar Abdel-Rahman (also known as the "Blind Sheikh") would move to America; the Berlin Wall would fall; and the issue of race relations would once again become front and center in American culture and politics—sparked by an incident on the streets of Los Angeles and by the nomination of a second black man to the Supreme Court.*

I. The Choppy Seas of the 1988 Election

Vice President George H. W. Bush had a distinguished career in public life. The son of a well-respected U.S. senator, he had enlisted in the navy in 1943, becoming the youngest pilot in the navy at that time, and he flew more than fifty combat missions in World War II, including one where he had to eject from his aircraft in a raid over Japan after his plane was struck by enemy antiaircraft fire.[1] Later, after a career in the oil business in Texas, George H. W. Bush went on to become a member of the House of Representatives from Texas, a U.S. ambassador to the United Nations, the chairman of the Republican National Committee, an envoy to the People's Republic of China, and the director of the Central Intelligence Agency.

Vice President Bush had faithfully supported Ronald Reagan through both terms of his dramatic and course-altering presidency. In a city notorious for "leaking," no leaks came from the Bush office. In an office often used for the stronger part of attack-style politics and sometimes more questionable public ethics behavior, Vice President Bush remained the consummate gentleman and clean-government professional—no Spiro Agnew or Richard Nixon, he. When he declared his intention to run for the Republican nomination for president, however, he found he had plenty of opponents.

For starters, there was the Kansan, Senate Republican Leader Bob Dole. A national figure for decades, he had run with President Gerald Ford as his vice presidential nominee in 1976.

Then there was Congressman Jack Kemp, Republican from New York, who represented the charismatic, young Supply-Siders (those who believed in economic growth through marginal tax rate cuts). Kemp was also a social conservative and foreign policy hawk. His base was tied to a philosophy of economic growth through tax cuts, social renewal, and tough rhetoric for the Soviet Union and its satellites. Kemp was the principal author and spokesman on Capitol Hill for the tax cuts that helped define the Reagan presidency and was known for such clever partisan jibes as, "The leaders of the Democratic Party aren't soft on Communism, they're soft on democracy."*[2]

Messrs. Dole and Kemp weren't the only opponents. The carefully laid plans of many Republican hopefuls (including Delaware Governor Pete du Pont and former Secretary of State Alexander Haig) were thrown into disarray by the entrance into the race of Rev. Pat Robertson (president of the Christian Broadcasting Network). Robertson's appeal to evangelicals was said to be equivalent in the GOP to Rev. Jesse Jackson's appeal to black Americans in the Democratic ranks. Robertson would prove to disrupt the candidacy of Jack Kemp (himself an evangelical Christian) with the ever-growing base of religious conservatives. In the 1987 bellwether Ames, Iowa, straw poll, Pat Robertson came in first place.[3] By early January 1988, the polls from Iowa (whose caucuses are considered key tests of strength in

---

* When I first met Jack Kemp in 1979, he said to me, "I didn't know you were interested in politics." I responded, "I'm not. I'm interested in football." (Kemp had been an outstanding quarterback for the San Diego Chargers and a star quarterback for the Buffalo Bills in the 1960s.)

presidential contests) validated Robertson's strength but showed Bob Dole in the lead. Indeed, Vice President Bush was having problems.*

Bush's nomination would typically have been a near coronation because he was the sitting vice president loyally serving a beloved president. Richard Nixon, for example, had had little trouble wrapping up the Republican nomination following eight years' service with the popular Eisenhower in 1960. As party machines began to fade over the years, however, it was becoming necessary to show real strength at the grassroots level and to actually earn the votes of primary voters and activists. Thus, in a split field, Bush's nomination was far from assured.

In January 1988, with polls showing him in second place in the February Iowa caucuses, Vice President Bush went on the *CBS Evening News with Dan Rather* for a wide-ranging interview. Dan Rather was, even then, considered a biased anchor, eager to embarrass Republicans. When Rather tried to badger Bush with questions about his alleged involvement in Iran-Contra, Bush pushed back—strongly. After a series of unremitting questions, the dialogue on national television went this way:

RATHER: I don't want to be argumentative, Mr. Vice President.
BUSH: You do, Dan.
RATHER: No . . . no, sir, I don't.
BUSH: This is not a great night, because I want to talk about why I want to be president, why those 41 percent of the people are supporting me. And I don't think it's fair . . .
RATHER: And Mr. Vice President, if these questions are . . .
BUSH: . . . to judge my whole career by a rehash on Iran. How would you like it if I judged your career by those seven minutes when you walked off the set in New York?
RATHER: Well, Mister . . .

---

* I had had an earlier run-in with my friend Pat Robertson on the direction of his campaign that the press picked up on. In a 1986 letter to supporters, he declared, "The Christians have won," when his delegates won a substantial number of Michigan precincts. I said at the time that this was the wrong way to campaign and think: campaigns should not be based on religious balkanization and sectarianism like that; that was not the way to celebrate electoral success. Robertson demanded an apology—I never gave one.

BUSH: Would you like that?

RATHER: Mr. Vice President . . .

BUSH: I have respect for you, but I don't have respect for what you're doing here tonight.[4]

As the interview began, I had no idea how it would turn out.* No one had ever talked back to one of the leaders of what was perceived as the establishment of elite public opinion on the air on his own program. But Vice President Bush traded fire for fire here, pointing out—on Dan Rather's own broadcast—that Rather had an imperfect past as well; for example, the previous year he had walked off his television camera set when the U.S. Open was still airing on his network even though it was time for the news. When the cameras went live to the news, many affiliates throughout the country had nothing to air because Rather was nowhere to be found.

For many years, George H. W. Bush had been seen as somewhat disconnected from the conservative grassroots of the Republican Party, too genteel to stand up for conservative principles, too close to the establishment, too Northeast preppy and not enough Midwest, Southwest, or just plain West as Barry Goldwater, Richard Nixon, and Ronald Reagan had been. For many grassroots conservatives who had long distrusted Bush's ties to the GOP's eastern establishment, the headline of a 1987 *Newsweek* cover and profile of the vice president said it all: "Fighting the Wimp Factor."[5] As presidential historian Timothy Naftali put it, "No one questioned the physical courage of the World War II veteran, and eternally young tennis player and jogger. It was his political courage that was in question."**[6] With this highly publicized clash with Dan Rather, Bush came close to erasing these doubts.

But not close enough for the voters of Iowa. Dole, as expected, won big in the Hawkeye State. Robertson came in second.

---

* I was in the Old Executive Office building at the time, watching the vice president's exchange and thought, *Just give him hell*. He did.

** I can attest to what a physically fit jogger he was. When we were together in Houston once, he asked me to join him for a morning jog to brief him on drug policy. When we returned to the hotel, a gaggle of press was waiting, and I was asked a question by the press about what I had briefed the president on. I was trying to conceal that I was gasping for air, and the president, without missing a beat, took my question and answered it, and without a break in his breathing. Even after he had finished his answer, I was still trying to catch my breath.

Bush was undeterred. He turned the tables in the next key contest, New Hampshire, and charged Dole with being a tax raiser. New Hampshire Republicans were (and are) famously averse to higher taxes. After aggressively retooling his campaign, Bush soundly won the New Hampshire primary. Dole came in second and Jack Kemp, third. Pat Robertson's campaign seemed an Iowa anomaly with little steam to continue nationally, and Jack Kemp was soon to realize it would be awfully difficult to persuade the public that he was a stronger disciple of Ronald Reagan's principles than Ronald Reagan's vice president—no matter how long Kemp had been a philosophical conservative. Following his defeat in New Hampshire, Dole was asked in a televised interview if he had a message for the vice president. Dole snarled, "Stop lying about my record!"[7] That unhappy comment, as much as his New Hampshire defeat, effectively ended Dole's run in 1988. Within just weeks, Bush swept the primaries of Super Tuesday and wrapped up the Republican nomination.

For the Democrats, Senator Gary Hart of Colorado had been regarded as the leading candidate. But he made the mistake of inviting a young woman, not his wife, to spend the night in his Washington townhome—after challenging the press to tail him. Hart denied all impropriety and denounced the reporters who "hid in the bushes" to trap him. Then a tabloid newspaper published a picture of him with the woman on his lap. They were shown aboard a pleasure boat eponymously named *Monkey Business*. Hart was quickly forced out of the race in 1987, leaving no obvious candidate, and a national conversation ensued. People debated the proper role of the media in its intrusion into the private lives of public figures (as they saw it) and the people's right to know (as the media defined it). This unresolved theme would loom large for the next twenty years and unfold at higher and higher levels with increasing dissonance and effect at every strain.

So, for the Democrats, the choices came down to, among others, Tennessee Senator Al Gore, Arizona Governor Bruce Babbitt, Missouri Congressman Dick Gephardt, Illinois Senator Paul Simon, civil rights leader Rev. Jesse Jackson, and Massachusetts Governor Michael Dukakis. Delaware Senator Joe Biden had dropped out of the race the year before, after the press had reported allegations of his plagiarism of a British politician's speeches and his fibbing about his college and law school records.

Gore played to his strength in the New South. He was young, vigorous, and a leader of those bright, well-educated politicians who had embraced the computer revolution, sometimes called Atari Democrats. He was also known as a bit more of a hawk on foreign policy than many liberals in the Democratic Party. Gore, however, came to grief in New York State. He had attempted to follow the Carter line on abortion; he favored the *Roe v. Wade* ruling, committed himself to legal abortion, but opposed federal funding for abortion-on-demand. Among the party's liberal activists, this position was anathema.

Babbitt attracted a flurry of press attention when he challenged his rivals in a televised debate to stand up if they favored a tax increase. Babbitt alone stood, and his elevated stance stood him few favors. Walter Mondale's bold assertion that he would hike taxes was praised as courage in 1984, but his staggering electoral defeat may have cooled liberals' ardor to try that again, and it was a massive turnoff to independents and to those known as Reagan Democrats.

Paul Simon was the last of the colorful prairie populists. He had been an Illinois editor, a student of Abraham Lincoln, and like the Emancipator, had never been to college. That last fact hadn't stopped him from writing a dozen books. But Simon's slicked-down hairdo, bowtie, and pendulous earlobes made him seem a throwback to the 1930s—even as he appealed to some voters with a thoroughly liberal voting record and a reputation for integrity.

Jesse Jackson renewed his wild-card status in the Democratic primaries. Party leaders dreaded the possibility that an offended Jackson might run for president as an independent. Such a move would doom the Democratic nominee's prospects. On the other hand, his open embrace of Third World dictators and terrorists such as Fidel Castro and Yasser Arafat caused deep distress in many quarters.

Dick Gephardt was a young member of the House of Representatives, but not very well known outside of Washington and Missouri. Proving how difficult and rare it can be for a member of the House to succeed, Gephardt won a few delegates and ran out of money fairly quickly.

Dukakis was a different story. Generous contributions from America's Greek community fueled his run for the White House. Justifiably proud of one of their own running for president, this community represented the success of America's appeal to hardworking immigrants. And the governor of a liberal state fit in perfectly fine with the Democratic Party's ideological commitments and regional preferences.

With strong sources of additional campaign funding, and no drama or awkward imagery surrounding him, Dukakis outlasted his opponents and cruised to a fairly easy nomination. For vice president, he selected an established Texan, Senator Lloyd Bentsen. The more conservative Bentsen could never have prevailed with liberal party activists in a race for the presidency (he hadn't even tried to run), but he seemed the perfect candidate to balance the national ticket both regionally and with some ideologically centrist appeal. The Boston-Austin alliance reminded party leaders of the successful 1960 ticket of Kennedy and Johnson.

Throughout the spring and most of the summer, Dukakis led George Bush by widening margins. Dukakis seized on his immigrant parents' story as an appeal to other first-generation Americans (the song played as he approached the podium at the 1988 Democratic Convention was Neil Diamond's "Coming to America"), and he even threw in a few lines of Spanish in his convention speech to strong applause. After the convention, Dukakis saw his poll numbers surge. When Bush arrived at his New Orleans nominating convention in August, he was down seventeen points in some polls.[8]

George H. W. Bush jumped over a generation of political leaders in his selection of a vice presidential nominee. He chose a politically conservative but youthful U.S. senator from Indiana. Dan Quayle was so energetic—perhaps too energetic, as the camera images showed the way he leaped onstage at his announcement for the nomination at a shirtsleeve rally in the steamy Delta city of New Orleans—that liberal journalists had a field day portraying him as an intellectual lightweight, owing to his youth and lack of national stature. The truth was, however, that Senator Quayle was forty-one years old at the time he was selected and had served in the U.S. Senate for eight years, having unseated the liberal lion Birch Bayh in his 1980 reelection effort. Prior to that, he had served in the U.S. House of Representatives.

The handsome Quayle, and a few others, had shared a townhouse during a golfing weekend with a woman, not his wife, some years back, and with that the press thought they had a story—and they attempted to tarnish his image the same way they had succeeded in tarnishing Gary Hart's. The townhouse at the golfing resort had, in fact, been occupied by several young congressmen. They were weekend guests of a Washington lobbyist.[9] The senator's wife, Marilyn Quayle, intervened and assured voters that if the choice was between philandering and golf, her husband, Dan, would choose golf. The story pretty much ended there.

Failing with that maneuver, the press then concentrated on the wealthy Quayle's alleged preferential treatment of getting into the Indiana National Guard during the Vietnam War. But his opponent, Lloyd Bentsen, had a son who served in the Texas Air National Guard at roughly the same time that Quayle was serving in Indiana. If it was wrong for the goose to have strings pulled, surely it was just as wrong for the gander.[10] And of course, criticizing service in the National Guard would only go so far before it would begin to offend others who were serving or had served in the National Guard.

In the midst of this storm of unfavorable press coverage, Dan Quayle was often tongue-tied. He occasionally tripped up in front of the microphone and cameras. Never mind that he had outdebated the highly articulate liberal Senator Bayh back in 1980. Never mind that he had earned respect in the Senate for his mastery of arcane defense issues. The press painted him as an intellectual lightweight and too young for the job. The tag stuck. Though this was a media theme throughout the rest of the campaign, as well as the basis for late-night television jokes and Democratic Party jabs, Quayle's perceived deficiencies did not attach further up the ticket.

Vice President Bush's acceptance speech in New Orleans turned the race around. He no longer spoke about the pollution of Boston Harbor (as if that was the Massachusetts governor's fault). He no longer pledged to be "the education president"; that just wasn't a strong enough motivator to people. Instead, he stressed the differences between himself and the liberal Massachusetts governor. He pledged "a kinder and gentler" America.*

---

* Some in Washington, including me, saw in Bush's "kinder and gentler" phrase a veiled criticism of Ronald Reagan. Bush's view of the matter, otherwise expressed in his memoirs, was that "Reagan was a kind and gentle man."

Then, fatefully, he said he would resist congressional demands for new taxes. Congress would push him, push him, Bush said, but he would reply: "Read my lips—no new taxes!" The crowd went wild.*

Bush's campaign manager, the tough political operative (and blues guitarist) Lee Atwater, vowed to drive up Dukakis's "negatives." In campaign parlance, that meant to flood the airwaves with comparative ads that would attack the opponent's record. Atwater's television attack on Dukakis would "strip the bark off the little bastard," he claimed.[11] (Surely, that was a curious way to achieve a kinder, gentler America.) Throughout modern American political history, what candidates say for public consumption about tactics and goals is often not the same as the way the candidates' operatives run campaigns.

As governor of one of the nation's most liberal states, Dukakis had built a strongly liberal record. While he had touted "competence, not ideology" in his campaign, Dukakis had always been unapologetically liberal. He proudly claimed, for example, that he was a "card-carrying member" of the American Civil Liberties Union (ACLU). Doing that was a serious mistake—not only in the membership itself—but even in his description of it. Words have meaning, and the phrase "card-carrying" had long been associated with "card-carrying member of the Communist Party." Moreover, millions of Americans heartily despised the ACLU. Two large voting blocs—Catholics and evangelicals—especially mistrusted it. Most Catholic families had at least one police officer among their relations. And many a family reunion in middle America has been regaled by an "Uncle Mac" telling horror stories of hardened criminals let out on the streets because of the intervention of the ACLU. For evangelicals, the ACLU was the prime mover behind the removal of prayer and Bible reading from the schools. (Conservative grassroots organizers typically referred to the ACLU as the Anti-Christian Litigation Unit.)

One issue that had come up in the campaign set off what were then becoming known as the culture wars—controversies over the defense of American values, patriotism, religious liberty, marriage and family, and the

---

* The line had been written by speechwriter Peggy Noonan, who was encouraged to put something in the speech just like that by Congressman Jack Kemp.

politics of the beginning and end of life. As governor, Michael Dukakis had vetoed a bill of the state legislature to require Massachusetts teachers to lead their classes in a voluntary morning recital of the Pledge of Allegiance. The Bush campaign seized on it. Dukakis had cited the famous 1943 Supreme Court opinion in *West Virginia State Board of Education v. Barnette* in justifying his veto.[12] That ruling had forbidden public school officials to compel children whose families were Jehovah's Witnesses to recite the Pledge. *Barnette* was entirely right. We, as a country, cannot compel any show of patriotism by children, who are required by law to attend school, when it offends their religious dictates. But Dukakis completely misunderstood the basis of the decision. Nobody has a right to be a Massachusetts teacher either. State employment is a privilege. If the people's representatives in the state legislature make it a condition of employment to lead children in *voluntarily* saying the Pledge, then no one's rights are violated. The unwilling teachers are perfectly free to teach in a private school or seek employment in another state. *Barnette* said students could be excused from reciting the Pledge; the Massachusetts law was about the teachers.

It was on this basis that I became embroiled in the 1988 presidential campaign. During an interview on *Meet the Press*, the host asked me about the Pledge issue and what it had to do with education. "It's the ABCs of civics," I replied. "If you have trouble with the Pledge, you're going to have trouble with a lot of the things down the road. . . . If you're the governor, and you're sitting there and someone brings the Pledge [legislation] for you to sign, do you look for a way to sign it or look for a way to avoid signing it? And with Mike Dukakis it was the latter."* Vice President Bush called me immediately after the show. He had seen it, and he told me how much he appreciated my speaking out on the issue. He said that I should stay in touch after the election.

Another, even stronger political problem for Dukakis emerged. Dukakis had supported a furlough system that allowed hardened criminals to leave state prisons on weekend passes. Under this system, one convicted murderer (named Willie Horton) had gotten out, left the state, and raped a woman in

---

* I recount this story in an earlier book: William J. Bennett, *The De-Valuing of America* (New York: Summit Books, 1992).

Maryland. Even after this atrocious incident, Dukakis stubbornly refused to consider repeal of the furlough system until the campaign for the presidency was under way.[13]

The issue was first used against Dukakis, unsuccessfully, by Al Gore in the Democratic primaries. In the fall campaign, however, the Bush team showed a grainy black-and-white film depicting criminals entering and leaving prisons through a subway turnstile.[14] Tough stuff, but surely within bounds for a political campaign. The Bush campaign never named Horton—that was done in a television ad released by an independent group, an ad with which the campaign disavowed any connection. But liberal critics pounced on the fact that the convict was a black man, and they charged the Bush campaign with racism.* These same writers never extended their criticism to Gore.

At one point, Michael Dukakis tried to show himself equipped to be commander in chief, and his advisors released photographs of him riding in an army tank. Any desk-bound politician might look uncomfortable riding around in one of these behemoths. Mike Dukakis, attired in an ill-fitting helmet, however, looked especially so. Dukakis was lampooned, compared to the cartoon character Snoopy, and generally made a figure of fun for trying to *look* like he could be commander in chief or like he was, indeed, tough when it came to defense policy. Bush ads featured the tank ride and contrasted them with Dukakis's liberal positions on national defense, including his one-time support of the nuclear freeze.

During the presidential debates, CNN newsman Bernard Shaw asked Governor Dukakis a question about capital punishment: How would he react if someone raped and murdered his own wife? The question was asked, no doubt, to elicit a sense of emotion from Dukakis, who carried himself with an impersonal, all-business, nonemotional demeanor.

SHAW: Governor, if Kitty Dukakis were raped and murdered, would you favor an irrevocable death penalty for the killer?

---

* George Bush came from a long line of civil rights advocates. His father, Senator Prescott Bush of Connecticut, had long campaigned for equal rights for black Americans. George H. W. Bush, himself, was no racist.

DUKAKIS: No, I don't, Bernard. And I think you know that I've opposed the death penalty during all of my life. I don't see any evidence that it's a deterrent, and I think there are better and more effective ways to deal with violent crime. We've done so in my own state.[15]

Dukakis then described at length how he would go after illegal drug use and begin with an international summit on the issue.[16]

Offered a rebuttal, George Bush said:

I do believe that some crimes are so heinous, so brutal, so outrageous, and I'd say particularly those that result in the death of a police officer, for those real brutal crimes, I do believe in the death penalty, and I think it is a deterrent, and I believe we need it. . . . And so we just have an honest difference of opinion: I support it and he doesn't.[17]

To be fair, Bernard's question had to have been the most personal question a member of the press had ever posed to a candidate for national office, but Dukakis's dry, matter-of-fact response was devastating to his chances. Even his strongest partisans despaired of his campaign skills. Few Americans saw past the controlled, careful public face of Michael Dukakis. How could they?

There was, indeed, another face. One journalist watched the 1988 Academy Awards ceremony in the offices of a caterer—en route to a campaign event with Michael Dukakis. As the envelope was passed for the Best Supporting Actress honors, Olympia Dukakis, Michael's cousin, was announced as the winner for the movie *Moonstruck*. Olympia waved the statuette at the camera upon receiving her award and shouted, "Let's go, Michael!" Undone by the emotion of the moment, the governor sat, starstruck, as tears coursed down his cheeks. It was a warm and human moment—and a side of the cerebral Harvard man that the voters never saw.[18]

From allegations about Michael Dukakis's record on crime, the Pledge of Allegiance, and his criticism of a hawkish defense policy, Vice President Bush succeeded in painting Michael Dukakis as a liberal, out of touch with the values of most Americans—he even used the word *liberal* derisively.

Many Dukakis supporters urged the governor to stand up for their ideology and to fight back. In one famous case, the composer and conductor Leonard Bernstein took to the op-ed page of the *New York Times* to defend the word and ideology, writing an essay titled "I'm a Liberal, and Proud of It."[19] That Leonard Bernstein was, among other things, made politically famous by the novelist Tom Wolfe for hosting a party with members of the Black Panthers in his Park Avenue home some years earlier probably proved more of George Bush's point than Leonard Bernstein's.[20]

Things were different down the ticket. Dan Quayle couldn't get a break. In the vice presidential debate he tried hard to establish his qualifications for the office that the press and his Democratic Party opponents had ridiculed. "I have far more experience than many others that sought the office of vice president of this country," he said at one point. "I have as much experience in the Congress as Jack Kennedy did when he sought the presidency." The dry-witted Bentsen was ready with a monumental put-down, perhaps the most famous of the campaign, perhaps one of the most famous quips of any presidential or vice presidential campaign: "Senator, I served with Jack Kennedy, I knew Jack Kennedy, Jack Kennedy was a friend of mine. Senator, you are no Jack Kennedy."[21] The crowd erupted with applause. Quayle tried to recover by saying, "That was really uncalled for, Senator," a comeback that elicited a bit of applause, but nowhere near what Bentsen received. Then Bentsen went in for the kill: "You are the one that was making the comparison, Senator—and I'm one who knew him well. And frankly I think you are so far apart in the objectives you choose for your country that I did not think the comparison was well-taken."[22] Quayle's stunned reaction—the deer-in-the-headlights look—and his inability to respond gave the debate to Bentsen, almost unanimously. It was a historical, political body slam.

Luckily for George Bush, presidential races are usually neither won nor lost with vice presidential selections or any particular vice presidential debate performance. The first vice presidential debate did not even take place until 1976; the 1980 campaign failed to feature the rhetorical sparring match. Even more luckily for Bush, he had other things lining up in his column. Ronald Reagan was a popular president, and the economy was doing well. The Misery Index (an economic calculation that combines our inflation rate and our unemployment rate) was far lower than when Jimmy Carter first popularized the metric against President Ford in 1976.*[23] Meanwhile, the Soviets seemed both to be loosening their internal vise grip with their domestic policies of glasnost and perestroika (economic and political liberalization) and cooling their anti-Western rhetoric.

The campaign began with a great deal of promise for the Democrats and the American left who had lived with eight years of the Ronald Reagan presidency. Americans like change, and the election offered an exciting story of an immigrant family's rise to the highest levels in U.S. society. Yet it ended with a stunning defeat for Dukakis. Bush won 49 million popular votes (more than 53 percent), carrying forty states for a near landslide total of 426 electoral votes. Dukakis trailed with just under 42 million popular votes (45.6 percent); his ten states—in the East, Northwest, and the northern tier of the Midwest—brought him just 111 electoral votes.[24]

Many journalists were soured by the campaign. They reacted as if it had been the height of absurdity for anyone in a presidential campaign to raise such issues as furloughs, the Pledge of Allegiance, and the ACLU (with its support of such policies as fewer restrictions on pornography, less religious influence—or reference—in the public square, and more rights for criminal defendants).[25] To them, it was undignified. To such writers and pundits, questions about patriotism, crime, and religious rights were a distraction from more important matters as they saw them. American democracy has often been raucous and unruly. Often, it is not pretty. But people instinctively understand that they do *not* decide the issues that are constantly talked about in the press. Instead, American voters like to decide who will decide how to handle those issues. In that sense, a probing, searching examination of the candidates' character and background, of their record and experience, is not absurd or trivial—it is commonplace in American politics. And quite often, seemingly small things often define much bigger things—or seemingly small decisions by people running for office will determine how they will handle much bigger decisions. And for a great many, issues regarding patriotism, crime, and religion are not small.

---

* The lower the index number, the better the economy. The index was over 13 when Jimmy Carter first brought it up, and it was between 17 and 20 when Ronald Reagan ran against Jimmy Carter in 1980. At the end of Reagan's second term, it was 9.57.

Although they made little progress in their quests for their parties' nominations, Robertson and Jackson changed the political landscape in different ways. Many in the major press missed it, especially those bent on criticizing Vice President Bush for trivializing the campaign with supposed "side issues," such as family values, patriotism, and crime. One acute liberal analyst well versed in theological and political currents, Garry Wills, noted the populist appeal of Robertson and Jackson. They "both deplored the loss of family values," he wrote, "the irresponsible sexuality of the young—what Jackson called 'babies making babies.'"[26] But it wasn't mere sexual morality and family decline. Wills flagged their twin concerns about drugs, crime, even school discipline.

Their populist agendas predictably diverged on issues like prayer in schools and abortion, but the divergence that mattered most to the frontrunners was how Bush and Dukakis managed the conversation that Robertson and Jackson started. Wills noted that Bush absorbed Robertson's message and many in his base as well. Dukakis, however, distanced himself from Jackson's message. "Robertson's cadres would be a quiet but key element in Bush's campaign, while Dukakis treated Jackson like an embarrassment. . . . This would lead him into his worse mistake, the renunciation of ideology, the attempt to build a middle constituency from scratch in the name of 'competence.' In effect, he fled his base instead of building on it."[27]

Robertson and Jackson would go on to play key roles in their public policy work and political outreach. Yes, they spoke out on social issues and family values, each in his own way, often with differing solutions. But when tapping in to large bases of support and interest, it is hard to consider those issues the province of low-minded political posturing.

Meanwhile, the campaign had virtually ruined Dan Quayle in many people's eyes. This would not be the first time the press would go after a vice presidential nominee with a no-holds-barred approach and create an image far different from the actual person himself (or herself). Typical of Washington insiders' reaction to Dan Quayle was a joke that Massachusetts Senator John Kerry had repeated (perhaps more famously than he had wanted): "Somebody told me the other day that the Secret Service has orders that if George Bush is shot, they're to shoot Quayle." After saying it, he quickly added, "There isn't any press here, is there?" Just as quickly, he apologized when his words were picked up in the Associated Press.[28] But Quayle was no lightweight and was known for surrounding himself with conservative intellectuals who took serious ideas seriously, people such as Bill Kristol, John McConnell, Spence Abraham, and Lisa Schiffren.*

In looking back at the 1988 election, one last thing Ronald Reagan did as president is worth mentioning for the profound impact it would have on our dialogue, future elections, and our democracy. President Reagan scrapped the so-called Fairness Doctrine in 1987. That regulation of the Federal Communications Commission had, for decades, stifled free and open debate on the airwaves. Radio and television stations that criticized the president or Congress could be required to air opposing views. In practice, Republican presidents could be vigorously criticized by broadcast journalists who had little fear that Congress—long in Democratic hands—would permit a crackdown. The result was like putting a lid on a serious exchange of ideas.**

The year 1988 almost ended with the major news story being the election and the upcoming transfer of the presidency from Ronald Reagan to George H. W. Bush. But it did not end that way. Just before Christmas, on 21 December, Pan Am Flight 103 exploded over Lockerbie, Scotland, killing all 259 people on board and another 11 on the ground.[29] It was no extraordinary aviation accident or tragedy due to mechanical or pilot error. The plane was blown up. The cause: a bomb in the luggage compartment planted by Libyan terrorists, led by one Abdel Basset Ali al-Megrahi. This was the deadliest terrorist attack on American civilians in our history—more than 180 Americans were on board, including dozens of college students coming home from their studies abroad.

The nation, its eyes still stained with tears, looked forward to a new year

---

* Kristol is the son of two leaders of the conservative intellectual movement, the recently deceased Irving Kristol and his widow Gertrude Himmelfarb; he is a Harvard Ph.D. and the editor of the *Weekly Standard* magazine and considered a leading conservative intellectual; he was also my chief of staff at the Department of Education. McConnell is a much sought-after conservative speechwriter; Abraham would go on to serve in the U.S. Senate and as a U.S. secretary of energy; Schiffren is a contributor to *National Review* magazine and a public essayist in her own right.

** The effect was to make liberalism the established opinion on the American airwaves. After 1987, syndicated radio talk shows became much more popular and much more available. It was, after all, in 1988 that a previously little known local talk show host in Sacramento picked up and moved to New York City and began a national radio show that began a revolution on the AM radio band. That talk show host was named Rush Limbaugh.

coming. Ronald Reagan bade farewell to the nation in a televised address on 11 January 1989. He warned the country to not neglect the teaching of American history. He said if we forget what we have done, we will cease to be who we are. It was a warning about forgetting that achieved a special poignancy in view of his later diagnosis with Alzheimer's disease. He spoke of high American ideals, especially freedom:

> And the image that comes to mind like a refrain is a nautical one—a small story about a big ship, and a refugee, and a sailor. It was back in the early eighties, at the height of the boat people. And the sailor was hard at work on the carrier *Midway*, which was patrolling the South China Sea. The sailor, like most American servicemen, was young, smart, and fiercely observant. The crew spied on the horizon a leaky little boat. And crammed inside were refugees from Indochina hoping to get to America. The *Midway* sent a small launch to bring them to the ship and safety. As the refugees made their way through the choppy seas, one spied the sailor on deck, and stood up, and called out to him. He yelled, "Hello, American sailor. Hello, freedom man."

Like that American sailor, Ronald Reagan *was* a freedom man.

II. A Scourge at Home

Few presidents had ever come to office with greater preparation than George Herbert Walker Bush, and that preparation was key to the years ahead. What issues the forty-first president would have on his plate in January 1989 would not—as with almost every president—be the same for which history, even recent history, would remember his presidency.

President Bush began his Inaugural Address with a prayer; many presidents invoked God in their Inaugural Addresses, but memory strains to actually recall a president reciting a prayer:

> My first act as President is a prayer. I ask you to bow your heads:
>   Heavenly Father, we bow our heads and thank You for Your love.

Accept our thanks for the peace that yields this day and the shared faith that makes its continuance likely. Make us strong to do Your work, willing to heed and hear Your will, and write on our hearts these words: "Use power to help people." For we are given power not to advance our own purposes, nor to make a great show in the world, nor a name. There is but one just use of power, and it is to serve people. Help us to remember it, Lord. Amen.[30]

Bush then continued, speaking on the wave of political and economic freedom sweeping through the world. "We know what works: Freedom works. We know what's right: Freedom is right. We know how to secure a more just and prosperous life for man on Earth: through free markets, free speech, free elections, and the exercise of free will unhampered by the State," intoned the new president.

He spoke of our national "will" being greater than our national "wallet" and that all citizens and government employees had their work cut out for them to conquer the issues of crime and "addictions" to "drugs, welfare," and "the demoralization that rules the slums" in America. He reiterated a call from his campaign that we needed "a thousand points of light," that was, "a new activism" which embraced "the community organizations that are spread like stars throughout the nation."[31]

He called for a new era of bipartisanship with the Democratic Party in the House and Senate:

To my friends, and yes, I do mean friends, in the loyal opposition, and yes, I mean loyal: I put out my hand. I am putting out my hand to you, Mr. Speaker. I am putting out my hand to you, Mr. Majority Leader. For this is the thing: This is the age of the offered hand. We can't turn back clocks, and I don't want to. But when our fathers were young, Mr. Speaker, our differences ended at the water's edge.[32]

And then the president got to the meat of his planned tenure, the key area in which he wanted to show marked improvement in his next four years, giving more words to it than any other policy issue in his Inaugural:

There are few clear areas in which we as a society must rise up united and express our intolerance. The most obvious now is drugs. And when that first cocaine was smuggled in on a ship, it may as well have been a deadly bacteria, so much has it hurt the body, the soul of our country. And there is much to be done and to be said, but take my word for it: This scourge will stop.[33]

George H. W. Bush had spoken out on the problem of illicit drug use before—several times in fact—and the issue was, indeed, receiving more and more of the nation's attention. Three years before President Bush's Inaugural, one of the most talented college basketball players in America who had just been drafted by the Boston Celtics, Len Bias, died of cardiac arrest (before his professional career could even take off) as a result of a cocaine overdose. That story grabbed the nation's attention. Nancy Reagan's "Just Say 'No'" campaign had proliferated through the media and into the schools. Still, by 1988, the drug problem in America was a big one with increasing stories of hospital emergency admissions for drug abuse going up,[34] and the latest national statistics we had at the time showed 18 million Americans were monthly users of marijuana, 5.8 million Americans were using cocaine, and about 500,000 Americans were injecting heroin.[35] Drug use, in and of itself, is never the only problem. The attendant problems then (as now) were the crime and the deaths from overdoses and accidents, the tens of thousands of emergency room admissions, the broken families, the children born into addiction, the family violence, and the waste and dependence that came along with such drug use. At the tail end of Reagan's second term, Joe Biden, then a Democratic senator from Delaware, championed the Anti-Drug Abuse Act. Congress and the president agreed, signed the bill into law, and thereby created the Office of National Drug Control Policy and its directorship position—the drug czar. But the job was thus far unfilled. In December 1988 I called President-elect Bush to congratulate him on his victory and tell him that I considered the drug issue so important that I would volunteer for the job. He was happy to hear that I was interested and told me he would check on the position.

I had already had some experience with this issue while serving as the secretary of education. (Although I had never used an illicit drug in my life, I had spent most of the 1960s and '70s on and around college campuses.) I was once asked on the *Today Show* if I considered drugs the biggest problem our nation's children faced in school. I replied that drugs were "the biggest outside impediment to learning in the schools. All the reform efforts that we're talking about . . . will come to nothing if kids are stoned or high." I had also made a plea that our nation's schoolteachers' unions require their members be drug free to maintain their membership to set an example to their charges. And I had called on school administrators that while they continued their drug education programs, they should also adopt policies that would toss kids out of school if they were using drugs. Finally, in one of my last speeches as the education secretary I had called for a greater use of the military in helping stop the shipment of drugs into this country as well as helping stop its production elsewhere. These statements and speeches were controversial, and they had received a good deal of attention (not all positive, not by a long shot), but they resonated with then Vice President Bush.

Prior to the inauguration, President-elect Bush offered me the job. I was later told that President Bush's incoming Chief of Staff John Sununu had also proposed my name to the president-elect for the position.

President Bush wasted no time. He made the drug scourge one of his domestic priorities and spelled out his thoughts in February 1989 during his first State of the Union (technically called an Address to Congress in a president's first year in office):

> My friends, that voice crying out for help could be the voice of your own neighbor, your own friend, your own son. Over 23 million Americans used illegal drugs last year, at a staggering cost to our nation's well-being. Let this be recorded as the time when America rose up and said no to drugs. The scourge of drugs must be stopped. And I am asking tonight for an increase of almost a billion dollars in budget outlays to escalate the war against drugs. The war must be waged on all fronts. Our new drug czar, Bill Bennett, and I will be shoulder to shoulder in the executive branch leading the charge.[36]

President Bush and I toured drug rehabilitation centers. I worked with national and local law enforcement officials as well as with the military, the Coast Guard, and leaders from other nations; and I delivered a good number of speeches intended to prod the nation's conscience about the issue. (All in all, I visited some 120 cities and communities as drug czar.) A popular issue in academia and among the press was that of drug legalization. One place I found legalization the least popular as an idea was in the inner cities where family members whose lives were being wrecked by drug use had wished for nothing but safer and cleaner neighborhoods.*

Another place drug legalization was highly unpopular was in the drug rehabs—no one I ever spoke to who was trying to get clean ever said, "I wished it were easier to have gotten hooked. I wished drugs were easier to obtain." I never bought any of the arguments for legalization, and neither did those, or the families of those, whose lives had been ruined by drug abuse. The rest of the argument, for me, was academic—and yes, we had plenty of those.**

There were colorful stories from our efforts (hundreds of them) involving dedicated people in both the law enforcement and the treatment communities. Take the story of one man I visited: Charleston, South Carolina's black, Orthodox Jewish police chief, Reuben Greenberg.

Greenberg posted uniformed police officers on street corners where drug

---

* Encouraged by Senator Ted Kennedy of Massachusetts to visit a school in his state, I went to the Joseph Lee Elementary School in Boston with Kennedy, Senator John Kerry, and Governor Michael Dukakis. The class of fifth graders was pretty well versed in the problem. When Senator Kerry asked them what should be done with drug dealers, one student said, "Fry the dealers." Another said, "Do something awful to them." When Senator Kennedy went into a long oration about poverty and root causes that he said led to some of the drug dealing, the students looked confused and did not respond much. As I wrote elsewhere, the kids were not sociologists; they were moralists. However, when I went to Harvard to talk about the problem, almost every question was about legalization—something seriously affected fifth graders or their parents did not think about.

** As I wrote in The De-Valuing of America, our best research showed that most drug criminals were into crime before they were into drugs. And most drug addicts who were not into crime before they were into drugs became criminals once they lost possession of their normal faculties and unadulterated judgment. Making drugs legal would end up simply enabling a habit. Drug criminals would continue to rob and steal to pay for food, clothes, and entertainment. And they would carry on with their drug trafficking by undercutting the legalized price of drugs and catering to teenagers who would (I assume) be nominally restricted from buying drugs at the corner drugstore. In my travels around the country, I have seen nothing (then or now) to support the legalizers' argument that lower drug prices would reduce crime. Drug enforcement officials will tell you crime rates are usually the highest where and when the drugs are the cheapest.

sales were common, reestablished foot patrols in dangerous neighborhoods, equipped his officers with cameras to take pictures of suspected dealers, and maintained a strict regimen of enforcement with public housing, seeing to the eviction of those involved in drug dealing and other illegal activities. Greenberg's tactics got the ACLU in a twist. The organization insisted that it observe the officers in the execution of their duties. Sensing a good story, the media then followed by insisting that they observe the observation. It was all part of Greenberg's strategy: when a drug dealer took to the streets in Charleston, he was liable to find himself tailed by a police officer, an ACLU observer, and the local press. Drug dealers took the hint, and many of them moved on. Greenberg cleaned up Charleston with his bully pulpit and his proper hectoring of those who would ruin lives and neighborhoods.

Another ally of mine was the man whom President Bush named his secretary of housing and urban development, Jack Kemp (his erstwhile challenger in the 1988 primaries). Secretary Kemp worked with me in our joint efforts to secure public housing from drugs by erecting fences and other security apparatuses around buildings and by giving residents official identification cards. Kemp argued that before Housing and Urban Development went into the business of fixing up, refurbishing, and improving public housing, it should make sure it was doing so for families and children who were obeying the law rather than for drug dealers making a mockery of it and the whole project.

No ally was, however, more important than the president. In any organization, most especially the federal government or the Executive Office and the White House, with the leader's support a great deal is doable; without it, change can be much harder, even undoable. President Bush was clearly moved by the drug issue (from addiction to its ties to family poverty and breakups to other destruction it wrought). One small story with large importance: early in his term, I needed to keep a part-time Defense Department official on loan to my staff for a longer period than he was assigned. Defense Secretary Dick Cheney and Joint Chief's Chairman Colin Powell thought the official should go back to his home at Defense, and they overruled my request. I explained to the president how critically I needed him to stay. The president understood that Defense could make do without him a few more months, called Cheney and Powell, and told them so. These kinds of turf battles occur by the hundreds each month in any administration—but that kind of early victory shows where the president stood, and it helped in our drug policy efforts a great deal.*

We also had assistance from outside, like the Partnership for a Drug-Free America and some in Hollywood like the then president of Disney studios who worked to create a "sobriety chic" in Hollywood, where drug use was simply not popular.

By the end of 1989, the nation had moved in the right direction; there was a greater consciousness about how bad for the person and the country drug abuse was, and we soon would see the results of this greater clarity. Our national drug control strategies included working with source and transit countries on tougher law enforcement, expanding treatment, making that treatment more accountable, and improving and focusing efforts at prevention and education. We received help from the military (using its eyes and ears). We intercepted drugs at the borders. We expanded drug intelligence throughout the country and funded and disseminated more research. In short, the majority of the country agreed on the nature of the problem and how to attack it—on both sides of the political aisle. The country got drug use down to record lows, from a high of 23 million to just under 13 million by 1990. It would go lower by 1992. By 1990, the country's cocaine use went down from almost 6 million users to 1.6 million users, and we saw a reduction in cocaine-related emergency room visits as well as a decrease in marijuana use.[37]

III. A New Set of Bricks and Tanks

While President Bush was busy trying to implement his domestic agenda, issues around the world were seemingly taking even greater precedence and

---

* Another story showing the president's sense of self: In one trip several of us made to Colombia (the president, me, Secretary of State James Baker, and others) after landing at Barranquilla, we were flying in a helicopter over the water on the way to Cartagena, and Secretary Baker asked me what my attention was on as I was looking out the window. I replied, "I'm looking for the fighter jets Secretary Cheney said would be here." Baker simply said, "Oh." I noted President Bush was not looking up out the window but down. I asked him about the accompanying jets and what he was looking for down in the water below us. He said, "I'm sure the F-14s are there; I was just wondering what the fishing is like here."

attention. The powerful movements for freedom that Reagan had helped to unleash throughout the world were felt even in China. In April 1989, thousands of students demanding liberalization of the Communist Party's stringent rule began gathering in Beijing's vast, historic Tiananmen Square following the death of the popular former Chinese Communist Party general secretary, Hu Yaobang.[38] Known as a "liberal-leaning party leader" and a "reformist," especially among the younger generations in China, Hu was greatly popular among those in China seeking more liberalism, more democracy.[39]

Meanwhile, the aging leader of China, Deng Xiaoping, had been responsible for helping end the madness of Mao's Great Proletarian Cultural Revolution. He pledged to put China on the path to modernization and permitted much greater economic opportunity for the 1.1 billion Chinese.[40] And as is so often the case when reforms toward liberalization and more freedom are instituted in autocratic or tyrannical regimes, the improved living conditions in China created what many in similar situations have called "a revolution of rising expectations."

Deng would, however, move only so far, and he had been responsible for ousting Hu from power in China a few years earlier when Hu allowed other student demonstrations to take place throughout China without cracking down on them. Those demonstrations—in 1985 and 1986—had already shown a youth interested in less repression and more freedom, as the students carried posters with slogans such as "Law, Not Authoritarianism" and "Long Live Democracy."[41]

In Tiananmen Square,* near the center of Beijing, thousands upon thousands of students gathered over the days and weeks; they read long lists of confusing, sometimes even contradictory demands. But they also read Chinese translations of America's *Declaration of Independence* and Lincoln's "Gettysburg Address" and erected a papier-mâché statue that was a Chinese version of the Statue of Liberty.[42]

Deng was not willing to share much power, and he would not tolerate a student revolt. His prime minister, Li Peng, played on the historic Chinese

---

* *Tiananmen* is translated to mean "Gate of Heavenly Peace."

people's fear of chaos. Li sent in tanks from the People's Liberation Army (PLA) to maintain control of the capital city. The world watched, amazed, as a young Chinese man wearing a neat white shirt and carrying a briefcase stood in front of a column of tanks. The image was televised worldwide. As the tank driver tried to maneuver around the man later identified as Wang Wei-lin, Wang stepped smartly aside and blocked the lead tank, again and again. It was a deadly ballet, like a bullfighter's carefully choreographed moves. Miraculously, the tank driver did *not* roll over the hero.*

In short order, however, more tanks ran over hundreds, killing them, and PLA soldiers fired their rifles into the masses of students. Within hours, fleeing students were hunted down and killed. Quickly, the Communist regime's forces cleared away hundreds of bodies, burned them, and hosed down the square, the ceremonial heart of ancient China.[43] Two days later, Deng went on Chinese national television to report to the people of China and congratulate the soldiers, saying, "They are truly the people's army, China's Great Wall of Steel." Of the dead, Deng said only this: "Their aim was to topple the Communist Party, socialism, and the entire People's Republic of China and set up a capitalist republic."[44]

Americans were outraged, horrified, as were people throughout the civilized world. President Bush had counseled calm and had urged the Chinese rulers to act with restraint. All through the crisis, President Bush had tried to maintain a close relationship with the Chinese leaders while pressing for lenient treatment for the students.

After the Tiananmen Massacre, the president sent National Security Advisor Brent Scowcroft to meet with the Chinese leaders. The Chinese government had warned Bush that they viewed American involvement in their internal affairs as a provocation. Scowcroft proceeded with ceremonial dinners, including the usual exchange of toasts. While Scowcroft did say, "I would not be honest if I did not acknowledge that we have profound areas of disagreement—on the events at Tiananmen, on the sweeping changes in

---

* Reports from Chinese refugees identified the man in Tiananmen Square. Whatever ultimately happened to Wang is unclear—various reports have said he was killed a short time later, mysteriously disappeared or was disappeared, or has been in hiding. The tank driver, these exiles had reported, was also put to death that day for *not* rolling over the brave Wang Wei-lin.

Eastern Europe . . . [still] we seek to outline broad areas where agreement is possible and to isolate for another time those areas of disagreement," what the world saw with this widely publicized image of the toast was this representative of the United States who seemed to be blithely unconcerned about the murder of hundreds, if not thousands, in China's capital city.[45]

Congress rang with denunciations of the massacre and with criticisms of President Bush for his failure to prevent it or say anything strongly against it. Of course such criticisms were short on realistic alternatives and the question of just what power he would have had to prevent the slaughter in China. Tougher rhetoric? Greater denunciation? *Yes.* Action? *What would it have been?*

President Bush proved unwilling to go along with congressional demands, from both conservatives and liberals, for severe sanctions against China for what it had done. One such demand—a domestic policy sanction—was sponsored by a recently elected Democratic congresswoman from California named Nancy Pelosi. Her bill would have allowed Chinese college students in America (especially those sympathetic to their activist brethren back home) to stay in the United States on extended visas.[46] President Bush vetoed the legislation but allowed Attorney General Dick Thornburgh to grant visa extensions administratively, without a law passed by Congress and signed by the president that the Chinese government had made clear would be met with unhappy diplomatic resistance.[47]

Ever since Nixon went to China in 1972, many Republicans had sought to use China as a counterweight to Soviet expansion and to do as much as possible to encourage trade and not ruffle Chinese leaders' feathers. Many in the Republican Party praised President Bush's efforts in these overtures. But there was no question they came at a cost to human rights.

On another front of the Cold War, President Bush still faced a dangerously unstable Soviet Union. He was trying to nudge, cajole, and persuade Mikhail Gorbachev to make greater reforms, to show more regard for human rights.

In April 1989, President Bush spoke in Hamtramck, Michigan (a city with a large Polish-American population). He outlined his vision for an Eastern Europe without an "imposed and unnatural" division. He told the

Hamtramck community, "We share an unwavering conviction that one day all the peoples of Europe will live in freedom."[48] And in July, President Bush traveled to Poland. He accompanied the Polish Solidarity leader Lech Walesa to the Lenin Shipyards in Gdansk, where he addressed a vast throng of 250,000.* Without inciting a revolt, he nonetheless made clear that the United States stood with Solidarity, with the forces of peaceful and democratic change. "It is Poland's time of possibilities. It is Poland's time of destiny, a time when dreams can live again," Bush told the crowd. America would stand with them.[49]

President Bush would soon speak of "a New World Order" based on human rights, democracy, and free trade. But change in Europe would come primarily from the ground up, with the occasional rhetorical push (and not too much more) from Washington, unsure as it was of what to make of great power shifts. President Reagan had spoken easily and worked hard toward tearing down the walls of communism; the Bush administration was more cautious, unsure of what would follow.

The changes were not long in coming. Poland's new spirit was contagious. The freedom revolution was spreading in Eastern Europe. Hungary and Czechoslovakia began to bubble with excitement. When Poland's first free elections resulted in a Solidarity sweep in the summer of 1989, the restive peoples of the rest of the captive nations could no longer be contained.[50]

East Germany, that rump state held under stern Stalinist rule for forty-five years, soon felt the upsurge of freedom. Defying the menacing gaze of the secret police—the Stasi—East Germans flocked to their once-empty Lutheran churches to hear passionate appeals for democracy and human rights. Czechoslovakia's and Hungary's new, more relaxed regimes opened their borders as well. The East German regime was supposedly their ally in the Warsaw Pact. Thousands of young East Germans bundled into their rickety Trabant automobiles and made their roundabout way for freedom into West Germany. The trickle soon became a flood.[51]

---

* Personal note: In all my service in government, the one person I have always wanted to meet—and never have—was Lech Walesa. At Ronald Reagan's funeral, at the National Cathedral in Washington, I saw on television footage (after the fact) that he was standing two rows behind me that day. To this day, I still wish I could shake his hand.

In short order, Chairman Gorbachev made it clear that he would not send in Soviet tanks to prop up the unpopular Communist regime in East Germany; this would not be Beijing all over again. Gorbachev knew that there were too many cameras, too many democrats, and that Asia simply was not Europe—no matter how hard the previous repression there had been. The whole world was, indeed, watching.

And then the Wall fell.

In 1961 the East German government had erected a physical Iron Curtain,[52] an ugly combination of cement and electrified fencing with armed guards, an internal barricade that separated the two nations and their brethren on each side. But at midnight, 9 November 1989, the government of East Germany finally gave permission to its citizens to peaceably pass through the gates of the Berlin Wall.[53] East Germans "surged through, cheering and shouting, and were met by jubilant West Berliners on the other side. Ecstatic crowds immediately began to clamber on top of the Wall and hack large chunks out of the 28-mile barrier."[54] Some years earlier, I had described something I called "the gates test." One can judge a country by which direction people run when the country erects gates: Do they flee in, or do they risk life and limb to get out? (Over the course of some four decades until 1989, some 2.5 million people had fled East Germany and many were shot trying to flee.) There was no better symbol of the gates test than the Berlin Wall.

Two years prior, President Reagan had gone to Berlin and described it as "a gash of barbed wire, concrete, dog runs, and guard towers." Perhaps the most famous words of Reagan's presidency were those he uttered that summer day in 1987: "General Secretary Gorbachev, if you seek peace, if you seek prosperity for the Soviet Union and Eastern Europe, if you seek liberalization: Come here to this gate! Mr. Gorbachev, open this gate! Mr. Gorbachev, tear down this wall!" And two years later, within hours of the granting of travel by the East German government, the German citizens were, themselves, taking pickaxes to the infamous Wall.

Thousands of young people—and not a few oldsters—scrambled to dance atop the symbol of Communist tyranny. There was no violence—miraculously. There was no settling of scores. Instead, a party atmosphere pervaded. The Wall was taken down to pieces with chunks of it sold as souvenirs. Today, many of those pieces of concrete and wire can be seen in museums across the world as well as here in America. The Wall has now become an artifact in that "sad, bizarre chapter in human history"—the words President Reagan had once used to describe communism.[55] Human freedom and hope had triumphed again. Within days, the rest of the physical Iron Curtain came down all over Eastern Europe. One after another, Communist governments either resigned or were simply voted out of office. In Czechoslovakia, a Velvet Revolution—nonviolent, democratic, and orderly—was led by the esteemed writer Vaclav Havel.

When Bush Press Secretary Marlin Fitzwater came to the Oval Office eagerly seeking a statement for the White House press corps, George Bush stopped him short. There would be no "dancing on the Berlin Wall." Steadily, Bush told his press chief: "Listen, Marlin, the *last* thing I want to do is brag about winning the Cold War or bringing the Wall down."[56] Bush emphasized for Fitzwater that crowing about the Berlin Wall would not be helpful in Eastern Europe.[57]

Bush would be widely criticized for failing to catch the mood of exhilaration, for being out of touch with the spirit of the times. But to be fair, there were several things to explain President Bush's seemingly calm attitude about the elation over what was happening a continent away. First, he knew that we were not out of the woods yet. And there was a bear in those woods. Who knew what the Soviet reaction would be? More recently, the journalist Robert Schlesinger related the following story with an accurate, descriptive conclusion:

The next day . . . [Ed] McNally [one of President Bush's speechwriters] sent [David] Demarest [White House director of communications] a four-page memo suggesting a full presidential publicity blitz: "Set forth below is a five-point plan for you to become the architect of the most popular presidency in modern history," McNally wrote. Bush should fly to Berlin the next day and go to the Wall. . . . "This is the real thing. History has offered the President a chance to place his stamp on an era— not at the end of an era, after it's proven itself out—but at the beginning, at the turning point. . . . What's happening at the wall probably *is* a turning point for the Cold War. And if we declare that it is, we may help the prophecy become self-fulfilling." Lech Walesa was to be awarded the Medal of Freedom in Washington, D.C., on Monday, November 13, and McNally suggested that the ceremony be moved to prime time and that Bush "declare Monday night that *the Cold War is over*."[58]

This certainly would have been the opposite of the president's more cautious and muted approach to the events in Germany. But as Schlesinger concludes: "Such theatrics would have given Bush an indelible Berlin Wall moment. But it would not have been Bush—not merely because he was trying to find a prudent path that would not spark a hard-line backlash, but also because placing his stamp on an historic moment was not the style of a president who disliked the word 'I.'"[59] That, indeed, was President Bush.

Still, others knew full well the United States' contribution to this great moment. West German Chancellor Helmut Kohl, for instance, after returning from Berlin told Bush, "Without the U.S., this day would not have been possible. Tell your people that."[60]

Several days passed before Bush addressed the nation on the events in Europe. On Thanksgiving Eve, the president spoke from the White House:

On other Thanksgivings, the world was haunted by the images of watchtowers, guard dogs, and machine guns. In fact, many of you had not even been born when the Berlin Wall was erected in 1961. But now the world has a new image, reflecting a new reality: that of Germans, East and West, pulling each other to the top of the wall, a human bridge between nations; entire peoples all across Eastern Europe bravely taking to the streets, demanding liberty, pursuing democracy. This is not the end of the book of history, but it's a joyful end to one of history's saddest chapters.[61]

He would then address his critics: "But to those who question our prudent pace, they must understand that a time of historic change is no time for recklessness. The peace and the confidence and the security of our friends in Europe—it's just too important."[62]

Some reasons for restraint were soon clear. In December 1989, the Romanian Communist dictatorship of the criminal Ceausescu family collapsed, but not without bloodshed. Thousands of Romanians died in clashes with the feared secret police, the Securitate. Ultimately, the dictator Nicolae and his politically powerful wife, Elena, were captured by resistance members. They were given a joke of a "trial" and shot—on Christmas Day.[63] By the end of the 1980s, what was now called the Soviet Outer Empire had collapsed. The Moscow-dominated Warsaw Pact simply dissolved, and aside from the brief, bloody end of communism in Romania, most changes had occurred peacefully.

President Bush met with Mikhail Gorbachev at Malta in early December 1989.[64] Not content with enough Soviet concessions in or over Eastern Europe, Bush now pressed Gorbachev to end Soviet military assistance to Nicaragua's Communist Sandinistas in our hemisphere, south of our border, in Central America. President Bush stressed the Soviets' signature of the 1975 Helsinki Final Act. That document had put human rights firmly on the agenda of all East-West summits.[65] Bush's patient, insistent demand for peaceful and orderly change, for democracy, was not U.S. meddling. It was something the Soviets themselves had agreed to. Only now, in the 1980s, had anyone actually expected them to abide by their agreements. By the end of the summit, the two countries had agreed to "reductions in troops and weapons in Europe."[66] And Mikhail Gorbachev stated, "I assured the President of the United States that I will never start a hot war against the USA."[67]

As the new decade dawned, attention in Europe focused on two questions: What would become of East and West Germany, and what would happen to the Inner Empire of the Soviet Union? In 1990, the first of those questions would be answered. President Bush quietly decided that the United States would stand for German reunification, provided that it occurred peacefully and by consent of the German people themselves. In taking this decision, he was guided by the United States of America's bound word. We had promised the Germans this for forty-five years. Bush would keep that promise. Others doubted the wisdom of such a stand. Prime Minister Margaret Thatcher, for example, was not so sure. Britain had spent much of the twentieth century preventing the rise of a Germany powerful enough to dominate all of Europe. France's Francois Mitterrand, similarly, hesitated.[68] Helmut Kohl felt isolated.

German reunification came in 1990 because George Bush firmly believed that America's word, once given, must be honored. He had refused to "dance on the Berlin Wall" so that he might usher in a new era in international life. Germany had been the flashpoint of the Cold War for almost half a century. The conflicts between the USSR and the Western Allies began almost as soon as Hitler shot himself in 1945. German issues dominated the headlines: the Soviet blockade of West Berlin of 1948, Soviet tanks crushing a revolt in East Berlin in 1953, the extended crisis of 1959–61 as Khrushchev threatened to drive the Western Allies out of West Berlin, and finally the monstrous Berlin Wall itself. If at any point during those years a serious analyst had said that East and West Germany would be reunited without bloodshed, that a unified Germany would remain within NATO, and that the Soviet Union would agree to all of this, people would have thought the analyst had gone mad. No thoughtful person believed it could happen. Without his patience and persistence—without George Bush's conception of "duty, honor, country"—the United States could not have played the peacemaker role that it did.

Europe was not the only place where freedom was breaking out, however. In Latin America, the long reign of the Communist Sandinista government in Nicaragua would come to a peaceable end as well. In 1990, Sandinista leader Daniel Ortega (once described on the cover of *Time* magazine as "The Man Who Makes Reagan See Red") was voted out of office and replaced by Violeta Chamorro (the widow of a popular slain newspaper editor in Nicaragua) in free elections that few once thought would resolve that country's problems, that few thought Ortega would allow to take place.[69] Nicaragua had been a longtime concern to the United States ever since the Sandinista takeover in 1979, and the United States had done everything it could to provide help to Sandinista opposition (including efforts that led to the Iran-Contra affair in the latter half of the Reagan presidency).* Meanwhile, the Soviet Union

---

* In 1987, on the two hundredth anniversary of our Constitution, I visited Nicaragua to speak to the supporters of the Contras (the opposition to the Sandinistas), telling the people there, "We will support the Contras. . . . To abandon the Contras is to enter on an irreversible course. Once abandoned, they are lost."

was doing all it could to prop up the Sandinistas. But as the Soviet Union was collapsing, and as the economy and curtailment of civil liberties in Nicaragua had taken their decade-long toll, and as free elections would take place, a Nicaraguan majority finally ousted Ortega. This was another major victory and story for freedom—not just in Latin America, but to and for the world.[70]

But a *Pax Central America* and a *Pax Middle East* were not so quickly in the offing—not yet. While the Cold War was ending, another war was breeding.

IV. A Scourge Abroad—A Just Cause

Manuel Noriega, the military leader and de facto head of Panama, had been a problem for some time—not just for the U.S. but for the citizens of Panama and the rest of Central America as well. A one-time U.S. ally, Noriega had become increasingly corrupt and criminal throughout the early to mid-1980s, aggrandizing to himself more wealth and power, and trafficking more and more in the illegal drug trade. He had allowed drug kingpins like Pablo Escobar and others working for the Medellin drug cartel to both secret themselves in Panama and ship their cocaine through Panama (on its way to infect Americans; about 80 percent of the cocaine in America came from the Medellin cartel).[71]

To be fair, not all of our past work with Noriega was commendable. As one congressional report put it, "Throughout the 1970s and 1980s, Noriega was able to manipulate U.S. policy toward his country, while skillfully accumulating near-absolute power in Panama."[72] General Noriega was, indeed, quite good at playing one side and one country against another side and another country—to his benefit.

But by 1989 the jig was up. The year before, two federal courts in the U.S. had indicted Manuel Noriega for, among other things, his efforts in helping Colombian drug smugglers.[73] By May 1989, General Noriega had nullified and rigged the national elections in Panama in his favor (former President Jimmy Carter—an observer of those elections—also claimed the election was stolen), and he unleashed a wave of violence that led to the brutalization of lead opposition candidate Guillermo Endara and his fellow candidates by paramilitary thugs during a protest in Panama City.[74] No one was safe. At the time tens of thousands of Americans were living in Panama, including military families, students, and businessmen; even Noriega's own people could run afoul of his paramilitary "Dignity Battalions" and suffer the consequences.[75] General Noriega was fast losing his grip on the country. Isolated from his people, isolated more and more from erstwhile supporters, he increasingly veered into troubled waters—a dangerous situation for a military dictator of any nation, even more dangerous for the world around him and especially the people in his country.

The United States had ten thousand troops in Panama, in large part to safeguard the Panama Canal, one of the world's most important throughways for international commerce; and with bipartisan support, President Bush sent additional troops to help out and further protect American interests and lives on the ground.[76]

On 15 December, General Noriega declared war on the United States, and the next day a U.S. Marine was shot to death by Noriega's soldiers in Panama City after an altercation.[77] The U.S. moved into action, and President Bush declared Operation Just Cause "to seize Noriega, protect American lives, restore democracy, and preserve the integrity of Panama Canal."[78] The president deployed the army and navy as well as their special forces, and the marines and the air force—the U.S. went in hard and it went in fast.[79]

The lightning-quick operation was so successful that "the high casualties and use of resources usually associated with all-out urban warfare did not occur."[80] But the general was at large. Asked at the time about his whereabouts, I answered, "Three days ago General Noriega was running Panama and running drugs, and now he is just running."[81] It turned out General Noriega was taking refuge from the U.S. military in the Vatican's embassy in Panama City. The Vatican had maintained a longtime policy of providing refuge for almost anybody who would seek it, particularly in Latin America. While ensconced, Noriega frantically sought asylum from any country that would take him. None would.[82]

Meanwhile, our military employed a particularly new kind of psychological warfare (psych-ops). They erected loudspeakers around the embassy and rattled the walls with songs such as "No Place to Run," "Voodoo Chile," and "You're No Good." Noriega, an opera lover, was no great fan of the play-list.[83] Weighing his options, finding few to none, and being driven crazy by the music, the former Panama strongman surrendered to the U.S. military on 3 January 1990. He sits in federal prison in Miami to this day, convicted of multiple drug and drug-related crimes.*

Operation Just Cause was a success, and the United States removed an international menace from his seat of power. But even with U.S. power still a marvel and a president proving he would take a no-nonsense approach to menacing dictators, even with communism collapsing across Europe, the world remained a dangerous place. Many were willing to celebrate the triumph of democracy; some, however, celebrated it a bit too soon.

V. Storms at Home

A provocatively titled essay in one scholarly journal (later turned into a best-selling book) set intellectual circles and university political science departments abuzz. In "The End of History and the Last Man," the intellectually conservative State Department official Francis Fukuyama argued that the collapse of communism revealed we were at "the end of history," and that the great ideological and philosophical debate about how best to organize forms of government was, for all intents and purposes, over:

> What we may be witnessing is not just the end of the Cold War, or the passing of a particular period of postwar history, but the end of history as such: that is, the end point of mankind's ideological evolution and the universalization of Western liberal democracy as the final form of human government.[84]

Fukuyama had few comments in his essay about the Arab world or Islam. "It is hard to believe that the movement will take on any universal significance," he said in one of his only references to the religion and

---

* As of this writing, Noriega is in legal limbo with the U.S. and France, which has also brought charges against him. By the time the reader is holding this book, Noriega may very well be serving the rest of his life in a French prison.

its political organizing principles and adherence in other countries. The Middle East, the Arab world—and political Islam in it and elsewhere— would, however, prove to be with us (and against us) for some time, in ways large and small. To most Americans, the Middle East was known for two things: it was the locus of much of the world's oil supply (except for Israel, which had no oil), and there was not one democracy in any of the more than twenty countries that comprised the Middle East (except, again, for Israel, which had a vibrant democracy—even Arabs voted and served in the parliament in Israel).

But here at home, neither history nor the end of politics had been reached; they never have been and it never will be. And yet, a president can never concentrate exclusively on foreign wars and foreign affairs, however compelling. In 1990, the hot Reagan economic recovery had begun to cool. Democratic leaders in Congress were determined to force Bush to break his "no new taxes" pledge. And with the Democratic Party in control of the House and Senate, President Bush was in a weak domestic policy bargaining position. Faced with few alternatives, Bush felt he had to give way to their budget requests, including an increase in taxes.

President Bush's 1990 budget compromise with congressional leaders kept the government functioning, but the new taxes they all agreed to did nothing to spur economic growth. There was no payoff. The economy stalled, the deficit continued to grow, and President Bush was forced to break an important pledge, arguably the defining pledge of his presidential campaign. When Bush took office, the national debt was approaching $3 trillion,* and "the federal government did not have the revenues for any large, new domestic ventures, nor did the political climate lend itself to enacting them."[85] It is worth reminding everyone at this point that the Democrats, who controlled Congress, were generally interested in increasing spending, raising taxes, and picking up more seats in the upcoming November elections while Republicans were generally interested in keeping spending as low as possible, cutting taxes, and minimizing Democratic gains in the House and Senate—if not picking up seats.

---

* Triple what it was in 1980.

With this stalemate, the president was at a logjam in budget negotiations with Capitol Hill, and after lengthy sessions with House and Senate leaders, he saw no choice but to raise taxes as a means of passing a budget and helping to reduce the deficit.[86] In a statement he issued to the press in June 1990, the president said,

> It is clear to me that both the size of the deficit problem and the need for a package that can be enacted require all of the following: entitlement and mandatory program reform, tax revenue increases, growth incentives, discretionary spending reductions, orderly reductions in defense expenditures, and budget process reform to assure that any bipartisan agreement is enforceable and that the deficit problem is brought under responsible control. The bipartisan leadership agree with me on these points.[87]

And with that sentence the pledge to "read my lips" was broken.*

President Bush's conservative grassroots supporters were increasingly unhappy. Republicans come to their party with a great many different personal, political, and ideological emphases on a great many issues, both foreign and domestic (some are more socially conservative than others; some are more hawkish than others). But almost all of them are united on lower tax rates, and certainly not increasing taxes. The important thing to remember is that George H. W. Bush had long been thought of as a socially liberal Northeastern Republican moderate, despite his living in Texas, and had been distrusted by many in the conservative grassroots of the Republican Party before becoming president. Indeed, even on tax policy, in his 1980 quest for the presidency, he had labeled Ronald Reagan's supply-side concept of cutting taxes to spur economic growth as "voodoo economics." In

---

* Toward the end of the year, RNC Chairman Lee Atwater had taken ill with a deadly brain tumor, and the president had asked me to replace him at the RNC. I was eager to help my old friend and boss, and new party, once again. (I had only switched to the Republican Party some four years before.) When I was told by some of the president's advisors that I would be expected to defend the tax hike, however, I said I could not. "It was only a pledge," one advisor told me. Yes, but pledges matter and important pledges matter even more, and this was *the pledge* (if not the most famous line) of the election; it was the rhetorical heart of the campaign for president. I did not ultimately take the job.

fact, although loyally serving President Reagan through two terms, part of the reason for his strong pledge to "read my lips, no new taxes" in 1988 was to solidify conservatives' support and disabuse the grassroots of any notion that he hewed to his pre-1981 economic philosophy. More than a politically savvy move by a smart candidate, the proof was in the pudding—Reagan's economic record was one of recovery and growth.

But with the 1990 tax hike, conservatives had cause to worry all over again. That year, the leading conservative magazine in the country, *National Review*, would editorialize that the White House's performance was "disastrous" and that the Republican Party was "more fractious" than it had been since Watergate.[88]

Worse, from the conservatives' point of view, President Bush used his first Supreme Court vacancy in the fall of 1990 to appoint a New Hampshire judge named David Souter. Even before the contentious 1987 Robert Bork confirmation hearings, the Supreme Court had become the leading indicator of political and cultural brawling, and divisive economic, environmental, and social policies were litigated there every session. The prior year, the court had overturned a Texas statute criminalizing flag burning, upsetting many patriotic Americans. And both the right and the left sought to jockey various aspects of their abortion-related agendas through the courts—the Holy Grail being to prevail before the Supreme Court.

David Souter was unknown nationally, and his record was undistinguished. Without controversial rulings or opinions in his baggage, he was thought confirmable; there was nothing for an opponent to attack. If there were doubts on this point, conservatives had little doubt about the nominee's commitment to strict constructionism (the belief that the founding documents should be adhered to in understanding current cases and controversies and that new rights or privileges should not be created to fit a politically desired outcome). Usually a strict constructionist's views are pretty well known within the conservative or strict construction movement.* But

---

* I was among this group of conservatives who had doubts about Souter, and I, and a few others (including Bill Kristol), went to Chief of Staff John Sununu to warn him about our misgivings. But the White House gave us assurances, as the saying goes, and Republican Senator Warren Rudman and the chief of staff (both residents of the Granite State) vouched for Souter. Rudman's support—given his liberal record—was, actually, one of the causes of our concern.

the Bush team wanted no repeat of the furor over the Bork nomination and wanted a nominee who would sail through the Senate and who, they thought, would uphold a commitment to conservative jurisprudence. They were right about the former: David Souter was confirmed by a Democratic Senate with ninety votes.[89] They were wrong about the latter: once seated, David Souter became known as one of the most liberal justices on the Supreme Court. Ever after, conservatives would be motivated to ensure Supreme Court nominations from their president would be well-established strict constructionists.

Notwithstanding the growing doubt from conservatives, President Bush faithfully vetoed any legislation that would have loosened restrictions on abortion. He strongly upheld President Reagan's Mexico City Policy, ruling out U.S. aid to international organizations that promote or perform abortions. And in gratitude for this continued support, the National Right to Life Committee (NRLC) and most mainstream pro-life groups continued to back President Bush.

VI. Storms in the Desert

Our attention to Europe and to domestic issues soon shifted to a tumultuous event we simply could not ignore. On 2 August 1990, Iraq's dictator, Saddam Hussein, invaded neighboring Kuwait.[90] Not only was Saddam's invasion a naked act of aggression; it also threatened a major realignment of the balance of power in the Middle East, especially as Hussein had threatened to turn Kuwait "into a graveyard" if any other country tried to stand in his way. If Saddam's aggression went unanswered, though, he would likely have seized Saudi Arabia as well—and Iraq, Saudi Arabia, and Kuwait were known for, basically, one big, important export: oil.

But it was not just "all about oil." Saddam Hussein used his oil revenues to finance his republic of terror. He maintained power by the sword—torturing his citizens, even gassing people to death as he had done to thousands of Iraqi Kurds two years before. Had his invasion of Kuwait been allowed to stand, had he followed up by overrunning Saudi Arabia, Saddam Hussein would have become the new Saladin; he would have claimed leadership of the Arab world. And he would have had the resources to make his claim stick.

George Bush wasn't having it. "This aggression will not stand," he said. He overcame some advice from the commentariat to not get involved and began building Operation Desert Shield to defend the Saudi kingdom from a Saddam attack.* He then immediately set about building an international coalition to force Saddam out of Kuwait, and the effort became Desert Storm. When Prime Minister Thatcher visited Bush at Camp David, she was widely quoted as saying, "This is no time to go wobbly, George." A year after liberating Panama, there was not much chance he would go wobbly. Now, he drew "a line in the sand" in the Arabian Desert.

Mrs. Thatcher could be forgiven for worrying about U.S. resolve, especially considering the U.S. Congress's oppositional position to President Bush. And worse, former President Jimmy Carter was lobbying furiously to stop a U.S.-led military effort against Saddam's invasion. Worth recalling is that he was president when Iran took American hostages, and he allowed those hostages to remain in captivity for 444 days. Drummed out of office by the American people, Carter now seemed to be playing to an international audience. Former President Carter had also long desired the Nobel Peace Prize. In these efforts, he worked tirelessly to undo President Bush's patient labor of coalition building. "I urge you to call publicly for a delay in the use of force," Carter wrote to Saudi King Fahd, Egypt's Hosni Mubarak, and Syria's Hafez al-Assad on 10 January 1991. He acknowledged that he was acting against U.S. policy, but he told these Arab rulers that they would find "the French, the Soviets, and others fully supportive."**[91]

Fortunately for President Bush, the Soviets were preoccupied at home. The Inner Empire was unraveling. The Baltic states of Lithuania, Estonia,

---

* It was at this time that a radicalized Saudi millionaire named Osama bin Laden, who had helped organize and fund Arab freedom fighters fighting the Soviets, offered to help the Saudi government defend itself and its oil fields from an Iraqi incursion. The Saudi government decided to put its trust in the American government instead. Angered by the U.S. presence on what was considered "holy land," bin Laden "felt betrayed" and moved to the Sudan. (See Lawrence Wright, "The Man Behind bin Laden," *The New Yorker*, 18 September 2002.)

** Such negotiations with foreign powers by a private U.S. citizen have been against the law since passage of the Logan Act in 1798. The reason such figures as Jimmy Carter, Ramsey Clark, and Jesse Jackson have not been prosecuted is their prominence, not their innocence.

and Latvia strained for their independence. And there were rumblings in the Ukraine as well. This meant that the Soviets' support for their Mideast client, Saddam Hussein, would not be forthcoming. President Bush asked Congress for a resolution authorizing the use of force. It passed by a wide margin in the House, but only narrowly in the Senate.

Over many years, President Bush had developed a trusting relationship with Mrs. Thatcher, King Fahd, Hosni Mubarak, and Mikhail Gorbachev. He observed to one friend that now it all came together—his experience at the UN, with the CIA, and as envoy to China.[92] He overcame Carter's efforts and went on to gain the UN's approval for the use of force to liberate Kuwait.

At the same time, Americans—along with much of the rest of the Western world—were beginning to familiarize themselves more and more with the maps, terminologies, and leaders of the Middle East. Contrary to much popular wisdom at the time, Saddam Hussein was not exclusively a secular Arab leader; at a minimum he was willing to use his religion as it suited his political purposes. In attempts to unite other Islamic states around him, he played up his theocratic tendencies. For example, Hussein ensured pictures of him praying to Allah were disseminated across the world, he had personally funded the building of Sunni mosques in Iraq and in other countries, and he changed the Iraqi national flag to add the words *Allahu Akbar* (God is great) in his own handwriting.[93]

Hussein's desired allies did not come, and the war did not last long. Following his strategic aerial bombardment plan, General H. Norman Schwarzkopf led a combined ground force of almost thirty nations. Americans, of course, made up the bulk of the half million that over-whelmed the dispirited Iraqis in Kuwait and southern Iraq. Schwarzkopf's brilliant success cut off the Iraqis in Kuwait. Thousands fled from Kuwait along the main road to Baghdad. It soon became "The Highway of Death" as U.S. warplanes decimated Saddam's vaunted Republican Guards. And Americans at home became used to regular briefings from top military personnel as they had not in a long time, perhaps since Vietnam. Secretary of Defense Dick Cheney and Chairman of the Joint Chiefs of Staff General Colin Powell (the first black man to become chairman of the Joint Chiefs) became household names. General Powell famously said on national television that the task was first to cut off the head of the Republican Guard "and then to kill it."

This is not to say Hussein did not wreak certain havoc. He did try to make good on one promise, in an attempt to turn Kuwait and one other nation "into a graveyard." He launched Scud missiles at Israel's capital city, Tel Aviv, as well as into Haifa, in an effort to do as much damage to Israel as possible and to unite other Arab nations around him. (Israel was a non-party to Desert Storm, at President Bush's pleading.)[94] And he lit Kuwait's oil fields on fire, "creating a large scale environmental disaster"[95] so immense it could be seen from outer space. CNN described it this way: "Day vanished into night, black rain fell from the sky, and a vast network of lakes was born . . . lakes of oil as deep as six feet. Saddam also poured 10 million barrels of oil into the sea. Thousands of birds perished, and the people of the Persian Gulf became familiar with new diseases."[96]

With the military liberation of Kuwait achieved, Bush stopped the war one hundred hours into major ground combat. General Schwarzkopf met Saddam's generals to negotiate a cease-fire. Incredibly, Saddam had survived the complete rout of his army and country in what he had called "the mother of all battles," as America quickly withdrew its forces but maintained northern and southern "no fly" zones in Iraq in an attempt to contain Saddam from further aggression. America erred, however, in urging Iraqi citizens to rise up and overthrow Saddam Hussein—we did not back them up, and he unleashed a new, postwar slaughter on the thousands of those who tried.[97]

President Bush, Secretary of State James Baker, Defense Secretary Dick Cheney, General Norman Schwarzkopf, and General Colin Powell were criticized by many on the right (including me) for not liberating Iraq from Saddam Hussein as well. But they would ever afterward defend their decision to not go all the way to Baghdad to topple Saddam and remove him from power (as we had done with, say, Noriega). To do so, they argued, would have split the coalition and gone beyond the UN's authorization of force. The Saudis were not eager to have a Shiite-led majority Muslim state on their border (Saddam Hussein was a Sunni dictator in a majority Shiite state—toppling him would likely give majority-governing status to the Shiites who, the fear was, would ally with Iran). The Turks would not have wanted Iraq's Kurds empowered (possibly to make common cause with Turkey's restive Kurdish minority). The French and the Soviets would have threatened hostile action at the UN. Given the conditions of the time—which President Bush keenly appreciated—it is hard to second-guess him, although many of us did. And then again, this would not be the last we heard from Saddam Hussein. History, it is said, does not reveal its alternatives.

America's impressive victory in the Gulf War was achieved by February 1991 and, like Operation Just Cause, with a minimal number of casualties. And many argued our "Vietnam Syndrome" was finally over. For years, many Americans were hesitant or gun-shy to deploy massive military force because the memory of Vietnam still rang too clearly in their heads. The combined effects of Just Cause and Desert Storm put an end to that—for the time being.

At home, despite some antiwar protests and antiwar teach-ins on college and university campuses, a new era of patriotism arose in the United States, and songs like Lee Greenwood's "God Bless the USA," written several years before, received new interest and popularity, topping the country charts all over again. Greenwood's song became "the second national anthem," as one radio insider put it.[98] Listenership to country music had a way of surging in turn-of-the-century America, especially in times of great loss or war. It was shortly after the Gulf War (as Operation Desert Storm was also known) that a whole new range of country music stars began to arrive on the scene and, indeed, to change the sound of country music toward a more modern and youthful beat and sound—adding a slew of new country music female artists, in a traditionally male genre, along the way.

But in the intellectual fight for the most important of causes, something old would come back too. Through his syndicated column and national television commentary, former Richard Nixon aide and Ronald Reagan White House Communications Director Pat Buchanan had become an important voice on the right in America. And in the lead-up to the Gulf War, he made news when he vocally opposed it (as few on the right did). He bluntly said on national television, "There are only two groups that are beating the drums for war in The Middle East—the Israeli Defense Ministry and its amen corner in the United States."[99] Earlier, he had called Capitol Hill "Israeli-occupied territory."[100] To many ears, this was a not-so-veiled attack on Jewish interests with an implied charge of dual loyalty.

In an oddly deduced acceptance of the "End of History" thesis, Buchanan pointed to the Soviets pulling out of Afghanistan, the Sandinistas voted out of office in Nicaragua, and the Communist bloc collapsing in Eastern Europe, arguing that the time had come for the U.S. to return to its policy of nonentanglement with world alliances. He called for a renewed commitment to "America First." Problematically enough, America First was the name of Charles Lindbergh's pre-WWII organization. It was Lindbergh who specifically blamed the British nation along with Jews in America for seeking to involve the U.S. in the war against Hitler. Many friends of Pat Buchanan—myself included—were dismayed (at the least) by his charge.

In truth, however, it was far more than just the Israeli Defense Ministry and its supporters who thought the invasion of Kuwait and the takeover of Saudi Arabia by a tyrant were bad for the world as well as America. Not to put too fine a point on it, the Bush administration was simply not susceptible to the charge of doing Israel's bidding: not one member of the Bush administration's cabinet was Jewish, some had been pretty critical of Israel in the past (and would be again in the future), and Israel—unlike some countries that did not even recognize Israel's right to exist—was not a part of the Desert Storm coalition.

VII. A New Attention to Race

Sometimes in America, an unfamous man can unwittingly cause a news storm and a cultural shift in currents. And so it was, in California, when racial anguish in this country was catalyzed in Los Angeles after the California Highway Patrol noted a seemingly regular case of speeding. It would become anything but "regular."[101]

Rodney King was speeding down the California 210 Freeway at more than one hundred miles per hour with two other passengers when the Highway Patrol and Los Angeles Police Department (LAPD) gave chase. "He ran a red light, nearly causing an accident, before finally coming to a stop."[102]

King would later say he didn't initially stop because he thought the speeding ticket would be a violation of his parole for second-degree burglary.[103]

King delayed but finally got out of his car. He seemed confused. LAPD officers ordered him to the ground, and King responded by lying down. While accounts vary about what happened next, it was determined that a police officer fired an electrical charge into King with a Taser gun and that an officer then beat King with a nightstick.[104] King, a black man, surrounded by several white officers, tried to get up, and two other officers joined in while the others stood by. About that time, a neighbor in the residential area started filming the episode with his video camera—unbeknownst to King or the police. This video would become "like wallpaper," as one journalist put it, because it was aired so many times on television. What the video then showed was one lunge attempt by King at an officer and then several more beatings on King with nightsticks while King tried to stand up again and again and was beaten again and again. When King was finally subdued, several officers turned him around on the pavement and began to handcuff him.

The whole video lasted just under two minutes—but Los Angeles was changed, as was much of the country. The public was rightfully horrified by the violent and persistent beating. Los Angeles Police Chief Daryl Gates asked the district attorney to file charges against and prosecute the officers.[105] Whatever the claims of the police on the scene were, the tough, no-nonsense, law-and-order Daryl Gates (with whom I had worked as drug czar) called for a prosecution, and a trial would be had. A new national dialogue on race would take place on college campuses and at dinner tables across the country.

And then, in the summer of 1991, Supreme Court Justice Thurgood Marshall announced his retirement. President Bush's second appointment to the Supreme Court, Clarence Thomas, would be an entirely different event from David Souter's—in politics, culture, and ease in confirmation. In fact, in short order, it would make the nomination of Robert Bork look and feel like a day in the park. Justice Marshall had been a pioneer in the civil rights movement, having argued the famous landmark case *Brown v. Board of Education* in 1954 and going on to be the first black justice on the Supreme Court (appointed by President Lyndon B. Johnson). There was a tradition for naming certain pioneer replacements to the Supreme Court that one could argue was established when the renowned Jewish scholar and Harvard professor Felix Frankfurter was named by President Franklin Roosevelt to replace Justice Benjamin Cardozo in 1939.[106] That seat, for example, would be held by several prominent Jewish Americans (after Cardozo first was nominated to it by President Herbert Hoover) over the years. After Frankfurter, successors to that seat would include Arthur Goldberg and Abe Fortas. President Richard Nixon interrupted that tradition following Fortas's resignation with the naming of Harry Blackmun.

With Justice Thurgood Marshall retiring, it was well established by the mood of the country—based on many of the successes of the civil rights movement—that his seat was the black seat on the Supreme Court. Some may call that a quota; others would argue that such a prominent position in our law and culture should be fairly represented by a member of the minority or black community, both for reasons of fairness and legitimacy. The first hitch for the administration was ideological. Many in the black community, especially what might be considered the elite or establishment black community (i.e., those in the professional classes like the legal community, like the leadership in the NAACP), were committed ideological liberals or Democrats. Still, usually, with few exceptions, a president was expected to appoint members to the Supreme Court who would share his ideology or help continue his legal worldview.

It was not entirely the case that all blacks in the professional classes were liberals, but certainly a great many were, especially in the professoriate and civil rights organizations. Many Republicans had tried to make inroads in the black community over the years, however, and it is worth remembering that the political fealty the black community had for the Democratic Party and its more liberal ideology was a relatively recent circumstance that began in the 1940s and '50s in, and just after, the New Deal. Still, there were exceptions. The legendary singer Pearl Bailey had endorsed and worked with Republican candidates,[107] as had Sammy Davis Jr.; Rev. Martin Luther King Jr.'s friend and collaborator, Rev. Ralph Abernathy, had voted for President Ronald Reagan;[108] the famous civil rights icon James Meredith had voted and worked for Republicans and had run on the Republican ticket for the U.S. Senate;[109] and football legend (and Bobby Kennedy's good friend) Roosevelt Grier had campaigned for Ronald Reagan's reelection in 1984. And others, like essayist Stanley Crouch, were hard to pigeonhole into a party or particular movement, because they had broken from some of the more liberal political nostrums—especially on issues like racial preferences in the law. In the academy, there was a rising group of younger black Americans who were also known for their conservative and Republican Party affiliations.

In the legal field, President Bush turned to Clarence Thomas, a Yale-educated lawyer who was the chairman of the Equal Employment Opportunity Commission under Presidents Ronald Reagan and George H. W. Bush. Thomas had been a Republican for some time, having worked for Republican Missouri Attorney General and U.S. Senator John Danforth, and he was greatly influenced in his thinking about natural law and the Declaration of Independence as interpreted by Professor Harry V. Jaffa, the well-known Abraham Lincoln scholar and conservative philosopher from the Claremont Institute and Claremont McKenna College.

The left in America, aided by Democratic Party activists and U.S. senators, would stop at nearly nothing to try and prevent Clarence Thomas's nomination. In his Senate Judiciary Committee hearings, chaired by U.S. Senator Joe Biden, he was savagely attacked when a former assistant, Anita Hill, raised questions about his personal conduct toward her. Miss Hill, a professor of law who specialized in sexual harassment, had never charged Thomas with a sexual harassment suit or filed a formal complaint. Instead, she vaguely claimed that he had made an off-color joke about a character in a pornographic movie and that he had once referenced, in her presence, to a part of the private anatomy. She maintained, too, that he had asked her on dates while she was under his employ. That Anita Hill had followed Clarence Thomas to work for him in a couple of different jobs seemed to discount her allegations, as had countertestimony from other friends and colleagues of Mr. Thomas.

For these allegations, Judge Thomas, a black man of formidable dignity, was subjected to what he dramatically termed a "high-tech lynching" on national TV, and he denied each and every one of Anita Hill's charges.

In the end, much of Anita Hill's testimony collapsed under the weight of probing questions from the Judiciary Committee's Senator Arlen Specter. President Bush continued to back his nominee and saw him through a close 52-48 confirmation in the Senate. Justice Thomas would, indeed, go on to be considered one of the more conservative members of the Court, and one of the only justices to continually look to and cite such founding documents as the Declaration of Independence to distill the founders' opinions on constitutional and legal matters before him.

That the language and references made during the Thomas-Hill showdown would become so common on national television and radio was a major turning point in our culture.* The culture, from high to low, had already started getting used to discussions of—if not anthems to—sexuality and private body parts on national television, on the radio airwaves, and in music stores.** Many of us at the time described this period as one of a general coarsening of the popular culture. Two years before the Thomas-Hill showdown, the country had become engaged in a national discussion on the public funding of pornographic art. The National Endowment for the Arts (NEA) had previously been almost an invisible federal agency. With a budget of less than $200 million,[110] it was nearly a forgotten entity. But under President Bush's chairman, John Frohnmayer, the NEA became a major battleground in a teeming cultural war. When it was revealed that the agency and its advisory commission were funding the promotion of performance art that was pornography by any definition, grassroots activists raised a hue and cry against the NEA.

As an example of this performance art, one "artist" would appear nude onstage, cover herself with chocolate sauce and bean sprouts, and talk about the oppression of women. Not many years before, such a "performance"

---

* I have substantially edited out a great deal of the graphic language and terminology that came out of the Clarence Thomas hearings, but those alive during the time will remember it well.

** Earlier in the decade, Tipper Gore (the wife of then Senator Al Gore) had become an activist for parental warning labels on the music that children would purchase (later, during the presidential candidacy of her husband, she would explicitly recant her position after complaints from show business activists), but by the latter part of the decade a new form of music, called gangsta rap, by such groups as NWA (Niggaz with Attitude), would take all that to a new level. They would release albums with track listings celebrating violence and very rough, misogynist, sexual violence.

would have been a scandal and shut down in certain neighborhoods. Now, it and similar performances were bringing in federal grants. Many religious Americans were horrified to learn about one grant recipient who had immersed an image of Jesus Christ on a crucifix in urine and displayed the photograph. Another exhibit involved inviting the public to climb a stairway, walking on the American flag.

Beyond the offense to their sensibilities, at a time of budget constraints and a weakening economy, many Americans simply thought the government was out of control. Hadn't the volunteers of the Reagan antitax rebellion risen up to quash just such foolish and wasteful government spending? A national debate erupted about the propriety of such funding, and Senator Jesse Helms, a Republican from North Carolina, sponsored legislation to end it. Helms and his supporters were opposed by those who argued that, as columnist George Will characterized their position, "government is obligated to support art and equally obligated not to think about what art is or is good for. They argue that government support for the arts serves the public interest, but that government cannot express an interest in the kind of art that is supported."[111] Will emphasized the middle ground between these two extremes: "There is a long American tradition of support on the grounds that the arts elevate the public mind by bringing it into contact with beauty and even ameliorate social pathologies. But if the power of art is profound, it need not be benign. And the policy of public subsidies must distinguish between art that serves an elevating purpose and art that that does not."[112]

Some years earlier, the social critic and founder of the neoconservative political movement, Irving Kristol, put the whole debate this way: almost any production deemed art (be it a book, a play, or a movie), at a minimum, carries with it a message or an intended instruction; to believe otherwise is to believe "that art is morally trivial and that education is morally irrelevant."[113] No artist, just as no educator, actually believes that Kristol argued. So, the debate was truly about whether the government (or, more to the point, the people of the United States) had the right to state what moral lesson and what public purpose its money would support.

George Will concluded his thoughts on the debate by giving the artists' argument, that nobody has the right to define their art, their due: "If, as some artists say, no one can say what art is (or, hence, what the adjective 'fine' means as a modifier), then art becomes a classification that does not classify. Then the NEA should be the NEE—National Endowment for Everything. It will need a bigger budget."[114]

Ultimately, Congress passed restrictions on NEA funding, and those restrictions were upheld by the Supreme Court—but not without a long, drawn-out fight and public argument.

VIII. Greatness and Gratitude

On Christmas Day 1991, the red hammer and sickle flag of the Soviet Union was lowered from the Kremlin towers for the last time.[115] Mikhail Gorbachev yielded his office to Boris Yeltsin as the president of a newly reconstituted Russian Republic.

"Free elections have become a reality. Free press, freedom of worship, representative legislatures and a multi-party system have all become a reality," Gorbachev said in a national address on live television. "Due to the situation which has evolved as a result of the formation of the Commonwealth of Independent states I hereby discontinue my activities at the post of president of the Union of Soviet Socialist Republics."[116]

The old red, blue, and white tricolor of the tsars was raised in Moscow and over Saint Petersburg. Lithuania, Latvia, and Estonia were independent for the first time since Stalin rolled over them in 1940. The Ukraine and Belarus were also independent, loosely aligned with the Russian Republic in a short-lived Confederation of Independent States. It was simply a fig leaf to cover the reality: the USSR had dissolved. Communism—formally at least—had been abandoned.

Margaret Thatcher loyally supported Presidents Reagan and Bush. They all had worked with a remarkable Polish pope, Pope John Paul II. Behind the Iron Curtain, men like Lech Walesa and Vaclav Havel played crucial roles. Aleksandr Solzhenitsyn's *Gulag Archipelago* battered the Communists' pretensions of humanitarianism intellectually. So did human rights activists within the Soviet Union like Andrei Sakharov and his wife, Elena Bonner,

Natan Sharansky, and others among communism's millions of prisoners of conscience. The honor roll is long, but not as long as it should be.

For all their courage, their vision, and their splendid achievement, it could all have come disastrously crashing down had it not been for the self-effacing modesty, patience, and diplomatic skill of George H. W. Bush. He worked tirelessly to make sure that the free world came through this most difficult passage peacefully.

For all this, he was pilloried on TV and in the press. "It wouldn't be prudent," mimicked *Saturday Night Live*'s Dana Carvey in a soon-to-be famous impression of the man who braved deadly enemy fire for his country while still in his teens. For his prudence, he was called a wimp by men who never flew anything more dangerous than a paper airplane. But President Bush took it all in stride with his sense of grace and humor—he even invited Carvey to the White House.

Great nations, it is said, are too often ungrateful nations. And we Americans have a great nation. But surely, for our gratefulness and greatness, no people can expect to show their thanks every time they have an election. And in the election year of 1992 gratefulness was at a discount.

Two

Rise of the Boomer

The 1990s was a decade of great possibility; many thought we had reached an "End of History." It turned out otherwise. To be sure, communism was finished in Eastern Europe, and the fear of a nuclear confrontation had receded. A new, young president would be inaugurated from the Democratic Party—a party that had been out of control of the White House for twelve years. Within two years of his election, the Republican Party would take back control of the House of Representatives—something it had not had in forty years. If there was no European Communist threat, there was a much larger one brewing as Middle Eastern terrorism would make its first strike inside the United States, as well as at U.S. outposts abroad. Senseless domestic violence would also strike at America, and the country would go through a state murder trial with national implications that was anything but satisfying in its outcome.

I. "It's the Economy, Stupid!": The Election of 1992

By the end of 1991, the bloom was off the rose for President Bush. His stratospheric approval ratings were at a record high of more than 90 percent after the miraculous victory of Operation Desert Storm—a high place to be, a high place from which to fall.*

---

* The peaking approval rating was so high (perhaps deceptively so) in early 1991 that I recall sitting on a panel at the National Press Club saying there was nothing to stop a second term for George H. W. Bush. I recall everyone on the panel, left and right, sharing my view.

The lightning-quick victory in the Middle East became a distant memory for many as the economy went south and took the president's approval ratings along with it. By November 1991 (one year ahead of the presidential election), his approval hovered just above 50 percent.[1] The low numbers were an invitation for opposition. The president soon faced an insurgency within his own party, the threat of an independent challenger, and a bevy of Democrats eager to take him on.

Pat Buchanan vowed to challenge President Bush in the Republican primaries of 1992. Quoting Thomas Jefferson, he said, "I hold it that a little rebellion now and then is a good thing, and as necessary in the political world as storms in the physical."* Warming to his theme, Buchanan referred to his "brigades" as "peasants with pitchforks." Once again, the famous wordsmith evoked a disturbing image: "Pitchfork" Ben Tillman was known for his anti-black views in South Carolina after the Civil War as much as anything else.

A more politically dangerous opponent soon arose in Bush's adopted home state. Texas billionaire and entrepreneur H. Ross Perot was increasingly angered by the partisan bickering over the budget in Washington. He began to send out hints during several appearances on the Larry King television show on CNN in 1992 that he would consider running for president as an independent. Perot was something of a hero, if not iconoclast, in the national mind. A Texarkana-born graduate of Annapolis, he had long supported the navy and other veteran causes and had earned a good deal of publicity for very generous personal funding efforts to help deliver food and gifts to our soldiers in Vietnam. In 1983 he became the subject of a famous novel (*On Wings of Eagles* by Ken Follett) for his successful, privately funded and planned rescue of two of his employees who were held in Iran against their will in 1979.**[2] To many, he was the living embodiment of the American dream and American patriotism. His was a rags-to-riches story, but he was also known for his old-

---

* Jefferson's famous "little rebellion" letter had been written to his friend James Madison while Jefferson was in Paris. It was his mild reaction to Shays's Rebellion in 1786. Madison never favored rebellions, little or large. Neither did George Washington, Alexander Hamilton, or John Adams. In fact, it was this little rebellion of Daniel Shays as much as anything else that prompted the founders to become framers. They would write a Constitution that empowered government to put down by force the very rebellions that Mr. Jefferson praised.

** To this day, *On Wings of Eagles* still sells as the thrilling story.

school ways. He was not a glamorous cocktail-circuit billionaire; he dressed and lived fairly modestly, and required his employees to remain clean-cut (they could not have beards or mustaches, and they had to follow a strict dress code). While most would have assumed that he was a Republican, he was not a fan of President Bush and had even opposed the Gulf War.[3]

Perot, like Buchanan, was tapping into an increasingly sour national mood. It might have been exhaustion. In addition to the Gulf War, the nation had won an incredible victory in ending the Cold War. That existential clash had threatened Americans with annihilation for four decades. Relieved of that burden, people focused on their personal situations. Heavy industry in the Rust Belt states—Pennsylvania, Ohio, Michigan, and Illinois—had been hit hard by the shift to an information and service based economy. American heavy manufacturers suffered from the effects of global competition. As one economic journalist has written of the period, "There were huge layoffs on Wall Street and much anxiety about the stability of the banking system. Savings and loans were failing everywhere. Real estate prices slumped."[4] The recession had ended by April 1991, but as with any recession, it took time to recover, including from job losses. The unemployment rate had gone from just over 5 percent when President Bush was inaugurated in 1989 to over 7 percent by the end of 1991.[5] The Misery Index we spoke of earlier had gone from 10.7 when President Bush was inaugurated to the 11 and 12 percentage ranges in the 1990–91 period and would not settle back down into the lower ends of the 10 percentage range until late 1992.[6]

Meanwhile, the Democrats had not had the White House since 1980 and were determined to regain it after more than a decade of Republican control. But there was one major problem: no nationally recognized Democratic leader was able to take the spotlight and run for president. Many had thought the charismatic and articulate Democratic governor of New York, Mario Cuomo, would run, but he inexplicably decided not to do so.* Perhaps many, like Cuomo, did not think (in 1991) their chances were too good against a

---

* To this day, it is uncertain why Governor Cuomo did not want to seek higher office. Over the years, he and I had become good acquaintances despite our partisan differences. In time, we became well-traveled debate duelers on the lecture circuit, but we also worked together on our mutual conviction, reducing illegal drug abuse, by co-chairing the Partnership for a Drug-Free America.

president who had been at record-high approvals and had steered us through a rapid war victory. By the end of 1991, though, such thinking would prove to make little sense as President Bush's poll numbers had dropped quite precipitously. Still, eleven months before an election is too late to start a presidential campaign.

Nonetheless, on the Democratic side, candidates lined up. Former Massachusetts Senator Paul Tsongas had a compelling personal story of triumph over adversity. He had left the Senate to spend more time with his family in 1984 when he was diagnosed with cancer. Through grit and determination, aided by the best medical care system on earth, Tsongas had pulled through. By 1992, he was in remission. Senator Bob Kerrey of Nebraska was the first Medal of Honor winner ever to run for president; he was a straight talker and war hero, having lost part of one leg in Vietnam. Former California Governor Jerry Brown (better known in the 1970s) threw his hat in the ring. And then there was the governor of Arkansas, William Jefferson Clinton.

Bill Clinton was a political *wunderkind* in that state. He had been elected five times in that solidly Democratic state but was still only forty-five years old. A Rhodes Scholar, with a law degree from Yale, he was glib, articulate, and he had the capacity to light up a room. His gift of gab was noticeable. Even though he had spoken too long at the 1988 Democratic Convention on behalf of Michael Dukakis, the nation took note of this otherwise energetic and charming speaker. He would later comment about his 1988 speech, saying, "Well, the people of Arkansas know I can give a good speech." Indeed, they did. Bill Clinton could speak extemporaneously on almost any subject. His range of knowledge and command of policy papers were impressive.*

Unfortunately for Bill Clinton, the "buzz" on him among Democrats was that he was unelectable because of what was politely called "the character issue." Rumors of his womanizing were legendary beyond Arkansas. He also had a tangled story to tell about his failure to report for the Vietnam-era draft. And he had a penchant for trying to satisfy almost any of his audiences. For this, Paul Tsongas dubbed him a "pander bear."

---

* I had known Governor Clinton a bit prior to his entry into the 1992 presidential race. We had debated on television in 1988 as surrogates for President Bush and Governor Dukakis, and before that, I had praised him for some of his efforts in education reform in Arkansas.

As he plunged into the New Hampshire primary, Clinton faced a national tabloid exposé. A woman named Gennifer Flowers had sold her story to the gossip sheets and claimed to have had a long-term affair with then Governor Clinton. Almost simultaneously, Clinton was confronted with a letter he had written to the head of the ROTC unit at the University of Arkansas. In it, he spoke of "loathing the military."

This double-barreled assault on his character and record would normally have been enough to destroy any candidate. Party professionals remembered the 1987 implosion of Gary Hart over the *Monkey Business* affair. But Clinton didn't flinch. He and his strong, supportive wife, Hillary Rodham Clinton, appeared on CBS News' *60 Minutes* broadcast on the night of the Super Bowl to answer some of these charges. Governor Clinton had also hired a different kind of political staff than previous Democratic candidates had hired—younger, more assertive, more aggressive. This group of new political combatants had put together what they dubbed "a war room" to answer every charge hurled at their candidate—from the personal to the political. They had learned from the earlier Dukakis campaign that everything needed to be answered and thrown back, hard. This group of young comers included names previously not known on the national scene, including Paul Begala, James Carville, George Stephanopoulos, and Bill Clinton's politically astute and combative wife. On *60 Minutes*, Governor Clinton, sitting next to his wife, denied the Flowers story, but he expressed regret for "having caused pain in my marriage." For millions of Americans, it was their first introduction to this amazingly coordinated and resilient couple.

The Clintons' performance struck many as the perfect response for a modern, sophisticated married couple who, having experienced difficult times, forgave one another and stayed together for the sake of their child (or children) and their vital work. And as a political strategy, it worked.

Clinton happily returned to the campaign trail, hammering away at the Bush economic record. The most famous of his strategists, always good for a television sound bite, was James Carville. With a strong Louisiana accent, he was nicknamed the "Ragin' Cajun." Aggressively, humorously, Carville pounded home the theme of the Clinton campaign: "It's the economy, stupid!" What he meant was that no matter what else anyone brought up—from Bill Clinton's character to President Bush's long résumé—they should always return to the issue of the economy. At a time of unemployment, when millions of Americans lacked health insurance, Carville and his team would argue how silly, how trivial it was to talk or even think about things like sexual misconduct or the Vietnam draft.

New Hampshire's jealously guarded "first in the nation" primary was poised to rock the American political system again in 1992. The question was: Could Bill Clinton survive the talk of scandal along with the fact that Paul Tsongas was practically a favorite son in New Hampshire (because he was from neighboring Massachusetts)?

Meanwhile, on the Republican side, Pat Buchanan had taken to scoring President Bush again and again on everything from the economy to foreign relations to cultural issues. Buchanan was tapping into a populist sentiment that few candidates since Ronald Reagan had been successful in attracting. Buchanan's version, however, was less cheerful than Reagan's version—more bitter, anti–free trade, more isolationist, and more distrusted by minority voters. But in the famously antitax state of New Hampshire, Buchanan made great hay of President Bush's tax hike—his leading television advertisement was called "Broken Promises."[7]

The Bush team was slow to take on Pat Buchanan and thought him more of a nuisance than a serious challenge. As time would show, that was a mistake.* Pat Buchanan scored nearly 40 percent of the vote in the Republican primary, compared to 53 percent for President Bush.[8] Usually, this would be considered a solid first-place win for a candidate—but not for an incumbent president running against a member of his own party. As so often happens in New Hampshire, the result was played up as a sign of weakness for the incumbent. Here, for example, is how the *New York Times* reported it: "President Bush received a jarring political message in the New Hampshire primary . . . scoring a less-than-impressive victory over Patrick J. Buchanan, the conservative commentator."[9] In some ways, Pat Buchanan

---

* I had seen the appeal of Buchanan from around the country and in conservative circles and had told President Bush's team that they were making a mistake letting Buchanan kick them around. I strongly urged them to go to New Hampshire and take him on. They needed to take his campaign seriously and go after him. Eventually, I went up myself.

had made Bush a better candidate—forcing him to roll up his sleeves a little earlier than he otherwise would have, getting the president on the stump, defending his record, and resharpening his campaign skills. New Hampshire was—as it turned out—a flash in the pan for Buchanan, and he ended up winning no primaries over President Bush and secured no major elected politician's endorsement.

New Hampshire's Democratic primary was similarly subject to a media spin. Former Senator Paul Tsongas won the field, but Bill Clinton came in second by losing to Tsongas by eight points. Normally, that would be a convincing win as well. But 1992 was not normal. Within minutes of the polls' closing, Clinton was on every news channel, buoyantly—*exuberantly*—proclaiming himself "the comeback kid," on the advice of his other talented strategist, Paul Begala. He was. The less-charismatic Tsongas was drowned in a flood of words. The quotable Clinton gave the reporters good ink, and the press likes a comeback story—as does America. Bill Clinton would go on to win big and important primaries in southern states like Georgia and South Carolina and, in short order, became the clear front-runner. He was a Democrat—at long last—that people thought could actually win a general election.

Clinton had proclaimed himself a "New Democrat." He had been a force in the Democratic Leadership Council—a group that struggled to make the party more competitive and centrist following disastrous defeats suffered by the party's dominant McGovern liberal wing. To this end, Clinton would stress his support for capital punishment—a sharp distinction from the politics of Michael Dukakis four years before. He pledged "to end welfare as we know it." He pitched his campaign to the forgotten middle class, "people who pay their taxes, obey the laws and play by the rules of the game." Abortion, he said, should be "safe, legal . . . and rare." And as a white southerner, Clinton was like Jimmy Carter in that he had established a strong, empathetic relationship with black Americans. This tie would prove critical to him throughout his political life.

Clinton surprised many when he chose Tennessee Senator Al Gore as his running mate, however. Gore was roughly the same age, hailing from a neighboring state. It was no "balanced" ticket—or was it?

Gore was seen as somewhat more hawkish than previous Democrats. He was known as a serious thinker and writer on environmental issues and defense. Gore added foreign policy heft to the ticket. But also, Al and Tipper Gore's marriage was famously free of any hint of scandal or dalliance. In selecting Al Gore, Clinton seemed to be saying to voters, "I know my own marriage has not been perfect, but I respect your traditional values and I will uphold them." The voters appreciated the compliment. If Bill Clinton was adventurous to the point of recklessness, Al Gore was steady, reliable, and maybe even a little boring. This was a new way of balancing the ticket. From the moment in June when Clinton named Al Gore, he was never behind in the public opinion polls.

Saying 1992 was not a usual election year may have been an understatement. A scourge had plagued the GOP—or at least the press portrayed it that way—that year in the form of former Louisiana State House member David Duke, who announced he, too, was running for president on the Republican ticket. Duke, who had been registered as a Democrat a few years before, was known more famously as a one-time prominent leader of the Ku Klux Klan. In 1991 he mounted a campaign for governor of Louisiana on the Republican ticket.* Close to the Louisiana election, President Bush did all in his power to read David Duke out of the Republican Party, saying at a D.C. press conference:

> When someone has a long record, an ugly record of racism and of bigotry, that record simply cannot be erased by the glib rhetoric of a political campaign. So I believe David Duke is an insincere charlatan. I believe he's attempting to hoodwink the voters of Louisiana. I believe he should be rejected for what he is and what he stands for.[10]

Duke ultimately lost the election in Louisiana but thought he could ply his trade nationally in 1992. His campaign drew some media interest—

---

* I, and others, had urged President Bush to denounce Duke as singularly unrepresentative of the Republican Party. I got through to the president on the telephone, and we had a good several-minute discussion about this. The president, initially unwilling to interfere too much in Louisiana's internal politics, ultimately came out with both barrels of his rhetorical shotgun.

especially because the one-time Democrat was now affiliating as a Republican. But the Republican Party tried to (and successfully did) bar him from running under their banner on many state ballots, and Duke's candidacy was mostly a side show; he won no delegates to the party convention.

When Ross Perot's new movement, the Reform Party, succeeded in gaining ballot access in all fifty states, however, President Bush's electoral fate was effectively sealed. Much of Perot's appeal was nonideological and intensely patriotic. Indeed, he picked (and could pay for) the best political consultants that money could buy on both sides of the aisle, including Ronald Reagan's famed campaign manager Ed Rollins, Jimmy Carter's campaign advisor and Chief of Staff Hamilton Jordan, up-and-coming GOP polling *wunderkind* Frank Luntz, and Democratic pollster Mark Penn. He heavily self-financed his campaign with staff and office space and equipment. Perot's appeal went beyond the Texan's ability for frank, plain talk. It was an appeal for the yearning of a leader who seemed above petty bickering and squabbling that many older voters—especially many retirees with time and money to donate—found so distasteful. These conservative citizens would normally have voted Republican, if they voted at all.

Perot's running mate was the widely admired Vice Admiral James Stockdale. Stockdale had been the leader of the American POWs in North Vietnam in the 1960s. His courage, character, and philosophical scholarship were admired by all. Perot's choice of Stockdale was a further message to the public of his deep and abiding commitment to (if not strategy to attract) military families. In the vice presidential debate, however, Stockdale was too philosophical, leading off on the wrong foot by asking questions such as, "Who am I? Why am I here?" Guffaws greeted Stockdale's questions. Shallow and immature observers thought the war hero was an out-of-touch has-been. They were wrong about Stockdale, a hero by any definition, but he was not on his game that night—of course politics had never been his game—and even had mentioned during the debate that he missed a few questions due to not having his hearing aids turned on. Still, his questions were entirely reasonable, and plenty of his answers to those questions were worthy of serious consideration. Stockdale was a student of the Greek Stoic philosopher Epictetus. One of that writer's most famous quotes could have served as a prophetic warning for American politics in the 1990s: "Control thy passions, lest they take vengeance on thee."[11] His debate performance—like others' before and since—was mocked on the late night television shows. But in another part of America he received high honor: the navy named and commissioned a destroyer after this worthy man.[12]

Perhaps Epictetus's quote could have applied to Ross Perot as well. His campaign is almost a faint memory now—and Mr. Perot has largely remained unheard from for the past decade. Yet his passions—even with the best political advice money could buy—got the best of him in his very rocky political campaign in 1992. He abruptly quit the presidential campaign in the summer of that year, in the midst of the Democratic Party's national convention taking place in New York. He had lost several of his advisors (including Ed Rollins) and said little at the time other than that he saw a "revitalized" Democratic Party and that he did not want to throw the election into the House of Representatives (which *could* have been the case if no candidate won a majority of electoral college votes).[13] But that was not the last of H. Ross Perot in 1992.

By October, Perot had changed his mind—again. A little more than a month before the election, Perot said, "I thought that both political parties would address the problems that face the nation. . . . We gave them a chance. They didn't do it."[14] By the end of October, he was citing different, stranger reasons for his return to the campaign. Perot claimed the real reason he left the campaign in the summer was that he had heard "that President Bush's campaign was scheming to smear his daughter with a computer-altered photograph and to disrupt her wedding."[15] He offered no proof, simply saying he received the information from friends and an unnamed "top Republican." Asked about these strange allegations, President Bush's press secretary, Marlin Fitzwater, said, "It's all nonsense. There's nothing to it. I don't want to attack Perot, but I don't know where he's getting it from. I mean, fantastic stories about his daughter and disrupting her wedding . . . it's all loony."*[16] What ultimately moved Perot in and out of and back into

---

* I was sitting with the president, having breakfast, when Perot was on one of the morning talk shows. We watched the performance, and the president turned to me, incredulous, shaking his head, saying, "Where does he come up with this stuff?"

the presidential sweepstakes in 1992 is anybody's guess, but his damage would be felt come November.

Meanwhile, far from the presidential politics taking place on the airwaves and in the preconvention period of the campaign, on the ground in Los Angeles other tempers were brewing. In April, a jury cleared the four police officers involved in the cruel beating of Rodney King the previous year. Almost immediately after the nation heard the verdict, riots, arson, and looting broke out in the streets and shops of L.A. That April night (the twenty-ninth), the nation saw a particularly horrific scene captured by news cameras when a white truck driver named Reginald Denny was stopped at a red light and dragged out of his truck by a group of black gang members and beaten senseless.[17] The following day, open gun battles took place on the streets, as well as between looters and shop owners (many Asian) defending their lives and property. Los Angeles Mayor Tom Bradley declared a state of emergency and imposed a curfew. Governor Pete Wilson deployed the National Guard to try to maintain order.[18] The following day, the cause célèbre, the man about whom all this started, Rodney King, maturely took to the cameras to plead with the citizens and rioters alike in Los Angeles:

People, I just want to say, you know, can we all get along? Can we get along? Can we stop making it . . . horrible for the older people and the kids? . . . It's just not right. It's not right. It's not . . . going to change anything. We'll, we'll get our justice. . . . Please, we can get along here. We all can get along.[19]

The quotation has entered our cultural lexicon as, "Can't we all just get along?" but what he asked was, "Can we all get along?" and as for a calm statement in the midst of a societal meltdown, it was about as appropriate as anything that could be said.

That same night, President Bush ordered thousands of military troops to Los Angeles, called for federal charges to be brought against the police who had beaten Rodney King, and said in a televised speech: "What we saw last night and the night before in Los Angeles was not about civil rights. It's not about the great cause of equality that all Americans must uphold. It's not a message or protest. It's been the brutality of a mob, pure and simple." The president went on to say, "In a civilized society, there can be no excuse, no excuse, for the murder, arson, theft and vandalism that have terrorized the law-abiding citizens of Los Angeles."[20]

Governor Bill Clinton also spoke that night, striking a more sociological note (and, of course, he had no power to order troops and quelling civil unrest was not his responsibility), saying, among other things: "I do understand what happened without condoning it," and that if we did not get to the root causes of social and economic unrest, "those people will be lost forever, and you'll have more of what you've seen in the last few days."[21] Governor Clinton continued on this theme for the next few days. For example, at a black church in Washington, he said, "If white folk killed white folk like this, all the law enforcement resources in the nation would be available. . . . When black folk kill black folk like this, we turn away." Meanwhile, Ross Perot criticized the president for not going to Los Angeles: "I would have to go see it, feel it and taste it. I cannot make good decisions remotely, and I'd be there."[22]

The truth is, the National Guard and federal troops stopped the riots, and by 4 and 5 May, they were pretty much over.[23] The federal troops stood down four days later. But the rioters had wreaked nothing short of havoc; by the end of it all, 55 people were killed, with another 2,300 injured, and more than 1,000 buildings burned.[24]

For all his talk about root causes and how reactions would have been different were the crime "white on white," Bill Clinton implicitly retracted such sentiments the following month in front of Jesse Jackson at a meeting of his Rainbow Coalition. Black rapper Sister Souljah had been quoted as saying, "If black people kill black people every day, why not have a week and kill white people?" She spoke at Jackson's Rainbow Coalition the day before Bill Clinton did. When it was his turn, Bill Clinton took her noxious words, quoted in an interview, to separate himself from such sentiments: "If you took the words, 'white' and 'black' and you reversed them, you might think David Duke was giving that speech."[25] Jesse Jackson was not amused and said Sister Souljah "represents the feelings and hopes of a whole generation of people."

This brief moment helped show Bill Clinton to be a centrist, willing to take on certain parts of the left-wing establishment in the Democratic Party— always appealing to independents and even disenchanted Republicans. Ever since, the phrase "a Sister Souljah moment" has come to stand for a politician or political leader taking a stand against type, or criticizing one of his own advocates or constituencies. It happens too rarely.

In the long end of the furor over the Rodney King riots (as they had become known), there was a great deal of misunderstanding indeed. But it was not the misunderstanding of root causes. The jurors were wrong, however they arrived at their decision, to find not one of the officers guilty of assault. But that would not be the first time a jury got something wrong, and the blame for what happened in Los Angeles after their verdict belonged with the rioters—nobody else. President Bush traveled to Los Angeles a few days after the riots had cooled down; the criticism that he did not go there at the time was unfounded. They had lasted only a few days. What more could he have done there? Would a presidential visit in the midst of a city in civil breakdown have actually been helpful or distracting to the authorities? Periodically, in American history, there have been calls for presidents to visit areas under civil or natural tumult, and those visits can be helpful, but they can also be distractions in medias res. A visit either during, or after, a catastrophe is often called by the press "a photo op" anyway as a form of criticism; better the visit happen when the local authorities can best accommodate it if criticism will come in any event.

The Sister Souljah episode was not, however, the most lasting or impactful moment of the campaign outside the conventions or debates. That belonged to Vice President Dan Quayle. The vice president made headlines once again when he spoke out against the popular TV show *Murphy Brown*. In one highly rated episode, actress Candice Bergen's on-screen character became pregnant and decided to bear the child; her character was unmarried, so the child would be out of wedlock. The portrayal therefore was to suggest that the professional career woman does not want marriage, but she does want someone to love. Quayle pointed out that such a conscious decision hurts the child and sends the wrong message to the rest of society. Fatherlessness is, after all, one of the most serious social, psychological, and economic issues confronting the country. As President Bush himself had said, "We bless young mothers when they choose life,"[26] but no one should think that a child born without a father is not hurt.

The prestige press branded Quayle a puritanical lightweight going after a fictional character, and they disdained his concern for the child's well-being. The truth—fictional context or not—was that the issue of fatherlessness in America was getting too little attention. As conservative essayist Richard Brookhiser wrote then for the *New York Times*: "American electioneering is so scorned for its emptiness and frivolity, for its ignorant armies clashing by sound bite, you'd think that a major political figure who addressed serious issues in a serious way would be thanked for his efforts." He went on to point out (as Quayle did in his speech):

> 68 percent of black families were headed by married couples in 1967. By 1991, less than half—48 percent—were. But the Vice President had another statistic: Among families headed by married couples, fewer than 1 in 17 are poor, while the poverty rate among families headed by single mothers is 1 in 3. Mr. Quayle knows it's a big, and changing, country. He simply asked us to question whether all the changes have been for the better.[27]

Taking on Hollywood is always a risky thing for a politician, all the more so in a political campaign. But what Quayle was pointing out was not only hard to argue with; it was also important—whether he chose a real-life example or a fictional one.* It would take some time (but not much) before what Quayle pointed out would become an *almost* commonplace concern across ideological camps. The following year, the widely respected Barbara Dafoe Whitehead weighed in with a powerful, well-researched article in the pages of the centrist *Atlantic* magazine titled "Dan Quayle Was Right." The epigraph (italics in the original) said it all:

---

* It's disturbing to note that today's numbers are even worse; today, 40 percent of all births in the nation are to single mothers. In 1991, that number was just over 25 percent.

The social-science evidence is in: though it may benefit the adults involved, the dissolution of intact two-parent families is harmful to large numbers of children. . . . Family diversity in the form of increasing numbers of single-parent and stepparent families does not strengthen the social fabric but, rather, dramatically weakens and undermines society.[28]

Today, almost anyone who remembers the popular *Murphy Brown* show remembers it in the context of the argument that Dan Quayle began over it.

While questions about the Bush (and Quayle) policies were the focus of the attention for the press throughout the campaign, the focus on Bill Clinton was otherwise. There were a good many allegations about Governor Clinton's extramarital dalliances, what became known as "bimbo eruptions" (a phrase coined by a Clinton confidante hired to try to squelch those rumors and stories).[29] And then there was the question of Governor Clinton's military record and why he did not serve in Vietnam. One particularly troublesome and, indeed, horrible statement came out in a letter (referenced earlier) he had written in 1969 to the head of the ROTC program at the University of Arkansas. In that letter, he thanked the colonel for "saving me from the draft." Such language implied he had received special treatment. If that wasn't problematic enough, he added, "I am in great sympathy with those who are not willing to fight, kill, and maybe die for their country." And he wrote that his letter was meant to explain to the colonel why he along with other "so many fine people have come to find themselves still loving their country but loathing the military." That "loathing the military" line stuck hard in the craw of many Americans and their family members who served in the military. There would be another line as well: "To many of us, it is no longer clear what is service and what is disservice, or if it is clear, the conclusion is likely to be illegal."[30]

Governor Clinton had a hard time explaining away that letter, but throughout the campaign, he would not sound like the typical caricature of a pacifist, arguing that while he had supported the Gulf War, he was not alone in standing with a good many others of his generation who did not support the Vietnam War. He then shifted the argument—as was his routine—by taking the press off his past and pointing the country to the future: "The real character issue and the real patriotism issue in this election is who has a vision for the country, a plan for the future, and the ability to get it done."[31] And by 1992, many people had been done with the hurt from Vietnam—how veterans were treated here, how protests were mounted, what was said to veterans at the time, and how we got into Vietnam as well as how we got out. Most Americans did not want to revisit that painful period, and most of the men Bill Clinton's age (he was forty-five years old in 1992) had not in fact served in Vietnam. The charges against Dan Quayle's service record in 1988 never stuck, and neither did the charges end up sticking to Bill Clinton in 1992.

Another issue that arose for this young candidate was whether he had smoked marijuana as a college student in the 1960s. Yet again, another phrase was birthed into our popular culture with the governor's (not altogether credible) response: "When I was in England I experimented with marijuana a time or two, and I didn't like it. I didn't inhale it, and never tried it again."[32]

While the Bush campaign tried to make an issue of Bill Clinton's character, the Clinton team was fierce in hewing to talking points about the economy and the future, not the past.

Bill Clinton was also aided by another cultural shift. The year 1992 was becoming known as the year of the woman: several female candidates from the Democratic Party were running for Senate, and it looked as if they would win. Bill Clinton's wife, Hillary, though running for nothing except the position of First Lady, became emblematic of this cultural era. Hillary Clinton was an outspoken and successful attorney in Arkansas, credited as an expert in children's issues and health care (a big theme for the Democrats in the 1992 election—especially given the higher-than-usual unemployment rates). Bill Clinton would say of his wife's familiarity with policy issues that by electing him, voters would get "two for the price of one."*

---

* There were ongoing jokes at the time about who in the Clinton marriage helped the other more. One went something like this: Bill and Hillary are driving through the town where Hillary grew up, when they stop for gas. As he is pumping gas, the attendant looks in the window and recognizes Hillary. "Do you remember me?" he asks Hillary. "We dated in high school." They chat for a little while, and then Bill pays for the gas and drives away. Bill is feeling superior and looks at Hillary and says, "I wonder how you think you would feel today if you had married the gas station attendant instead of me?" Hillary replies, "Oh, I'd feel the same because you would be pumping gas and he would be president!"[33]

Character and history issues aside, the campaign moved to a circuitous end. The three-way debates included Ross Perot because he was cresting above 15 percent in many polls—and he proved great entertainment with his homespun, nothing-to-lose-or-prove wit. It was hard to pin down exactly his positions on many issues, but he always provided some sport, whether he meant to or not. Once, he responded to a questioner with a pat answer, then said, "If anyone has a better plan, let me know. I'm all ears." The audience roared with laughter at the jug-eared Texan's witty rejoinder.

Through much of the fall campaign, President Bush seemed tired, almost as if he were going through the motions, as if campaigning were not to his taste, and as if he were more than a little surprised by the support many in the populace were showing for a character-challenged young governor whose experience and national service were so much less than his own. At one rally toward the end of the campaign, some of this showed when the president shouted, "My dog Millie knows more about foreign policy than these two bozos!" The audience loved it—but then again it was an audience of President Bush's base. Generally it doesn't appear too presidential for the president to call his opponent a "bozo," and again, while few knew as much about foreign policy as President Bush, the voters were mostly thinking about the economy.

President Bush was never the natural-born campaigner that Ronald Reagan was (let alone the famously gregarious Bill Clinton), and the cameras could be unkind. During one debate, he seemed bored, and he looked at his watch. In the way of TV debates, analysts immediately seized on the gesture. "Time's up!" his opponents crowed. It wasn't exactly as it was portrayed, however. The president later explained that he was looking at his watch to see how much time there was left to work in certain points he wanted to make during the debate. Now, some candidates don't even wear watches when they debate.

President Bush's frustration with the campaign and the direction of the populace's mood was evident when he was asked in the first debate about how he would create jobs and he responded:

What I'm going to do is say to Jim Baker when this campaign is over, all right, let's sit down, now you do in domestic affairs what you've done in foreign affairs, be kind of the economic coordinator of all the domestic side of the House, and that includes all the economic side, all the training side, and bring this program together.[34]

As we noted, small things often say big things in campaigns. Farming out the answer to the relatively unpopular Jim Baker said too much and too little. Bill Clinton seized on this point in the final debate, saying,

> You know, in the first debate, Mr. Bush made some news. He'd just said Jim Baker was going to be secretary of state and in the first debate he said no, now he's gonna be responsible for domestic economic policy. Well, I'll tell ya. . . . The person responsible for domestic economic policy in my administration will be Bill Clinton.

President Bush was quick with a verbal parry. "That's what worries me," he said, to great applause. But the damage was done. President Bush looked hands off on the economy, and Bill Clinton, famous for telling audiences "I feel your pain," seemed hands on.[35]

Bill Clinton was also an effective public speaker and a better debater, and given his young age, he represented a generational shift in electoral politics. Clinton could ham it up like few other candidates in recent memory. Americans were delighted when candidate Clinton sported dark glasses and played his saxophone on the *Arsenio Hall Show*. Clinton supporters joked that their candidate had more "sax appeal" (never mind the allegations of infidelity from earlier in the campaign). That kind of effort by the candidate was taken as it should have been—good fun.

Bill Clinton was elected with almost 45 million popular votes (43 percent) and a comfortable 370 electoral votes. President Bush received just over 39 million popular votes (37 percent) and 168 electoral votes. Perot won close to 20 million popular votes (19 percent). Because his support was not concentrated in any state or region, though, Perot won no electoral votes.[36] In the end, the voters had voted on the economy. There was a general exhaustion with the GOP, even after winning so many foreign policy battles, and the plurality of voters saw fit to put the economy at home into the hands of a governor who, it seemed, knew and could relate to poverty himself. It is not always fair, but one truism of American politics is the party or president in office gets the credit when the economy does well and the party or president in office takes the blame when the economy performs poorly. Though the unemployment rate had started out at a relatively low 5.4 when President Bush took office in 1988, it had reached 7.8 by the middle of 1992. It had begun to go down from there on, but by November 1992 it was still 7.4.[37]

Analysts noted quickly that Bush had lost 9 million votes in four years. Had he retained his 1988 supporters, he might have prevailed. George Will scolded the president for squandering the Reagan legacy and losing the Republican electoral lock on the White House that Will had often written about. On one television show he said President Bush—especially in his turning James Baker into the czar of domestic policy—"made a sow's ear out of a silk purse." Conservative columnist Charles Krauthammer was kinder in saying that Bush's was not so much a failed presidency as a completed one. Truth be told, having twelve years of Republican rule from the White House is a historically, anomalously long run. There had not been anything like it since the 1920s and early '30s (Harding-Coolidge-Hoover), and there may not be a period like it again for a very long time.

Bush took his defeat with typical grace. When he later started skydiving, he told audiences that his wife, Barbara, said she had not seen him take such a plunge—"since the '92 campaign."[38]

Retrospect is a great thing—and one nonpartisan Washington journalist, Jonathan Rauch, summed up the presidency of George H. W. Bush quite nicely in writing that President Bush was overcriticized by both the right and the left in America and he kept a steady hand on the ship of state during some awfully troubling crises. Things could have gone terribly wrong for this country from 1989 to 1993, but they did not:

A modern president is pretty darned good if he can cope adeptly with a crisis and otherwise avoid serious mistakes. The second criterion—avoiding major blunders—is especially hard for romantics and pundits to appreciate. But politics is a stream of temptations to pander, grandstand, and overreact. Consistently resisting those temptations requires maturity and toughness.[39]

That was President Bush. Such maturity and self-discipline (and no small measure of achievements internationally) may be George H. W. Bush's lasting legacy.

II. "We Force the Spring"

Bill Clinton began his Inaugural parade in Charlottesville, Virginia. There, at Thomas Jefferson's Monticello, he paid tribute to the founder of the Democratic Party. William *Jefferson* Clinton and his official party rode in a bus convoy north to Washington through the frosty, rolling hills of Virginia's wintry hunt country. It was a promising start for an administration that claimed it shared the Apostle of Liberty's dedication to learning and reason.

In his Inaugural Address, President Clinton graciously saluted President Bush and all the members of what was soon to become known as "the greatest generation." He thanked them for their steadfastness and sacrifice, for leading America in triumph over depression, fascism, Nazism, and communism: "This ceremony is held in the depth of winter. But, by the words we speak and the faces we show the world, *we force the spring.*" He did not open with a prayer, as President Bush had done four years before, but he closed his Inaugural speech saying:

And so, my fellow Americans, at the edge of the 21st century, let us begin with energy and hope, with faith and discipline, and let us work until our work is done. The scripture says, "And let us not be weary in well-doing, for in due season, we shall reap, if we faint not." From this joyful mountaintop of celebration, we hear a call to service in the valley. We have heard the trumpets. We have changed the guard. And now, each in our way, and with God's help, we must answer the call.[40]

Early in 1993, President Clinton had very real reasons for wanting to move fast, to force the spring. He would have barely a year and a half to rack up a substantial legislative record. He had promised to "focus like a laser" on the economy. And he had Democratic majorities in both houses of Congress. If he did not succeed, there would be no one else to blame.

Staffing his cabinet proved his first challenge. His first two nominees for attorney general (Zoe Baird and Kimba Wood) had to be withdrawn due to reports that they had hired undocumented immigrants as housekeepers and nannies. President Clinton then settled on his third choice (still, the first woman to hold the post as U.S. attorney general), Dade County, Florida, prosecutor Janet Reno. Reno was single with no children (and would not have a "nanny problem"), and she was known as a tough prosecutor in Florida.[41] But President Clinton soon made other news in filling jobs to complete his administration and fulfill his campaign promises.

By the end of his first month in office, he named his wife, First Lady Hillary Rodham Clinton, as the chairman of his newly created Task Force on National Health Care Reform, complete with a staff and office in the West Wing of the White House. It was the first time a First Lady was given such stature and authority in a presidency.[42] She was in charge of creating the administration's policy on health care reform. Many, especially those following the oddness of his wife's defense of him throughout the various "bimbo eruptions," had assumed it was a payoff or trade-off that the Clintons had arranged for themselves in their marriage: she would stick by him while he would ensure her seats of authority, power, and responsibility to carry out official duties for which she was passionate. She would not be a typical First Lady; she would be able to craft a policy record she could establish for herself.

But on his own public policy, he was knocked off his stride early on by an issue in which few thought he should have been embroiled in the first place, at least so early in an administration trying to prove itself. During the campaign, he had promised to end the long-standing military ban on allowing openly homosexual people to serve in the U.S. armed forces. And he attempted to make good on that promise as one of his first acts as president.

Among those opposed to ending the ban (based on tradition, the military's own views, and unit cohesiveness) was Joint Chiefs of Staff Chairman General Colin Powell. General Powell had said lifting the ban "would be prejudicial to good order and discipline."[43] When he initially made known his desire to end the ban, via an executive order, President Clinton received a resounding response of criticism and vocal dissent from members of the military, their family members, and supporters. He held back, as if he feared to give General Colin Powell a direct order. What if this supremely dignified, universally respected military professional simply resigned rather than carried out that order?

General Powell's prestige as the first black man to become chairman of the Joint Chiefs of Staff was higher than that of President Bush or President Clinton. And the general had thrown down the gauntlet in a commencement address to the midshipmen at the Naval Academy in early January 1993, telling the audience, if they found the imminent policy on gays in the military "completely unacceptable and [if] it strikes at the heart of your moral beliefs then I think you have to resign."[44]

Facing the backlash from so many pro-military quarters, and realizing he might be forcing (or springing) something that the country was not yet ready for, Clinton decided he would not sign an executive order. Liberals were seriously upset over the issue; conservatives were outraged for different reasons; and many in the press corps wondered why the president would start off his presidency on such a controversial and noncritical imbroglio.

Meanwhile, senators and congressmen went on fact-finding missions to military bases and submarines. What they learned was that the military does not billet heterosexual men and women together on submarines, where the *racks* (bunk beds) are just eighteen to twenty-two inches apart. Similarly, they found the military could not create "sexual tension" in the ranks by forcing acceptance of open homosexuality in such intimate environments. Resistance to Clinton's plans for the military was deep and intense.

Clinton was in a bind. On the one hand, his "loathing the military" letter circulated widely during the campaign, and now this social experiment with one of the most crucial, traditional, and well-working parts of the federal government confirmed many people's worst fears. On the other hand, because of his role as commander in chief, he could not afford to jeopardize respect from the armed services. Clinton blamed Republicans for raining on his Inaugural parade by arguing the issue. Elizabeth Drew, a veteran of the Washington press corps, wasn't having any of it. She said it might have been the first example in his presidency of his "tendency to lay the blame off on others."[45]

Ultimately, and in pretty short order, President Clinton put the issue off with a compromise policy (ratified by Congress) known as "Don't Ask, Don't Tell," crafted in large part by General Powell and Democratic Georgia Senator Sam Nunn, the chairman of the Senate Armed Services Committee.[46] In the end, the "compromise" was not much of a change from previous policy and came to stand for the proposition that "the government would no longer 'ask' recruits if they were gay; and so long as military personnel didn't 'tell' anyone of their sexual preference—and didn't engage in homosexual acts—they were free to serve."[47]

If President George H. W. Bush (with his expertise in foreign policy) saw his term, beginning in 1989, as overseeing a kind of imminent post–Cold War period that would allow him to focus on domestic issues only to find himself more engaged in international issues, President Clinton was resolute to ensure his term, beginning in 1993, would indeed stay focused on domestic policy (where his expertise most surely was, having little foreign policy under his belt). Thus, President Clinton was, indeed, more successful with his economic and education plans, especially as he had a Congress of his own party to work with (unlike President Bush before him).

President Clinton quickly reversed himself on the middle-class tax cut he had promised during the campaign, pushing through one of the largest tax increases in history.[48] It included an increase in marginal tax rates as well as higher federal gasoline taxes. He kept most of President Bush's America 2000 education plan, renaming it Goals 2000. Many centrists and conservatives who took him seriously as a "New Democrat" were interested to see how—and when—he would make good on other centrist promises such as "ending welfare as we know it" and making abortion "safe, legal, and rare." Those promises would have to wait.

Conservatives were more successful, however, the following year, when the Clintons overreached on education. An obscure amendment offered by liberal Congressman George Miller, Democrat from California, was quietly slipped into a 1994 education bill. The Miller Amendment could have outlawed homeschooling by requiring all teachers to be state certified in all subjects they taught. Mike Farris and his Home School Legal Defense Association rolled up its sleeves, as did Dr. James Dobson's Focus on the Family organization and other conservative groups concerned with education reform. Soon, tens of thousands of homeschoolers and their supporters were telephoning Capitol Hill. The telephones rang for eight days. Many members could not reach their own offices because the phone lines were so tied up. Crying "uncle," Congress sheepishly removed the Miller Amendment. It was a signal victory for grassroots democracy.

But 1993 seemed as if it would be the liberal moment in American politics and legislation. Bill Clinton had promised to insure the uninsured with a government-sponsored health care plan "that no one can ever take away." His pledge appealed strongly to Americans who had lost their jobs—or those in fear of losing their jobs. That comprised many millions. Since the 1940s, America had developed a health insurance system that linked health care to employment. As a result, with a rapidly changing economy and workers changing jobs more frequently, anxiety about continuous coverage mounted.

The task of reforming health care belonged to the First Lady. Despite the uniqueness of such a high-profile position for an unelected and unconfirmed official, Mrs. Clinton was known as a serious policy professional. Highly educated and constantly probing public issues, she was qualified for the task. The difficulty was that, since she was the president's wife, none of his advisors could credibly criticize her work. President Clinton would have to become "wedded" to the task force's final recommendations in a way no president is if he is merely surveying the work of subordinates.

When the Clintons' plan became public, it immediately became the source of a great political and philosophical debate. And despite Democratic majorities, it is not accurate to say the president "controlled" both houses of Congress. Much of the task force's work was done in private—and longtime Democratic Party legislative champions and experts on health care (such as New York Senator Daniel Patrick Moynihan of New York) were excluded.

Bill Kristol, formerly Dan Quayle's chief of staff, leaped into action from the Republican side. Using the cutting-edge technology of the early 1990s (today, a dinosaur, the fax machine), he developed a network of public officials, journalists, and lobbyists. He distributed detailed and well-researched daily reports criticizing various aspects of the task force's efforts. He was determined to defeat the Clintons' plan, which would have empowered the federal government to control over one-seventh of the U.S. economy.

Kristol was not alone. George Will reached millions with his columns and TV commentary. Typical of his argument: "Fifteen presidential appointees . . . not you and your doctor, would define the 'medically necessary' and 'appropriate' care a doctor could give you. There would be 15-year jail terms for people driven to bribery for care they feel they need but the government does not deem 'necessary.'"[49] Will explained the impact of the Clintons' plan to control prescription drug prices: "For every drug that becomes profitable, 1,000 do not. Thus the Clintons' plan would certainly suppress research that might spare millions of persons some of the ravages of AIDS, Alzheimer's, breast cancer and other diseases."[50] At the end of the day, while there was much to say and do about health care in America, a great many Americans were concerned that a government-run plan (often criticized as importing "socialized medicine" to America) would ruin the best parts of our health care system, including—perhaps more than anything—choice.

Efforts by activists and commentators such as Kristol and Will, plus televised ads, talk radio, and several conservative think tanks, sparked an extraordinarily high level of public debate. Congress slowed the rush to enact the Clinton plan; then, buffeted by sustained criticism, the members finally abandoned it altogether. Something better would have to be found.

In essence, the debate over the Clinton health care plan was a debate over freedom. Both sides contended for freedom. The Clintons argued that Americans who feared a health emergency without insurance, or who feared the loss of health coverage when they lost their jobs, were not truly free. The other side argued that, still, there was a great deal of freedom in the health care they did have—including the freedom of physicians to prescribe what they saw best without government interference. And they fought for freedom too. They wanted Americans to be free to choose their own doctors, their own plans, their own medicines.

Like the issue of gays in the military, health care reform was teaching a lesson to this New Democrat. He saw some of the problems that President

Jimmy Carter faced when he came to Washington: *You may have a majority on the Hill, and you may be electable to the White House as an outsider, but you still have to work with us or we will not work with you.* A president has four years, but majorities on the Hill are susceptible to change every two years, and committee chairmanships as well as sizable majorities in both the Senate and the House matter for House and Senate members too.

III. Trouble in Texas

While President Clinton wanted to focus on domestic policy, unpredictable events intruded from within and afar as has proven to be the case again and again. The president and his attorney general were faced with a burgeoning problem near the city of Waco, Texas. There, in February 1993, a local paper published an article on a little-known cult leader, David Koresh (born Vernon Wayne Howell).[51] Known as the Branch Davidians, this group of almost one hundred members, according to the article, was holed up in a compound, waiting for the end of the world but maintaining "a large arsenal of high-powered weapons" including ".50-caliber weapons, AK-47s, AR-15s, Israeli assault rifles and 9mm handguns."[52] Investigations by private detectives and reporters alleged that Koresh (who claimed he was Jesus Christ incarnate) "abuses the children of his followers, boasts of having sex with underage members, claims at least 15 wives and believes all women in the world belong to him."[53] When Alcohol, Tobacco, and Firearms (ATF) agents entered the property to serve warrants and investigate the weapons charges, "they were met with immediate gunfire" from the compound, and four ATF agents were killed, while fifteen others were injured in the gunfight and taken to the hospital.[54] In a telephone interview with CNN after the shootout had ended and the federal agents stood down and back, Koresh admitted that he and his followers were "heavily armed," as if that needed any further verification.[55]

With intermediates and negotiators going back and forth between federal agents and Davidians inside the compound, Waco became a news center. Many Texas citizens took coffee, doughnuts, and other refreshments to the police and federal agents surrounding the compound over the next fifty days. The FBI joined the ATF in Waco as they worked on plans for ending the standoff—including such ideas as using tear gas in the compound.

In the meantime, negotiations were going nowhere slowly, and at one point the "Davidians held children up in windows with signs that said 'Flames Await,' among other things."[56] Worried about another Jonestown-like massacre or some other cultish mass suicide or other violent action, Attorney General Reno approved plans to have FBI vehicles insert tear gas into the compound; as they did so, Davidians opened fire again on the federal agents, and fires broke out in the compound.[57] Soon, the compound was engulfed in flames, and the remaining men, women, and children (some eighty of them) within it died, some with gunshot wounds.[58]

Rage rose with the flames. Both the right and the left criticized Reno for forcing the tragedy, and citizens, commentators, and congressional members traded allegations about the genesis of the fire. Was it started by Koresh and his followers, or did it happen when the federal agents knocked holes into the compound with tear gas? Surely, however, the former director of the ATF, Steve Higgins, was correct when he wrote in the aftermath that "the law requires that when served a warrant, we comply with that warrant and let the judicial systems determine our ultimate guilt or innocence."[59] We don't open fire on federal agents, we don't threaten further violence, and we especially do not do any of that when women and children are held within such a compound with serious allegations of their abuse being reported. If Koresh and his army thought they were in the right, Koresh could have acted like the real Jesus he said he was and faced the authorities civilly, making his case orally and vindicating himself in the public mind (gaining more adherents) or becoming a martyr to the civil justice system. Koresh shouldn't have brought about his own group's Armageddon at such a great cost of life.

President Clinton, throughout the standoff, allowed new Attorney General Reno to stand point and remain in charge of the entire episode. She faced serious questions and criticism from both parties in the press and in congressional hearings. Liberal Democrat John Conyers of the House Judiciary Committee, for example, excoriated Reno: "When in God's name is law enforcement at the federal level going to understand that these are very sensitive events, that you can't put guns, barbed wire, the FBI and the Secret

Service around them, sending in sound 24-hours a day and then wonder why they do something unstable?"[60]

Reno was clearly shaken by the event and its conclusion. (As a Florida prosecutor, she had the reputation of seeking justice for and having great empathy with children.) During the hearings that ensued, she stood strong in taking responsibility, however, and was unwavering in defending her department and the federal agents. Among other things, she said, "Nobody will ever know what the right answer was," and this otherwise impassive public servant ultimately showed the emotional toll she went through in describing how lonely she felt the night of the takedown of the compound. Tearing up before the committee, she said, "The first call I got was from my sister. She said, 'Atta girl.' The second call I got was from the president of the United States. 'Atta girl.'"[61]

The last official word was given by a fact-finding commission headed by Republican Senator John Danforth of Missouri. In its findings it exonerated the federal agents, concluding that their efforts did not start the fire in the compound and that David Koresh and his confederates were responsible for the events that unfolded in early 1993.[62]

IV. A Bomb in the World Trade Center

As disturbing as the Waco incident was, it was not (despite the body count) the most important event, not even the most important violent event, of early 1993—nowhere near it. On Friday, 26 February, a little past noon, an explosion rocked the World Trade Center in New York City. It was no ordinary explosion. The physical plant of the building hummed along just fine; nobody fumbled a candle or cigarette in one of the offices; no car overheated; no exhaust system backfired. No, this was a 1,400-pound urea nitrate bomb stashed inside a Ryder van and driven into the World Trade Center parking garage.[63] And when it detonated,

> the hyper-intensive shockwave bored a six-story canyon into the bowels of the complex. Seven people were killed (one of the six officially listed murder victims having been well along in her pregnancy), over a

thousand were injured, and the structural damage—from a device that had cost only a few thousand dollars to build—would cost nearly a billion dollars to repair.[64]

The FBI and its New York Joint Terrorism Task Force investigated immediately—their instincts were that it was Middle Eastern–based terrorism.[65] In short order, thanks to great investigative work and a team that had been monitoring Islamic radicalism, the FBI traced the rented van to one Mohammad Salameh and several other suspects: Nidal Ayyad, Mahmoud Abouhalima, and Ahmad Mohammed Ajaj (Salameh was a Palestinian, Ayyad was a Kuwaiti, Abouhalima was from Egypt, and Ajaj was a Palestinian).[66] The mastermind of the operation was a Kuwaiti national of Pakistani descent named Ramzi Yousef—but he remained at large, having fled the country shortly after the bombing. These men had pulled off what had been called and surely was at the time "the most brazen attack against the American homeland since Pearl Harbor."[67]

Why had Middle Eastern–style terrorism come to us in 1993? Had we not been a net help to so many Muslims from Kuwait to Afghanistan? And while we were rightfully credited with helping save Afghanistan from its Soviet occupiers, just as we were rightfully credited with saving Kuwait and Saudi Arabia from their Iraqi neighbors, many restive Islamic radicals remained dedicated to their continued Islamism. Psychologists can study to the end of time why adherents to a radical theology in failed societies become angered with others outside their society, especially those who have helped them. At the end of the day, though, the philosopher Hannah Arendt probably had it right: nothing can be so blinding to reality as the power of ideology. Or as in this case, radical violent theology as ideology.

The Middle East had long been a hotbed of terror and ideology, sometimes fueled by Arab nationalism, sometimes by Islamic theology, and sometimes by the very toxic confluence of both. Israel, as a Jewish state, had known this terror for decades, before and since its founding. Other Western countries had as well. Not so much the United States, the most powerful Western nation in the world. The United States had not adopted Islam as its religion, it did not neighbor a Muslim country, and its Muslim population was a small minority. The United States did sponsor democracies like Israel and we helped support the more stable Middle Eastern states that wanted to be our allies (troublesome as many of them were).

Still, the radical Islamic state of Iran had long targeted U.S. interests, military personnel, and civilians abroad. Factions of Palestinian terrorists had also killed U.S. citizens in Israel. And it is worth recalling, although we saw these incidents as isolated events over long stretches of time, the U.S. had not been fully immune from a train of terrorist attacks over the years. For example, Sirhan Sirhan, the Palestinian assassin of U.S. Senator and presidential candidate Bobby Kennedy, claimed that Kennedy's support for Israel led him to murder Kennedy.[68] Other examples include:

- Palestinian terrorists killing U.S. Ambassador to the Sudan Cleo Noel and his Charge d'Affairs George Curtis Moore in 1973;
- Hezbollah terrorists killing hundreds of U.S. embassy officials and military service members in two separate truck bombings in 1983;
- Islamic Jihad terrorists killing U.S. embassy official William Buckley in Lebanon in 1984;
- Palestinian terrorists killing an American civilian on the cruise liner *Achille Lauro* in 1985;
- Libyan terrorists killing scores of Americans in 1989 in blowing up Pan Am 103; and
- An American-born rabbi and former Israeli member of the Knesset (parliament), Meir Kahane, being gunned down in 1990 after a speech at a Manhattan hotel by an Egyptian-American named Sayyid Nosair.*[69]

---

* Meir Kahane was not just any rabbi. For years he had been associated with initiating various organizations of Jewish self-defense both in America and in Israel. He founded the Jewish Defense League in the 1960s, teaching Jews to take up arms in their self-defense, and he had led rallies against the Soviet Union to publicize the Soviet policy of refusing civil rights to Jews. His group had resorted to violence in both causes. When Rabbi Kahane immigrated to Israel, he founded a political movement there based on instilling a more religious character in the Jewish state and expelling Arabs from Israel for purposes of Jewish security. He served one term in the Israeli parliament and since then had traveled back and forth between Israel and the United States, warning of Arab terrorism, threats to Israel, and the need for more Jews to emigrate to Israel.

But terrorism was hardly a normal or familiar struggle for us as it had been for others. While the Kahane killing made big news in Israel, as well as among Jewish supporters and opponents of Kahane in the U.S., it was largely ignored as a major event in and for the U.S. To paraphrase terrorism specialist Steve Emerson, Kahane's killing was seen as one extremist killing another. But who was Nosair and who were the men who had tried to take down the World Trade Center in 1993? We would soon find out there was more than a unifying geography or theology.

In investigations of the *how* and *who* of the 1993 World Trade Center bombing, a common thread was revealed: the terrorists worshiped at the same mosques in Brooklyn and Jersey City. And they didn't just know each other—they also knew Sayyid Nosair. They knew someone else too. At these mosques a character soon to be recognized as the face of terror in America did much of the preaching: Omar Abdel-Rahman, also known as the Blind Sheikh. (He wore darkened glasses hiding his eyes, which were blinded at an early age due to childhood diabetes.) The Blind Sheikh had moved to America some three years before. Unlike so many immigrants who came here seeking religious freedom, his professional life did not start in America; it had a longer history abroad, and his purpose in coming here was about a lot of things—but freedom was not among them.

Rahman (or the Blind Sheikh) was well known in his home country of Egypt—and throughout many precincts of the Middle East. The Blind Sheikh was known there for his denunciations of secular leaders of Egypt like Gamal Abdel Nasser and Anwar Sadat. He headed an organization based in Egypt called the Islamic Group and issued fatwas (Islamic religious declarations or rulings) encouraging, and giving permission to use, violence against Christians and less fundamentalist Muslims.[70] When Anwar Sadat was assassinated in Egypt in 1981 by Islamic fundamentalists, the Blind Sheikh was imprisoned for encouragement, having declared that "heretical leader(s) deserved to be killed by the faithful."[71] While he was in prison he met another Egyptian radical leader named Ayman al-Zawahiri.

In less than a year, Egyptian officials released the Blind Sheikh from prison because he was not seen as having directly singled out Anwar Sadat by name as one suited for assassination by "the faithful."

The Blind Sheikh would go on to establish himself as a teacher and preacher throughout the 1980s, a career that included traveling to Pakistan and Afghanistan as a counselor, religious advisor, and fund-raiser for Arab mujahedeen fighting the Soviet Union.[72] At that time the Sheikh made some interesting friends and acquaintances, among them a wealthy Saudi Arabian named Osama bin Laden.[73] In various ways, the most extremist Muslims who declared against the secular Arab rule of Egypt and inspired Arab mujahedeen fighters in Afghanistan against the Soviets were inspired by, encouraged by, and financed by three main men: the Blind Sheikh, Ayman al-Zawahiri, and Osama bin Laden.[74] The last name was not one many people outside Saudi Arabia or Afghanistan knew, although Osama bin Laden had helped raise funds for Sayyid Nosair's legal defense (sending money of his own as well). He had financially supported the Blind Sheikh's efforts in America,[75] and his name was on a list of people the 1993 World Trade Center terrorists had called from their safe house.[76] Although bin Laden had never been to America, Ayman al-Zawahiri made a trip to the United States raising money for his teaching and "charitable" causes not five weeks after the World Trade Center bombing.[77]

So, in the Middle East and Afghanistan, a new, radical temper was brewing against the United States—it was "new" in the sense that the terrorism directed against us was fueled not just by Palestinians or Hezbollah or Libyans anymore. It was both "new" and "radical" in that individuals were no longer targeted; mass civilian areas (like the World Trade Center) were. The 1990s was the decade that delivered a new radical and deadly Islamic distemper to the United States.

While Ramzi Yousef and an Iraqi accomplice had fled the United States, the Joint Terrorism Task Force and the U.S. attorney's office did an excellent job in rounding up and prosecuting most of the terrorists (including the Blind Sheikh) responsible for the bombing and their foiled their plots to blow up other New York City landmarks. In part because the death toll was relatively small (even if the damage and the aims were not), in part because this kind of violence was so new to the country, people wanted to believe it was a one-off event. People held to this notion because they did not want to believe, or could not bring themselves to believe, that their country was so hated by such a vast number of people. Also due to the legal success of the prosecutions that would ensue (prosecutions led by two particularly excellent, young assistant U.S. attorneys, Andrew C. McCarthy and Patrick Fitzgerald), the nation's attention, by and large, moved on from the bombing of the World Trade Center. Treating this kind of terrorism as a legal matter and not as a part of a wider war against the United States has become known as "lawfare." That was how we dealt with the New York City terrorists. With the exception of a handful of federal prosecutors and officials from the FBI and CIA, almost everyone else believed there was no conspiracy or worldwide Islamic declaration of war against the United States.* But the many were wrong; the few were right.

Perhaps, too, our national concentration on the terrorist attack in New York City was diluted by the distraction of other issues. The year 1993 was very eventful, as most new presidents' first years in office often are. Though these issues would prove much less important over time, they occupied much of the attention of the media and the pundit class. Aside from pushing health care reform and a deficit-reduction plan, the president found himself embroiled in a growing number of early controversies. In May, the head and staff of the White House travel office were fired, bringing with the summary dismissal the allegation that the Clintons wanted to staff the office with their friends. The FBI opened an investigation of the matter.[78]

V. A Rare Flash of Temper and an Attempt at Peace

In June, President Clinton announced Federal Appellate Judge Ruth Bader Ginsburg as his nominee to the Supreme Court to replace Justice Byron White, who had announced his retirement in March. His announcement of Judge Ginsburg in the Rose Garden showed an early flash of the president's

---

* This is not to say the issue of Islamic terrorism at home and abroad was completely ignored outside government's precincts. Honorable mention here should be made of two private citizens who had begun making a career out of documenting and trying to publicize the terrorist threat to America from within and without, journalist Steve Emerson and Middle East historian Daniel Pipes. Many took them seriously; too many, however, had ignored them or written them off as Cassandras.

well-known but usually private temper when ABC White House correspondent Brit Hume asked the president how he arrived at the choice of Judge Ginsburg when other names (for example, then Interior Secretary Bruce Babbitt and Federal Judge Stephen Breyer, who would become a later Supreme Court appointment) had been floated as likely candidates. "We may have created an impression, perhaps unfair, of a certain zigzag quality in the decision-making process here," said Hume. "I wonder if you could walk us through it and perhaps disabuse us of any notions we might have along those lines. Thank you." Hume was getting at something the president knew was on the press's minds: Why the floating of other names that legal insiders thought were up for the job, and why the relative surprise of Judge Ginsburg? The president snapped at Hume, "I've long since given up the thought that I could disabuse some of you of turning any substantive decision into anything but political process. How you could ask a question after the statement she just made is beyond me."[79]

The president was referring to the statement just given by Judge Ginsburg about how monumental her nomination was in light of the discrimination she had faced in her early career. Later, we would find out how relevant Brit Hume's question was—it turned out that Bill Clinton had in mind a whole line of other nominees, including New York Governor Mario Cuomo, before he settled on Judge Ginsburg.[80] Judge Ginsburg was not unqualified; she just seemed a curious, little known choice. In any event, both the right and the left lined up for a summer of confirmation hearings for the super bowl of judicial nominations, a seat on the Supreme Court.

But there was no major battle for the Supreme Court in 1993. It took backseat to the other big headline news of what was turning out to be a very tumultuous year. Judge Ginsburg was confirmed by a sweeping majority vote in the U.S. Senate in August by a vote of 96–3.[81] The Republicans in the Senate did not believe in doing to Democratic appointees what had been done to Robert Bork and Clarence Thomas. There was no question Judge Ginsburg was qualified as a good judge (even if her opinions were on the left), and *generally* the prevailing view at the time was that a president should be entitled to naming the appointees he chooses so long as they are not beyond the pale in ideological extremism and have no conflicts of interest or personal baggage that would tarnish their or the Court's reputation.

But the energetic President Clinton, trying to accomplish his agenda and make good headlines solidifying his tenure, moved on two other big fronts in the fall: Middle East peace and the North American Free Trade Agreement with Mexico and Canada. Israel's very existence was long a thorn to the Arab nations. Since its founding in 1948, Israel was deemed anathema to the Arab states; only Egypt even recognized its right to exist, and not until the late 1970s. As a result, Israel fought at least five wars with its Arab neighbors from its founding until 1993, wars for its survival, wars waged against it to eradicate it and its Jewish character. In the meantime, not only did Israel have to protect itself from other Arab countries, but one of its main threats was an internal terrorist organization, the Palestine Liberation Organization (the PLO).

The PLO was founded in 1964 and by the 1970s and '80s had achieved a long line of terrorist accomplishments against Israeli civilians. Its leader, Yasser Arafat, was the epitome of a modern-day terrorist. He had even addressed the UN in 1974 with a gun on his hip. To get a sense of the PLO's ambitions, one need only look at its official emblem, which consists of the Palestinian flag flying over the entire State of Israel.[82] The Fatah faction of the PLO, the largest faction, Yasser Arafat's faction, also has an emblem: it consists of the entire State of Israel covered by two rifles and a hand grenade.[83] For better or worse, over the course of the 1970s, '80s, and early '90s, the PLO had come to be recognized as the sole political representative of the Palestinians.*

Middle East peace had been a desideratum for several U.S. presidents from the 1940s onward, and interest in it had significantly increased after the oil embargo of 1973. Intransigence by the various parties had made the accomplishment impossible for most presidencies, and nearly impossible to achieve. But Jimmy Carter's efforts with Egypt and Israel in the late 1970s

---

* The story of how a terrorist organization could become recognized as a responsible, diplomatic player on the world scene and in the eyes of the U.S. is both sad and tragic, as is the fact that Yasser Arafat could win a Nobel Peace Prize. This story has been dealt with well by others. See, for example, Jeane Kirkpatrick's piece in *Commentary*, "How the PLO Was Legitimized" (http://www.aei.org/docLib/20030829_KirkpatrickPLO.pdf).

proved somewhat of an exception and instigated hopes in future presidents.* Bill Clinton thought, with a Labor (liberal) government in Israel and an aging Yasser Arafat—and his own personal charm—that he could, he would, have success where others had failed.

And he did get something. On the morning of 13 September 1993, on the White House lawn, with literal, physical nudging from the president, Israeli Prime Minister Yitzhak Rabin and Yasser Arafat shook hands in front of the world as they agreed to a Declaration of Principles toward peace. Those principles, boiled down, included Israel's recognition of the PLO and a commitment to withdrawals from the Gaza and West Bank territories. The PLO, in turn, was to renounce the use of terrorism, recognize Israel's right to exist, and alter its charter committed to those historic principles of organization.[84] There was a great deal inherent in each of those pregnant promises,** but suffice to say, for now, a historic first was reached: the world's face of Middle Eastern terrorism was invited to the White House for the first time; and also for the first time, the prime minister of Israel and the head of the Palestine Liberation Organization shook hands. The Israeli war general and the master Arab terrorist shook hands at the behest of the president of the United States—(for better or worse) not a small accomplishment.

But all was still not quiet in that volatile region known as the Arab world. In April 1993, while former President Bush was traveling in Kuwait, Iraqi terrorists with ties to Iraq's intelligence service had tried to assassinate President Bush with a car bomb. The plot had all of the designs of the Iraqi government. Kuwaiti authorities had foiled the effort, seized

---

* Many would say Jimmy Carter was the vessel allowing Egypt and Israel to come together, that by the time of the rapprochement between Egypt and Israel, Egypt realized it could not fight another war with Israel. Anwar Sadat's recognition of Israel, among other things, would ultimately cost him his life at the hands of Islamic radicals. And many would say the peace between the two nations was rather cold from the beginning, not much beyond *de jure* recognition of Israel's existence. Nonetheless, Jimmy Carter did preside over the two nations' accords during his presidency.

** Included among the pregnant questions: Would Arafat define the violence that had been his stock and trade as *terrorism*, or would he consider it as justifiable liberation efforts as he had before? Would Israel withdraw from all of the West Bank and Gaza or parts, and where did the West Bank begin? Would Arafat amend the PLO's charter with a wink and a nod, or would he do it in the very specific manner the Charter itself mandated? All of these questions surrounded the handshake, but for then it was a historically symbolic moment.

the car bomb—hundreds of pounds of explosives—and arrested eleven Iraqi nationals involved in the effort.[85] In response, in late June, President Clinton ordered a missile attack on the Iraqi intelligence service headquarters in Baghdad.[86] U.S. Secretary of State Madeleine K. Albright went to the United Nations to detail the evidence against Iraq in its efforts to kill the former president and justify the U.S. missile attack. Aside from affirming what had been going on for three years (that Iraqi President Saddam Hussein had been continually abrogating cease-fire resolutions from his invasion of Kuwait), the secretary said,

> I come to the Council today to brief you on a grave and urgent matter, an attempt to murder a President of the United States by the intelligence service of the Government of Iraq, a member of the United Nations. Even by the standards of an Iraqi regime known for its brutality against its neighbors and its own people, this is an outrage. The attempt against President George Bush's life during his visit to Kuwait last April was an attack on the United States of America. I'm not asking the Council for any action, but in our judgment, every member here today would regard an assassination attempt against its former head of state as an attack against itself and would react.[87]

Many had thought President Bill Clinton might be somewhat hawkish in his foreign policy as a self-proclaimed New Democrat. His posture toward Iraq here, coming as it did in his first year of office, along with the strong words of his secretary of state, was—indeed—not that of a dove, was not the approach of Jimmy Carter, and was not the appeasing policy that others had worried about with more outwardly liberal candidates for president in the recent past. It would not be the last we heard from Saddam Hussein, however, nor the last he would hear from us.

VI. Scandal Brews

In July, Deputy White House Counsel Vince Foster (a friend and associate of the Clintons from Arkansas) was found dead in a Washington area public park. The death was labeled a suicide, but curiosities were piqued when "federal investigators [were] not allowed access to Foster's office immediately after the discovery," although White House aides were permitted into his office. This gave "rise to speculation that files were removed from his office and some thought there was more to the Vince Foster story than met the eye."[88] Foster was in charge of issues related to Whitewater, a land-development deal back in Arkansas the Clintons were involved in with a colorful businessman named James McDougal.

From the 1992 campaign on, questions about the Clintons and Whitewater cropped up from time to time, questions such as:

> whether state regulators under Bill Clinton extended favors to [a McDougal-owned] savings and loan in exchange for campaign funds, whether the Clintons properly paid taxes on the Whitewater business, and whether McDougal might have illegally channeled money from the savings and loan to the Whitewater project.[89]

The Clintons had been slow in turning over requested Whitewater documents to the press and investigators, and their response inspired even more questions. Due to questions about Whitewater and foot dragging by the Clintons, Attorney General Janet Reno in January 1994 appointed a special counsel (Robert Fiske) to investigate all Whitewater-related allegations.

But the home front wasn't the only place the fires were burning. In Mogadishu, Somalia, the U.S. had suffered the horror of seeing our Army Rangers killed by Muslim extremists in October. Our military had gone into the country for the most noble of reasons. In 1991, Somalia had collapsed into a state of clan-on-clan, warlord violence—by 1992 the U.S. had begun airlifting food supplies into the war-torn country to aid UN and other relief-effort missions. But it was not enough, as "lawless gangs seized relief supplies and used them to buy local loyalties while letting thousands starve."[90]

In short order, President Bush had ordered more of our military in a UN-ratified mission to help settle down Somalia and ensure a degree of order and a smooth flow of supplies to Somali civilians. Once the U.S. military, along with other nations' efforts, had restored a degree of presence and order, things did stabilize—until May 1993 when the UN mission expanded in Somalia. The main warlord, Muhammed Farah Aideed, was having none of it, wanting the run of the country to himself, and he soon led an ambush against Pakistani soldiers, killing twenty-four of them.[91] The U.S. carried out air strikes against Aideed's forces and sought his arrest.

As violence from Aideed's forces increased, so too did our deployment of further troops, including the air force and Navy Seals. Our forces remained under fire much of the time, even as we captured more of Aideed's guerrillas, and soon we were taking heavy artillery hits from rocket-propelled grenades. On 3 October, on a mission to capture two of Aideed's leading lieutenants, we had successfully captured some twenty-four Somali militants when a Black Hawk helicopter was struck from the air by a rocket-propelled grenade and all hell broke loose:

> Ground fire struck two more MH-60s (Black Hawks), with one going down less than a mile south of the first destroyed helicopter while the other limped to safety at the airport. A Somali mob overran this second crash site and, despite a heroic defense, killed everyone except one of the pilots, whom they took prisoner.[92]

The aftermath of this battle was broadcast on television for the world to see; and what they saw were two of our brave young soldiers, shot, and their naked bodies dragged through the streets of Mogadishu, the rebel capital, with a mob of cheering Somalis in the background.* Although many in our armed forces wanted to bring the fighting to an end by fighting to the end, President Clinton and Defense Secretary Les Aspin would soon begin to withdraw U.S. forces from that troubled country prior to any decisive victory. It was no Desert Storm. It was a shame. And it was the third time within less than a decade that the U.S. military had come to the aid of Muslims abroad, and had paid a heavy price for it.

Not many in political leadership at the time paid a great deal of attention

---

* The story of this incident is best told by journalist Mark Bowden in his book *Black Hawk Down*. A movie based on the book had a profound impact on part of a young generation in America that saw it, a generation that had not known much of Vietnam or past wars.

to the ignominy of the events in Somalia. But we would learn in time that others were watching the broader implications. Osama bin Laden was well aware of the goings on in Somalia and had sent a handful of his men to work with the guerrillas there, perhaps even helping train them in the use of rocket-propelled grenades.[93]

Meanwhile, back at home, conservatives geared up to challenge the Clinton presidency on every front, from policy to ethics. The editorial page of the *Wall Street Journal, National Review* magazine, and national talk radio (especially Rush Limbaugh) would lead the tough—but mostly fair— challenges to the administration. Others soon joined in, including, with a vengeance, the *American Spectator* magazine.

In December, the *Spectator* (under then journalist David Brock's byline) released a piece that (for those who had not heard of the magazine) would put it on the map; it was a big story, at least to Clinton's critics. Headlined "His Cheatin' Heart," the story alleged several extramarital affairs of then Governor Bill Clinton in the 1980s and early '90s, and went on to also specu- late that Vince Foster's death was more than a depressive suicide. There was little doubt by those who read the article that the reporting of the affairs was accurate in many ways, as far as it went, but the Foster allegations and the "lurid, extraneous, and unverifiable details" in the story were over the top and left the article open to a great deal of criticism.[94]

But the *Spectator* article did one more thing: it mentioned a woman named "Paula" as one of the women the governor had approached for an assignation at the Excelsior Hotel in Little Rock. The *Spectator* was not the only publication with this story; later in December, the *Los Angeles Times* published a similar story with many of the same sources (Arkansas State Troopers responsible for the governor's security detail), absent the charges about Vincent Foster. The allegations would soon be known as "Troopergate," based on the main sourcing for the stories and the efforts of the troopers who claimed they helped the governor with his liaisons.* The White House vigorously denied the allegations. In the words of Clinton Senior Assistant Bruce Lindsey, "These allegations are ridiculous. Similar

---

* After the Nixon Watergate scandal, almost every Washington-based scandal attached the suffix "-gate" to it.

charges were made, investigated and responded to during the campaign. There is nothing that dignifies a further response."[95]

VII. Reclaiming the Agenda

The Congress passed and President Clinton signed a tax hike as well as the Brady Act (named after former press secretary to Ronald Reagan, James Brady, who was shot in 1981) which imposed a five-day waiting period on handgun purchases. And the Clinton administration attempted to overhaul the health care system—this all after attempting to impose a social experiment on the military. Meanwhile the questions of ethics that had begun to surface about the president were receiving more and more attention. As a result, by the end of 1993, conservatives and Republicans in America were reenergized—looking forward to the next year's congressional elections. If there seemed to be little bipartisanship in Washington, D.C., there was one success the White House achieved with the help of Republicans, or most Republicans anyway: the North American Free Trade Agreement, which broke down trade barriers among the United States, Canada, and Mexico.

NAFTA had become—as with any international trade debate—a contentious issue pitting various interests against each other. Free Trade Democrats had to fend off opposition from the labor unions worried about job losses due to exporting manufacturing in other countries without labor protections. Free Trade Republicans had to fend off opposition from economic isolationists in the party (recall the Smoot-Hawley tariff of the Great Depression was sponsored by Republicans) and many in their grassroots who were distrustful of international agreements. Vice President Al Gore would debate the leading opponent of NAFTA, Ross Perot, in a highly watched debate on CNN. Perot, as during the campaign, deployed a lot of great slogans, but Gore proved the superior debater with a better command of the facts. One major poll gave the debate to Vice President Gore by a whopping 59 to 32 margin.[96]

The Congress passed NAFTA with 132 Republicans and 102 Democrats voting for it in the House and 27 Democrats and 34 Republicans voting for it in the Senate.[97] It was a rare moment of bipartisanship in an otherwise highly rancorous year. But as is often the case with a new president's first year of his first term, it set the course for the next three years, a template of the debate and first term of the Clinton presidency. That template would be—depending on your party—a mixture of the economy and/or taxes, the Middle East peace process and/or terrorism, and domestic extremism and/or personal responsibility and ethics.

If 1993 seemed like a big year, a watershed 365 days of consequential events and politics, 1994 was even bigger. The year opened well for President Clinton on his agenda. In January he traveled to Russia and met with Russian President Boris Yeltsin, a democratic reformer who had taken the reins of government after the dissolution of the Soviet Union, promising to further move Russia toward a freer economy, a continued liberalization of domestic politics, and better relations with the West.

In Yeltsin, Clinton had an ally of similar temperament and easy mutual relations. In Moscow, President Clinton spoke at a town hall meeting extemporaneously, charming the newly free Russian people: "I come here as a friend and supporter of the democratic changes going on in this nation," he said. "I hope that my nation and I can make a positive contribution, in the spirit of genuine and equal partnership."[98] Clinton and Yeltsin agreed to end the targeting of each other's nation with their leftover strategic missile arsenals. While the agreement was more symbolic than anything else (with no circumscribed verification procedure), it was awfully good symbolism.[99]

Entering his second year in office, the president began his January State of the Union with a jape—as the TelePrompTer (the almost invisible screen that shows the speaker his prepared speech text) had a malfunction. He opened: "Mr. Speaker, Mr. President, members of the 103rd Congress, my fellow Americans, I am not sure what speech is in the TelePrompTer tonight, but I hope we can talk about the State of the Union."[100] Not a bad laugh line, or insight into the president's ability to charm and remain comfortable in front of any camera—and he carried on with his speech extemporaneously without the TelePrompTer for several minutes.

He then got to the main text of his prepared remarks (which were, ultimately, correctly loaded into the TelePrompTer). He spoke of his previous year's accomplishments and went on to outline the upcoming year's desired agenda, focusing mostly on a renewed effort to reform health care. But he did have a few other interesting comments on other policy issues, including welfare and family policy. On welfare, he seemed to be making good on his campaign promise to "end welfare as we know it," saying the then current welfare system "doesn't work; it defies our values as a nation. If we value work, we can't justify a system that makes welfare more attractive than work if people are worried about losing their health care." He continued:

> If we value strong families, we can't perpetuate a system that actually penalizes those who stay together. Can you believe that a child who has a child gets more money from the government for leaving home than for staying home with a parent or a grandparent? That's not just bad policy, it's wrong and we ought to change it.[101]

January would be nearly the last time Bill Clinton and the Democratic Party would be ascendant that year, upbeat, on offense. Attorney General Reno had, that same month, assigned an independent counsel to look into the Whitewater affair. And while the president would go on the road to tout the health care reform his wife had worked so hard on, it ran into political buzz saws throughout America and in Washington. The liberal magazine that had endorsed the Clinton-Gore ticket and was perhaps the most respected magazine in the liberal movement, the *New Republic*, featured a widely circulated—and controversial—critique of the Clinton health care proposal titled "No Exit." A Manhattan Institute scholar named Betsy McCaughey provided a road map to the opposition for Clinton-style health care reform.

Her piece was cited by columnists and talk show hosts throughout the nation—and it was given added credibility coming from a liberal magazine. Another person who found the article persuasive was Congressman Newt Gingrich of Georgia. Many outside the Washington, D.C., Beltway did not know Congressman Gingrich at that point in early 1994, but his fame was growing; two groups of Americans were paying more and more attention to him: almost every politician in Washington, and C-SPAN's national television audience where Gingrich saw the value of delivering speeches on the floor of the House of Representatives aimed directly at viewers of C-SPAN.

A voracious reader with ceaseless energy, Newt (as he was known) was a former history professor with a Ph.D., and he had already begun to revolutionize the way Republicans did business on Capitol Hill. Earlier, he had formed the Conservative Opportunity Society in the House with a group of Reaganite-Republicans who wanted to continue in the Reagan tradition of cutting taxes and proposing bold ideas. He had helped engineer the ouster of former House Majority Leader Jim Wright on ethics charges, and he had worked his way up the chain of leadership to become the minority whip for Republicans in the House. He had the ear of many conservatives in Washington, and they had his—he was the go-to conservative leader on Capitol Hill by early 1994.

Aside from televised ads, conservative columnists, and Bill Kristol's active fax machine, there was also private industry. One famous moment showing the opposition from the private sector came in April in a town hall meeting the president held in Kansas City (with bigger audiences looped in via television satellite in other locations). The vice chairman of the National Restaurant Association and head of Godfather's Pizza, Herman Cain, was given the opportunity via satellite to ask the president a question:

> The cost of your plan is simply a cost that will cause us to eliminate jobs.
>
> In going through my own calculations, the number of jobs that we would have to eliminate to try to absorb this cost [of covering those who do not have employer-related health care] is a lot greater than I ever anticipated. . . . On behalf of all those business owners that are in a similar situation to mine, my question is, quite simply, if I'm forced to do this, what will I tell those people whose jobs I have to eliminate?[102]

It was a zinger of a question coming from a well-dressed, articulate, respected businessman (who also happened to be black) that simply caught the president unprepared. The president rattled off a series of numbers and percentages about employment and then went on to say that Cain and his competitors could raise the price of pizzas. And there, on television, people could see the ultimate trade-off for the president's plan: it would increase the price of consumer products or lead to job loss. Cain's question ran not only on national and cable television but also throughout talk radio and in follow-up columns. And Cain explained further, in a well-circulated column he wrote for the *Wall Street Journal,* how President Clinton's numbers did not add up.

After several versions, the health care bill went back and forth in the House and Senate, and it ultimately died by September. Some would say the left had overreached by trying to push a bill that was too big and too expensive; some would say Clinton's other pieces of domestic legislation distracted enough of Congress's attention to work out a satisfactory health care bill that could pass muster with the natural give-and-take compromises that accompany any piece of major legislation; some would say the legislation was too hard to explain in a simple manner; some would say the televised ad campaign against it (featuring a fictional couple known as "Harry and Louise" sponsored by the health insurance lobby) was too persuasive to too many; some would say physicians' groups were strong in their worry about regulated fees as business owners were strong in their worry about costs to their own bottom lines. But Bill Kristol (who led the policy fight against the health care reform legislation from Washington) probably had the best explanation at the end of the day:

> Clinton's plan failed because of its very nature. He thought the middle class would accept an expansion of government in return for "health security," and I think he radically underestimated the American people's mistrust of big government liberalism. He thought he was elected to carry forward, to enact the final piece of the New Deal, Great Society agenda, and it turns out the American public is more interested in reversing course now rather than continuing that course. . . .
>
> I think the key moment was when the quality argument came to the fore. Americans might have tolerated a little more bureaucracy or a few more regulations for the sake of covering the uninsured. But when it became clear that the Clinton plan threatened the choice of

doctors and the quality of medical care available to Middle America, or available to most Americans, they . . . turned against it.[103]

As the United States faced the 1994 midterm elections, few journalists sensed the political earthquake that was rumbling below the surface. For better or worse, more and more people were beginning to distrust the administration. This, despite the fact that not since FDR and Eleanor had the White House seen the president and First Lady so thoroughly involved in the day-to-day workings of the government. But the First Lady and her husband, by the end of 1994, had not fared too well in her signature issue.

VIII. A Weakened President

The president had had a difficult 1993 and half of 1994. Waco had raised many doubts about "competence." The failed attempt to transform our nation's health care system appeared to many like a fundamental threat to liberty. Taxes were raised, pleasing few. And scandals (some tawdry from the past, some financial and complicated) were becoming more and more discussed. Furthermore, Bill Clinton in the White House seemed to lack the dignity and integrity Americans like in their president—whatever comparison to FDR or JFK seemed to end there, at dignity.

When the conservative *American Spectator* revealed that Clinton, as governor, had used state troopers to procure women for him, the story was denounced as gossip mongering. Then the liberal *Los Angeles Times* essentially confirmed the outlines of the story. The Clintons' Whitewater land dealings in Arkansas had come under scrutiny by the *New York Times* during the 1992 campaign, but they had not affected the election outcome. Now, in 1994, following the suicide of White House Counsel Vince Foster, many new conservative media outlets charged a broad pattern of corruption against the Clintons.

In May, yet another shoe dropped on the eroding dignity of the White House—"Paula" from the *American Spectator* essay became more than an "eruption." In February, after her first name had been published in the

American Spectator, Paula Corbin Jones held a press conference in Washington explaining the 1991 incident. One of the then governor's troopers told her the governor would like to see her in his hotel room. At the time she was a state employee for the Arkansas Industrial Development Corporation. She went, escorted by said trooper, to the governor's room, where, she alleged, the governor made sexual advances and statements to her that she ultimately rebuffed and, then, walked out of the room some fifteen minutes later. She said, too, she had supporting corroboration from a colleague and a friend whom she told about the incident.[104]

Paula Jones said she wanted to clear her name from any negative implication in the *Spectator* story and had sent a letter to the president asking for an apology. No apology came, and the White House Press Secretary Dee Dee Myers denied the entire incident from 1991, saying the story was "just not true."[105] Jones took this and other White House denials as defamation, saying she was being called a liar. In May 1994, before federal statutes of limitations had run out on her claims, she filed a civil lawsuit against the sitting U.S. president claiming a violation of her civil rights as a state employee, infliction of emotional distress, and defamation.[106] It was a big first, and it landed heavily in the newspapers, television, and talk radio. Nobody could remember any time in recent history when a sitting president had been sued for actions he had allegedly committed before he was president.

To say this lawsuit and these accusations were precisely what President Clinton did not need would be an understatement; and he hired one of the best-known and most respected lawyers in the country to defend him and try to get the case dismissed, Robert S. Bennett. Bennett was a Washington-based litigator who had represented any number of prominent individuals, including President Reagan's former Secretary of Defense Caspar Weinberger.* Bennett was not only fierce in a courtroom, he was a Washington legal insider's insider, and he was also pretty quick with a sound bite in the court of public opinion. Upon Jones's filing, he told the press, "This is tabloid trash with a legal caption on it." The problem for Clinton was that where there was

---

* Robert Bennett is also my older brother.

smoke, there was often fire, and in the president's case, this was not the first billow (or the last).

IX. Los Angeles

Meanwhile, outside of presidential politics, outside of Washington, another Southern Californian was making legal news that would—again—shake the country, but this time the man was well known. In June, Nicole Brown Simpson, the ex-wife of former NFL running back O. J. Simpson, was found murdered along with her friend Ronald Goldman outside her home near Los Angeles. Upon learning that the police had found certain evidence that he was the lead suspect for the double murder, and realizing that he would soon be arrested, O. J. took a friend's white Ford Bronco and led the police in a fairly slow, surreal, but long chase that was broadcast on live television as millions of stunned Americans watched. At the end of the "chase," O. J. was arrested and indicted for the double homicide. His plea in open court: "100 percent not guilty."[107] His trial would commence in January.

O. J. Simpson's case was perhaps *the* dominant story of the year, but it was not the only news story involving major sports figures in 1994 and 1995. Baseball fans the country (and world) over became disgusted with the sport (many saying they would never watch another World Series again) after the baseball players went on strike that year over salary caps.[108] And due to the strike, there was no World Series in 1994. America rewards its star athletes very well, as it rewards its movie stars and top music entertainers, but most fans saw greed in their favorite teams' actions. The average baseball player salary was $1.2 million then, and some players made several times that amount.[109] The storied institution, our "national pastime," restored itself to most fans once the strike ended in 1995, and a few years later, baseball greats Mark McGwire and Sammy Sosa competed in a historic home run chase in the 1998 season, breaking all previous baseball records and drawing fans back to the stands and to their television sets to watch it happen.*

---

* Regrettably, the reputations of Sosa, McGwire, and other baseball greats were later marred by reports about positive tests for performance-enhancing drugs. See http://www.nytimes.com/2009/06/17/sports/baseball/17doping.html?_r=2&hp (visited 20 Sept. 2009).

X. The Republican "Revolution"

Back in the less surreal world, while movement conservatives were raising up anti-Clinton sentiment, the Republicans on Capitol Hill needed to start thinking about a November strategy for the upcoming elections. Newt Gingrich—ever the strategist—came up with a plan for November with Ross Perot's former pollster Frank Luntz, and they called it the "Contract with America." Gingrich thought of this Contract as an unprecedented and abbreviated party platform to be offered for a midterm election.

The Contract effort was a bid for the Republicans to take over Congress for the first time in forty years. Gingrich and Luntz had identified several agenda items that the congressional Republicans would promise America they would enact if they were given a majority in November. They made local congressional elections a national referendum on the Democratic direction and leadership in Washington. They publicized the Contract in new places as well, reaching ever larger grassroots audiences.

One striking note about the Contract was that it had nothing about what many had come to think the Republican Party stood for most: social issues and family values; instead, the Contract mostly was about restoring faith in government and fiscal responsibility. Among the contractual promises were such things as requiring all laws that apply to the rest of the country to apply equally to the Congress; conducting a comprehensive audit of Congress for waste, fraud, or abuse; and requiring a three-fifths majority vote to pass a tax increase. There were also promises of limiting tenure for congressional chairmanships, reforming welfare, and balancing the budget.[110]

The Contract was a flash of genius. It energized the activists, like those from the Christian Coalition under the leadership of the young and talented Ralph Reed, who in turn energized the base. The Republican victory in November delivered an astonishing rebuke to the Clintons and to the Democrats in Congress. Along with the Contract, Gingrich and the Republicans made a point of the culture of arrogance and corruption in which the Congress at the time wallowed. Too many House members were becoming known for living off too many perks unavailable to the rest of

America, including some perks that rose to the level of scandal—such as overdrawing their House banking accounts without penalty and, in the case of House Ways and Means Chairman Dan Rostenkowski, charges that he was using congressional funds for gifts for friends and keeping "ghost employees" on his official payroll.[111]

The 1994 elections, called by many the Republican Revolution, were an elephant stampede. The GOP gained fifty-two seats in the House of Representatives. The party won a majority of the House for the first time since 1954. The Senate, too, became Republican. And the mastermind of so much of this, Newt Gingrich, became the Speaker of the House of Representatives. Stung by the voters' rejection, Bill Clinton had to scramble to face the new, assertive GOP opposition in Congress. He was nothing if not agile. Gingrich and his allies succeeded in passing many meaningful reforms, but they soon overreached. During 1995, the House Republicans demanded that Clinton commit to balancing the federal budget in seven years "using CBO numbers." This meant the nonpartisan Congressional Budget Office (CBO) had to "score" the final budget agreement. Americans outside the Washington Beltway thought the battle—as important as it was—was a tempest in a teapot. Few average citizens had any idea what "using CBO numbers" meant. And when Republicans allowed the federal government to be shut down for lack of funding, there was a predictable backlash against Speaker Gingrich.

The Republicans' talk of "revolution" proved to be unsettling to many voters. And, as remarkable as the 1994 elections were, they did not fairly compare with the vast electoral sweeps of Franklin Roosevelt in 1932 or 1936.

XI. Terrorism Homegrown

Clinton cleverly exploited Gingrich's often bold statements. When the worst case of domestic terrorism occurred in America, it occurred in a stunning incident in Oklahoma City in April 1995. Although many initially thought it might be another case of Islamic terrorism, it turned out otherwise. Two homegrown American boys, who were angry at the federal government for any number of reasons (including the storming of the Branch Davidian compound in Waco), timed their attack to commemorate the debacle in Texas.[112] The cowardly and deadly bombing took the lives of 168 Americans (including those of 19 children) and destroyed the Alfred P. Murrah Federal Building in Oklahoma City. Oklahoma Governor Frank Keating, who had just recently been elected, rose to the national conscience as a steady and responsible hand mobilizing emergency efforts amidst the bombing and the sorrow. And in response to this national issue (and an attack on a federal building), President Clinton quickly comforted a stunned and grieving country. At a memorial service in Oklahoma, the president was at his Baptist-upbringing best, saying,

> This terrible sin took the lives of our American family, innocent children in that building, only because their parents were trying to be good parents as well as good workers; citizens in the building going about their daily business; and many there who served the rest of us— who worked to help the elderly and the disabled, who worked to support our farmers and our veterans, who worked to enforce our laws and to protect us.[113]

Before he headed to Oklahoma, the president had received word that one Oklahoma schoolgirl had suggested everyone plant a tree to remember those who were killed. The president said he and his wife had planted one at the White House that morning, and he concluded his remarks in Oklahoma: "My fellow Americans, a tree takes a long time to grow, and wounds take a long time to heal. But we must begin. Those who are lost now belong to God. Some day we will be with them. But until that happens, their legacy must be our lives."[114]

The right words from the man in the right job at the right time. But like his political nemesis, Speaker Gingrich, President Clinton could also overreach, and a few days later he said at another address,

> We hear so many loud and angry voices in America today whose sole goal seems to be to try to keep some people as paranoid as possible and the rest of us all torn up and upset with each other. . . . They spread

hate. They leave the impression that, by their very words, that violence is acceptable. . . . I'm sure you are now seeing the reports of some things that are regularly said over the airwaves in America today. Well, people like that who want to share our freedoms must know that their bitter words can have consequences, and that freedom has endured in this country for more than two centuries because it was coupled with an enormous sense of responsibility.[115]

Many in the talk radio and conservative community took this as a not-so-veiled slap at their work and opinions. While the president did not single anybody out by name, many concluded he had in mind radio host Rush Limbaugh or some of the newly empowered congressional Republicans. If so, it was an irresponsible charge—it would be difficult, indeed, to find a political opponent of the president such as Rush or an elected official in Washington saying anything inspiring terrorism. Indeed, we had learned, *if anything*, the inspiration for the two Oklahoma bombers was opposition to the actions of the Clinton administration, not the words of those who opposed it. Regardless, nobody is responsible for terrorism except terrorists, and there is no excuse for their action—ever—no matter what kind of legitimacy they may claim. And if nothing else, the 1994 election proved that the democratic process works just fine to check power one opposes. As Abraham Lincoln put it, "Among free men, there can be no successful appeal from the ballot to the bullet."[116]

But there was more violence in the air in 1995—and not just in Oklahoma. Another domestic terrorist known as the Unabomber had sporadically mailed letter bombs to American citizens, such as university professors and corporate leaders, since 1978. He had severely injured dozens of people and by 1995 had killed three.* Five days after the Oklahoma bombing, the Unabomber struck again, killing a forestry executive in California.[117] Again, the motives for this terrorist were far beyond sane but, to him, included the "dehumanizing influences of post-industrial society."[118]

---

* One of his targets was my good friend Professor David Gelernter of Yale University; his book on the Unabomber, *Drawing Life*, is one of the single, best pieces of nonfiction to be published in the 1990s.

XII. State v. Simpson

And of course, there was that other story of the year that had spawned endless hours of cable news and radio chatter, speculation, and commentary: O. J. Simpson. In October, a jury had found Simpson not guilty of the murder of his ex-wife Nicole Brown Simpson and her friend Ronald Goldman. This verdict rocked the nation. The verdict and the televised trial were the dominating cultural and entertainment events of 1995. And they caused more than a little dismay.

Simpson had hired the best legal team that money could buy, a collection of attorneys known as "the Dream Team." This team included Los Angeles attorney Robert Shapiro, civil rights attorney Johnnie Cochran, and one of the legends of the law, F. Lee Bailey. For good measure, Simpson also hired one of the great legal scholars of the age to advise in the background and prepare for any possible appeal, Harvard Law professor Alan Dershowitz.

The worst move of the trial was the judge's, allowing the trial to be aired on television—this helped feed the hysteria and the playing to the cameras and the national audience by the attorneys and witnesses involved. The second worst move was by the prosecution: it had not properly prepared or done a thorough enough background check on some of the key witnesses. In one famous moment of the trial, Bailey exposed a policeman who was a prosecution witness as having used racial epithets in the past—even as he denied ever doing so on the stand in front of the jury.

And then there was the famous glove incident. In a telling moment of the trial, the prosecution did the visual equivalent of asking a question it did not know the answer to when it decided to ask Simpson to put on a glove (in front of the jury) that had been found at the scene, with his and the victims' blood on it. When Simpson put the glove on his left hand, he showed the judge and jury that it was too small. The glove didn't fit, and thus, his message was, "It can't be mine." This fed into the defense's legal theory that O. J. Simpson was being framed, no matter how hard the prosecution tried to then show how such gloves could have shrunk.[119]

In his summation argument to the jury, Johnnie Cochran played up the glove to fare-thee-well. He—as others—identified the glove moment as the "defining moment of the trial." In his closing arguments, Cochran said what would be the single, most memorable line of the trial: "Mr. Darden [the prosecutor] asked Mr. Simpson to try on those gloves and the gloves didn't fit, remember these words; if it doesn't fit, you must acquit."[120] Cochran used that refrain, "if it doesn't fit, you must acquit," several more times. The Dream Team also played up the race angle and the framing angle when they alleged evidence tampering. To the victims' families, to those present in the courtroom following the case closely, to those watching closely on television, indeed, to most Americans, there was little question that O. J. Simpson was guilty. While there may have been some irregularities in the prosecution's argument, and with the evidence, it still stood up, and Simpson was, in reality, the only one who could have committed the double homicide.

But members of the jury had other things on their minds—and they were aided by the *razzle dazzle* of the Dream Team that gave them just the excuse. Race was, in fact, all over this case. The Rodney King trial was still in the air. Allegations of police racism were thick throughout the black community. Nicole was white; Simpson was black. And when the jury delivered its verdict of not guilty, "Simpson smiled thinly and mouthed the words 'thank you' as the not guilty verdicts were read. Two jurors smiled back. Another, Lionel (Lon) Cryer, raised his left fist in a [black power] salute toward Simpson as the panel left the courtroom."[121]

The nation was stunned, asking: How could such an evidently guilty man be exonerated like this, race issues or not? Is racism worse than murder? Sadly, the view by many was that this was the black community's payback for the excusal of the police in the Rodney King trial. The polling showed it: 71 percent of black Americans regarded O. J. as innocent of the murders when he was acquitted; 72 percent of white Americans saw him as guilty.[122] Over time, as a free O. J. Simpson acted more and more obnoxiously (a brazen book about the case, arguments with his children, a robbery charge), and as the memory of Rodney King's injustice faded, those numbers would change, with a majority of black Americans later saying they thought he was, indeed, guilty.[123] And in a side note to both the original King and Simpson verdicts, it is worth noting that some level of justice ultimately marked both cases. A federal jury had found some officers in the

Rodney King beating case guilty of violating King's civil rights, and a civil suit filed against Simpson by Ron Goldman's father found Simpson liable for Goldman's wrongful death. No riots attended the Simpson circus, but the discussion of race, racism, and violence continued anew in America.

Violence was still much with us in 1995. Israeli Prime Minister Yitzhak Rabin was assassinated in Israel by a right-wing Jewish zealot who had thought Rabin was selling Israel out to Yasser Arafat and his cohorts. Whatever the merits or demerits of the Israeli-Palestinian peace accords, Americans (with typically strong ties to the Jewish state) grieved over such a violent act.

As the year was closing out, however, politics loomed large again, especially as the following year was the Republicans' chance to unseat President Clinton. With the 1996 election before them, Republicans felt they had made a pretty good case against Clinton's policies, they felt they had become a semi-majority party again with the taking back of Congress, and the president's personal ethics were shown to be less than dignified to a people who appreciated dignity in the White House.

On the policy front, outside of Congress's quarters, many were working on promoting issues such as family integrity, welfare reform, educational choice, and crime reduction.*

XIII. Social Thought at Home
and the 1996 Elections

Fatherlessness had become one large issue that many in the think tank and journalist communities were talking about—and many of us thought it was the Rosetta Stone for many societal ills. The prior year, *Newsweek* had declared it "The Year of the Father," writing that "fathers have become almost mythic figures—manning (as it were) the barricade safeguarding

---

* Although I would become known as one of President Clinton's chief critics, especially on ethics, I had not said too terribly much about them up to this point. I had recently published a few books, one, a large best-seller, and was working with Jack Kemp and Jeane Kirkpatrick at a think tank we had founded (Empower America). The three of us and our staff were offering up just these kinds of policies, testifying before Congress, writing books and policy papers and op-eds, and giving speeches around the country.

America against further decay."[124] And one of the founders of the modern conservative movement, Irving Kristol (Bill's father), had penned a widely discussed piece in the *Wall Street Journal* titled "Life Without Father," detailing the societal ills that had come about from out-of-wedlock births or fatherlessness. For example, Kristol had found, "Almost two thirds of rapists, three quarters of adolescent murderers, and the same percentage of long-term prison inmates are young males who grew up without fathers in the house."[125]

I had detailed, to some popular media note, other social ills in a book titled *The Index of Leading Cultural Indicators*. The *Index* showed, for example, that a lot of bad things were taking place in America, often under the radar of the national news media: increasing crime rates, increasing out-of-wedlock and teen births, lower educational achievement, and higher rates of divorce and welfare dependency.*

Trying to find positive role models for our nation's youth and, at the same time, trying to bridge some of the gulf in our race relations, several of us pushed to draft General Colin Powell for president. The general was widely hailed as "the black Eisenhower."[126] He was considered the first black man who had a realistic chance of being elected president. He had presided over the splendid success of the Gulf War. Older conservatives, however, opposed General Powell's liberal stances on abortion and racial quotas. Nonetheless, the Republican Party lost its *only* real chance for victory in 1996 when the general withdrew his name from consideration. Bill Clinton would prove more than a match for the GOP.

And still, the culture needed help. Many, from all political backgrounds, had become increasingly concerned with the kind of entertainment being produced and broadcast to our children from gangsta rap lyrics to trashy television. This kind of "entertainment" was not only debasing to the listeners but polluting to the general atmosphere as well. There were lyrics

---

* While much of the religious-inspired conservative movement was working on issues from gay marriage to abortion (issues on which I generally agreed with them), around this time I had given a speech to the Christian Coalition where I told them: "The behavior of the middle class has been [a] negative model. . . . In terms of damage to children in America, divorce is far more destructive to the children of American than issues such as gay marriage. The statistics about divorce are increasingly discouraging, because it indicates a failure of commitment."

by popular artists that promoted violence against women, the police, and others—not to mention sexually explicit imagery that advocated everything from pedophilia to sadism.[127] I and others would speak to the corporate board meetings of the entertainment companies that distributed the material, trying to shame them by reading out loud the lyrics they were publishing, writing op-eds, and giving public speeches on the issue.

Democratic U.S. Senator Joe Lieberman of Connecticut and civil rights activist Delores Tucker were the two most prominent public figures who joined in our campaign. Lieberman was particularly forceful, speaking as an elected official known for his moral probity and strong Democratic Party ties. Near the holiday season in one of our news conferences, he would say of one music corporation, "They are literally marketing death and degradation as a twisted form of holiday cheer."[128] At one point during this effort, *Time* magazine (owned by the Time Warner corporation) gave its front-page cover to the debate, with red, white, and blue lettering in bold, asking, "Are Music and Movies Killing America's Soul?" Another *Time* magazine article subtitled a story, "Reformers Decry the 'Cultural Rot' of Daytime Talk Shows."

Our group had also advised Senate Majority Leader Robert Dole, who was gearing up for a presidential run, to take on this issue, to go to Hollywood and speak about the violent movies the industry was making. We helped him with his speech in Hollywood where he spoke of reaching a "point where our popular culture threatens to undermine our character as a nation," and condemned some of the worst films for promoting "nightmares of depravity."[129] It was one of the few times Dole would speak about the culture and the challenges facing it—an issue Dan Quayle had taken on before him, an issue grassroots conservatives like those involved with Gary Bauer's Family Research Council or the Christian Coalition were concerned with.

Cultural issues aside for the moment, though, Senator Bob Dole seemed the general consensus Republican candidate going into 1996—he had been around a long time, and people felt he deserved his shot. He faced Pat Buchanan and others such as former Tennessee Governor Lamar Alexander* and businessman Steve Forbes in the New Hampshire primary in a race

---

*I was Lamar Alexander's National Co-Chairman at the time.

nobody could predict. Buchanan won a narrow victory there with Dole finishing second.[130] It was to be Buchanan's high-water mark, however, just as he had made New Hampshire his best showing in early 1992. But Buchanan didn't leave New Hampshire without a lot of enthusiasm. Even though his support was more deep than wide, he could still energize his very loyal base, and he had a way with words. He instructed his followers on the eve of New Hampshire's results with typical Buchanan rhetorical gusto: "They're going to come after this campaign with everything they've got. Do not wait for orders from headquarters, mount up everybody and ride to the sound of the guns."[131]

Those guns didn't roar, and Dole soon wrapped up the Republican nomination, albeit not without a strong challenge from Steve Forbes who had campaigned on the supply-side idea of a flat-tax rate for all Americans. President Clinton had no opposition for the Democratic nomination. His campaign was to run TV ads against Dole throughout the spring. So effective were these ads in putting the worst light on some of the thousands of Senate votes Dole had cast over his long career that Dole never came close in the polls.*

In the meantime, as was his master ability, President Clinton had brought into the White House a political consultant who had worked with him in Arkansas but who had mostly worked for Republicans—Dick Morris—to help him shape centrist strategies and language, if not policies. And at Morris's urging, Bill Clinton finally made good on a campaign promise on which many Republicans had held his feet to the fire: welfare reform. The Republicans in Congress had passed the massive reform—linking welfare to work, ending the federal entitlement, and block granting the money to states—twice already, although the president had vetoed the reforms. Dick Morris had warned the president he could not veto it a third time. And in the summer of 1996, the president, with three former welfare mothers at his side, signed the legislation.[132]

---

* At the time, I—primarily in televised debates with Governor Mario Cuomo—had begun trying to bring up the issue of personal ethics, saying that there was enough worry about the mounting scandals surrounding President Clinton. I predicted that more would be found out, more would come if Americans gave him another four years.

Welfare reform—and a Democratic Party president signing it—was no small matter; indeed, it angered many of his more liberal supporters and advisors. One major hallmark of the domestic policy work of Franklin Roosevelt's New Deal and Lyndon Johnson's War on Poverty, the federal welfare program had become not just a badge of accomplishment for many Democrats, but a symbol of what they could achieve to help the poor. But as conservatives pointed out, while the intentions might have been altruistic, the realities were not.

President Clinton signing this legislation ending the federal entitlement was a momentous event. To conservatives, welfare was one of the most discouraging and intransigent programs to reform; it was something they had campaigned against since at least Ronald Reagan's 1980 presidential run. For liberals, it was a program whose only desired reform was to put more money into it with the thought that the country simply wasn't spending enough on it. Yet the numbers told the tale: a leading advocate and researcher for welfare reform, Robert Rector, pointed out throughout the 1996 debate that not only had the hundreds of billions of dollars spent on welfare over the years not reduced poverty; the funding had created dependence and fueled illegitimacy (one of the key eligibility conditions was single motherhood), and "among the nearly 5 million families" who at the time were welfare recipients, far from its being a temporary fix, "the total time spent on welfare" averaged about thirteen years.[133]

I had become involved in the debate, arguing for the reform as a matter of helping the poor end their cycle of dependence and strengthen their families. In the pages of the *Washington Post*, for example, New York Democratic Senator Daniel Moynihan and I debated the merits of reform when he wrote that I (along with others arguing for reform) would set social policy on a path of "unforeseeable consequences, many of which will surely be loathsome."[134] I had responded that while changes in poverty legislation would not come easily and there would be challenges, social welfare policy had to change, or there would come a day of social ruin. I went on to state:

> Can welfare reformers guarantee that fundamental reforms in welfare
> will not cause some dislocation and suffering? Of course not. But the

relevant question is: compared to what? The burden of proof rests not on those who would try something new but on those who would defend the horrors of the status quo. After all, proponents of welfare reform can make a plausible case that the current system is exacting a far higher cost than what will replace it.[135]

The president finally agreed with the reformers and Dick Morris, and signed the legislation. It ended up being smart social policy, ultimately halving the welfare rolls. And it proved a good election-year strategy as well.

As to November, Senator Bob Dole's World War II heroism was honored throughout the country, but in 1996, World War II was a fading memory, and it certainly had not meant much for George H. W. Bush in his reelection bid four years earlier. To give a sense of the age difference, Bob Dole had actually won his medals for valor in World War II the year before Bill Clinton was born. Although Dole was in remarkable physical and mental condition, he was seventy-three years old, and the president, having recently turned fifty, still maintained a youthful, energetic demeanor.

In order to give a shot of B_{12} to the GOP ticket, Dole chose his former Republican rival, Jack Kemp, as his running mate.* And Kemp's youthful, athletic demeanor and tax-cutting energy truly energized the grassroots of the GOP. The Republicans were never able, however, to gain traction. When stories surfaced about the Clinton campaign taking large amounts of money from corporations that were selling high technology to the People's Republic of China, Bob Dole plaintively asked, "Where's the outrage?" Few were listening. Clinton was still a great campaigner and public speaker; Bob Dole was not. And the president was earning points for the economic recovery.**

Clinton had attacked the senior George Bush in 1992 for "coddling the butchers of Beijing." Now, he was garnering major campaign donations from Chinese nationals. One American, Johnny Chung, served as a conduit

---

* Senator Dole had asked me if I would like to be his running mate, and I had to turn him down based on greater interest in policy work and writing.
** Unemployment had gone down nearly two full points since Clinton had taken office. See http://www.miseryindex.us/URbymonth.asp.

for senior Chinese military leaders to funnel vast sums into Clinton campaign coffers.[136]

Chung wasn't the only person involved. Defense analyst Mark Helprin related in *National Review* some of the dangerous losses to America's national security that Clinton allowed through another shadowy figure in the burgeoning Chinese campaign contribution scandal:

> John Huang met secretly with Chinese officials in Washington nine times, six times in the Chinese embassy. China has walked away with a great deal of what it needs [to modernize its military] . . . guidance, MIRV, busing, fairing, and failure-analysis technology for missile design and testing; highly classified antisubmarine warfare techniques; night-vision technology; machine tools necessary for military production beyond the ken of Chinese manufacture; plans for every nuclear warhead in the U.S. inventory; nuclear legacy codes; and high-capacity computers.[137]

Nonetheless, nothing seemed to throw candidate Clinton off stride. Not even the uncomfortable news for the president from just before the summer campaign and convention season that the U.S. Supreme Court had ruled Paula Jones could go forward with her lawsuit against the president.* When Clinton and Dole met in debate, the president boldly stood apart from his lectern with his arms folded across his chest. He smiled as Dole launched into a fierce attack on his record. Clinton, the master of body language, seemed to be saying: "Go ahead, Bob, take your best shot."

When Dole tried another tack—criticizing Clinton for the dozens of very liberal federal judges he had appointed—Clinton grinned and deflected the charge: "You voted for 'em!" Dole's attack, in fact his whole campaign, collapsed. Clinton was right. Dole *had* gone along with most of the appointments.

---

* A lower court had tossed out the Jones suit—a big victory for the president (and my brother). The night the lower court had dismissed the suit, my brother was greeted with a standing ovation when he went out to dinner at the Palm Restaurant in Washington to celebrate. On appeal, though, an appellate court, and now the Supreme Court, had reinstated the suit. Also, around the same time Jim McDougal, his wife, and the Arkansas governor (Jim Guy Tucker) were convicted of fraud in the first trial to emerge out of the Whitewater investigation.

Bob Dole hoped that Clinton's veto of the bill to ban partial-birth abortion would help him defeat the president.* Three million postcards arrived at Capitol Hill from the nation's Catholic parishes, urging an override of the president's veto. All to no avail. Clinton would never compromise on abortion or racial quotas.[138] Pro-life Democrats accused Senator Dole of scheduling the vote late in the campaign season solely to embarrass their party. There was, in this, a measure of truth. Not that it proved very effective.

On Election Day, Bill Clinton triumphed. Just two years after the voters had punished Clinton and his party, they now returned him to office. He was the first Democrat since Franklin D. Roosevelt to be elected to a second four-year term.** Clinton won 47 million popular votes (49.2 percent) and 379 electoral votes to Bob Dole's 39-plus million popular votes (40.7 percent) and 159 electoral votes. Ross Perot's Reform Party had largely collapsed in the polls.[139]

XIV. Terrorism and Peace Abroad

But the election was not the only thing going on with the United States in 1996. The nation's intelligence agencies had opened up a dossier on Osama bin Laden, finding him to be of possible increasing danger to the United States. Among other things, the year before he had written an open letter to the king of Saudi Arabia (a U.S. ally) that urged the king to wage a campaign against the U.S. forces stationed in Saudi Arabia.*** In that rambling letter, bin Laden wrote: "It is not reasonable to keep one's silence about transforming the [Saudi] nation to an American protectorate to be defiled

---

* The horrific procedure involved partially delivering a live unborn child, feet-first, but leaving the head within the mother's womb. Then the abortionist used scissors to create a hole at the base of the skull and thrust in a catheter to suck out the child's brains. The mere description of the procedure caused a shudder of revulsion in such sensitive liberal columnists as the *Washington Post*'s Richard Cohen. He and many others urged Clinton to sign the bill.

** Harry Truman was reelected in 1948, but he had served out the remainder of FDR's fourth term. In all, however, Truman served seven years and nine months.

*** U.S. forces were stationed in Saudi Arabia to help protect that country from Saddam Hussein and to enforce international sanctions against Hussein, sanctions he had continually violated. One such violation was his invasion of the Kurdistan city of Irbil for which President Clinton issued another missile strike on Iraq.

The terrorist bombing of Pan Am Flight 103 killed 270 people, including more than 180 Americans.

© Hudson-Landevin-Nogues/Sygma/Corbis

© Peter Turnley/CORBIS

A German youth

© Bettmann/CORBIS

One man blocks the path of a tank convoy along the Avenue of Eternal Peace near Tiananmen.

George H. W. Bush takes the Oath of Office, accompanied by wife, Barbara.

Michael Dukakis rides in an M1A1 Abrams tank during the 1988 campaign.

Drug Czar, Bill Bennett, burns marijuana plants.

Bill Bennett (right) with President H. W. Bush.

President H. W. Bush visits Los Angeles to stand with the community against drugs.

Secretary of Housing and Urban Development, Jack Kemp.

General Colin Powell (left), General Norman Schwarzkopf (center), and Paul D. Wolfowitz at a press conference during Operation Desert Storm.

An American soldier stands on top of a destroyed Iraqi tank while Kuwaiti oil wells burn in the distance.

Clean-up efforts after the riots following the Rodney King trial in Los Angeles.

Rodney King (right) calls for an end to violence.

O. J. Simpson leads police on a chase as bystanders cheer him on.

© Les Stone/Sygma/Corbis

Workers stand near a makeshift memorial at the site of the Oklahoma City bombing.

© Mike Segar/Reuters/Corbis

Diana the Princess of Wales holds hands with Mother Teresa, the foundress of the Missionaries of Charity, after a meeting in New

© Wally McNamee/CORBIS

President Bill Clinton stands between Yitzhak Rabin (left) and Yasir Arafat (right) during the signing of the Israeli-Palestinian Peace Agreement

President Bill Clinton denies sexual relations with Monica Lewinsky, while Vice President Al Gore stands at the side.

Former White House intern Monica Lewinsky hugs President Bill Clinton

Speaker Newt Gingrich, who led the 1994 Republican resurgence

by the soldiers of the Cross with their soiled feet in order to protect your crumbling throne and the preservation of the oilfields in the kingdom."[140]

In June 1996, another terrorist attack struck at America—Americans—abroad, in Saudi Arabia, when a truck bomb blew up the Khobar Towers where American soldiers were housed. It killed 19 American soldiers and wounded 372.*[141] In August 1996, bin Laden openly declared war on America in a fatwa (a religious ruling) he had issued: "Declaration of War against the Americans Occupying the Land of the Two Holy Places." In that fatwa he had written, "There is no more important duty than pushing the American enemy out of the holy land. No other priority, except Belief, could be considered before it."[142]

The previous year, we had learned of another plot against the United States that was discovered by the Philippine government when an accidental fire alerted the police in Manila to the apartment that Ramzi Yousef and his uncle (one Khalid Sheikh Mohammed) were using. On Yousef's computer was found a manifesto that said, "All people who support the U.S. government are our targets in our future plans."[143] Their plan was to place bombs on a dozen U.S. airliners flying to the U.S. from Asia and to assassinate the pope.[144] In September 1996, Ramzi Yousef was convicted in U.S. federal court for his role in the Manila plot.

By this time, bin Laden was expelled from the Sudan and had moved his headquarters and his team of associates to Afghanistan.[145]

Peace seemed at hand elsewhere, outside the Middle East, and President Clinton had made headway in even stronger relations with Russia. On other fronts, Clinton had sent former President Jimmy Carter to North Korea in 1994 to negotiate an agreement to keep the Communist dictator Kim Il Sung from developing nuclear weapons. "When the Great Leader and the Man from Plains first laid eyes on each other, it was all smiles, as if they had known each other for years," historian Douglas Brinkley wrote. "From Carter's born-again perspective, Kim was not by nature evil," Brinkley said.[146] Americans were relieved. But critics knew there was nothing in the evangelical Christian doctrine professed by Carter to assure us that Kim

---

* The Khobar bombing was the work of Iran's Hezbollah.

was *not* evil. A man who was responsible for millions of deaths in his long-suffering country could be nothing but evil. To conservative critics, Carter's mission served only to "kick the can down the road."

"The world," wrote George Will, "is less menacing than at any time since the 1920s."[147] Charles Krauthammer would later write that during this time, we were living in a "bubble," with Americans thinking we pretty much had reached the end of history. We would be sadly mistaken, and that bubble would burst in future years. But as we headed into 1997, the country seemed quite calm. And in 1997, the press took up this theme. "Why is this happening on my watch?" *USA Today*'s Walter Shapiro moaned.[148] ABC's Cokie Roberts added, "There is no real news here."[149]

Three

Into the Fire

If things were relatively quiet at home, hot spots from Afghanistan, where religious fanaticism marched into power, to Pakistan, which became the first Muslim nation to test a nuclear weapon, were getting hotter. All the while, Saddam Hussein would continue to rule and ruin Iraq, and several more efforts would be made at solving the Israeli-Palestinian conflict. Meanwhile, far removed from the klieg lights of the nation's political and financial capitals of Washington, D.C., and New York City, another revolution was taking place—a technological and informational boom that was years in the making, set off by the most ubiquitous and commonplace ingredient known to man: the grain of sand. By the end of the 1990s, America would become wealthier and wiser, but "safer" would remain another question to be answered once the century turned. And the country would go through a searing national drama ending in the impeachment of a president.

I. Lessons in the Lull

Dick Morris had mastered the art of triangulation for Bill Clinton's successful reelection bid in 1996. This would help Clinton stand between the Republican-controlled Congress and his fellow Democrats. Clinton would talk about "values" and speak out for school uniforms and teacher testing. These were matters that had been poll-tested to elicit a favorable response, especially from the new key political demographic known as "soccer moms."* And in quiet times, they were good things to talk about, requiring little action. Dick Morris joked, "Everyone wondered after the election if he'd go to the left or to the right. Nobody thought he'd go to sleep!"[1] But Clinton wasn't going to sleep. He still had a Republican Congress to deal with and a legacy to think about.

The year 1997 truly was a slow news year for the United States—with two exceptions of loss. This was the year two non-Americans with very close followings in the United States (and much of the rest of the world) died: the elegant and charitable Princess Diana of Great Britain and the saintly and even more charitable Mother Teresa of Calcutta. Diana was killed at the young age of thirty-seven in an odd automobile accident in Paris. She had been loved as so many Americans had loved Great Britain's royal family, but she was respected even more so for her charitable work for AIDS and her campaign against landmines. Mother Teresa died five days later at the age of eighty-seven. Few people in the world were as respected for their humility and work on behalf of the underprivileged and diseased as Mother Teresa and her Missionaries of Charity. She was also known as a strong proponent of the seamless web of life and could deliver a powerful message about life in the most touching way. Anybody who attended her 1994 appearance at the National Prayer Breakfast in Washington, D.C., remembers her plea on behalf of the unborn and adoption:

> We are fighting abortion by adoption—by care of the mother and adoption for her baby. We have saved thousands of lives. We have sent word to the clinics, to the hospitals and police stations: "Please don't destroy the child; we will take the child."

She continued:

> Please don't kill the child. I want the child. Please give me the child. I am willing to accept any child who would be aborted and to give that child to a married couple who will love the child and be loved by the child.

---

* educated young mothers from the suburbs

From our children's home in Calcutta alone, we have saved over 3,000 children from abortion. These children have brought such love and joy to their adopting parents and have grown up so full of love and joy.[2]

To the political members of both parties, pro-life and pro-choice, including the president and vice president, it was a rare, strong, and touching moment.*

While the national media covered Princess Diana's funeral in full, with the major news anchors traveling abroad to attend the event, many had wondered whether the coverage of this beautiful young woman was not a bit overdone, especially in comparison to the death of Mother Teresa at the same time. Well-known columnist and commentator Mike Barnicle had asked on PBS:

> If you believe in God, or a higher being, it's almost as if God tapped the news media around the world on the shoulder at about 1 o'clock this afternoon and said, "It's time to straighten your priorities out. Mother Teresa is dead."
>
> For five straight days we have been making Princess Diana larger than life. She seems like a very wonderful woman, a nice woman. She was 36 years of age [sic]. A woman died in Calcutta today who spent all of her life touching the poor and helping the poor. And I'm going to be interested, and I think many Americans would be interested to see if Peter Jennings and Dan Rather and CNN and Tom Brokaw go to Calcutta.[3]

They did decide to go; they were "shamed" into going according to CBS's *60 Minutes* veteran news reporter Mike Wallace.[4]

The other stories out of 1997 were, indeed, media related. As personal computers became more and more ubiquitous, the Internet became more and more useful for work, school, and personal use with businesses, news gatherers, and non-profit organizations setting up Web sites. With this

---

* And to many, especially the pro-life crowd, Mother Teresa's strong words were seen as a public rebuke to the Clintons and Gores. Never before in recent memory had such a strong moral voice in control of the microphone said anything so powerful to those pledged to the pro-choice position.

technology came greater demand for more and more information about the world and all manner of individual interests. In part as a response to the media attention over such stories as the O. J. Simpson trial, in part as a response to the noted interest in the 1996 political election, in part as a result of proliferating media personalities becoming pundits of opinion, and in part as a response to the quest for a more democratic demand for information, two new twenty-four-hour cable television news networks were also launched in 1996: MSNBC (a partnership between NBC and Microsoft) and the Fox News Channel (created by Australian-American media mogul Rupert Murdoch and former political operative Roger Ailes). Now there was increasingly little excuse for people to be uninformed about the world around them or the happenings in their country. That is, so long as viewers and Internet users were able to filter out whatever bias or error such a flood of information would—by force of necessity—often provide.

One other phenomenon in the media that was attaching to this expansion of news information was a Hollywood-based citizen newshound and sometime gossip trafficker named Matt Drudge. Drudge started an e-mail list and then a Web site that received increasing attention. Titled the Drudge Report, this site provided a collection of different kinds of news stories. Sometimes his news was hard and specific about a national story or international story; sometimes it was based on rumor. But with more and more people going online and more and more Web sites popping up, people who wanted to double-check a story or the facts of a story from Drudge, or any other news source, now had more and more ability to do so.

If 1997 was a slow news year, 1998 would surely make up for it.

II. The Tangled Web

On 21 January 1998, readers of the *Washington Post* saw a page one story alleging that President Clinton had asked an aide to lie.[5] Two days prior to that, the Drudge Report had alleged that *Newsweek* was holding a story about an alleged affair the president had with a White House intern named Monica Lewinsky. When the *Post* ran on 21 January, the headline was "Clinton Accused of Urging Aide to Lie." And it was not just any lie, but a lie under oath. These allegations, if true, were the serious crimes of suborning perjury and obstruction of justice.

Even to a country used to smiling or winking at or making some peace with the allegations of their chief executive's past skirt chasing, the story that quickly came out was one of stunning recklessness and tawdriness. Lewinsky was only six years older than the president's eighteen-year-old daughter. The *Wall Street Journal* on 22 January quoted former Clinton communications director George Stephanopoulos that sex with a twenty-four-year-old intern in the White House Oval Office could lead to Clinton's impeachment.[6] The *Journal's* distinguished editor, Bob Bartley, expressed the shock and dismay of much of the country: "Now comes the outrage, pouring out of the mouths of every Beltway pundit with access to a TV talk show. The ceiling is caving in on Mr. Clinton's presidency on the testimony of two or three courageous women."[7]

High-level Clinton administration officials were shocked at the alleged recklessness. They wondered whether he should resign.

Clinton immediately responded to the crisis by denying everything. Wagging his finger at the cameras, he angrily said, "I did *not* have sexual relations with that woman, Miss Lewinsky." Soon the country would learn that Monica Lewinsky had made dozens of visits to the White House, including after her internship was over, had received gifts from Bill Clinton, had gotten help finding a job from top White House legal advisor Vernon Jordan, and had received a post-internship job offer from UN Ambassador Bill Richardson.

How this came to be revealed was a long story—but it started with Paula Jones's lawsuit against President Clinton. In almost any legal allegation of sexual misconduct, attorneys for the plaintiff will try to prove a pattern and practice of such conduct by the defendant. When Jones's lawyers had learned of the possible extramarital liaison between the president and Monica Lewinsky, they sought an affidavit from her, but she denied any relationship with the president. When Jones's lawyers deposed the president, he also denied the relationship to them. But before that, in 1994, the Congress had reauthorized the independent counsel statute allowing for an authorized independent investigator to follow allegations of wrongdoing by the administration (any administration), and the president had signed that law.

Meanwhile, the three-judge panel overseeing the independent counsel had appointed a former federal Court of Appeals judge, Kenneth Starr, as that independent counsel. When Kenneth Starr received tapes made of conversations between Lewinsky and a friend of hers, he smelled impropriety that could have legal consequences (for example, Lewinsky confided that the president had asked her to deny their affair in the Jones inquiry). Starr then asked Attorney General Janet Reno for permission to pursue this possible illegality, and she signed off, giving him permission to do so.[8]

If there was ever a chance for Republicans to force Clinton out of office, it was in those first days of shock and rage over what it appeared he had done. The Republican leaders of Congress—Speaker Newt Gingrich and Mississippi Senator Trent Lott—might have gone to their Democratic counterparts. They might have approached Vice President Al Gore. They might have put the case plainly to them: "This is intolerable. The country cannot afford the distraction of a lengthy impeachment or a severely ethically compromised commander in chief. Bill Clinton must be forced to resign."* That this did not happen may be attributed to several causes—Bill Clinton's intransigence, his popularity, the successful stewardship of the economy, which was ever-growing, the deep mistrust between the Republican and Democratic leaders in Congress, and the fact that (unknown to most) Clinton's chief nemesis, Speaker Newt Gingrich, was then involved in his own adulterous liaison.

And there was a sense of unseriousness about this from both the White House and some of the conservative grassroots. On the *Today Show* on 27 January, the First Lady was asked about the scandal and said,

> We've [she and the president] talked at great length and I think as this matter unfolds the entire country will have more information. But

---

* Early in the news of the scandal, Jack Kemp and I paid a visit to Senator Lieberman to tell him he was the prophet Nathan to Bill Clinton's King David and it was his duty to explain to the president that he had, if not "despised the word of God," defiled the office of the presidency; that the job had fallen to him to tell the president to resign and not drag the country through a scandal such as this. Senator Lieberman, appreciative of the perhaps overwrought analogy, took our counsel but, beyond a public speech in the Senate denouncing the president's behavior, did not take our advice.

we're right in the middle of a rather vigorous feeding frenzy right now, and people are saying all kinds of things, and putting out rumor and innuendo, and I have learned over the last many years, being involved in politics . . . that the best thing to do in these cases is just to be patient, take a deep breath and the truth will come out.

She continued, "The great story here for anybody willing to find it, write about it and explain it is this vast right-wing conspiracy that has been conspiring against my husband since the day he announced for president."[9] *Wait one moment,* the columnist George Will thought, *we will have more information? Couldn't,* Will sardonically asked, *the First Lady say to her husband at breakfast:*

Pass the marmalade, and by the way is *The New York Times* right that Monica Lewinsky met alone with you late last month, two weeks after being subpoenaed by Paula Jones' lawyers and a week before Lewinsky filed her affidavit saying she had not had sexual relations with you? Help yourself to the bacon, dear, and what did you and "that woman" talk about, other than saving Social Security?

And over at the annual grassroots meeting of conservatives known as the Conservative Political Action Conference, minions in the crowd were delighting in the president's troubles and the tawdry accusations, making hay of the whole series of allegations.*

"The big news is that I was standing there," Bill Clinton later recalled.[10] The "there" was the well of the U.S. House of Representatives. On 28 January 1998, President Bill Clinton appeared before a joint session of the Congress to deliver his annual State of the Union Address. The initial shock of his

---

* A regular speaker at these conferences, I addressed the crowd that January day and criticized those who were reveling, saying this was no time to cheer or take joy in what was being reported. The White House and the office of the presidency were being disgraced. I told them the moral sensibilities of the president have led the country downhill and that the president was winking at us and his own behavior, but if he is found out and forced out of office, he will have nothing but disgrace. We should not shame ourselves by making light of any of this, I told them. They seemed to agree on reflection as I spoke. I was not alone in saying this; others, like Republican U.S. Senator John Ashcroft of Missouri, made much the same point.

Oval Office sexual misconduct had already begun to wear off as he was trying to move away from the story, ignore it, and act presidential.

"If we balance the budget for next year," Clinton began, "we'll have a sizable surplus in the years that immediately follow. What should we do with that surplus?" He looked out directly at the members of the Republican majority: "I have a simple four word answer: Save . . . Social . . . Security . . . First!"[11]

The Democrats were on their feet with long, loud, sustained applause. Brilliantly, Bill Clinton had changed the subject, and the immediate effort to remove him from office had been dealt a serious blow. Here he was, despite the dark cloud of scandal swirling around his head, behaving in a most presidential manner. He not only appeared to be performing the essential tasks of his office, but he threw a Hail Mary pass for Social Security. He had slipped the noose, at least for the time being.

But people would not stop speaking about it, writing about it, and—on the one side—asking, "Is this not a scandal?" "Was there no lying in a legal proceeding by the president?" On the other side, people defended the president: "This is Bill Clinton's personal life and even the president is entitled to a zone of privacy." "This is between Bill Clinton and Hillary Clinton and a matter of personal—not public—morality." Many argued back: "No matter what the claim of privacy, the chief law enforcement officer of the United States cannot be lying in legal proceedings."

Speaker Gingrich wanted Special Prosecutor Ken Starr to do the House's work. Starr would have the task of searching out evidence of Clinton's law-breaking and presenting a report to the whole House. That task would take months, everyone knew. That was what Gingrich wanted. He thought that if the scandal could be stretched out until November, the Republican Party might win another forty House seats in the midterm elections.

III. And Yet Duty Still Called

Meanwhile, all was not quiet on the Middle Eastern front. Saddam Hussein had been thwarting UN weapons inspections in Iraq, one of the conditions he had agreed to in order to gain the cease-fire following Desert Storm. The president was receiving intelligence that, at the same time he was avoiding inspections, Hussein was maintaining a stockpile of offensive weapons of mass destruction.[12] In an event mostly forgotten, the president went on television to announce he was sending more military forces to the region in case a military strike needed to be ordered to force Hussein into compliance.

At the same time, the president dispatched Secretary of State Madeleine K. Albright, National Security Advisor Sandy Berger, and Secretary of Defense William Cohen to a televised forum with the audience at Ohio State University to discuss the threat from Iraq and his proposed missile strike.[13] Many at the time thought the president had sent his defense policy team to a forum he should have attended but could not, given his credibility issues back home. The forum did not go well as protestors continually shouted down the three speakers, arguing against another war and the use of military force.

While Secretary of Defense Cohen seemed lost, even dazed, facing this opposition, Albright (a former college professor, not unused to campus politics) lectured: "No one has done what Saddam Hussein has done, or is thinking of doing. He is producing weapons of mass destruction, and he is qualitatively and quantitatively different from other dictators." She went on to say, "Iraq is a long way from Ohio, but what happens there matters a great deal here. For the risks that the leaders of a rogue state will use nuclear, chemical or biological weapons against us or our allies is the greatest security threat we face."[14]

But February was a busy month on another front as well. On 23 February, Osama bin Laden and his lieutenant Ayman al-Zawahiri had issued another declaration, a "Jihad Against Jews and Crusaders."[15] Among other calls to action, bin Laden and al-Zawahiri wrote, "The ruling to kill the Americans and their allies—civilians and military—is an individual duty for every Muslim who can do it in any country in which it is possible to do it," and they laid out their list of top three grievances:

First, for over seven years, the United States has been occupying the lands of Islam in the holiest of places. . . . Second, despite the great devastation inflicted on the Iraqi people by the crusader-Zionist alliance . . . the Americans are once against trying to repeat the horrific massacres as though they are not content with the protracted blockade imposed after the ferocious war or the fragmentation and devastation. . . . Third, if the Americans' aims behind these wars are religious and economic, the aim is also to serve the Jews' petty state and divert attention from its occupation of Jerusalem and murder of Muslims there.[16]

Saudi Arabia . . . Iraq . . . Israel. Again, the first two were intertwined: American troops were in Saudi Arabia (at the request of the Saudi government) to protect it from a Hussein invasion. We were maintaining sanctions on Iraq (under UN auspices) to contain the Hussein regime. As for the "occupation of Jerusalem and murder of Muslims there," well, few historians and legal scholars thought Jews didn't have a right to their country, Israel, and the "murder of Muslims there" was a longtime piece of propaganda. It didn't help Iraq's case to know that Saddam Hussein was also sending tens of thousands of dollars' worth of checks to the families of suicide bombers in Israel.

By the end of the year, President Clinton ordered four days of missile strikes on Iraq and signed the bipartisan-authored Iraq Liberation Act, saying:

The United States looks forward to a democratically supported regime that would permit us to enter into a dialogue leading to the reintegration of Iraq into normal international life. . . . The evidence is overwhelming that such changes will not happen under the current Iraq leadership.[17]

As all this was unfolding, the Justice Department indicted Osama bin Laden in federal court in June on conspiracy charges to attack the United States and for complicity in the attacks on our soldiers in Somalia.[18] But that was not the only news of bin Laden for America. In August, two American embassies (in Kenya and Tanzania) were simultaneously bombed, killing more than two hundred people (including twelve Americans) and injuring thousands more.[19] Learning of the various ties between bin Laden and the African Embassy terrorists, the president ordered missile strikes on sites in Afghanistan, where bin Laden was thought to be, and on a pharmaceutical plant in Sudan, where it was thought bin Laden was manufacturing chemical weapons.[20]

Several had claimed these actions by the president were to distract Americans from his legal and ethical problems back home—something that would be known as a "wag the dog" scenario.*

IV. The President Hangs On

At home, as the presidential scandal dragged on, Americans refused to support the ouster of the president. Public opinion polls consistently showed that Americans were angry and disappointed, but unwilling to support impeachment. Many suspected that the Republicans were "playing politics" with the issue.

And not all of the left or the media were condoning or excusing Clinton's conduct, which seemed to be much as the original stories implied. Jack Germond expressed the dismay felt by many liberals:

> I dislike judgmental people. But a President . . . is not free to act as his glands dictate. Quite apart from whatever obligation he feels to his wife, he has a responsibility to the people who got him there, to his political party, to those who serve on his staff or in his administration, and, finally, to his constituents.[21]

There were others, like Michael Kelly of the *Washington Post* and Christopher Hitchens, who would write a best-selling book on the president's scandals, denouncing them with his biting, British wit.**

As for his staff, it appeared the president was lying to them as well, and summoning their support to defend him at the same time. Nevertheless, every member of the Clinton administration publicly backed him.

But the facts were closing in on the president. When Lewinsky's blue

---

* A movie by that name had come out around the same time with an eerily similar fictional storyline. As for those arguing Clinton was engaging in a factual wag-the-dog scenario, most conservatives in America—myself included—spoke to the media saying we did not believe it and that politics should stop at the water's edge, and the president should be given the benefit of the doubt on foreign and defense policy.

** Over lunch once, Kelly (a lifelong Democrat) told me that because of the Democrats covering for Clinton, he would never vote Democrat again.

cocktail dress was shown to contain Bill Clinton's DNA, his lies were exposed, and Monica Lewinsky ultimately testified under a grant of legal immunity. After much legal defensiveness, President Clinton finally appeared before a Washington grand jury during this same hot, summer month. It was something no president had ever had to do before. His appearance was compelled by the Jones sexual harassment lawsuit. The country and the world watched as Bill Clinton testified under oath for four hours. The most remarkable part of his testimony was his attempt to avoid answering one question about the Lewinsky affair by saying: "It depends on what the definition of *is* is."[22]

That evening, at the urging of one of his longest serving and most trusted advisors, Paul Begala, President Clinton went before the nation in a televised speech. He admitted that he had had an "improper relationship." He did not go into detail, and mercifully he did not try to suggest that oral sex was not sex. It was a somewhat bitter, defensive speech, very uncharacteristic of the normally sunny Bill Clinton. If there was an apology to the nation for dragging it through this spectacle, it was couched in the vaguest of rhetoric: "I know that my public comments and my silence about this matter gave a false impression. I misled people, including even my wife. I deeply regret that."[23] Unlike his usual orations, this was as short as it was sad. The entire speech was less than one thousand words and lasted less than four minutes.[24]

When Clinton and his wife and daughter rapidly departed Washington for a vacation on Nantucket Island, cartoonists had a field day. Clinton was shown walking his lively young chocolate Labrador retriever. "And he wants to have *me* neutered," Buddy the dog told readers in one cartoon.

By fall, Ken Starr presented his report to the House of Representatives, together with thirty-six boxes of evidence. There was, he said, "substantial and credible information . . . that may constitute grounds for an impeachment."[25] It was too late. Already, the Clinton White House political defense—led by James Carville—had succeeded in demonizing Ken Starr. He was cast as a bluenose, a snooper, an uptight, moralistic, religious crank.

The debate about the public and private ethics of public and private persons raged throughout the country. Aside from the legal allegations of lying in a deposition and before a grand jury, in a civil rights case no less, many still believed the prosecution of the president for sexual encounters had gone too far. The veteran newsman Ted Koppel (long of ABC's *Nightline*) summed up the moral debate quite poignantly, however, in a C-SPAN broadcast of a commencement speech he delivered to Stanford University that year:

> We follow the evolution of "that mess in Washington" with a sense of discomfort that is eased only by a reliance on precisely the two devices that society employs when logic fails. We mix ourselves a toxic little cocktail of privacy and hypocrisy: "I don't care what he does in his private life," we tell one another with a nudge and a wink. "The economy's doing great." Which poses at least one potentially troubling question: If the economy collapses, does a focus on the president's character then become more appropriate?
>
> What we have done in America today is to turn ethics into a commodity. Virtue may still be its own reward, but we lose touch with its meaning when we allow it to be defined by the standards of the marketplace or the political arena. The equation really couldn't be much simpler: When people, in large numbers, consistently reward bad behavior, then, inevitably, we perpetuate that sort of behavior. To suggest that a vibrant economy somehow renders questions of morality irrelevant reduces ethics to a business proposition; one set to be applied when things are going well, another when the economy is in trouble.[26]

People were of a mixed opinion on all of this throughout the year, the Koppel argument and others' notwithstanding.*

---

* I had become endlessly involved in this argument in op-eds, speeches, debates, and television interviews. I also wrote a book on the whole matter, *The Death of Outrage*. That my brother was one of Clinton's defense attorneys proved endlessly interesting to the media with him on one side and me on another. One *New Yorker* cartoon depicted a homeless man on the street with a cup held out for alms. The bubble caption title was "The Third Bennett Brother," and his bubble-captioned thoughts were, *I don't know what to think*. In another moment around this time, my brother and I were walking out of the famed Palm Restaurant after lunch, and cameras had assembled. My brother waved me aside and said, "I'll handle this." Turning to the reporters who were wondering just how the two of us could get along at this point, my brother said, "If James Carville and Mary Matalin can stay together, I can have lunch with my brother." Mary Matalin is and was a well-known Republican operative and advisor who was married to Clinton strategist James Carville.

The 1998 midterm elections produced not an increase of forty Republican seats, as Speaker Gingrich had confidently predicted, but a *loss* of five. And that wasn't all. In short order, a Republican House revolt forced Gingrich to resign not only from the speakership but also from Congress. And Gingrich, we soon learned, was also having an adulterous affair with a woman who worked on the staff of a committee in Congress. Gingrich maintained the relationship with her and married her. His successor as Speaker, Louisiana's Bob Livingston, stepped aside when it was revealed that the powerful chairman of the House Appropriations Committee had also had an adulterous affair. He, too, resigned from the House. While there were no allegations of lying under oath or perjury regarding Gingrich or Livingston, clearly marital fidelity was not just a Democratic problem in Washington.

The Republicans believed that they had met their responsibilities to the American people by pushing out Gingrich and Livingston. But it was only on a narrow, party line vote that William Jefferson Clinton was impeached on 19 December 1998 by the House of Representatives on two counts—perjury and obstruction of justice. He thus became only the second president in history to be impeached.*

As 1999 dawned, Americans gave Clinton high approval ratings and strongly opposed his conviction and removal from office. The House impeachment managers labored hard to show that they were not impeaching him for sexual misconduct, but instead for lying under oath and for obstructing justice. They pleaded for the rule of law. But the argument was being won neither with the American public at large nor in the Senate. The economy was strong, the budget was balanced, and people seemed to have had enough of scandal.

The Senate vote was a foregone conclusion. Despite publicly scolding Bill Clinton for his irresponsibility and for his "reprehensible" conduct, those considered to be the conscience of the Senate, senators like New York's Pat Moynihan, Connecticut's Joe Lieberman, and Nebraska's Bob Kerrey,

---

* Andrew Johnson was impeached by the House of Representatives in 1868. The Senate failed by one vote to convict him. Richard Nixon *resigned* in 1974 rather than face all-but-certain impeachment and removal from office. (He thus preserved his substantial presidential pension and perquisites.) The House can impeach by a majority vote, but it takes two-thirds of the Senate to convict and remove from office.

joined every one of their fellow Democrats in voting not guilty. Several Republicans also voted not guilty. Pennsylvania Republican Arlen Specter offered a "Scottish verdict"—not proven.

V. Beyond Politics 1999 to 2000

Both sides had exhausted themselves in the struggle over impeachment. The nation faced another two years with a president who had been politically neutered. Although he continued to be personally popular, he was wounded and considered a "lame duck," perhaps a year earlier than most presidents finishing their second term. Sadly, the low the country felt was not isolated to politics.

On the culture front, the nation was shocked in April 1999 when two students at Columbine High School in Colorado went on a shooting rampage, killing twelve fellow students, a teacher, and themselves. Thankfully, a bomb they planted in the school cafeteria never detonated, or the death count would have been in the hundreds.[27] Trying to determine the motivation of the two killers became an endless round of speculation and allegation based on their clothing (trench coats and combat boots), their activities in their spare time (playing violent video games), and their behavior at school in the weeks leading up to the massacre (fellow students reported seeing the two assassins giving Nazi salutes to each other and noted a fascination with Nazi principles by at least one of the students).[28]

The debate about guns, teens, school safety, ideology, and video game imagery surfaced again. Beyond a greater awareness by teachers, administrators, and parents about teen violent expression, imagery, and writing, little could be resolved or concluded about how to prevent the triggers in the minds of seriously disturbed youths who could or would kill like this. As one psychologist looking into the Columbine massacre put it, "These are not ordinary kids who played too many video games. These are not ordinary kids who just wanted to be famous. These are simply *not ordinary kids*. These are kids with serious psychological problems."[29] Tragically, Columbine was not the last school shooting in America.

America is a big country, and while the tragedies cry out, often other important things take place slowly, over time.

VI: The World Pivots on a Grain of Sand

If the mid- to late 1990s were dominated by presidential scandal and national lectures about constitutional law out of Washington, something else was going on in the rest of the country—a technological and business revolution that would change not only this country but also the rest of the world. Thank the grain of sand (from which silicon comes) as the flint stone that sparked this bloodless revolution. When asked what he would put in a time capsule that best represents America in the twenty-first century, business magazine mogul and former presidential candidate Steve Forbes once answered: "In addition to the Declaration and the Constitution, I'd have a grain of sand, because that's the basis of silicon—the whole information age. It shows what a free people can achieve and only a free people can achieve writing whole worlds on grains of sand. A true symbol of American inventiveness."[30]

Today, we take for granted communication and research devices such as BlackBerrys and iPhones, Internet connections, e-mail, personal computers, laptops, and Wi-Fi. Roughly 80 percent of Americans now have computers in their homes and use the Internet. Percentages are even higher for cell phone ownership.[31] But it was not always so, and it was not long ago that it was a much different world of communication, research, and business (and, yes, not a little trouble).

Cell phones are now the size of a deck of cards or smaller and getting smaller all the time, but twenty years ago they were the size of a brick for those who had cell phones unattached to a case or automobile. Home computers twenty years ago were the size of a medium suitcase and attached to a hard drive that was equally large. They were used primarily for word processing, games, and number crunching. Going "online" or "e-mailing a document" was scarcely available, and most Americans (never mind anyone anywhere else) would not have known what was meant by those terms back then. Just ten years ago, e-mail was hardly something that could be done away from the home or office. The BlackBerry and iPhone, as we know them now, were not on the market yet.

While once we thought of mobile phones on the shoe of Maxwell Smart or the watch of Dick Tracy as fantasies; while once we used modified type-writers with a ruler-sized screen that held 5k of memory to process word documents, this all changed as the decade of the 1990s began—changed into reality.

As far back as the 1950s, two American engineers, Robert Noyce, born in Burlington, Iowa, and Jack Kilby, born in Jefferson City, Missouri, independent of each other, were inventing integrated circuits (now known as microchips or microprocessors).[32] Kilby was at Texas Instruments while Noyce went on to cofound Intel, where he brought in a coworker, Andrew Grove, from his previous firm. Grove, who was born in Hungary, would take Intel into the modern age after becoming its president and CEO in the 1980s. Grove "is credited with having transformed Intel from a manufacturer of memory chips into one of the world's dominant producers of microprocessors" that supplies most of our home and work computers today.[33] What did Grove and Intel render? In 1997, *Time* magazine made Grove the Person of the Year and noted the mass-produced microchip's impact: "Millions of transistors, each costing far less than a staple, can be etched on wafers of silicon. On these microchips, all the world's information and entertainment can be stored in digital form, processed and zapped to every nook of a networked planet."[34]

Of course Grove was not alone in transforming our use of computers or the way we store memory on them—far from it. Credit goes to a great many other innovators who had unique ideas about our burgeoning information age and the businesses they could start in order to mass-market them and change the economy, our lives, and the world. There was the king of the hill, Bill Gates, who founded Microsoft after dropping out of Harvard. Building operating systems for computers, he became the wealthiest man in the world with his ideas about home and office computing.*[35] Indeed, the tech boom created many multimillionaires, but Gates stands head and shoulders above the rest. His billions (close to $100 billion in net worth at the time of this writing) made him one of the wealthiest Americans of all

---

* Bill Gates dropped out of Harvard in 1974 to form his company with longtime friend Paul Allen. I was a proctor at Harvard, the proctor to Gates's proctor (John Curnutte), and I spoke with Gates, urging him that his life would be so much better if he would stay in school. So much for the good sense of this proctor's advice.

time—not as wealthy as a John Rockefeller or Cornelius Vanderbilt even in today's dollars, but close.[36]

There were other revolutionary innovators. For instance, Michael Dell, who also dropped out of college to start his own company, built customized computers. His idea, beyond the design of the hardware, was to sell directly to customers rather than through third parties. This kept prices down and allowed clients to more finely tailor their orders to their individual specifications.[37] All along the way, two other college dropouts, Steve Jobs and Steve Wozniak, were perfecting their concept of easy-to-use home computers bearing the name Apple. By the late 1980s and early '90s, Apple computers were preferred by graphic design artists and college students, and in short order Apple created ever more modern-looking computers known as iMacs that would expand into yet more and more home and small business use.

Then there were the Internet gurus who saw e-commerce possibilities, taking the World Wide Web from a research, personal interest, and information tool to a global shopping market. The Internet started as a Department of Defense project that then became a tool linking university research communication systems. As it gradually opened to public use in the early 1990s, it became a place of international commerce. Internet browsers like Microsoft's Explorer and Netscape competed against each other to become the standard browser. Gates and Microsoft soon dominated the race by bundling their browser into personal computer operating systems that individuals purchased from other computer companies, ultimately making Netscape a memory.

There was America Online, founded by Steve Case. AOL brought the Internet and e-mail to a general audience with rudimentary understandings of the new World Wide Web and e-mail systems. Amazon, founded by Jeff Bezos in 1994, started an online book-selling venture that expanded into selling everything from vacuum cleaners to computers. Amazon ultimately created its own electronic book, ironically challenging the need or desire for the very product it began selling in the mid-1990s.[38] Bezos's and Amazon's accomplishments were enough to land him as a *Time* magazine Person of the Year in 1999. By the end of the twentieth century, consumers were buying some $15 billion of consumer goods over the Internet.[39] Today online consumer spending is in the hundreds of billions.[40]

Then there was also eBay, under the leadership of Meg Whitman. E-Bay further democratized the American and international marketplace with an online auction house where anyone could sell anything and buyers could bid on the items. The company ultimately boasted more than 100 million users and created its own industry of people who made their living selling through the site.[41]

Then there were the search engines, from Yahoo! to Google, that made searching for information possible to those not subscribed to fee-based services such as Nexis and Westlaw. And there were news sites like the Drudge Report. So pervasive would the Internet, e-commerce, and personal computing become that, today, we can laugh at this 1995 report from the Pew organization: "Few see online activities as essential to them, and no single online feature, with the exception of E-Mail, is used with any regularity. Consumers have yet to begin purchasing goods and services online, and there is little indication that online news features are changing traditional news consumption patterns."[42]

Business could be conducted without a telephone or an in-person conference as e-mail and telecommuting became more popular. Wanting to know the value of a stock in Japan was as close as five seconds away via the Internet. Wanting to send a draft essay to a publication or editor could be done instantaneously, with edits going back to the author just as fast. No longer would one have to go to a government office to file certain forms; one could do that online. Want to know what was written by a favorite writer in a newspaper across the country? Look it up online as you read the whole newspaper or any part of it. Want to know how many members of a given party sit in the Australian Parliament? Three clicks away at most. Want to know the biography of a certain prospective hire or employer? "Google it." As recently as Bill Clinton's reelection, this was all brand new.

The late 1990s saw explosive technological and related economic growth from all this, creating what would later become known as the *dot-com boom*. Indeed, many new companies were started, and many new millionaires were made. The computer, the microchip, the Internet, e-mail, and e-commerce literally changed America and the world—and fast.

How much wealth, how many jobs, and how much freedom (political and personal) were created by all this is difficult to quantify. Some comments of economic historian John Steele Gordon lead to certain conclusions, though:

> In 1954 the gross domestic product of the United States—the sum of all the goods and services produced in the country that year—was about $380 billion. In 2003 it was $10.9 trillion. . . . [As of this writing, the gross domestic product is about $14 trillion.][43]
>
> The reason is plain enough: the computer. It is the most profound technological development since the steam engine ignited the Industrial Revolution two centuries ago, perhaps since the agricultural revolution ignited civilization itself 10 millennia ago. None of the biggest changes in business in the last 50 years would have been possible—or would have evolved as they did—had it not been for the computer.[44]

The boom itself did not last, at least not as it started and promised. And a great many Internet start-ups or tech stocks were also overvalued and failed, leading to the early twenty-first-century *dot-bomb*.* Beginning in 2000, more than eight hundred companies trying to make it as tech start-ups failed, and a lot of stock market value went with them (numbering in the trillions).[45] In subsequent years most of that money was made up for as the new era of the technological revolution sorted itself out and as the surviving companies stabilized and new companies came to the fore after learning the lessons of overevaluation on the stock market.

But if the news out of our nation's capital was slow in the late 1990s, the news and changes throughout the rest of the country were measurable in mega- and gigabytes.

VII: America and Islam Again

But not all was completely quiet in the rest of the world or Washington. In the spring of 1999, President Clinton acted again in the international arena, again committing U.S. help to beleaguered Muslims, when he committed

---

*I have been involved in helping found two dot-com education businesses: one succeeded, one failed.

U.S. forces to Kosovo in the Balkans. The breakup of Communist Yugoslavia had brought to power a vicious ethnic Serb named Slobodan Milosevic. He had engaged in a brutal policy of "ethnic cleansing." Serbs used rape, murder, and torture to drive Kosovar Muslims out of their disputed region. The brutality was ongoing throughout the 1990s. Milosevic signed and then ignored agreement after agreement. Britain's former Prime Minister Margaret Thatcher had called for concerted action against the rampant Serbs.

Finally, Bill Clinton ordered U.S. jets to join with NATO forces in striking at Milosevic and his Serb nationalists. In this Clinton was supported by some leading Republicans in Congress and by the influential conservative journal the *Weekly Standard*. The magazine's editor, Bill Kristol, had staunchly opposed the Clintons' health care plan. Now, more reliant on e-mail and the Web than the fax machine, he fully backed the use of force against the ruthless Milosevic regime. Fortunately, the mission was a quick success. The U.S. lost no lives in its "surgical strike" against the Serb military.

Part of the tragedy of Bill Clinton's lack of self-control was that he could not rally Americans to understand and support this important and humanitarian application of force. It should have been his moment. It should have been his legacy. A worthwhile military operation, it brought credit to all who participated, but it had an unreal quality. The president was simply not taken seriously as a war leader, and as for being any other kind of leader, he was seriously compromised.

In the closing of 1999 two stories from our borders would have resounding implications. Out of Florida came a story about a young boy shipped to freedom in America. On Thanksgiving Day, a six-year-old boy from Cuba, Elian Gonzalez, was rescued from shark-infested waters off the coast of Florida, clinging to an inner tube, after his mom took him with her, seeking the liberty her relatives had known in America.[46] His mom died in the waters, and Elian was the sole survivor of the group of Cubans fleeing Castro's tyranny. Elian's Miami relatives opened their arms to welcome him. In Havana, however, Cuba's Communist dictator, Fidel Castro, was enraged. The boy's father, who stayed in Cuba, had "rights" that were being ignored, Havana claimed. Soon, the American government would intervene.

While much of the country was worried about computer and other technology systems that would automatically turn their dates over to recognize the year 2000 on 1 January, and whether certain computer and infrastructure systems would shut down because of programming bugs known as "millennium bugs," a lot of joint efforts went into repairing these computer problems. The transition to the new year took place, technologically, safely, and without incident.

So too did Los Angeles International Airport (LAX) remain safe, thanks to the skeptical eye of a border patrol agent in Port Angeles, Washington—on the American-Canadian border. There, an Algerian named Ahmed Ressam was arrested by a suspicious U.S. Customs agent, Diana Dean.[47] Ressam had spent time at an Osama bin Laden training camp in Afghanistan, learning about firearms and explosives, and had lived in an apartment in Montreal, Canada, that would later be discovered as being run by bin Laden's operatives.[48]

Throughout the summer and fall of 1999, Ressam was making plans to bomb LAX. When he arrived at the Canadian-American crossing in Port Angeles on 14 December, Agent Dean became suspicious of Ressam, who was "nervous, fumbling, and sweating" and refusing to answer her questions.[49] When agents then searched his car, they found more than one hundred pounds of explosives; Ressam attempted to run away, but the agents gave chase, caught, and arrested him. This thwarted entry of Ressam into the United States of America would later be named "the millennium bomb plot."

In October 2000, the USS *Cole* was docked in the Aden port of Yemen on a refueling stop. The *Cole*, a naval destroyer, was in the Middle East to help enforce UN sanctions against Saddam Hussein's Iraq. On the morning of 12 October, while the *Cole* was refueling, two men in a small inflatable boat loaded with high explosives approached the destroyer and detonated a blast, blowing a hole the size of a house into the *Cole*'s side.[50] The blast was so strong, it shook the buildings near the port. Seventeen U.S. sailors were killed—as were the suicide bombers. And for days, to anyone paying attention, one could see the images of the *Cole* listing with the scarred blast hole in its side. As the national press had broadcast in the aftermath of the bombing, Osama bin Laden and his network were immediate prime suspects. Bin Laden and his number two, Ayman al-Zawahiri, had spent a good deal of time in Yemen, preaching and recruiting, and both Yemeni and

American investigators were focusing on a bin Laden associate (Tawfiq bin-Attash) as one of the *Cole* operation's masterminds.[51]

But the *Cole* bombing was not all they had in mind. In short order, bin Laden's terrorist camps would soon fill with new recruits and money, and bin Laden had ordered the head of his media operation—one Khalid Sheikh Mohammed—to create a video reenactment of the *Cole* bombing to use for propaganda and further recruiting.[52] At the same time, bin Laden began dispersing his leadership in Afghanistan, wagering his camps would be targeted by an American military retaliation.[53] Bin Laden's camps were never bombed.

The question of why there was no retaliation against bin Laden and his Afghanistan-Taliban hosts is a deeply troubling, confusing, and disputed one that comes with different answers depending on who was or (to this day) is being asked. A later bipartisan commission gave a sense of the goings-on at the time just after the *Cole* bombing:

> [President Clinton] did not think it would be responsible for a president to launch an invasion of another country just based on a "preliminary judgment."
>
> Some of Secretary Albright's advisers warned her at the time to be sure the evidence conclusively linked bin Laden to the *Cole* before considering any response, especially a military one, because such action might inflame the Islamic world and increase support for the Taliban. Defense Secretary Cohen [said] it would not have been prudent to risk killing civilians based only on an assumption that al Qaeda was responsible.
>
> [NSC Counterterrorism Advisor] Richard Clarke thought that there was not much White House interest in conducting further military operations against Afghanistan in the administration's last weeks ... [and that] President Clinton, [Sandy] Berger, and Secretary Albright were concentrating on a last-minute push for a peace agreement between the Palestinians and the Israelis.[54]

While this conversation—some called it "dithering"—went on among the various agencies and portfolios of interest, some people inside the administration were pushing for action against the Taliban and Osama bin Laden, Richard Clarke among them. But such action never came. And it is true: while bin Laden was building his terrorist network, after having declared two wars against the United States, the president was almost singularly focused on forging a peace plan between the Israelis and the Palestinians. Bin Laden had escaped—at least for now.

VIII. The 2000 Election

Meanwhile, 2000 was an election year. Vice President Al Gore had supported his beleaguered chief loyally through the yearlong struggle of impeachment. Had Gore ever publicly expressed his dissatisfaction with the president, there might well have been a "palace revolt" against Clinton. Instead, he had held a well-publicized press conference on the South Lawn of the White House during the impeachment and proclaimed, "I believe [President Clinton] will be regarded in the history books as one of our greatest Presidents."[55] New York's liberal Senator Chuck Schumer noted that what "kept us close to the President was the Republicans. Their extreme nastiness pushed Democrats into Bill Clinton's arms, even those who didn't like him very much."[56]

Now, Al Gore, the dutiful son of a U.S. senator, the faithful husband, the devoted dad, the straight arrow, felt he had *earned* his party's nomination for president. He faced only token opposition in the Democratic primaries. Within weeks, he had defeated former New Jersey Senator Bill Bradley. Bradley, a Princeton graduate, Rhodes Scholar, and pro Basketball Hall of Famer, ran to Gore's left. He attacked Gore's long abandoned opposition to federal funding of abortion. He denounced Gore's support for one of the great achievements of the Clinton administration—welfare reform. Bill Bradley had a compelling biography, and he offered a stern liberal critique of the more centrist Clinton-Gore administration. He should have been a powerful contender in the Democratic primaries. Had he not been a famously flat speaker, he might have given Al Gore a run for his money. But aside from Bradley's lack of charisma on the campaign trail, the economy was doing well, and it was a hard case to make that Al Gore did not deserve the Democratic Party's nomination.

Among Republicans, the race included two heavyweights—Texas Governor George W. Bush and Arizona Senator John McCain. The others—magazine publisher Steve Forbes, conservative grassroots activist Gary Bauer, former Ambassador Alan Keyes, and columnist Pat Buchanan—were dispatched fairly quickly, although Keyes would not step out of the race until very late—thinking his superior rhetorical skill and appeal to the right of both Bush and McCain would light up an ultimate grassroots fervor. But Republican voters hungered to retake the White House and had no patience with candidates who had no previous experience winning an election of any size and were determined to make a statement. They agreed with the old Hollywood line: if you want to send a message, call Western Union. Former Vice President Dan Quayle took a shot, as did Senator Elizabeth Dole (wife of Bob Dole) and Lamar Alexander—but they left the race fairly early as well, as neither had enough money or votes coming their way.

John McCain was a navy aviator who had spent five years in North Vietnam's "Hanoi Hilton" as a prisoner of war. Though he had been beaten and tortured, McCain did not make too much of his service and heroism and would dismiss his suffering by saying simply: "They didn't put a chocolate on our pillows at night." But for all of his humility, John McCain had attained almost mythic status for millions of veterans and admirers.

George W. Bush, son of the former president, Yale and Harvard graduate, had grown up in West Texas. Whenever he was asked what the difference was between him and the father he loved and respected, he answered: *Midland*.

There was a sense throughout much of the country that George W. Bush was being coronated for the nomination. Most of the Republican Party fund-raisers and conservative think tank personnel were behind him; and between him and John McCain, Bush would appeal more to the religious activists in the party.* Unlike his father, George W. Bush was

---

* George Bush's campaign was headed by the political autodidact Karl Rove, who had constructed a "front porch strategy" of bringing in various conservative thinkers and writers to meet with George Bush in Texas. At my meeting with the governor, he inquired of me whether I might like to toss my hat in the ring as his running mate—I told him that I would not, that I was working on too many other fronts at the time. Ultimately, the man he had put in charge of his vice presidential search, former Defense Secretary Dick Cheney, after a long vetting process, recommended himself for the job.

comfortable speaking about being "born again" and how Christ had changed his life. That was not a tradition of John McCain. McCain and his streak of independent-minded supporters defeated Bush handily in New Hampshire, and the Texan's operation had to scramble to create a "firewall" in the South Carolina GOP primary. The campaign, regrettably, produced some ugly incidents. McCain's wife was slurred in a widespread telephone whispering campaign in South Carolina, and false rumors were rampant about a child whom the McCains had adopted from abroad.

From the McCain side, George W. Bush's speech to the fundamentalist Bob Jones University was attacked in anonymous phone calls to Catholic voters in Michigan. Some virulently anti-Catholic statements of the university's founder *from 1924* were spread around Michigan *as if George Bush knew and approved them.* It was an absurd charge, but it helped create the widespread impression that George W. Bush was anti-Catholic. "W", as he became known in campaign shorthand, protested. His *own* brother Jeb was a Catholic convert, he said. These ugly rumors and counterrumors only strained the relationship between Bush and McCain—and their supporters.

But after Bush's victory in South Carolina and his own in Michigan, McCain unwisely attacked two leading figures of the Religious Right— Pat Robertson and Jerry Falwell—comparing them with the Reverend Al Sharpton and Minister Louis Farrakhan. He had called these religious and political leaders "agents of intolerance." While it was true that both Robertson and Falwell were unpopular in the country at large and had been criticized in their own evangelical community on occasion, it was a ridiculous stretch to compare them to Sharpton and Farrakhan. Sharpton at the time was known for leading riots in New York, and Farrakhan was known as the leader of the Nation of Islam, which, aside from some rather odd theology including space ship visions, was virulently and vocally anti-Semitic.

With his remarks, McCain provoked a stunningly bad reaction, and evangelical voters throughout the South and Midwest flocked to the polls for Bush.* Those who had no particular dog in the fight, or strong dislike or

---

* I, too, had criticized McCain in the *Wall Street Journal* in a piece that was quoted some, especially since I had introduced him at events earlier in the campaign.

like for Robertson or Falwell in any event, thought McCain at least politically reckless for taking on such leaders when there was little reason to do so. McCain was showing his independence, however, trying to prove himself a different kind of Republican. But there are arguably better ways of doing so than attacking the base of one's own party. Meanwhile, Governor Bush had no problem showing where his religious views were: in one primary debate, asked to name his favorite philosopher, he replied, "Jesus Christ—because he changed my heart." By contrast, Steve Forbes had answered John Locke, and John McCain had answered Teddy Roosevelt. There was no question about who was the candidate most comfortable courting the religious voters.

Long before their respective conventions in Philadelphia and Los Angeles, Bush and Gore had wrapped up their parties' nominations. Both enjoyed remarkably unified ranks. The fall campaign would be a battle of titans with arms. And almost every poll showed the country evenly split.

Bush sensed the public's distaste for Clinton-bashing. He would not replay the ugly partisan battles of the two previous years. Instead, he pledged to restore "dignity and honor" to the White House. Americans were smart, he figured. They would get it. And George Bush had made no secret of the fact that he had lived a youthful life of too much partying and drinking. But he had changed his ways after a religious conversion and with the help of personal counseling from Billy Graham. Bush was a repentant man who had, as they say, been there and done that—and was long ago finished with all that.

Throughout the campaign, Al Gore kept his distance from Bill Clinton. To suggest a distance without openly breaking with Clinton's philandering, Gore selected Connecticut's Joe Lieberman as his running mate. Lieberman, a practicing Orthodox Jew, had spoken the most critical words about Bill Clinton's conduct of any Democrat (even though he would not vote to convict him on impeachment charges) and was known for nothing so much as his upstanding personal character. Within the Democratic Party, he created excitement as the first Jewish candidate on a national ticket.* Enjoying a

---

* Barry Morris Goldwater, an Episcopalian, was the son of a Jewish merchant, but that did not make him Jewish (as religion passes through the mother in Jewish law). He used to joke that he had once been excluded from a country club golf course. "I'm only *half* Jewish," he said. "Can I just play nine holes?" Joe Lieberman was the real thing.

surging economy and apparent peace throughout the world, Gore thought he could coast to an easy victory.

The conventions did not make much news, but one could see the outlines of the campaign in the nomination speeches the candidates delivered. Vice President Gore signaled something in his approach to the stage as he took his wife, Tipper, in his arms and gave her a prolonged kiss on the mouth that lasted for what seemed a very long time—as if Gore had just returned home from a warfront to greet his beloved back home. Even if staged as it was, this display was unprecedented in fidelity and passion in political memory. Gore went on to discuss the accomplishments of the previous eight years and promised to expand on the Clinton administration's successes. He then took an interesting turn on the notion of "family values," a phrase usually more at home at Republican conventions:

> But there's something at stake in this election that's even more important than economic progress. Simply put, it's our values; it's our responsibility to our loved ones, to our families.
>
> And to me, family values means honoring our fathers and mothers, teaching our children well, caring for the sick, respecting one another—giving people the power to achieve what they want for their families.
>
> Putting both Social Security and Medicare in an iron-clad lock box where the politicians can't touch them—to me, that kind of common sense is a family value.[57]

The idea of a "lock box" would become the most memorable if not monotonous phrase Gore would speak throughout the campaign and in the debates. It must have tested well in his internal polls; but it was not something that would make most people storm a mountain for a candidate.

As for the religious file, that was left to the person of Joe Lieberman. For years it has been recognized that Jew or Christian, serious members of either faith respected serious members of the other faith. And Joe Lieberman was, indeed, an Orthodox Jew who was not shy to speak of his heritage, even at the convention:

In my life, I have seen the goodness of this country through many sets of eyes. I have seen it through the eyes of my grandmother. She was raised in Central Europe, in a village where she was often harassed because of the way she worshiped God. Then, she immigrated to America. On Saturdays, she used to walk to synagogue, and often, her Christian neighbors would pass her and say, "Good Sabbath, Mrs. Manger."*[58]

Governor Bush's speech had more rhetorical flourish than Vice President Gore's; he was not of Washington, and he was not ungifted with the TelePrompTer when it matched what he felt in his heart. One of his most moving lines was in imparting his religious conviction while at the same time showing, yet again, he was a reformed man from his earlier, wilder days:

I believe in tolerance, not in spite of my faith, but because of it. I believe in a God who calls us not to judge our neighbors but to love them. I believe in grace because I've seen it, and peace because I've felt it, and forgiveness because I've needed it.[59]

In those simple but well-cadenced lines, Governor Bush spoke volumes about two issues that would demark the major themes of his campaign. As his father had spoken of a "kinder, gentler nation," Governor Bush spoke of his "compassionate conservatism." What that meant was a conservatism that embraced the power of nongovernmental entities to help the poor—something that would soon become known as his faith-based initiative, his plan to help the poor and addicted in the country through

---

* Senator Lieberman was not particularly politically conservative, mind you—he was, for example, as pro-choice as most Democrats. But he had a feel of conservatism, and his work on cultural pollution with Delores Tucker and me was just one example of that. And he was a foreign and defense policy hawk. It is noteworthy: nothing he or we did on the culture front resulted in any major legislation; that was not Lieberman's interest in the culture battle in which we were engaged. In sum, he could sound conservative, but perhaps like Daniel Patrick Moynihan before him, he voted fairly liberal. We did get into a public dispute during the campaign when liberal groups criticized him for his work with me on condemning the excesses of the entertainment industry. He said he was "noodging" the industry, not more. I said, "It was more than a noodge," but we ultimately decided we did not want to get into a Talmudic disputation over the word *noodge*.

faith-based organizations. Rarely had a Republican running for office spoken so much about the impoverished and so specifically about the best ways to help them overcome the causes of their poverty. While many were distrustful of the mechanisms of the state working with church organizations, Governor Bush was unremitting in making the case for this new kind of welfare reform.

The sense that America was in a postwar period—an "end of history," at best; a "bubble," at worst—permeated the American mood, and the campaign focused primarily on domestic policy. To a fault. Until the eruption of the Elian Gonzalez story. The case of Elian Gonzalez was unfolding in Florida in the early part of 2000, and both major candidates *tried* to speak as little about it as possible, trying to steer clear of the debate over the father's right to have his son back in Cuba versus the denial of human rights that awaited Elian upon his return to Cuba.

Both candidates attempted to walk delicately through the trip wires of Elian's fate by stating that the case should be decided by the courts, although Governor Bush specified that the case should be decided by the "family courts" in Florida (which were deemed more favorable toward Elian staying in the United States) and said that his preference would be for the boy to stay in America. And the Republican National Committee chairman, Jim Nicholson, had pushed the inference even further, stating, "If Elian gets sent back, the Cuban community will remember which party wanted to hand a small child back to Fidel Castro across a barbed-wire fence."[60] The vice president was caught between trying to defend the administration (which was set on a path of trying to return Elian to Cuba) and not upsetting the Cuban American community in Florida, which empathized with young Elian's plight.

Vice President Gore, knowing how important the vote in Florida would be to his election chances, had subsequently—including late in the case of Elian's fate—switched his position several times, and he erratically called on Congress to pass a law granting Elian U.S. citizenship.[61] As commentators noted at the time, that was a significant break from the Clinton administration he was still serving and fodder for Governor Bush, who could then say, "I'm glad the vice president now supports legal residency for Elian

Gonzalez. . . . I wish he could convince the rest of the administration of the wisdom of that approach."[62]

Things began to move fast in Florida as Attorney General Janet Reno had met with Elian's dad, who was given a visa to come to the United States to meet with (and bring back) his son. By mid-April 2000, federal agents under orders from Attorney General Reno seized Elian from the home of his relatives in Miami to reunite him with his father and send them on their way back to Cuba. The *New York Times*'s lead paragraph summed up the horror so many felt at seeing the pictures of the raid with armed agents in helmets storming Elian's family's house to seize the innocent child: "Armed United States immigration agents smashed their way into the Little Havana home of Elian Gonzalez's Miami relatives before dawn today, took the sobbing 6-year-old boy from a bedroom closet and flew him to a reunion with his father outside Washington."[63]

One does not hear much about Elian Gonzalez anymore—the latest news is that the government of Cuba guards his privacy and that he has since joined Cuba's Youth Communist Union.[64] With federal agents snatching a young boy from the freedom that his mom literally died to provide him, to return him to Cuba where his de facto father would be one of the Castro brothers, the image of the American in government uniform as a "Freedom Man," as Ronald Reagan noted, was put at a severe discount.

Without sharp differences to debate, the two candidates' styles were endlessly contrasted. Gore, the taller man, actually seemed to stalk Bush during one debate. At another debate, he sighed audibly, giving the impression that he was exasperated by his opponent's wrong-headedness. Governor Bush was not as skilled a policy expert as Gore, but for all his specific talk and sighing into the microphone during the presidential debate, Gore was parodied devastatingly on *Saturday Night Live*. He came across as a stiff know-it-all. Bush was satirized too, but as a not-too-bright regular guy, a frat jock with a penchant for mangling the English language. *SNL*'s Bush gave us "strategery," but "W" himself would give us "misunderestimate."

Bush was slightly ahead in most polls leading up to Election Day. Few could have predicted the monthlong nightmare to come.

IX. The Contested Contest

When the closest election in U.S. history appeared to give Florida and the majority of the Electoral College votes to George Bush, Al Gore telephoned his rival to concede. As he was on his way to Nashville's War Memorial Auditorium to make the announcement public, however, his campaign aides called and begged him to wait.[65] By then, the difference in Florida was down to two thousand votes *and dropping*. It was too soon to concede, they pleaded. Gore decided to cancel his announcement and call Governor Bush again.

That was not the only cancelled announcement that evening. The television networks, along with CNN, had done the reverse earlier in the evening, calling the state of Florida for Vice President Gore, only to withdraw the call later in the evening.*[66]

When Governor Bush spoke to Vice President Gore by telephone on election night, learning Gore was calling back his concession, Bush said coldly, "Let me make sure that I understand, you're calling to retract that concession?" Gore, annoyed, shot back: "You don't have to get snippy about it." When Bush said that his "little brother," Florida's Governor Jeb Bush, had assured him he'd carried the state, Gore answered sharply: "Let me explain something. Your little brother is not the ultimate authority on this."[67]

On that, Al Gore was absolutely right. It will forever be amazing that the 2000 election came down to 537 disputed votes in the one state out of fifty where the brother of the Republican presidential nominee was the elected chief executive. Dramatists could not plot something so improbable. The fact that the two Bush brothers were in their precise positions at that precise moment will forever appear to some as a conspiracy. It matters little that the charges of systematic disenfranchisement of Democratic voters that would be alleged were found false. It matters little that to believe such charges, one

---

* Doing analysis for CNN that evening, I openly criticized CNN on air for calling the state of Florida too early and, seemingly at that point, wrongly. Off air, a CNN host told me I should not criticize the network on air like that, but the fact was, they knew they were wrong and others at CNN knew my criticism was nothing short of what others were thinking and saying throughout the rest of broadcast television: in the rush to call a state for one candidate, they moved too soon in giving Florida to Al Gore, and everyone knew it.

must believe that these voters were systematically defrauded by Democratic election officials in overwhelmingly Democratic counties.

One thing became clear in Florida in 2000: members of the Cuban American community were enraged by what they saw as the Clinton administration's kidnapping of little Elian Gonzalez. Cuban Americans rallied behind George and Jeb Bush at every point in the thirty-six-day conflict of judicial wrangling and recounting of votes.* It may be no exaggeration to say that George W. Bush was elected by a six-year-old boy who was no longer even in the country. In 1996, the Democratic ticket of Clinton-Gore had prevailed in Florida over the Republican ticket of Dole-Kemp for the first time in several elections—and the Elian Gonzalez dispute cost the Democrats a good deal of the support they had begun to receive from the Cuban American community (in Miami-Dade County, alone, Gore received seventy thousand fewer votes than Clinton did four years earlier).[68]

Of course another factor in Gore's loss of Florida was the candidacy of consumer advocate and left-wing activist Ralph Nader, who took some ninety thousand votes in Florida that many assume would or could have gone to Al Gore.[69] Ralph Nader's defenders dispute this claim, however, citing evidence that most of his voters were "new voters" and not inclined toward Al Gore in the first place.[70]

But whatever excuses may have been lodged for such a close vote in Florida, one thing is eminently clear: Al Gore lost his home state of Tennessee along with its eleven electoral votes. Had Gore won his home state, he would have won not only the popular vote but also the Electoral College vote and become president. One has to go back to George McGovern's 1972 campaign to find a candidate who lost his home state.

Still, amazingly enough in the new century that had brought us cable

---

* It is hard to retell how animated partisans were during the recount of Florida. While voting officials argued about scrutinizing an intent of a voter's ballot and what a *hanging chad* on the ballot meant, protesters in Florida and Washington, D.C., proliferated on the streets; in D.C., Republicans stood in front of the vice president's official house on Massachusetts Avenue with signs that read: "Al Gore, Get Out of Dick Cheney's House." Bumper stickers appeared as well. Republicans had stickers that read "Sore-Loserman" with Gore campaign colors; Democrats had bumper stickers after Bush was declared the victor that read "Hail to the Thief." Others making sport of the whole imbroglio had stickers that read "Florida: where your vote counts . . . and counts . . . and counts."

and satellite news, the Internet, and several other forms of new high-tech industry, for several weeks after the election of 2000, due to the alleged irregularities on the ballots and the legal fighting over them in Florida, there was still no definitive answer about who won Florida and, thus, who won the presidency.

During these weeks, known as the "Florida recount," teams of election officials—and lawyers from both campaigns who had swept into Florida—tried to assess voters' intentions in ballots that had been discarded for error because they were not fully punched or read as fully punched. (The term *hanging chad* would describe a dangling piece of paper from the ballot that did not completely separate after punching; other terms included *dimpled chads* and *pregnant chads* for ballots that seemed marked but did not separate from the ballot at all.) Then there was the claim of mistake from older voters about the *butterfly ballot* that had the names of the candidate on one side but a corresponding number to select that name on the other side. Numerous recounts and rules for recounts came from various election boards and Florida courts in what seemed to be an interminable legal and election process confusion.

The U.S. Supreme Court finally had to step in to resolve the situation. On 12 December 2000, the court ruled for George Bush in *Bush v. Gore* and put an end to the endless recounts of disputed ballots. Four weeks of hanging chads and pregnant chads had brought the country perilously close to a constitutional breakdown. Al Gore conceded the election on the day following the Supreme Court's ruling.

After the election, *USA Today*, the *Miami Herald*, and the Knight-Ridder newspaper chain conducted a canvass of some 64,000 disputed ballots. Under *three of four scenarios*, Bush won. Under the rules demanded by the Gore-Lieberman ticket, Bush won.[71]

Ironically, Gore won 540,520 more popular votes nationwide than Bush. The U.S. Electoral College system was set up by the founders to reduce this possibility, but not to eliminate it entirely. George Will compared the Electoral College's requirement of a majority of the electors from fifty states to be like the requirement that a World Series winner must be the first to win *four of a possible seven* games. It does not matter if the Yankees blow out the Dodgers 13-1 in the first game and then drop four straight games by scores of 1-0, 2-1,

3-1, and 4-1. In this imaginary World Series, the Yankees score 16 runs to the Dodgers' total of 10. The Dodgers still win if we play the Series by the rules of the game. To this day, many of Al Gore's supporters are still sore because the Supreme Court did not allow them to change the rules of the game.

Americans could, nonetheless, be grateful to Al Gore for conceding the election on 13 December 2000. Had he refused to accept the Court's ruling, the election might have been determined by the House of Representatives. That had happened in 1800 and 1824. Bush would have won easily there. When the House decides, each state has just one vote, and Bush's fellow Republicans still controlled the House. Still, for the sake of national unity and stability of government in the nuclear age, Gore's ultimate concession was an act of statesmanship for which he should be praised.

But as disputatious as October, November, and December 2000 had been at home in America, what had happened thousands of miles away, in Yemen, was even more important.

X. The Middle East Gets Closer Than Ever Before

Five days after the attack on the *Cole*, the final presidential candidates' debate took place. While the questions all came from the audience in this debate, not one question was asked about the *Cole* or terrorism. Vice President Gore and Governor Bush each took a moment in answering the first question posed to them (about health care) to say a consoling word to the families of the victims of the *Cole* bombing, but that was the extent of it.[72]

When it came to the Middle East, Bill Clinton had been consumed with Israel and the Palestinians. Notwithstanding that Yasser Arafat never changed the PLO charter to recognize Israel according to the charter's terms or that Arafat had unleashed several violent uprisings (or *intifadahs*) in Israel, no foreign leader visited the White House more from 1993 to 2000 than Yasser Arafat—and the United States, for the first time in its history, would fund various Arafat-controlled Palestinian entities.[73] Ultimately, President Clinton and the Israeli government, through all of the various negotiations President Clinton had put together, offered Arafat control of

Arab Jerusalem (which would become the Palestinian capital), 97 percent of the West Bank, and all of Gaza. To all this, Arafat said no, and President Clinton would not have a Middle East peace process of which to boast.[74]

As for Afghanistan and bin Laden, while some, like Richard Clarke, were pushing for an effort to take out Osama bin Laden in Afghanistan, others—outside government—were warning of a domestic attack as well. As far back as 1997, terrorism expert Steve Emerson had warned of terrorist cells in America in the pages of the *Middle East Quarterly* with an article titled "Get Ready for Twenty World Trade Center Bombings."[75] And in New York City, Rick Rescorla, the head of security for Morgan Stanley located in the World Trade Center, had thought—after the first World Trade Center bombing in 1993—that the terrorists would not stop and would next time use airplanes to take down the Twin Towers.[76] Rescorla

> pressed the company to conduct regular drills even though some employees grumbled and joked about them. Every few months, all 2,700 employees in the South Tower would be marched, with Rescorla at the bullhorn, in an arduous trek down the long winding stairwell of one of the world's highest skyscrapers and out of the building, just for practice.[77]

The year 2000 ended as would soon the presidency of Bill Clinton. There was no substantial action against Osama bin Laden, there was no conversion of Yasser Arafat, and Saddam Hussein was still running Iraq—and thwarting international inspections. There was more to come.

Four

Bush and the Age of Terror

The new millennium came and passed without many alarms and excursions. After the late 1990s presidential impeachment, much of the country seemed exhausted. The next presidential election, however, was anything but tranquil—and for the first time in our nation's history the result was thrown to the Supreme Court. A new president with an old name, George Bush, was elected. The son of the former President Bush came to office on a promise of "compassionate conservatism," as a "uniter and not a divider." He had set out to heal racial strife and cure impoverishing ills with greater assistance from our country's faith-based organizations. He began that course. But it was interrupted, as was all the business of the nation. Another day of infamy would come to America, but this time it targeted civilians. It was a slaughter, at the hands of Islamic terrorists. Almost every time the United States had taken up arms over the previous two decades, it had been on behalf of Muslims: from Afghanistan to Kuwait to Somalia, to Bosnia and Kosovo. Nevertheless, a grievance-minded group of Islamic radicals attacked the United States, using civilian airliners, and the civilians in them, as missiles. For the first time in a long time, America saw the face of evil directly, it suffered from the hand of evil directly, but America also showed the many, many more hands of goodness, of self-sacrifice, of decency. We prayed. And then we took up arms and fought.

I. Bush Begins

When George W. Bush took the oath on 20 January 2001, he became the first man since John Quincy Adams to occupy the same high office his father had held. And as was the case with the younger Adams, his father was in good health to savor the honor. After eight years of conflict, controversy, and scandal, Americans once again longed for domestic tranquility. The prospects seemed bright. President Bush claimed to be "a uniter, not a divider." He reached out to his opponents and to his supporters. Bush concluded his unexpectedly eloquent Inaugural Address with this exhortation:

> Americans are generous and strong and decent, not because we believe in ourselves, but because we hold beliefs beyond ourselves. When this spirit of citizenship is missing, no government program can replace it. When this spirit is present, no wrong can stand against it.
>
> After the Declaration of Independence was signed, Virginia statesman John Page wrote to Thomas Jefferson: "We know the race is not to the swift nor the battle to the strong. Do you not think an angel rides in the whirlwind and directs this storm?"[1]

For Republicans and conservatives, it was a time of great excitement. Former President Bush's son had bested former President Clinton's vice president, and with his youthful indiscretions long behind him, it was hoped George W. Bush would bring new respectability, new honor, and new dignity to the White House. Not all was new, however. George Bush knew what he knew (mostly domestic policy), and he knew what he did not (foreign and defense). While his vice president, Dick Cheney, was a veteran of Congress and a former secretary of defense, Bush chose as his secretary of state the former Chairman of the Joint Chiefs of Staff, General Colin Powell. His national security advisor was Stanford Provost Condoleezza Rice. These two black Americans, in such high-profile positions in an administration, all the more so a Republican administration, were—and were considered—

deserved and landmark appointments.* For his secretary of defense, Bush also went with experience, Donald H. Rumsfeld.** But given his expertise and passion, Governor-cum-President Bush had his eyes and heart set on domestic policy, primarily education and poverty issues.

The economy had done rather well in the late 1990s, especially with the boom in the high-tech and Internet industries that had become successful. Names like Yahoo! and Intel became commonplace. Java suddenly meant more than a cup of coffee or an exotic locale. And online "day traders" became the Wild West gunslingers of the "new economy." Federal Reserve Chairman Alan Greenspan, along with President Clinton's secretaries of the treasury, had borne testimony to all kinds of new and creative financial instruments that would help in the home loan and housing markets. Yet by the beginning of 2001, the boom was showing a bust, and many Internet companies known as *dot-coms* were becoming known as *dot-bombs*. Jack Kemp had written a syndicated op-ed in January 2001, the opening line of which was, "Virtually everyone agrees that George W. Bush confronts a rapidly weakening economy as he assumes the presidency."[2] One headline in the *New York Times* in early 2001 read, "Economy Grew at Slowest Rate in 5 Years in 4th Quarter," and the article went on to cite experts debating whether the United States was heading toward a recession.[3] We were.

For the first time in history, President Bush—to great fanfare by some, debate and concern by others—opened an Office of Faith-Based Initiatives

---

* As written earlier, the Republican Party had had a hard time recovering the black vote, and indeed, George Bush had won only 9 percent of the black vote in 2000.

** Known for his sense of humor, when the newly installed defense secretary appeared at the Pentagon for his second tour of duty, he remarked: "*Charlie's Angels* is back and so am I!" (*Charlie's Angels* was a popular television series in the 1970s, and the 2000 movie based on the television series was a blockbuster hit with the public).

I had been close with the Powell, Cheney, and Rumsfeld families for years. Alma Powell (the general's wife) had long been involved with a youth character development program, Best Friends, of which my wife (Elayne) was the founder and president; I had worked with and known both Dick and Lynne Cheney in various capacities over the years; and Don Rumsfeld sat on my and Jack Kemp's board of directors at our think tank, Empower America. I was close with others in the administration as well: Bush's drug czar, John Walters, had been my deputy at the drug czar's office under the first President Bush, and Pete Wehner, a longtime friend and associate of mine in various jobs, had become part of President Bush's speechwriting staff under Michael Gerson, who had worked with me at Empower America as well.

in the White House to run and implement what he had promised on the campaign trail: a program of freeing up faith-based organizations to address such issues as poverty and addiction. On the campaign trail he had spoken of this as part of his "compassionate conservatism" agenda. "It is not enough to call for volunteerism. Without more support and resources—both private and public—we are asking [religious charities] to make bricks without straw," the governor had argued.[4]

For example, President Bush—as governor—had been taken with the work of ex-Watergate felon and, since then, prison reformer Chuck Colson.* Colson's Prison Fellowship, which ran a very successful program in Texas (to Bush's notice), had been so successful that it had grown over the years to run religious and educational programs for inmates in more than eight hundred prisons in forty countries.[5] Something else had piqued social scientists' interests as well: Prison Fellowship graduates were showing 17 percent re-arrest rates compared to almost a 63 percent re-arrest rate of non–Prison Fellowship graduates.[6] Other religiously inspired programs were also working better than government-run programs, the former governor and newly elected president had argued.

To run his Faith-Based Initiatives Office, President Bush chose one of the premier social scientists in the country, John Dilulio of the University of Pennsylvania. Dilulio, a Democrat, was a big believer in the work of religiously inspired programs and the change in the soul of the poor, the addict, and the criminal that could take place where other programs had failed that person.** Many people were suspicious of such an office and such a program, and Dilulio was given a hard time of it as he promoted these ideas to various groups, liberal and conservative. Would it violate the rules separating church and state? Would it replace government funding for social

---

* Chuck Colson was interested in many issues, not just prison reform (which was his main interest). For example, he had helped work with many evangelical Christians in bringing attention to the slaughter of non-Muslim minorities in the Sudan for years; indeed, my first meeting at the White House in 2001 was with Colson—he and I met with Karl Rove to talk about the crisis in the Sudan.

** John Dilulio was and is a close friend of mine—and we had coauthored a book a few years earlier. The best description I've read of this barrel of a man with a super-high IQ was author David Kuo's: "The mind of Einstein, the heart of Mother Teresa, and the disposition of a longshoreman."

services? Would an organization keep people from one religion out of its dispersal of services if they did not hold to the same faith as that organization? Ultimately, the faith-based initiative was watered down by both sides of the partisan aisle to stand for (and expand the reach of) a proposition known as Charitable Choice, something that was begun in the 1996 federal welfare reform law. Charitable Choice stood for the proposition that faith-based organizations should not be discriminated against in applying for government funding to provide social services—so long as proselytizing was not part of the service that would be provided. That was the big social welfare domestic debate in early 2001.

The president wanted to take on two other big issues on the domestic front: taxes and education. In his first address to Congress in February, President Bush outlined his campaign promise of a tax cut and defended it based on the surplus in the government's budget and as a way to spur the economy: "The growing surplus exists because taxes are too high and government is charging more than it needs. The people of America have been overcharged and, on their behalf, I am here asking for a refund."[7] While he did not get taxes cut as steeply as he wanted, he was able to pick up Democratic votes in the Senate (Dianne Feinstein's of California, for example) by compromising on the amounts he would cut—and every taxpayer received a tax cut in 2001. The Bush tax cuts included new savings accounts for education as well as child tax credits and cuts in estate taxes. The top marginal rates were lowered; they had been at 39.6 percent for the highest earners in America, and that would fall to 35 percent; people in the 36 percent bracket would see their rates go down to 33 percent; those in the 31 percent rate went to 28 percent; and those in the 28 percent rate went to 25 percent. Those at the lower income levels received tax cuts too: they went from 15 percent to 10 percent.[8]

President Bush had a strong passion for education reform (as many reform-minded governors did) and had selected as his secretary of education the former Houston School Superintendent Rod Paige.* But the major effort for school reform would come early in 2001 as a major piece of federal education legislation, the Elementary and Secondary School Act, was coming up for

---

* Rod was yet another friend. In fact I had recommended him as secretary of education.

renewal. President Bush made a big effort at bipartisanship here,* and brought in two other Texans to work on the legislation: White House Domestic Policy Advisor Margaret Spellings and Special Assistant Sandy Kress (a Democrat and friend of President Bush from Texas who worked on school reform issues back in the Lone Star State).

The law, named No Child Left Behind, would, indeed, have large bipartisan support—mostly due to concessions made to Senator Ted Kennedy and Democratic House Education leader George Miller of California. The bill would be the largest increase in federal funding for education programs in history, but it required states receiving federal money to show results for that money. Many on the conservative side of the aisle were unhappy with the amounts being spent and thought the consequences and flexibility offered to states too narrow. Several of us spoke out against the legislation and its compromises.**

The White House was upset by such conservative dissent, echoed as it was by many other conservative and education reform think tanks, publications, and pundits. But it was happy to have Kennedy and the Democrats on board. Ultimately, No Child Left Behind passed with large majorities. Federal education funding was not something many Republicans had been successful at scuttling in the past, and the reforms were more serious than most offered by Democrats previously, even though the unprecedented monies were large and the requirements for reform rather weak.

On social policy, President Bush was known to be more conservative than his father and much more attuned to the moral aspects of domestic policy. He could not change domestic abortion policy with the stroke of a pen or anything like it, but throughout the campaign, he was known for speaking up on behalf of the unborn. But there were a few things he could do on this front. For instance, he had told the Christian Coalition in 2000: "I will lead our nation toward a culture that values life—the life of the elderly and the sick, the life of the young and the life of the unborn,"[9] and he had promised

---

* Although he had largely sidelined his secretary of education in drafting the White House's education policy.

** My former colleague at the Department of Education, Chester E. Finn Jr., and I wrote an op-ed in the *New York Times* criticizing the compromises made in the name of bipartisanship.

to sign a ban on partial-birth abortion. President Bush first, then, restored the Mexico City policy by executive order, holding back U.S. funding to abortion providers abroad (reversing President Clinton's executive order before him).

On 9 August, President Bush used his first nationally televised evening address to explain his policy on the controversial issue of stem cell research. He strongly endorsed federally funded research on *adult* stem cells, encouraged the use of stem cells from newborns' umbilical cords, and allowed research on *embryonic* stem cells only if the work had begun prior to enacting the policy. He stated, "Research on embryonic stem cells raises profound ethical questions, because extracting the stem cell destroys the embryo, and thus destroys its potential for life. Like a snowflake, each of these embryos is unique, with the unique genetic potential of an individual human being."[10] In cases "where the life and death decision has already been made," the new policy would permit federally funded research.[11]

Some in the pro-life community criticized this decision, saying the Bush policy was not funding the killing of human embryos, but it was funding the destruction of embryos already slated to be killed. Most in the pro-life community, approved the president's decision and vocally supported him. Just as loudly, pro-choice critics and many in the medical research community denounced the president's decision. Some accused him of a crass indifference to human suffering, claiming he did not care if cures for Parkinson's, Alzheimer's, stroke, cancer, heart disease, or AIDS were found. The advocates of this position saw no ethical problem with using human embryos as objects of experimentation. And experimentation it was.

Faith-based initiatives, taxes, education, stem cell research—these issues started dividing Americans and put millions at odds with their new president. And the Left was still angry over the Supreme Court decision vindicating the Bush election in the first place.

Then came 11 September.

II. "Let's Roll!"

Eleven September 2001 is one of those dates—like 7 December—that changes the landscape, that tilts the earth. On the East Coast, 11 September

2001 was a beautiful morning. I had walked a few blocks in downtown Washington to a recording studio to tape some statements on education; some of my staff was meeting (as it had every Tuesday morning at the offices of Empower America) for a regular Bible study, overlooking the White House and Old Executive Office Building on Seventeenth and Pennsylvania Avenue.

The lead articles on page one of the *New York Times* that day carried headlines such as "Key Leaders Talk of Possible Deals to Revive Economy" and "Scientists Urge Bigger Supply of Stem Cells"; Pulitzer Prize–winning columnist Thomas Friedman had an op-ed about the failed peace process in the Middle East; in the arts section, there was a profile of the just-published autobiography of a retired domestic terrorist named Bill Ayers ("No Regrets for a Love of Explosives; In a Memoir of Sorts, a War Protester Talks of Life with the Weathermen"). Ayers spoke of his anti-Vietnam activities from the 1960s and '70s, but for those who did not remember Ayers or his movement from the past, the opening sentences of that story were unmistakably jarring: "'I don't regret setting bombs,' Bill Ayers said. 'I feel we didn't do enough.'"[12] And on page fifteen, a too-little-noticed man received the wrong kind of attention: "The day after a suicide bombing aimed at Ahmed Shah Massoud, the leader of the last remaining opposition to the ruling Taliban, conflicting reports persisted today over whether he had survived."[13] As would soon be learned, Massoud, one of the United States's best allies in Afghanistan, was killed. But other news came first.

For those who were tuned in to the leading morning news show, the *Today Show*, that day at nine o'clock, the news unfolded in real time, at first slow and surreal and then in a rush of shock and horror.

Following a commercial break, news anchor Matt Lauer shared the breaking news that a plane had flown into the World Trade Center. Cameras trained on the building and Lauer guided viewers. "You can see fire and flames, or smoke, billowing from that tower," he said. "There's a gaping hole on the north side of the building. That's the side you're seeing to the left-hand side of your screen right now." After a brief comment about the presence of people in the building, Lauer jumped to what brimmed on the minds of many: "This is the World Trade Center that was the center of a terrorist bombing some years ago. So the questions have to be asked, was this purely an accident or could this have been an intentional act?" The answer would have to wait, but not for long.

Katie Couric next took the screen to introduce an eyewitness, Elliott Walker, a *Today Show* producer who was taking her daughter to school at the fateful moment. They spoke by phone. Asked what she saw by Couric, Walker responded, "[W]e heard a very loud sound, the kind of sound you hear when a plane is, you know, going fast past you 'Nnnnnn,' followed by an enormous crash and an immediate explosion." From her vantage point she could see the tower through other buildings. She described seeing "an enormous fireball that must have been 300 feet across" and "a three-block cloud . . . of white smoke." She said smoke was billowing from several floors and "hundreds of dozens of pieces of paper . . . are just sort of floating like confetti."

Then, while Couric asked about emergency crews and whether people were then being brought out of the tower, Walker interjected. "Oh, my goodness. Oh, another one just hit," she said. "Something else just hit, a very large plane just flew directly over my building. . . . Can you see it?" By then all the focus was on the Trade Center, all eyes and cameras fixed upon the devastation. Everyone saw. Walker asked if there was an air traffic control breakdown. But no one wanted think what became so quickly obvious, as terrorism hurtled itself into American minds and lives.[14]

There were no air traffic control problems. As we all soon learned, three civilian airliners had been hijacked and turned into enormous human and fuel-carrying missiles aimed at targets in New York City and Washington, D.C., and a fourth, also destined for D.C., crashed over Shanksville, Pennsylvania. Nineteen young men—fifteen of them from Saudi Arabia—took over the jetliners using box cutters as weapons, and they used these airplanes and the people inside them as weapons of mass destruction. And mass destruction and slaughter were what America got.

The two jets that crashed minutes apart into the World Trade Center caused hundreds of deaths on impact, including all the people on board who died instantly. The fires the planes started resulted in both skyscrapers collapsing in less than two hours. Their structural steel skeletons first buckled from the heat, and then the upper floors pancaked downward, killing thousands. The death toll of nearly three thousand (2,975 to be exact) from the attacks in New York, at the Pentagon, and at the hijacked plane crash in Shanksville, Pennsylvania, exceeded the total numbers of dead from the last major attack on America at Pearl Harbor (2,388 killed). But unlike the attack at Pearl Harbor, the 9/11 attacks were specifically directed against civilians.

The stories of death and tragedy, the stories of heroism and survival from this horrific day are too numerous, far too numerous, to detail. There were the stories of the policemen and women and the firemen and women who ran up the towers to save as many people as possible—as those people were running down the stairs for their lives—and were killed. There's the story of Father Mychal Judge, the chaplain for the New York City Fire Department, who was killed after giving last rites to another fireman. Before he went into the towers, New York City Mayor Rudolph Giuliani saw him and shouted out to him: "Mychal, please pray for us," to which the priest shouted back: "I always do."[15] In his pocket was a prayer he had composed and would often hand out:

> *Lord, take me where you want me to go;*
> *Let me meet who you want me to meet;*
> *Tell me what you want me to say, and keep me out of your way.*[16]

There were, of course, the children too. In Washington, D.C., on American Airlines Flight 77, children Asia Cottom, Bernard Brown, and Rodney Dickens (and their teachers James Debeuneure, Hilda Taylor, and Sarah Clark) were on their way to California on a *National Geographic*–sponsored field trip. For some, it was their first airplane trip. Flight 77 was also carrying my friend, attorney and commentator Barbara Olson (the wife of the Solicitor General of the United States), and flight attendant Michelle Heidenberger, whose sister and sister's children were friends of my family. Flight 77 smashed into the Pentagon killing all on board as well—and 125 Pentagon employees on the ground.[17]

Defense Secretary Donald Rumsfeld was in his office in the Pentagon when he heard the crash in the building he was in charge of. "The 69-year-old former Navy pilot was jolted and rushed to the scene. 'He went outside the building and was helpful in getting several people that were injured onto stretchers,' said a Pentagon spokesman, Rear Adm. Craig Quigley. 'He was out there 15 minutes or so helping the injured.'"[18]

Back in New York City, there were the two hundred people who jumped from the Twin Towers to their deaths; they chose to jump rather than be burned to death. And as they jumped, with makeshift parachutes, "the force generated by their fall ripped the drapes, the tablecloths, the desperately gathered fabric, from their hands" as they lived out their final ten seconds of life in free fall.[19]

There was Rick Rescorla, the security chief of Morgan Stanley, who had spent the last part of his professional career practicing evacuation strategies and died while helping others escape from ground zero; his last recorded words were, "As soon as I make sure everyone else gets out." He said those words in response to Morgan Stanley regional manager John Olson, who was yelling at him: "Rick, you've got to get out, too!"[20] There was the former assistant director of the FBI, John O'Neil, who was on bin Laden's case in the 1990s and after the USS *Cole* attack; he had left the agency to become the head of security at the World Trade Center. There were so many.

Then there were other responders, like retired marine Dave Karnes, who left his accounting job in Connecticut, donned his marine uniform, stopped by the barbershop to get a regulation marine haircut, and went to the World Trade Center site to help any way he could—and ended up rescuing two police officers who were buried in the rubble and are alive to this day.[21]

So many untold stories of tragedy and heroism on and after 9/11, but perhaps none grabbed the attention as that which took place over Shanksville, Pennsylvania. On US Air Flight 93, businessman Todd Beamer picked up an airplane telephone and transmitted information to the GTE operator, who filled him in on the other flights. Beamer told the operator that he and a few others were planning to try and take the plane back from the terrorists. Beamer prayed the Lord's Prayer with the operator, and then "after the prayer was finished . . . Beamer dropped the phone, leaving the line open. It was then that the operator heard Beamer's words: 'Let's roll.' They were the last words she heard. The phone went silent, and the plane crashed, killing all 44 people aboard." Flight 93 went down in an open field in Pennsylvania (and the terrorists did not complete their mission of attacking the White House), thanks to the efforts of a handful of everyday, hardworking Americans. "Let's roll" became a popular bumper sticker and a watchword in post-9/11 America.[22]

As people tried to figure out just what had taken place, how many were killed, and who was responsible, Mayor Rudy Giuliani was the man in charge in New York City—commanding all aspects of the emergency response. When a reporter asked him how many people he thought had died, he replied, "The number of casualties will be more than any of us can bear."[23] And right he was—it was an unbearable shock to the country and most of the world, except in those shadowy corners where the evil rejoiced. Columnist Charles Krauthammer had speculated that Americans lived in a bubble, "a holiday from history," throughout the 1990s and, channeling Robert Frost, that the bubble would somehow burst by ice or by fire—it turned out to be fire.

The next day, 12 September 2001, the *San Francisco Examiner*'s single-word headline in bold said what much of the nation was thinking: "*BASTARDS!*"[24]

And on Friday, the president told the nation and the world what America was thinking too. At the National Cathedral he led the country in a memorial service but said, "The conflict was begun on the timing and terms of others. It will end in a way and at an hour of our choosing." That was the American way in war: first Americans prayed, and then they prepared to fight. Later that day, standing on a pile of rubble in New York City, President Bush was thanking rescue workers via a handheld megaphone as the crowds were shouting, "USA! USA!" When some yelled they couldn't hear the president, the crowd quieted, and he shouted: "I can hear you. The rest of the world hears you. And the people who knocked these buildings down will hear all of us soon!" At that point, there was no doubt—the president was resolved, the nation was resolved, and the war that was declared and inflicted upon the United States would be joined.

On 17 September, what many know to be Constitution Day, President Bush spoke at a Washington, D.C., mosque to assure the Muslim community in America and throughout the world that the U.S. would not be declaring a war against Islam—against terrorists and terrorism, yes; Islam, no. There, the president said:

> Both Americans, our Muslim friends and citizens, tax-paying citizens, and Muslims in nations were just appalled and could not believe what we saw on our TV screens. These acts of violence against innocents violate the fundamental tenets of the Islamic faith, and it's important for my fellow Americans to understand that. . . . The face of terror is not the true faith of Islam. That's not what Islam is all about. Islam is peace. These terrorists don't represent peace. They represent evil and war.[25]

It caused no little amount of concern to many that the mosque where the president chose to speak, like so many other mosques in America, was built and funded with Saudi Arabian money. It had been documented, too, that the anti-Semitic screed, *The Protocols of the Elders of Zion*, had been sold at that mosque.[26] And many others became worried about our nation's long and cozy relationship with Saudi Arabia. Further concerning was the question of just how many terrorists or terrorist sympathizers were living in America.

On 20 September, President Bush addressed a joint session of Congress and rallied the nation:

> Our response involves far more than instant retaliation and isolated strikes. Americans should not expect one battle, but a lengthy campaign, unlike any other we have ever seen. It may include dramatic strikes, visible on TV, and covert operations, secret even in success. We will starve terrorists of funding, turn them one against another, drive them from place to place, until there is no refuge or no rest. And we will pursue nations that provide aid or safe haven to terrorism. Every nation, in every region, now has a decision to make. Either you are with us, or you are with the terrorists. From this day forward, any

nation that continues to harbor or support terrorism will be regarded
by the United States as a hostile regime.[27]

By that time, it was becoming ever clearer that the attacks were the work
of Osama bin Laden and his terrorist organization, Al Qaeda.* Americans
all over the country started delving into who Osama bin Laden was and just
what kinds of things were going on in Afghanistan and in the rest of the
Arab world—a world many of us had not focused on for many years. And
President Bush instructed further—as he threatened the Taliban government
in Afghanistan with war if it did not turn over the leaders of Al Qaeda:

> They [the terrorists who attacked America] are recruited from their
> own nations and neighborhoods and brought to camps in places like
> Afghanistan where they are trained in the tactics of terror. They are
> sent back to their homes or sent to hide in countries around the world
> to plot evil and destruction. The leadership of al Qaeda has great influ-
> ence in Afghanistan and supports the Taliban regime in controlling
> most of that country. In Afghanistan we see al Qaeda's vision for the
> world. Afghanistan's people have been brutalized, many are starving
> and many have fled.
>
> Women are not allowed to attend school. You can be jailed for
> owning a television. Religion can be practiced only as their leaders
> dictate. A man can be jailed in Afghanistan if his beard is not long
> enough. The United States respects the people of Afghanistan—after
> all, we are currently its largest source of humanitarian aid—but we
> condemn the Taliban regime.[28]

But the Taliban would not hand over bin Laden and his minions.

Americans rallied around the flag in the days after the attacks. Certainly
most public officials—those who had to answer to the electorate—supported
the president's call for a war on terror. A few, especially those who felt secure
in their tenured faculty posts, spoke out against America's response. A

---

* In Arabic, *Al Qaeda* translates to "the base."

speaker at a University of North Carolina teach-in called on the president to apologize to "the widows and orphans, the tortured and the impoverished, and all the millions of other victims of American imperialism."[29] A Rutgers professor complained that whatever "the proximate cause" of 11 September, its "ultimate cause is the fascism of U.S. foreign policy over the past decades." Reuters news service refused even to designate the 9/11 attackers "terrorists." "We all know that one man's terrorist is another man's freedom fighter," Reuters said.[30]

The late Meg Greenfield understood the habitual dissidents' mind-set. They were the kind of people, she once wrote, who, if put in a pot by a cannibal chieftain, would always try to see the matter from the cannibal's point of view.

Thankfully, in the immediate aftermath of 9/11, such disloyal sentiments were completely unrepresentative of most Americans' reactions. Most Americans were serious and got serious. Bible sales skyrocketed. Church and synagogue attendance increased. Recovery meetings filled up. There were even reports from divorce lawyers of families seeking to settle their differences out of court and to make another go at it with their families they had been separated from.*

Once the Taliban refused to surrender bin Laden or any part of his terrorist ring, the president ordered U.S. forces into Afghanistan to take down the Taliban regime that had harbored Al Qaeda. America's war in Afghanistan would have strong support from a broad coalition. Britain, Canada, France, and Germany supported the U.S. drive to liberate millions of Afghans—especially women—who had been so cruelly oppressed by the Taliban.

Still, many worried about a backlash here in America from the Muslim community and about just how many sympathizers with the terrorists there might be. Was Islam a religion of peace as the president had said? Was bin Laden's a minority viewpoint? What were the distances between a peaceful adherent to the Muslim faith and the views of bin Laden? And, of course, there was the worry of another attack on America—many analysts at the time

---

* Another indication of the mood: my phone rang off the hook with calls from young business executives in the private sector asking if I could recommend to them jobs in national security, in either the public or the private sector. They wanted to serve.

assumed there would be one. These were the questions on many Americans' minds. In Washington, D.C., those questions were further fueled by reports such as the one in the *Washington Post* about a private Muslim school in Potomac, Maryland, where the reporter asked the students their views, and one eighth grader, speaking on behalf of others, said, "If I had to choose sides, I'd stay with being Muslim. . . . Being an American means nothing to me. I'm not even proud of telling my cousins in Pakistan that I'm American."[31]

What President Bush and most Americans were trying to assure was that there was, there should be, no distinction between being a Muslim and being an American: Muslims were as free in America to practice their faith as Jews or any other minority—perhaps freer in America than any other country. Indeed, this country had even gone to war several times on behalf of Muslims. And America was about to do so again.

Despite some calls from the pacifist left, Congress was nearly united in authorizing the military to go into Afghanistan—the Senate was unanimous, and only one vote in the House opposed military force, that of Representative Barbara Lee of California, who said on the House floor, "Our deepest fears now haunt us. Yet, I am convinced that military action will not prevent further acts of international terrorism against the United States. . . . As we act, let us not become the evil that we deplore."[32]

There were legislative efforts as well, directed at protecting the home front. The president proposed the Patriot Act to expand and strengthen the legal tools available for fighting terrorism. The legislation codified a good deal of law used in other enforcement matters (like drug and organized crime cases) for terrorism investigations. It removed "legal barriers that prevented the law enforcement, intelligence, and national defense communities from coordinating information," so that government could better "connect the dots" in tracking down terrorist plots.[33] "The FBI could get a wiretap to investigate the mafia, but they could not get one to investigate terrorists," said Delaware Democratic Senator Joe Biden, who supported the bill. "To put it bluntly, that was crazy! What's good for the mob should be good for terrorists."[34] And said North Carolina Democratic Senator John Edwards, "We simply cannot prevail in the battle against terrorism if the right hand of our government has no idea what the left hand is doing."[35]

The act passed in October 2001 with near universal approval in the Senate (Wisconsin Democratic Senator Russ Feingold was the lone opposing vote), and with all but sixty-six votes in the House.[36]

The mood in America outside Washington and New York was marked by both sadness and a strong disposition to vengeance. Country music, the most popular genre on the American radio dial, captured the mood of the nation perhaps better than any other. Country superstar Alan Jackson performed for the first time a live song at the Country Music Association Awards ceremony in November. It was a tear-jerker he had written in the wake of 9/11, "Where Were You When the World Stopped Turning":

> *Did you shout out in anger*
> *In fear for your neighbor*
> *Or did you just sit down and cry.*[37]

And on the other side of our national emotions, another superstar, Toby Keith, excited concertgoers with a song that would soon also top the country charts, "Courtesy of the Red, White, and Blue":

> *Soon as we could see clearly through our big black eye,*
> *Man, we lit up your world like the 4th of July.*[38]

Throughout the months of October, November, and December, Secretary of Defense Donald Rumsfeld delivered his newly famous and typically well-received press briefings. Rumsfeld had become popular as a spokesman for common sense and welcomed any and all questions from the press, even as he enjoyed staring them down on occasion when he thought their questions worth mocking a bit. It was always a friendly joust, and the press enjoyed it as much as the secretary did. One press briefing stands out from the late fall of 2001 when the secretary of defense, grinning broadly, displayed photos of American Special Forces chasing Al Qaeda through the rugged mountains of Afghanistan—on horseback. The forces of freedom had come full circle. With Global Positioning Systems linked to satellites, with unmanned drones capable of killing fleeing Taliban chieftains helping

America fight the war, on the one hand, the military now had also returned to the weapon of first resort—the cavalry.

The question of whether 9/11 could have been prevented would prove a long and complicated one. To be sure, there would be plenty of blame and excuses to go around. Bin Laden had declared war on America twice in the 1990s, and his general whereabouts was known. After the attack on the USS *Cole*, arguments about what to do ended in deadlock. The new administration was briefed on the threat from bin Laden and even the director of the CIA, George Tenet, was aware of *something* going on in America. On the morning of 9/11, he was having breakfast in Washington at the St. Regis hotel when an aide told him of the hijackings. His immediate response was, "This has bin Laden all over it." He speculated, "I wonder if it has anything to do with this guy taking pilot training."[39] The fact was, FBI agents had reported suspicions about possible terrorists in several flight schools. The fact was, certain parts of the FBI were not allowed to talk to other parts of the FBI. The fact was, the CIA and the FBI guarded too much of their own information and did not share information between agencies. The fact was, America had been struck again and again by terrorists from Africa to the Middle East and had done next to nothing in response. The fact was, America did not want to go to war—unless it had to.

But when it did, it took the terrorists' breath away. There were other attacks planned on the United States, including in Chicago and Los Angeles—but they did not happen. The planners were scattered and their plans disrupted. In Afghanistan, America did light up the sky (and the ground), and within about two months of operations there our military and intelligence agencies had captured or killed about a quarter of Al Qaeda's known leadership.[40] The leader of the Taliban, Mullah Omar, did escape Afghanistan, as did Osama bin Laden. But as writer Christopher Hitchens put it, the campaign in Afghanistan was the first time in history that the United States had bombed a country "out of the stone age." At the same time, the president organized a new cabinet-level agency along with new efforts to coordinate our national security intelligence. The Department of Homeland Security was created—and in short order, every kind of travel in America became a little more difficult and a lot safer.

In the aftermath of 9/11 national security and terrorism experts were arguing that never again should America be hit like it was on 11 September. "It is time to drain the swamps," many had argued. Would Saudi Arabia be next? Pakistan? Syria? Iran? Iraq? Just how serious was the president about what he said in September? One thing Americans knew for certain: President Bush, despite all his plans for the economy, education, and welfare, had become a wartime president. The big question before him, however, was how much war he could wage and under what conditions. Would America or should America strike other places before terrorists there struck America? Should the country, in fact, drain the swamps and engage in preemptive war?*

As Americans debated these issues, they knew Afghanistan and the homeland were not and could not be the only fronts in the battle, the war, against terrorism. On 21 December, Richard Reid, a British convert to Islam who had been trained in Afghanistan and reported to Al Qaeda operations chief and 9/11 mastermind Khalid Sheikh Mohammed,[41] was stopped in the middle of his terrorist operation: blowing up American Airlines Flight 63 from Paris to Miami. Reid had boarded the flight from Paris with a sophisticated shoe bomb he was trying to ignite in flight when a flight attendant noticed the smell of a match he had lit. "Somebody help me!" the flight attendant screamed, and another attendant doused Reid—and his flammables—with a bottle of water. Reid was restrained, and Flight 63, which would have been blown out of the sky with its 185 passengers had Reid succeeded, landed safely in the United States.[42]

After 2001, for a time at least, nobody would look at an airliner in the sky the same way as before, and nobody would fail to think about terrorism as he planned a trip on a commercial airline. If one of the intents of

---

* I, and others, had worried that although the country was fairly united after 9/11 to engage in a long twilight struggle, the nation would lose its resolve. With the financial help of philanthropist Lawrence Kadish of New York, and the assistance of former Clinton CIA Director James Woolsey, we started a group called Americans for Victory Over Terrorism to bolster public opinion for the long haul. We went to several college campuses and argued for a vigorous prosecution of the war, including the necessity of taking on Iraq. At times we were joined by others, including columnist Charles Krauthammer and terrorism expert L. Paul "Jerry" Bremer. We received a lot of press and television coverage, some in criticism as many said we were foolish to think public opinion would ever swing against the war.

terrorism is to plant fear (or suspicion) in a civilian population, the terrorists had accomplished at least that. There was more than one reason former Israeli Prime Minister Binyamin Netanyahu had said after 9/11, "Today we are all Americans."*

As if the unprecedented terrorist attack on the United States of America were not enough to shake our confidence in the latter half of 2001 and beyond, as if it did not disrupt the national economy enough (setting aside the unprecedented human death toll for the time being), another institution in America collapsed in the fall of 2001: trust in the American corporation, or at least several big corporations. The Enron Corporation was the symbol. It was one of the largest corporations in America and the sixth-largest energy corporation in the world.[43] But due to internal and external accounting manipulations, its market capitalization—which was as high as $60 billion, with a stock trading price closing in on ninety dollars a share—was overvalued, its financial success was a ruse, its books were "cooked." Enron's stock price and market capitalization were, in reality, seventy times its earnings and six times its book value.[44]

By October 2001, the jig was up when the company announced a more than $600 million loss. By December, Enron had declared bankruptcy.[45] Thousands of employees were laid off, pensions were lost, and shock struck employees and investors alike—as well as the nation. Enron's top two executives, Chairman Ken Lay and CEO Jeffrey Skilling, would become household names and the faces (and hands) of the Enron collapse. In short order, nineteen Enron executives would face criminal charges, with Lay and Skilling being found guilty of perpetrating one of the largest corporate frauds in American history.[46] Ken Lay would die from a heart attack after his conviction, but his and his associates' crimes laid the groundwork for not only a long-lasting inherent distrust of many corporate executives but also a series of laws that Congress would pass, and the president would sign, to make corporations and their boards more accountable and more transparent.

---

* Upon hearing this from my old friend, I said on CNN, "Actually, today we are all Israelis." Whichever the case, after 2001, this country was clearly no longer immune from what a democracy like Israel had been facing: Islamic terrorists who hated our existence and would do anything they could to end it.

But Enron and Lay and Skilling were not alone. The following year, telecommunications giant WorldCom filed for bankruptcy after disclosures that billions of dollars were unaccounted for, and its CEO, Bernard Ebbers, was convicted of fraud.[47] There were others, from manufacturing giant Tyco to cable provider Adelphia. If people—and the government— were shocked by the corporate wrongdoing, some of the lavish spending by the executives (such as Tyco's Dennis Kozlowski's $2 million birthday party for his wife) shocked the conscience even further.[48] I had written at the time, "An economic system like ours depends on trust—trust between consumer and vendor, auditor and employee, shareholder and executive. When that trust is broken, the economic system itself is damaged."[49] And the economic system was damaged, as were honest and reliant employees and retirees and investors in these companies, as was the public and private trust.

This was very damaging and probably more harmful to the financial markets than the terrorist attacks. Nevertheless, the war that was waged against us, and our response to it, was still the dominant story and concern in America's—if not much of the world's—eyes, hearts, and minds.

III. The Next Phase

In his State of the Union speech in January 2002, President Bush readied the nation for an even greater national response to the terrorist threat, beyond the battlefield of Afghanistan. Leading up to his speech, many in Washington thought it would be a groundbreaking speech. They knew that his gifted speechwriting team had put their noses to the grindstone and that the president wanted a speech for the ages.* He—and they—delivered on that. The president opened by saying,

> Mr. Speaker, Vice President Cheney, members of Congress, distinguished guests, fellow citizens, as we gather tonight, our nation is at war, our

---

* At this point, Bush's team for such speeches was led by Michael Gerson with the very gifted group of John McConnell, Pete Wehner, Matthew Scully, and the conservative intellectual and author David Frum.

economy is in recession and the civilized world faces unprecedented dangers. Yet the state of our union has never been stronger.[50]

The president went on:

> The American flag flies again over our embassy in Kabul. Terrorists who once occupied Afghanistan now occupy cells at Guantanamo Bay. And terrorist leaders who urged followers to sacrifice their lives are running for their own.
>
> America and Afghanistan are now allies against terror. We will be partners in rebuilding that country. And this evening we welcome the distinguished interim leader of a liberated Afghanistan: Chairman Hamid Karzai.

He listed the problem as beyond Al Qaeda: "A terrorist under-world—including groups like Hamas, Hezbollah, Islamic Jihad and Jaish-i-Mohammed—operates in remote jungles and deserts, and hides in the centers of large cities." He said America was operating "elsewhere," beyond Afghanistan. And while the president would also speak about the economy and domestic exertions, the take-away, the most remembered, and the most debated was this:

> Our second goal is to prevent regimes that sponsor terror from threaten-ing America or our friends and allies with weapons of mass destruction.
>
> Some of these regimes have been pretty quiet since September 11, but we know their true nature. North Korea is a regime arming with missiles and weapons of mass destruction, while starving its citizens.
>
> Iran aggressively pursues these weapons and exports terror, while an unelected few repress the Iranian people's hope for freedom.
>
> Iraq continues to flaunt its hostility toward America and to support terror. The Iraqi regime has plotted to develop anthrax and nerve gas and nuclear weapons for over a decade. This is a regime that has already used poison gas to murder thousands of its own citizens, leaving the bodies of mothers huddled over their dead children. This is a regime

that agreed to international inspections then kicked out the inspectors. This is a regime that has something to hide from the civilized world.

States like these, and their terrorist allies, constitute an *axis of evil,* arming to threaten the peace of the world.[51]

"Axis of evil." Rare were the times that presidents had spoken of true good and evil. Even more rare was the identification of a country, or countries, as "evil." People had to reach back to recall the last time they could remember such a prominent designation: Ronald Reagan's, describing the Soviet Union. To the hawks in America, the words sounded just right. To those more used to the modern or postmodern vernacular of values-free realism and diplomacy, the words were a clanging sound. Sounding more convincing or clanging, depending on one's position, was what the president said next:

By seeking weapons of mass destruction, these regimes pose a grave and growing danger. They could provide these arms to terrorists, giving them the means to match their hatred. They could attack our allies or attempt to blackmail the United States. In any of these cases, the price of indifference would be catastrophic.[52]

Was America going to war with North Korea, Iran, or Iraq? There had been speculation about Saddam Hussein and Iraqi complicity in 9/11—most of it came to naught. But there were questions on the table, such as whether America expected another terrorist-sponsoring state, or state being sponsored by terrorists (as Afghanistan was), to someday attack. If that were the case, shouldn't America attack it or them first? And if America was facing weapons of mass destruction (WMDs), is the imperative not so much the greater? Heck, many hawks argued, civilian airliners had been turned into WMDs, and nineteen men created havoc with those—how much worse would it get with real weapons and an even larger set of terrorist operatives?

As it was, several envelopes of anthrax had been sent through the U.S. mail to offices on Capitol Hill and media outlets in a curious series of cases that remained unsolved. Saddam Hussein had experimented with and used chemical and biological weapons. He had declared the U.S. an enemy, had tried to assassinate a former president (President Bush's father), was continuing to thwart cease-fire agreements from the first Gulf War, and had been subsidizing suicide bombers in Israel. And had not President Clinton signed the Iraq Liberation Act less than four years earlier? Americans would later learn that Saddam had also sought a meeting with Al Qaeda after the first Gulf War and that, as recently as 1998, Iraqi officials went to Afghanistan to meet with bin Laden's second in command, Ayman al-Zawahiri, to discuss relocation of Al Qaeda to Iraq.[53] And in 1999, Americans would learn, al-Zawahiri and a Jordanian terrorist named Abu Musab al-Zarqawi traveled to Baghdad to attend an Islamic conference sponsored there.[54]

This "axis of evil" line stuck in the craws of many who thought the administration was taking a new turn, one from retaliation to preemptive attacks on other countries. The left wing in America was out of power, but it had begun building a bigger presence for itself and an anticonservative audience on the Internet and on radio and television interviews. Was this not somewhat of a departure from the unarticulated consensus in America: that the country would go after those who had attacked it? Would not America ruin sorrowful goodwill toward this country by going after others who had not attacked it—yet? There was one other matter: midterm elections for the House and Senate were coming up that November, and the Democrats—as any party out of power would—wanted to make a strong showing and reclaim something, even if the White House was out of reach just then.

Still, if Americans needed a reminder that they were at war, they were treated to occasional jolts about just how vicious the enemy could be. Perhaps few things shocked the conscience more, after 11 September, than the slaughter of *Wall Street Journal* reporter Daniel Pearl. In February of 2002, Pearl was in Pakistan, on his way to interview a fundamentalist Islamic cleric, when he was abducted. Soon, the terrorists who captured him released a gruesome video of what they had done to him: after demanding he read anti-American statements and a confession that "I am a Jew," they decapitated him. This was the hand and (masked) face of evil that simply would not stop itself after 9/11 and would not leave our mind.*

---

* Later, Khalid Sheikh Mohammed would state he was the actual terrorist who beheaded Pearl.

Politics and war were the hot buttons of 2002, and whether America would engage Iraq, or some other country, as it had Afghanistan, was much on the nation's mind. Indeed, other terrorist states were on the administration's mind—most prominently Iraq. In early February, Secretary of State Colin Powell (though a retired general and former chairman of the Joint Chiefs of Staff, not known as one of the administration's more hawkish members) testified to the Senate:

> With respect to Iran and with respect to North Korea, there is no plan to start a war. . . . With respect to Iraq, it has long been, for several years now, a policy of the United States government that regime change would be in the best interests of the region, the best interests of the Iraqi people. . . . And we are looking at a variety of options that would bring that about.[55]

Although no decision had been made to take out Saddam, it was becoming fairly apparent that such a thing was very much on the table. General Tommy Franks, the head of the U.S. Central Command (who had overseen the ouster of the Taliban from Afghanistan and would be similarly in charge of any campaign in Iraq), would reiterate that no plans had been finalized at this point, no decision had been made—but clearly plans were in the works.

In the past, Osama bin Laden had said America was a "paper tiger," and he was surprised by American "weakness," especially in Somalia—that "after a few blows [Americans] ran in defeat."[56] In a videotape of a meeting he held shortly after 11 September, bragging about the operation, he said, "When people see a strong horse and a weak horse, by nature, they will like the strong horse."[57] This, it was thought, was the mind-set of not just bin Laden and his minions but Arab terrorists throughout the world.

The Middle East scholar and Princeton professor Bernard Lewis (who was informally talking with members of the administration) had said that "anxious propitiation" to the Arab or Arab terrorist world was one of the chief causes of their "growth industry," recruitment, and action. Resolution and strength would still them or make them rethink an attack.[58] There was

much in recent history to back this up: not attacking bin Laden's operation had not prevented him attacking us. The shuttle diplomacy with Syria
in the early years of the Clinton administration had not pacified Syria.
The endless negotiations with Yasser Arafat and the attempts to grant his
organization statehood had not pacified him or the Palestinian terrorists.
Indeed, all quite the opposite; after each showing of goodwill and effort,
they had all grown more belligerent. With Saddam Hussein, this was turning out to be true as well. He never accepted defeat in the first Gulf War, the
economic sanctions had not made him capitulate in his actions or rhetoric,
and leaving him in power had not turned his heart in any way. Thus, for
the administration, it was not enough to take out the Taliban and Al Qaeda
in Afghanistan; more force and more resolve needed to be shown. And if
such resolve would protect America from a "mushroom cloud," as National
Security Advisor Condoleezza Rice would put it, so much the more urgent
to do so.*

There was no question of a diplomatic—as well as a domestic bipartisan—cost to the administration's position on Iraq, and it did not take
long to reveal itself. As early as mid-February 2002, other nations started to
weigh in on possible U.S. action against Iraq. The Chinese and Russian governments were saying they would not be on board, and the French foreign
minister had said the U.S. was being "simplistic" in its axis of evil thinking.
Secretary Powell defended the U.S. position and thinking and responded
to his foreign colleagues that they were "getting the vapors" and that the
European Union's minister of foreign affairs, who had warned against a U.S.
invasion of Iraq, would need "a word, as they say in Britain."[59]

Inside the president's cabinet and at the secondary levels, there was
a good deal of division about the wisdom and benefit of taking on Iraq.
While Vice President Cheney and his Chief of Staff Lewis "Scooter" Libby,
along with Defense Department officials Paul Wolfowitz and Doug Feith,
were strongly in favor of ousting Saddam Hussein, Secretary of State Powell
and his deputy, Richard Armitage, were much more skeptical and at times

---

* Aware that our intelligence was never perfect—as 9/11 itself had proven—Condoleezza Rice's
  framing of the threat from Iraq was quite attention grabbing when she deployed it later in 2002:
  "We don't want the smoking gun to be a mushroom cloud."

strongly opposed—despite Powell's public support for the administration's position. Powell and Armitage had developed the "Pottery Barn" rule, telling the president that "if you break it, you own it."[60]

While Hussein kept thwarting international weapons inspections, Americans studied up on Iraq—and what they found was not only a regime that would not come clean about its weapons programs but a regime of horrific human rights abuse as well. Just what was Saddam Hussein doing in his country, to his country, during his tenure as its dictator?

He had used chemical weapons on his own people and started two wars in the Middle East—one against Kuwait, one against Iran; by most accounts, he had actually killed more Muslims than any other person in modern history. Saddam Hussein had also violated more than a dozen United Nations resolutions relating to weapons of mass destruction, and the UN Security Council had found Iraq "in flagrant violation" of prior demands that it destroy such weapons. President Clinton had signed the 1998 Iraq Liberation Act and had said, "Some day, some way, I guarantee you he'll use [his] arsenal." The chief of the German Intelligence Service had recently said, "It is our estimate that Iraq will have an atomic bomb in three years." And Richard Butler, who headed the UN team investigating Iraq's WMD program, had said, "Saddam Hussein is a homicidal dictator who is addicted to weapons of mass destruction."[61]

Inside his own country, Saddam Hussein's record of terror and repression was as abominable as it could possibly be. In the words of Kenneth Pollack, the former director of Gulf Affairs at the National Security Council under President Clinton:

> This is a regime that will gouge out the eyes of children to force confessions from their parents and grandparents. This is a regime that will crush all of the bones in the feet of a two-year-old girl to force her mother to divulge her father's whereabouts. This is a regime that will hold a nursing baby at arm's length from its mother and allow the child to starve to death to force the mother to confess. This is a regime that will burn a person's limbs off to force him to confess or comply. This is a regime that will slowly lower its victims into huge vats of

acid. . . . This is a regime that applies electric shocks to the bodies of its victims. . . . This is a regime that in 2000 decreed that the crime of criticizing the regime would be punished by [the] cutting out of the offender's tongue.[62]

Aside from indictments like these, there were others, like that from liberal British Member of Parliament Ann Clwyd, who took testimony that "there was a machine designed for shredding plastic. Men were dropped into it and we were . . . made to watch. Sometimes they went in head first and died quickly. Sometimes they went in feet first and died screaming."[63]

Despite these serious indictments, there was at the same time a growing and serious antiwar movement both in America and abroad. America retaliating for an attack on its homeland may have been one thing; America initiating an attack before being struck was another. As other foreign allies were issuing their reservations, dissents, and opposition to joining the U.S. in forcing Hussein from power, including mass protests on the streets of Europe, the president knew one ally in particular was key: Prime Minister Tony Blair of Great Britain.

Just as America stood with Britain in World War II, Britain—under Blair's leadership—would stand with the U.S. in the war against terror and, specifically, Iraq. In early September, before leaving Britain for a meeting in the U.S. with President Bush, Blair spoke about his support for ousting Hussein should Hussein not allow full-fledged inspections into his country and come clean about his covert weapons program. Blair told a press conference:

> If Britain and if Europe want to be taken seriously as people facing up to these issues do, then our place is facing them with America—in partnership, but with America. . . . The threat posed by the current Iraqi regime is real. . . . Either the regime starts to function in a completely different way, or the regime changes. . . . The United Nations resolutions he stands in breach of are there for a purpose. . . . You would think with the debate going on in the last few weeks, it was somehow us who were in breach of the United Nations resolutions and Saddam who was the one being compliant.[64]

A more articulate and forceful ally the U.S. would not have. A few days later, speaking at Camp David, Prime Minister Blair disabused any notion he was not with President Bush on Iraq when he further stated, "The policy of inaction is not a policy we can responsibly subscribe to."[65]

The day after the anniversary of 11 September, President Bush made his case against Iraq to the United Nations General Assembly. The tenor of his speech was that ousting Saddam Hussein from power, if he would not comply with UN disarmament resolutions and inspection orders, was an effort to vindicate the UN as much as it was an effort to protect the free world. He opened by stating, "After generations of deceitful dictators and broken treaties and squandered lives, we've dedicated ourselves to standards of human dignity shared by all and to a system of security defended by all. Today, these standards and this security are challenged."[66]

President Bush continued:

Twelve years ago, Iraq invaded Kuwait without provocation. And the regime's forces were poised to continue their march to seize other countries and their resources. Had Saddam Hussein been appeased instead of stopped, he would have endangered the peace and stability of the world. Yet this aggression was stopped by the might of coalition forces and the will of the United Nations.

To suspend hostilities, to spare himself, Iraq's dictator accepted a series of commitments. The terms were clear to him and to all, and he agreed to prove he is complying with every one of those obligations. He has proven instead only his contempt for the United Nations and for all his pledges. By breaking every pledge, by his deceptions and by his cruelties, Saddam Hussein has made the case against himself.

President Bush then recited the UN resolutions in which Saddam Hussein was in breach, including the sanctions provision that allowed Hussein to use oil revenues to buy food for the people of Iraq. "Saddam Hussein has subverted this program," he said, "working around the sanctions to buy missile technology and military materials. He blames the suffering of Iraq's people on the United Nations, even as he uses his oil wealth to build lavish palaces for himself and to buy arms for his country."

The president further stated:

Delegates to the General Assembly, we have been more than patient. We've tried sanctions. We've tried the carrot of oil for food and the stick of coalition military strikes. But Saddam Hussein has defied all these efforts and continues to develop weapons of mass destruction. The first time we may be completely certain he has nuclear weapons is when, God forbid, he uses one. We owe it to all our citizens to do everything in our power to prevent that day from coming.

And he asked:

The conduct of the Iraqi regime is a threat to the authority of the United Nations and a threat to peace. Iraq has answered a decade of U.N. demands with a decade of defiance. All the world now faces a test, and the United Nations a difficult and defining moment. Are Security Council resolutions to be honored and enforced or cast aside without consequence? Will the United Nations serve the purpose of its founding or will it be irrelevant?[67]

IV. The Politics of War

Back at home, the president sent a request to Congress on 19 September to authorize the use of force against Iraq, and he dispatched Secretaries Powell and Rumsfeld to make the case on Capitol Hill in person. The draft resolution stated, "The president is authorized to use all means that he determines to be appropriate, including force, in order to enforce . . . United Nations Security Council resolutions . . . defend the national security interests of the United States against the threat posed by Iraq, and restore international peace and security in the region."[68]

There was actually little initial dissent from most Democrats and Republicans on Capitol Hill upon receipt of this authorization request.

What Democratic leaders signaled was that they would likely change some of the wording to make it more specific and less wide ranging, beyond Iraq. The language of "restore international peace and security in the region" was deemed too universal; the senators believed they could be writing a blank check for war against countries beyond Iraq. "We are interested and determined to keep the focus on Iraq, not on Iran or other countries in the region that also pose a threat to the United States," said Democratic Senate Majority Leader Tom Daschle. Senator Biden of the Foreign Relations Committee stated, "I'm sure the president isn't specifically asking us for unilateral authority to move against Syria or Lebanon if there's not peace on the Lebanese border. So what does it mean?"[69]

It was clear there would be a resolution, but what that resolution would say was to be debated so that it would be circumscribed to Iraq.

And while many would say the administration's increasing impatience with Iraq, if not the president's bellicose rhetoric, was dividing America and shaking the alliances it had formed abroad, there was no shortage of intemperate rhetoric from the American left. The previous year, Republican Senator Jim Jeffords of Vermont had left the Republican Party for reasons that were not entirely explicable. In announcing he would move from the Republican Party, become an independent, and caucus with the Democrats, he had stated, "I understand that many people are more conservative than I am, and they form the Republican Party. Given the changing nature of the national party, it has become a struggle for our leaders to deal with me and for me to deal with them."[70] His move delivered to the Democrats a one-seat majority. His move had perplexed many in his party who could not quite understand what was so different in the Republican Party of which he had been a member for years. Was the party of Ronald Reagan more liberal than the party of George W. Bush? Were the pro-life and lower tax rate planks in the party platform new? The answer to both questions was no.

Nevertheless, with a mere one-seat majority in the Senate, the left looked outside Washington for further leadership, and former Vice President Al Gore was happy to take up that microphone for them, perhaps leading to another run at the presidency, perhaps giving the left a voice it felt it did not have with Democratic senators hanging on to power in Washington by the skin of their teeth.

And so, in a well-publicized speech at the Commonwealth Club in San Francisco in September 2002, Al Gore delivered. He took on the case for war against Saddam Hussein full bore by beginning his indictment of it, saying, "The president is proclaiming a new, uniquely American right to preemptively attack whomsoever he may deem represents a potential future threat."[71]*

Still, Gore continued, "Iraq's search for weapons of mass destruction has proven impossible to completely deter, and we should assume that it will continue for as long as Saddam is in power."[72] But the language that struck the hardest was one sentence he delivered in discussing the legal and moral case for preemptive war: "Two decades ago, the Soviet Union claimed the right to launch a preemptive war in Afghanistan, we properly encouraged and then supported the resistance movement, which a decade later succeeded in defeating the Soviet army's efforts."[73] In so saying, Al Gore had put on par America's efforts to take out one of the world's worst dictators and abusers of human rights with the Soviet Union. In his view, President Bush's case for war against Saddam Hussein was equivalent to the wholly unjustifiable Soviet invasion of Afghanistan in 1979 at the height of the Cold War. America was little different than its worst enemy, and by implication, George W. Bush (Al Gore's domestic political opponent in 2000) was little better than Leonid Brezhnev (America's international rival). Little, it would seem, could have been more divisive and fray our domestic political consensus and cooperation more than such a comparison as that—two months before the congressional elections no less.**

But something actually could be more divisive—and at the most unlikely

---

* This country had gone to war against Germany in World War II, even though Germany had not attacked us at Pearl Harbor but was in league with those who, in Lincoln's phrase, would "blow out the moral lights around us." Further, it was not just President Bush who was claiming Saddam Hussein a future threat but Al Gore's own President Clinton and other nations' intelligence services. And President Bush had submitted a request to authorize the use of force against Iraq, which was pending on Capitol Hill.

** At the time of Gore's speech, I took to the pages of the *Wall Street Journal* to pen an op-ed claiming this speech of Al Gore's would mark the beginning of the end of his political career. Whether I was correct or not remains to be seen: he has not run for office again, but he has remained a very popular figure, especially on and with the American left.

of places, a memorial service. U.S. Senator Paul Wellstone of Minnesota was one of the more liberal Democrats in Congress and had staked out his political career in the Senate as a sincere left-of-center Democrat. Tragically, he died in a plane crash in Minnesota in late October on his way to a political debate. His memorial service was attended and watched by many. Even those who had disagreed with him vociferously, respected his sincerity and lack of artifice so often seen in too many other politicians. Agree or disagree with him, Paul Wellstone was the real deal. His memorial service was not—it became a highly charged partisan rally that so shocked even the rough-hewn governor, former professional wrestler Jesse Ventura, that he walked out in the middle of it.[74] The memorial service was so partisan that when Republican Senate Minority Leader Trent Lott walked in to pay his respects to his fallen colleague, he was booed.[75]

After attending the memorial, one liberal journalist, William Saletan, wrote, "The solemnity of death and the grace of Midwestern humor are overshadowed tonight by the angry piety of populism."[76] He continued to describe the event this way:

> As the evening's speakers proceed, it becomes clear that to them, honoring Wellstone's legacy is all about winning the election. Repeating the words of Wellstone's son, the assembly shouts, "We will win! We will win!" Rick Kahn, a friend of Wellstone's, urges everyone to "set aside the partisan bickering," but in the next breath he challenges several Republican senators in attendance to "honor your friend" by helping to "win this election for Paul Wellstone." What can he be thinking?[77]

If the Democratic left outside Washington thought it could start a prairie fire that would reach the Democrats in Congress and force them to stand against the impending resolution to liberate Iraq militarily, it was mistaken. The authorization to use force in Iraq passed the House in mid-October, 296–133; voting yes were 81 Democrats and 215 Republicans.[78] In the Democratic-controlled Senate, the vote was 77 to 23.[79] Among the prominent Democrats voting for the resolution were House Minority Leader

Dick Gephardt, Pennsylvania Congressman Jack Murtha, and Maryland Congressman Steny Hoyer; U.S. Senators Hillary Clinton, Joe Biden, Dianne Feinstein, John Kerry, Harry Reid, and John Edwards; and Senate Majority Leader Tom Daschle.[80]

Among the Democrats who had voted for the resolution, there was fairly unanimous agreement about the danger that Saddam Hussein had posed. On the eve of his vote, John Kerry had stated, "I will be voting to give the President of the United States the authority to use force—if necessary—to disarm Saddam Hussein because I believe that a deadly arsenal of weapons of mass destruction in his hands is a real and grave threat to our security."[81] On the eve of her vote, Senator Clinton said:

> In the four years since the inspectors left, intelligence reports show that Saddam Hussein has worked to rebuild his chemical and biological weapons stock, his missile delivery capability, and his nuclear program. He has also given aid, comfort, and sanctuary to terrorists, including al Qaeda members. . . . It is clear, however, that if left unchecked, Saddam Hussein will continue to increase his capacity to wage biological and chemical warfare, and will keep trying to develop nuclear weapons.[82]

And on the eve of his vote, the Senate Intelligence Committee's Jay Rockefeller declared:

> There is unmistakable evidence that Saddam Hussein is working aggressively to develop nuclear weapons and will likely have nuclear weapons within the next five years. . . . We also should remember we have always underestimated the progress Saddam has made in development of weapons of mass destruction. . . . I do believe that Iraq poses an imminent threat.[83]

Of course not all of the Democrats believed in ousting Saddam Hussein—several thought he could still be contained, even though he was not coming clean on his weapons of mass destruction. And others, like a then little-known state senator in Illinois named Barack Obama, had given a speech at an antiwar rally in Illinois. The antiwar crowd of about one thousand people in Chicago was led by Rev. Jesse Jackson as the audience sang songs like "Give Peace a Chance" and held rally signs such as "War Is Not an Option."[84] Barack was not the main speaker that day, but sometimes little-known speakers from Illinois can have larger ripple effects down the line, to a time not immediately seen. That day, 2 October 2002, State Senator Obama told the crowd he was not opposed to all wars and would have supported World War II and the Civil War, but

> what I am opposed to is a dumb war. What I am opposed to is a rash war. What I am opposed to is the cynical attempt by Richard Perle and Paul Wolfowitz and other armchair, weekend warriors in this administration to shove their own ideological agendas down our throats, irrespective of the costs in lives lost and in hardships borne.
>
> What I am opposed to is the attempt by political hacks like Karl Rove to distract us from a rise in the uninsured, a rise in the poverty rate, a drop in the median income—to distract us from corporate scandals and a stock market that has just gone through the worst month since the Great Depression. That's what I'm opposed to. A dumb war. A rash war. A war based not on reason but on passion, not on principle but on politics. Now let me be clear—I suffer no illusions about Saddam Hussein. He is a brutal man. A ruthless man. A man who butchers his own people to secure his own power. He has repeatedly defied UN resolutions, thwarted UN inspection teams, developed chemical and biological weapons, and coveted nuclear capacity. He's a bad guy. The world, and the Iraqi people, would be better off without him.
>
> But I also know that Saddam poses no imminent and direct threat to the United States, or to his neighbors, that the Iraqi economy is in shambles, that the Iraqi military [is] a fraction of its former strength, and that in concert with the international community he can be contained until, in the way of all petty dictators, he falls away into the dustbin of history.[85]

Still, for all the anger the antiwar movement was showing at the time, focusing on administration officials like Karl Rove (the president's political advisor) and semiofficial advisors like Richard Perle (a former Reagan Defense Department official, now an advisor to the Pentagon and a fellow at the American Enterprise Institute think tank), there was one other question that seemed unanswered: Why put the blame for ousting the then worst dictator in the world on just Republicans? Were not the majority of Democrats voting to authorize the use of force? Did not President Clinton and his national security team in 1998 and 1999 make it U.S. policy to liberate Iraq and warn of the dangers of Saddam Hussein? Did not intelligence agencies from Britain, Germany, Israel, and other countries come to the same conclusion that ours did about Saddam Hussein's stockpile and interests?

Many on the left would blame many on the right for angling to oust Saddam Hussein from even before 11 September 2001. There was truth in this charge; many conservatives did want Hussein gone. They thought he was a danger before 11 September, just as Bill Clinton and his team had thought. As early as January 1998—several months before Clinton signed the Iraq Liberation Act—many of us, including Bill Clinton's former CIA director Jim Woolsey, had signed an open letter to President Clinton. The letter, organized by Bill Kristol and his Project for a New American Century (a small think tank he had formed), said in part:

> We urge you to seize that opportunity, and to enunciate a new strategy that would secure the interests of the U.S. and our friends and allies around the world. That strategy should aim, above all, at the removal of Saddam Hussein's regime from power. We stand ready to offer our full support in this difficult but necessary endeavor.[86]

The left made great hay of the fact that several signatories of that letter had ended up in the Bush administration, including Paul Wolfowitz, Donald Rumsfeld, John Bolton, Elliott Abrams, and Richard Armitage. Richard Perle had not gone directly into the administration but did head an outside advisory committee to the Pentagon and, given his prolific writing and passion on the issue, was seen by the left as one of the longtime ring leaders to oust Hussein from power.*

While the left tried to show some conspiracy about this letter and its signers, it was open for the world to see, and not one of the signers was embarrassed about the letter; it said nothing less than what others had been saying, including Democrats on Capitol Hill. Moreover, once the Bush administration had taken office, it was clear to all within the administration that at least one signer of the letter had become one of the most cautious insiders about using force to oust Hussein, Deputy Secretary of State Richard Armitage.

It should also be noted there was not a unanimous consensus on the right in America about the use of force to oust Hussein. Many prominent Republicans (or erstwhile Republicans, as was the case with Pat Buchanan) either were opposed to taking on Saddam Hussein militarily or kept their counsel rather quiet, neither supporting the administration's efforts nor opposing them in public. Jack Kemp, for example, was vocally opposed to the use of force to liberate Iraq. Jeane Kirkpatrick said little either way in public. And a handful of others were skeptical that Iraq needed to be dealt with militarily. While not opposing the liberation of Iraq, former Reagan official and prolific writer and thinker Michael Ledeen, also at the American Enterprise Institute, was fairly quiet on Iraq and argued that Iran was the bigger threat.

At the same time, some on the left were very much in favor of and outspoken in their support for ousting Hussein with military force, like the author and columnist Christopher Hitchens. And while not exactly men of the traditional far left (as Hitchens might have been categorized), Prime Minister Tony Blair of Great Britain was the leader of the liberal Labour Party there, and U.S. Senator Joe Lieberman had a liberal voting record in the Senate and had been Al Gore's running mate for vice president on the Democratic ticket two years before. Some of these traditional liberals were several of the most articulate spokesmen for the ouster of Saddam Hussein, arguably even more articulate and forceful in their rhetoric than President Bush.

---

* I, too, was a signatory to the letter.

V. Midterm Elections and Troubles on the Right

During this time, the president remained highly popular. He hit the campaign trail for Republicans in Congress. The country was now at war, the economy was coming back to life, out of its recession from the previous year, and Republicans were arguing for more tax cuts. In addition, Democrats had not made a good showing of how they differed with the president or the Republicans' policy, and the country was gearing up for another front on the war on terrorism. That concatenation of issues and events spelled trouble for the Democrats in their efforts to decisively take back the Senate and increase their numbers in the House (where they were still the minority party) in the midterm elections in November 2002. And they lost. The Senate picked up two more Republican seats, putting the Republican Party back in charge there; the House races saw a pickup of eight seats for the Republicans.[87]

And do you recall the Senate seat in Minnesota that was open due to Paul Wellstone's death and the memorial service cum political rally for Wellstone? Former Democratic Vice President Walter Mondale ran for Wellstone's seat that November but was defeated by Republican Norm Coleman, the former mayor of St. Paul. *Time* magazine reported on all this after the November elections this way:

> A backlash against the politically charged service almost certainly helped Norm Coleman beat Walter Mondale for Wellstone's Minnesota Senate seat. And a private poll by Bill Clinton's former pollster, Mark Penn, suggests the service backfired on Democrats nationally as well.
>
> Penn found that 68% of voters knew about the service, a high awareness of an event broadcast live nationally only on C-SPAN. What's more, 49% of voters said the service made them less likely to vote for a Democrat, and 67% of independents said they felt that way.[88]

Not all was immediately happy for the GOP after its November election victory, however. At another small event, newly minted Republican Senate Majority Leader Trent Lott would create national headlines and controversy in a birthday toast to one-hundred-year-old South Carolina Senator Strom Thurmond. Thurmond was a legend in politics—in South Carolina and nationally—and had had a colorful career. A one-time segregationist and Democrat, he ultimately had changed his views as well as his party, but as far back as 1948, he ran for the presidency on a states rights and segregationist platform. In toasting his birthday in December 2002, Lott said, "When Strom Thurmond ran for president, we voted for him. We're proud of it. And if the rest of the country had followed our lead, we wouldn't have had all these problems over the years, either."[89]

The story and quote were picked up by bloggers, who were expanding political debate in the nation while also gaining influence in the public square. Bloggers had the ability to report what the mainstream didn't, couldn't, or just thought plain unnewsworthy. But soon enough the mainstream press did pick up on the quote, and it left people wondering just what Senator Lott had meant: Did he really think voting for a segregationist in 1948 was a good idea? Had Thurmond been elected in 1948—as opposed to Harry Truman—would the country truly not "have had all these problems over the years"? What problems was he talking about? And why resurrect a part of a man's past that even that man had long ago dispensed with? Lott had tried to explain that he was just being kind to the aging senator, but still, the point of historical reference was troubling. And as some historians had pointed out—even historians who were conservative or Republican—Senator Lott had a long history of mixed statements and views about the pre–civil rights efforts of the South, correcting its past so valiantly as it did.*

It was not a pleasant moment in Republican circles, even as Lott apologized and tried to explain his comments, at one point even consenting to an interview on Black Entertainment Television where he, incredibly, stated he supported affirmative action. Lott, for the good of the party and upon not

---

* Historian Al Felzenberg had written, "In 1984, in Biloxi, Mississippi, deep in the heart of the old Confederacy, the future Senate majority leader Trent Lott declared that 'the spirit of Jefferson Davis' now lives in the Republican party. It's a mystery quite how the party of Abraham Lincoln, born in the moral outrage of the great northern abolitionists, could become in the minds of some of its most visible modern leaders the party of Davis." I, and other Republicans, had also criticized Lott for his statement about Thurmond.

a few demands from within it, stepped down as majority leader. Journalist John Podhoretz called Lott's "the Internet's first scalp," a sign that a new era was coming along with the new year.[90]

Before the year closed, however, the country's largest church, the Catholic church, delivered the conclusion to a scandal that had rocked the nation. Reports had been surfacing about a number of Catholic priests who had abused young boys in their parishes. The focus of this scandal was in Boston, where Cardinal Bernard Law had presided and reportedly had, along with others, chosen "repeatedly to keep in ministry priests who had sexually molested children and adolescents."[91]

The problem was not, however, exclusive to Boston. It reached throughout the nation, from Pennsylvania to Florida to California and many parishes in between. But given Boston's especially strong Catholic population and culture, and Cardinal Law's international reputation, he became the emblem of it. In all, throughout 2002, more than three hundred Catholic priests across the nation would resign or be forced from their ministry for this very un-Catholic and illegal behavior.[92] Commissions were established to investigate what went wrong and what the church could and should do to clean up its act and make recompense to the victims. My brother, Bob Bennett, was called on to chair the investigative committee of the National Review Board of the Catholic Church to examine the problem.* By the middle of December 2002, Cardinal Law resigned, and the church as a whole would begin a process of self-examination and, equally important, recuperation for the purpose of its important work and mission.

VI. Eyes on Iraq

The year 2003 began with one major issue on everyone's mind: Iraq. The Democrats on Capitol Hill had given the go-ahead, the Republicans were now united in their national majority, and most of the country (and much of the world) had understood Saddam Hussein to be nothing short of a

---

* And I, who was as disgusted by these scandals as anyone, to say the least, had been speaking out rather strongly against the church for the coverups and had publicly called upon Cardinal Law, a friend, to resign.

menace—and an unstable and threatening one at that. There was one major bow to tie, however, before the U.S. could act: the United Nations.

In late January, President Bush delivered his State of the Union address and commenced with an update on the progress his administration had made on several domestic issues, including the recovering economy and his 2001 tax cut, saying, "Some might call this a good record. I call it a good start."[93] He promised to work on expanded tax cuts, Medicare reform, energy independence, and the problem of drug addiction; he asked the Congress to ban the practice of partial-birth abortion; and he spoke up for a new initiative of his to help curb the scourge of AIDS in Africa, seeking $15 billion to do so.[94]

Then he turned to an update on the war on terrorism. We'd delivered heavy blows to Al Qaeda by then, having arrested in excess of three thousand suspected terrorists across the globe. But that was prelude. Bush then moved to Iraq. He started by saying that America had urged the United Nations to act, to demand Iraq's disarming, and from there he laid out the case for U.S. military involvement:

> Twelve years ago, Saddam Hussein faced the prospect of being the last casualty in a war he had started and lost. To spare himself, he agreed to disarm of all weapons of mass destruction. For the next 12 years, he systematically violated that agreement. He pursued chemical, biological and nuclear weapons even while inspectors were in his country. Nothing to date has restrained him from his pursuit of these weapons: not economic sanctions, not isolation from the civilized world, not even cruise missile strikes on his military facilities. . . .
>
> It is up to Iraq to show exactly where it is hiding its banned weapons, lay those weapons out for the world to see and destroy them as directed. Nothing like this has happened.[95]

President Bush detailed other depredations taking place in Iraq, as well as other intelligence about weapons of mass destruction. He said, among other indictments, "The British government has learned that Saddam Hussein recently sought significant quantities of uranium from Africa."[96]

These would later be known as the famous "sixteen words," to which we shall return.

When it came to taking the case against Saddam Hussein to the UN, President Bush asked Secretary of State Colin Powell to do that—he was not only one of the most credible people to serve in the president's cabinet, but he was also one of the most credible Americans, period. It also made sense for the secretary of state, responsible as he was for relations with other countries and for foreign policy generally, to address the UN. Powell readily agreed.[97] President Bush and his senior staff had done all they could to marshal as much evidence as possible against Saddam Hussein, in making up their own minds, persuading the public, and persuading other nations. In December 2002 when the president wanted one more go-round on the intelligence regarding Saddam Hussein's arsenal and pursuits, he asked CIA Director George Tenet, "George, how confident are you?" Tenet replied, "Don't worry, it's a slam dunk"; Tenet would say "slam dunk" three times in that meeting.[98]

Just days before the president's State of the Union, Chief UN Weapons Inspector Hans Blix had testified to the UN that Iraq simply would not come clean: "Iraq appears not to have come to genuine acceptance—not even today—of the disarmament which was demanded of it and which it needs to carry out to win the confidence of the world and live in peace."[99] And Secretary Powell had said, "Time is running out. We've made it very clear from the very beginning that we would not allow the process of inspections to string out forever."[100]

On 5 February 2003, Secretary Powell made his case to the UN, and the world was watching. He started his case as a prosecutor in a courtroom:

> Last November 8, this Council passed Resolution 1441 by a unanimous vote. The purpose of that resolution was to disarm Iraq of its weapons of mass destruction. Iraq had already been found guilty of material breach of its obligations stretching back over 16 previous resolutions and 12 years.
>
> Resolution 1441 was not dealing with an innocent party, but a regime this Council has repeatedly convicted over the years.

Resolution 1441 gave Iraq one last chance, one last chance to come into compliance or to face serious consequences. No Council member present and voting on that day had any illusions about the nature and intent of the resolution or what serious consequences meant if Iraq did not comply.[101]

He then played audio of Saddam Hussein's generals admitting to hiding information about their WMD program and detailed the Iraqi government's efforts at obfuscating what international inspectors authorized by the UN had demanded, saying about a report Iraq had submitted: "You saw the result. Dr. Blix pronounced the 12,200-page [Iraqi] declaration rich in volume but poor in information and practically devoid of new evidence. Could any member of this Council honestly rise in defense of this false declaration?"[102] He went on to show satellite imagery of WMD production and concealment, detailed more intelligence, and said, "Ladies and gentlemen, these are not assertions. These are facts corroborated by many sources, some of them sources of the intelligence services of other countries."[103]

He noted the threat from Saddam Hussein's biological weapons program and said, "There can be no doubt that Saddam Hussein has biological weapons and the capability to rapidly produce more, many more. And he has the ability to dispense these lethal poisons and diseases in ways that can cause massive death and destruction." He spoke of Iraq's chemical weapons and its nuclear ambitions and its ballistic missile capabilities. He then turned to the already present issue of Iraq and terrorism:

Iraq and terrorism go back decades. Baghdad trains Palestine Liberation Front members in small arms and explosives. Saddam uses the Arab Liberation Front to funnel money to the families of Palestinian suicide bombers in order to prolong the Intifadah. And it's no secret that Saddam's own intelligence service was involved in dozens of attacks or attempted assassinations in the 1990s.

But what I want to bring to your attention today is the potentially much more sinister nexus between Iraq and the al-Qaida [sic] terrorist network, a nexus that combines classic terrorist organizations and modern methods of murder. Iraq today harbors a deadly terrorist network headed by Abu Musab al-Zarqawi an associate and collaborator of Osama bin Laden and his al-Qaeda [sic] lieutenants.[104]

Secretary Powell spent further time linking Iraq to international terrorism and concluded:

> The United States will not and cannot run that risk for the American people. Leaving Saddam Hussein in possession of weapons of mass destruction for a few more months or years is not an option, not in a post–September 11 world.
>
> My colleagues, over three months ago, this Council recognized that Iraq continued to pose a threat to international peace and security, and that Iraq had been and remained in material breach of its disarmament obligations. . . .
>
> My colleagues, we have an obligation to our citizens. We have an obligation to this body to see that our resolutions are complied with. We wrote 1441 not in order to go to war. We wrote 1441 to try to preserve the peace. We wrote 1441 to give Iraq one last chance. . . .
>
> Iraq is not, so far, taking that one last chance.
>
> We must not shrink from whatever is ahead of us. We must not fail in our duty and our responsibility to the citizens of the countries that are represented by this body.[105]

To those inclined to think Saddam Hussein had to go, Secretary Powell's case was the real "slam dunk."

When the administration realized it would not be able to receive another UN Security Council vote, based mostly on the immovability of France's and Russia's leadership, the U.S. and Great Britain knew they were going to go into Iraq without the UN's ultimate blessing. *So be it*, many here thought. *The UN cares about borders, not people.* That sentiment was not unfounded. The UN had proved useless in preventing terrorism or war against any democracy, and it had stood by any number of dictators throughout its history. Accusations of UN failure mounted on talk radio, conservative publications, and blogs. And public sentiment was increasingly augmented by many scholars who argued that the notion of "anticipatory self-defense" was a fully legal doctrine. The dean of Princeton's Woodrow Wilson School of Public and International Affairs, Anne-Marie Slaughter, had taken to the pages of the *New York Times* to argue that while an explicit UN sanction was a debatable proposition, the UN "cannot be a straitjacket, preventing nations from defending themselves or pursuing what they perceive to be their vital national security interests."[106] With France blocking a UN authorization, Americans started changing the name of "French Fries" to "Freedom Fries."

But not everyone in America was supportive of going into Iraq without another UN resolution—or going into Iraq at all. There was still an antiwar movement both here and abroad, and one big surprise would come from a trio of Americans in London in March 2003. The Dixie Chicks were three very talented female country music singers—and as popular and prolific in country music as any other top group or other performer. The three women hailed from Texas, and in a concert in London the lead singer, Natalie Maines, had told the audience there, "Just so you know, we're ashamed the president of the United States is from Texas."[107] Her comments shocked on several levels.

As a matter of general political conversation, Americans usually refrained from criticizing their president while abroad, especially in times of war. But even more shocking was that the country music audience was generally a culturally, if not politically, conservative audience—supportive of the military, supportive of the president, and again, all the more so in a time of war. If there was one group thought of as "red state voters," one would be hard-pressed to identify them without including or thinking of country music fans. One commentator at the time had said this statement by the Texas trio was the greatest example he could think of when it came to turning on, or attacking, one's very base of support. Indeed, the Dixie Chicks would remain unmoved and maintain their opposition to the war and to the president and later even record a song about it. And, indeed, they soon faded from the fame and popularity they had once known, with their songs played less and less frequently on country radio.

Meanwhile, as the lead-up to the confrontation with Iraq was taking place, the hunt for other al Qaeda operatives had not been ignored. The U.S. was fighting a multifront war already, and in the first week of March 2003, Americans were reminded of that with the biggest capture of an al Qaeda terrorist yet: Khalid Sheikh Mohammed in Pakistan. Mohammed, the uncle of Ramzi Yousef (who was responsible for the 1993 World Trade Center bombing), was the mastermind of the 11 September attacks in 2001 and the most senior Al Qaeda leader after bin Laden and Ayman al-Zawahiri. "Mohammed has been at the vortex of every major operation going back a decade," said one terrorism expert, "from the first bombing of the World Trade Center to 9/11 to the most recent incidents."[108] When pictures of him were shown upon his arrest, the Western world had a pretty good laugh: he was shown in a dirty T-shirt too small to cover his chest, and he had unkempt hair that reminded people of something between John Belushi and *Seinfeld*'s Kramer. He looked like nothing more than an average skid-row drunk. Nevertheless, he was one of the world's most dangerous men, and with the help of Pakistani intelligence services, America now had him.

How the United States captured Khalid Sheikh Mohammed would not be without some degree of controversy in later years, but it would appear to have taken place with a mixture of intelligence surveillance using National Security Agency cell phone monitoring, and intelligence gathered from other al Qaeda operatives the government had captured. These men were interrogated using what intelligence agencies had labeled "enhanced interrogation" techniques (procedures on which Intelligence Committee members of Congress had been briefed as early as 2002).*[109] Controversial or not—Khalid Sheikh Mohammed was responsible for the deaths of thousands of Americans, and America had him.

But for now, Iraq was the focus of military attention. On 17 March

---

* Among those briefed by the CIA were Representatives Nancy Pelosi and Jane Harman of the Intelligence Committee. The *Washington Post* would later report that during these briefings, which described such techniques as waterboarding, objections were not raised, and the sense of the congressmen briefed was in the form of a question to the CIA: Were the methods "tough enough"? It has also become pretty clear that the 2002 capture and enhanced interrogation of other Al Qaeda operatives, like Abu Zubaydah, helped identify and lead us to Khalid Sheikh Mohammed as well as thwart a second wave of post-9/11 attacks. See, for example, Marc A. Thiessen, "The CIA's Questioning Worked," *Washington Post*, 21 April 2009.

2003, President Bush took to the national airwaves in an address from the Oval Office and stated that while the UN would not act, "a broad coalition" was forming behind U.S. efforts, and that even several Middle East countries had done their part, urging Saddam Hussein to leave office. The president then stated, "Saddam Hussein and his sons must leave Iraq within 48 hours. Their refusal to do so will result in military conflict, commenced at a time of our choosing."[110]

Two days later, with Saddam Hussein remaining defiantly attached to power, the U.S. and its allies, known as "a coalition of the willing," launched Operation Iraqi Freedom.

VII. The War Begins

Secretary of Defense Donald Rumsfeld, from the outset of early 2001, had been working to "transform" the Pentagon and U.S. military so that they could operate with lighter footprints, less bureaucracy, and less manpower in their foreign operations. Transformation would convert the typical military uses of "brute strength" with "special forces, high technology, and more creative war plans."[111]

The beginnings of the transformation were under way when the U.S. went into Afghanistan, and now, with Iraq, the phrase that had pleased the nation about how the U.S. would liberate Iraq with a lighter force than was used to liberate Kuwait was "shock and awe." While several hundred thousand troops participated in the first Gulf War to liberate Kuwait, the Pentagon—under Secretary Rumsfeld's leadership and the president's sign-off—debated the force numbers necessary for the liberation of Iraq. And indeed, America did go into Iraq with several hundred thousand troops less than were deployed in the first Gulf War. While some generals, most famously Eric Shinseki, the U.S. Army Chief of Staff, had argued that the military would need a much larger number of troops, others argued that the smaller force was adequate and, importantly, would not appear like an occupying force. Secretary Rumsfeld would maintain he and the president ordered the number of troops the generals on the ground had requested.

As the U.S. and its allies entered Iraq, most Democrats were still supporting the president, but many people across the nation and in other countries were protesting. One former public official looking to the 2004 presidential election was becoming louder in his opposition to the use of force and in his criticism of fellow Democrats who had not challenged the president or the gear up to war: "This is not Iraq, where doubters and dissenters are punished or silenced. . . . Based on enduring principles of peace and justice, concerned Americans should continue to speak out."[112] Few would think, given the protests on campuses and in public parks, anyone was being punished or silenced. With the Internet and other newer and less-expensive access to information and communication technology, dissent and protest in America never seemed to be at a higher watermark. But former Vermont Governor Howard Dean was right about one thing: more elected Democrats in Washington had supported the liberation of Iraq than not.

Many antiwar protesters would argue that it was a "war for oil" or that America did not have the same international coalition and goodwill of other countries as it had in the Gulf War. The truth was, America had almost as many countries supporting its efforts as in the Gulf War—thirty-one as opposed to thirty-four in the earlier war; in both wars troops from Great Britain, Poland, and Australia went right into Iraq alongside American troops. And the initial invasion of Iraq and ouster of Saddam Hussein and his government went as well as anyone could have expected. Indeed, many Americans even got a chuckle out of the daily briefings from Iraq's information minister, Muhammad Saeed al-Sahhaf, who would deliver the news from Iraq's side of the war—clearly lying as his government around him was crumbling and running for the hills and caves. Nicknamed "Baghdad Bob," al-Sahhaf would say such things as Americans "are going to surrender or be burned in their tanks. They will surrender, it is they who will surrender," and he held one press conference stating American troops were nowhere near Baghdad when our troops were, in reality, just a few hundred yards from his very press briefing.[113]

By early April, Baghdad was in coalition hands, and many Iraqis, as many coalition partners watching from abroad, were further buoyed when television crews showed Iraqis tearing down posters of Saddam Hussein, throwing shoes at his images, and with the help of the U.S. Marines, toppling a huge statue of him in one of Baghdad's central squares.[114]

At the beginning of May, President Bush famously copiloted a navy jet onto the USS *Abraham Lincoln* off the coast of California to deliver a nationwide address, declaring, "Major combat operations in Iraq have ended," to cheering troops on board the *Lincoln*.[115] It was the first time a U.S. president had landed on an aircraft carrier by plane. And President Bush, who was a fighter pilot in the National Guard, could not have been happier about the perfect landing or the announcement he was making. In the backdrop of his statement to the troops (and the world) was hanging a huge banner that read, "Mission Accomplished."

But there was much more "mission" ahead.

Five

In War and Culture: A Clash of Values, A New Media, A New Election

The country was in the midst of war, and Iraq and Afghanistan were the major battlefields. The remarkably articulate British Prime Minister Tony Blair addressed the American people to buck them up in the cause of the war against terrorism. Meanwhile, the left flexed its muscles with a populist filmmaker and anti-Bush hatred began again, while the united good will in America that followed 9/11 had disappeared. The warfront in Iraq became more and more unpopular and politicized, especially as Weapons of Mass Destruction were not found. In short order, Washington experts were taking to the papers, the airwaves, and the publishing industry to question the wisdom of the preparedness for and response to 9/11, as well as the wisdom and effort to take on and take out Saddam Hussein. The left and right in America would see new power and persuasion abilities with the Internet, especially in the blogosphere, and another scalp would be taken. In the American political sweepstakes, the presidential election of 2004 would take place and the first Catholic since John Kennedy was nominated to head a major ticket. Values issues—from media bias to the definition of life to marriage initiatives to patriotism—came roaring back in this election as hadn't been seen in sixteen years.

I. Big and Complicated

Massachusetts Democratic Senator John Kerry, who was gearing up for a run for the presidency the next year, started voicing his opposition to the president and trying to change the conversation about what was a military victory: "The president's going out to an aircraft carrier to give a speech far out at sea . . . while countless numbers of Americans are frightened stiff about the economy at home."[1] And soon there would be other questions to be raised, such as where were Saddam Hussein and those closest to him, his two sons? And where were the stockpiles of WMDs?

Not all liberals were angling against the administration, however. British Prime Minister Tony Blair stood with the United States from the moment the planes crashed into the Twin Towers, and in July he was invited to address Congress. His speech was meant to reassure and console Americans—just as the words of Churchill had done in World War II:

> As Britain knows, all predominant power seems for a time invincible, but, in fact, it is transient. The question is: What do you leave behind? And what you can bequeath to this anxious world is the light of liberty.
>
> And I know it's hard on America, and in some small corner of this vast country, out in Nevada or Idaho or these places I've never been to, but always wanted to go. I know out there there's a guy getting on with his life, perfectly happily, minding his own business, saying to you, the political leaders of this country, "Why me? And why us? And why America?"
>
> And the only answer is, "Because destiny put you in this place in history, in this moment in time, and the task is yours to do."[2]

Tony Blair was a godsend to Americans looking for international kudos for having liberated Iraq of its insane tyranny, even if there were still questions to be asked about how long the United States would be there and what it would find there.

On the domestic front, President Bush was using his political capital and his congressional majority to make good on other promises and priorities. He had signed another tax cut as passed by Congress, and in November he had signed the partial-birth abortion ban that Congress passed and his predecessor had vetoed, pleasing his political base and the traditional concerns of conservatives at home.

Still, questions about Iraq persisted. Bob Schieffer of CBS News spoke for many when he said, "It's now clear the job is bigger and more complicated than officials expected."[3] Even though two world-famous Palestinian terrorists were found in Iraq—Abu Nidal (one of the most famous terrorists of the 1970s and '80s) and Mohammed Abbas (a longtime associate of Yasser Arafat who masterminded the *Achille Lauro* hijacking)—and American troops had killed Hussein's two sons (known for their barbarism among the Iraqi populace as well as their rape chambers), several problems in Iraq were beginning to make people nervous.

If reminders of terrorism in Iraq were needed beyond the violence inflicted on the coalition's military, Americans were shocked to see a Daniel Pearl–like video released of a Pennsylvania communications expert and civilian, Nick Berg, who had traveled to Iraq on his own to do what he could to help the cause there and perhaps even start a business. The video showed Iraqi terrorists beheading the twenty-five-year-old Berg. Terrorists had also blown up the UN offices in Baghdad, killing the UN envoy and others there. And the military coalition, as well as Iraqi allies it was training, was facing shootings and car bombings in other areas of Iraq. It was known that Abu Musab al-Zarqawi was in Iraq, but most wanted to see the final end of the long psychodrama of Iraq by seeing the capture of Saddam Hussein and the cache of weapons he had been amassing.

President Bush had appointed L. Paul Bremer to run the Coalition Provisional Authority in Iraq, effectively becoming the head of the civil administration or proconsul there. He would deliver regular briefings as he tried to organize a new civilian and military leadership made up of Iraqis. For news on the ground there, Bremer was the spokesman.* One of Bremer's first major orders was the "de-Baathification" of the Iraqi leadership (removing

---

* "Jerry," as he is known to his acquaintances, went to Iraq with great promise. He was a respected voice of analysis about terrorism in the U.S. media, and I had gotten to know him fairly well through my project Americans for Victory Over Terrorism. A clean-cut, well-dressed man of great learning, who was quick on his feet to address protesters and dissenters as I had witnessed him do at various conferences and joint panel appearances, he was also actually quite humble. At a quick dinner he, Jim Woolsey, my colleague Seth Leibsohn, and I were having in Los Angeles before a speaking event, the news of the day was that Woolsey was likely to be appointed the head of the Coalition Provisional Authority. When Woolsey got up to wash his hands before eating, we asked Bremer what he knew of this, and he said, "He'd be absolutely great at that job!" A few days later it was publicly announced Bremer was the actual choice.

those who had pledged their support to and affiliated with the Baath Party in Iraq) and the dismantling of the Iraqi army. It seemed to be a good idea at the time to some, but it would have consequences down the line that would serve as a major criticism against him. As one analyst put it, "Thousands suddenly found themselves not only unemployed but also alienated. Simultaneously with this order, the army was disbanded, making in effect approximately 400,000 soldiers jobless."[4]

As weapons of mass destruction were not found at anywhere near the levels Americans thought they would be, other questions were being asked from the strident political bumper stickers about being "lied" into war to whether intelligence was faulty or doctored. One major op-ed in the *New York Times* shortly after the liberation of Iraq asked the following question in its opening sentence: "Did the Bush administration manipulate intelligence about Saddam Hussein's weapons programs to justify an invasion of Iraq?"[5] The author of that piece was someone not too many people outside Washington had heard of, "Joseph C. Wilson 4th," as he identified himself. His tag line said he was the "United States ambassador to Gabon from 1992 to 1995" and "an international business consultant."[6]

But beyond his opening question, he had a long story to tell in his op-ed that would be much discussed soon after its summer appearance. According to Wilson in his op-ed, the vice president's office had questions about allegations that Saddam Hussein was seeking to purchase uranium from Niger. (The purpose of such uranium would be for the building of a nuclear weapon.) Wilson wrote, "I was informed by officials at the Central Intelligence Agency," and "agency officials asked if I would travel to Niger to check out the story."[7] Wilson added that he spent "eight days" in Niger "drinking sweet mint tea and meeting with dozens of people" from the government there as well as others "associated with the country's uranium business. It did not take long to conclude that it was highly doubtful that any such transaction had ever taken place."[8]

Wilson then told officials at the CIA and the State Department of his findings, or nonfindings as the case was. Given what he told the CIA and Department of State officials, he wrote how surprised he was to hear President Bush speak of "Iraqi efforts to buy uranium from Africa."[9] Recall those sixteen words from the president's State of the Union: "The British government has learned that Saddam Hussein recently sought significant quantities of uranium from Africa."

This op-ed raised a good many questions—not only about the uranium claim but also about Joe Wilson. Just who really was this former ambassador making claims that the administration had lied to the American people about the war? And how was he chosen by the administration to investigate its own intelligence? One particularly well-known columnist, the late Robert Novak of the *Washington Post* and CNN, who had supported neither the first Gulf War nor Operation Iraqi Freedom, smelled something particularly odd here and opened his Rolodex to go sniffing. Shortly thereafter, he wrote the following in his *Washington Post* column:

> Wilson never worked for the CIA, but his wife, Valerie Plame, is an agency operative on weapons of mass destruction. Two senior administration officials told me that Wilson's wife suggested sending him to Niger to investigate the Italian report. The CIA says its counterproliferation officials selected Wilson and asked his wife to reach him. "I will not answer any question about my wife," Wilson told me.[10]

Almost immediately, Wilson and others, particularly those on the left or opposed to the war, shouted, "Foul!" and argued that the administration had leaked to Novak a covert operative's name (Valerie Plame's) to punish Joe Wilson for his column. Wilson himself would soon charge that Karl Rove and other political figures in the administration were to blame. While Novak would not divulge his sources, neither had he thought he had done anything terribly wrong or been used to make a political point or seek political revenge. He had said, "Nobody in the Bush administration called me to leak this," and as Novak was doing his investigation on the origins of Wilson's trip, an administration official had mentioned that Wilson's wife had recommended him for the job.[11] When Novak checked with the CIA, he said, he was told, "according to a confidential source at the C.I.A., Mrs. Wilson was an analyst, not a spy, not a covert operative, and not in charge of undercover operatives," and thus he had little reason not to publish what he had found out.[12] Novak had also said two other things: (1) he actually had learned of Valerie Plame's name from Joe Wilson's entry in *Who's Who* (clipped copies of which proving that was the case soon boomeranged around the Internet), and (2) the person who told him Wilson's wife worked at the CIA was "not a partisan gunslinger." The CIA referred the matter to the Justice Department, and in short order the Democrats were pushing for an independent counsel investigation. By the end of 2003, Joe and Valerie—evidently milking all the controversy and celebrity they could—were on the front cover of *Vanity Fair* magazine in a posed photo shoot in a convertible.

As investigations and allegations unfurled, one had to wonder at this point why, if Wilson were so concerned about his wife's identity, would he take to the *New York Times* to write a column alleging the falsifications by the Bush administration when a very practical and logical question about how he obtained his original mission would likely be asked? And why over such a small piece of evidence as uranium from Niger, which was hardly any major part of the case against Saddam Hussein and which the president had attributed to British sources anyway? The White House did indeed later say that citing the uranium claim was a mistake and they should not have done it, but the British government investigated this claim and stood by its substance.[13]

An entire book could be written on the rest of the fallout of this story (and Wilson, indeed, wrote one), but suffice it to say in summary, a special prosecutor, Patrick Fitzgerald, was appointed by the administration to look into the leak. Over the course of months and millions of dollars of expenses—by prosecution and defense alike—almost everyone in Washington seemed to have been dragged in front of his grand jury, including Karl Rove, NBC's Tim Russert, the vice president's Chief of Staff Scooter Libby, and reporters from *Time* and the *New York Times*. It was quite the parade. At the end of it all, nobody was prosecuted or even indicted for leaking Plame's profession or name to the press. What did come about was an indictment against Scooter Libby (the vice president's chief of staff) for lying to FBI investigators and the grand jury during the investigation. Libby would maintain he did not deliberately lie but had misremembered certain events and time frames.[14]

Libby was ultimately convicted—and then had his sentence commuted by President Bush.

In sum, bloggers on the right had documented all manner of questions about Joe Wilson's charges and so, too, bloggers on the left about the administration's alleged complicity. But nobody was ever charged with violating the law the Wilsons claimed was violated. Ultimately the country would find out that the source for Robert Novak was not even Scooter Libby but one of the less hawkish, more doubtful-about-going-into-Iraq-in-the-first-place administration officials: longtime Colin Powell friend and Deputy Secretary of State Richard Armitage. That Armitage never stood up to say anything or admit his actions during the months of investigations and charges continues to be a great mystery and disappointment to many.*

Odd as the allegations and political fighting from the Wilson story had been, there were two very good pieces of news by the end of 2003. In mid-December, as families at home were thinking about their loved ones on the battlefield and the holidays were fast approaching, Jerry Bremer held a news conference from Iraq and said, "Ladies and gentlemen, we got him." Saddam Hussein was captured by U.S. forces who found him in a dug-out hole, living the life of a long-bearded hermit, in a small house near Tikrit. Images of him being inspected and arrested soon surfaced throughout the world.

A few days later, another piece of unexpected news would come. Libyan dictator Muammar Khaddafi—the terrorist-sponsoring scourge of several U.S. presidential administrations over the decades—publicly announced he would surrender and cease all nuclear weapons acquisition; he would surrender his own WMD program. He saw what the U.S. was capable of doing after 11 September, and fearing for his own safety and leadership, he began negotiating such a surrender just as the U.S. was going into Iraq. By December, he had capitulated.[15]

---

* One could use barrels of ink to further detail the whole Wilson-Plame affair, including the back-and-forths between the Wilsons and the administration and the endless commentary about it. Indeed, I spent considerable time, hours and hours, on my radio show discussing it, as had others. And the Brothers Bennett had their involvement here too: Bob Bennett was hired as counsel to one of Patrick Fitzgerald's targets, Judith Miller of the *New York Times*, when he went after her for refusing to testify about her sources. I had been publicly critical of the Wilsons and had donated money (and my name) to the Scooter Libby Defense Fund.

II. The Struggle at Home Begins

January 2004 marked the beginning of a major presidential election year. President Bush's poll numbers were good, but they were not insurmountable. President Bush—as anyone in politics—well remembered how high his father's ratings were before he suffered electoral defeat. And eleven months out from the election, President Bush was running some nine points ahead of the generic Democratic Party's nominee.[16] Meanwhile, President Bush's campaign strategist, Matthew Dowd, was telling his team, almost regardless of what happened in the news (i.e., the economy, the war), the presidential election would be decided—one way or the other—by between a four- and five-point margin.[17]

True, the economy had picked up, and unemployment rates were going down, but there were a great many uncertainties in the year ahead—including who the Democrats would choose to run against President Bush and which direction they would gather their attack on him vis-à-vis the war. Massachusetts Senator John Kerry entered his name as a long-serving liberal senator who was famous for having worn the uniform in Vietnam only to come back home to oppose the war. Former NATO General Wesley Clark entered as a Clinton friend who had military credentials and who had the feel of a centrist. U.S. Senator John Edwards of North Carolina entered as a southern candidate who would focus on his passion—poverty in America. And a few others as well, including the Reverend Al Sharpton and defense policy hawk and Connecticut Senator Joe Lieberman. But the one candidate most people had trained their eyes and attention on at the beginning of January was former Vermont Governor Howard Dean.

Dr. Dean (a former family physician) was little known outside Vermont prior to 2003. But he had been making news and numbers as a vociferous and articulate critic of the Iraq War, opposing it from the get-go and criticizing it ever since. He was a hero with antiwar crowds and had a great attraction to more youthful voters with his rolled-up sleeves, caffeinated energy, and willingness to speak so strongly against the war when most Washington Democrats had, at least initially, been willing to support it.

How would those—especially Edwards and Kerry—appease their

increasing liberal base on the issue of Iraq, given their vote of approval for it? Soon would come the charges that President Bush had misled the country into war by fear-mongering and trying to tie the attacks of 9/11 to Iraq. The other Democratic defense for voting to authorize force was, Kerry and Edwards maintained, that it was an *authorization* to use force *if* all other options were off the table and, to their thinking, *if* the president would go to the UN again.

There was actually little anyone in the administration had said about an Iraq connection to 9/11, but the argument was that by speaking so much about preventing another 9/11, the president had used the issue to solicit support for war in Iraq. And hadn't others done much more than the administration on this front—including Osama bin Laden himself? In a 2003 audiotape, bin Laden had said, "We want to let you know and confirm to you that this war of the infidels that the U.S. is leading with its allies . . . we are with you and we will fight in the name of God. . . . Our brothers the mujahedeen in Iraq, don't worry about America's lies and their powers and their military might."[18]

Even General Wesley Clark had gone further than almost any administration official who could come to mind, having said in 2002,

Certainly there's a connection between Iraq and al Qaeda. . . . It doesn't surprise me at all that they would be talking to al Qaeda, that there would be some al Qaeda there or that Saddam Hussein might even be, you know, discussing gee, I wonder since I don't have any scuds and since the Americans are coming at me, I wonder if I could take advantage of al Qaeda?[19]

One other important question needing parsing as well: Just why would the administration think it a politically useful strategy to lie to the American people in order to roll the dice by invading another country, the outcome of which would be uncertain at best, especially if the administration knew it was lying? As to the Democrats' argument that they voted for a resolution that required President Bush to go back to the UN: The actual congressional resolution of 2002 had detailed all of Saddam Hussein's violations of the UN resolution and, in fact, read, "The President is authorized to use the Armed Forces of the United States as he determines to be necessary and appropriate."[20]

Still, with numbers showing the campaign in Iraq increasingly unpopular, with the daily drumbeat of the death toll, the Democrats had their issue— just as George McGovern had run against the war in Vietnam in opposing Nixon, just as Walter Mondale had run against a hard-line policy against the Soviet Union in opposing Ronald Reagan, and just as Michael Dukakis had run against George H. W. Bush's hard-line policies, the Democrats would pick up the mantle as the antiwar party. To any observer of this list, one thing becomes immediately apparent: all those Democrats had lost. Indeed the only Democrat in that time period who had unseated a Republican and also won reelection was Bill Clinton, who had run as a moderate and even to the right of George H. W. Bush on some foreign policy issues.

But Clinton was an anomaly in the Democratic Party's more recent history. Gone were the days of the Democrats standing for a muscular, Truman-like or John Kennedy–like foreign and defense policy. And on domestic policy, while Bill Clinton had given the Democrats what they wanted on taxes (more, not less), his signing of the Welfare Reform Bill had angered many in the base, as had one other thing: his signing of the Defense of Marriage Act (DOMA)— defining marriage in federal law as the union of one man and one woman, and allowing states that did not redefine marriage the right to deny marriage licenses to same-sex couples who moved into those states.

The race began in Iowa. All eyes were on Howard Dean. Could he make it there? Could he make it through the debates and retail campaigning without him losing his temper? Was his appeal to the youth vote enough? Democrats wanted the White House; they did not want to roll the dice with an unknown who seemed more comfortable rousing at rallies than being able to appear presidential. And Dean was prone to making gaffes, including one about the Confederate flag (an issue that usually tripped up Republicans). In Iowa, Dean had said, "I still want to be the candidate for guys with Confederate flags in their pickup trucks. . . . We can't beat George Bush unless we appeal to a broad cross-section of Democrats."[21] What kind of southern strategy was that? people asked. Dean wants to appeal to racists?

Those who think the Civil War is not over? And coming from a state with so few minorities, Dean became ever more vulnerable on the race issue. In the final televised Iowa debate, Al Sharpton zeroed in on Dean and race, hammering him for not having minorities in his cabinet back in Vermont.*

In the end, in Iowa, the more risk-averse voters of that state handed Howard Dean a surprise; he came in third to John Kerry and John Edwards. Dean had a great youth following, but as one political scientist in Iowa put it, "You can't run a professional presidential campaign on a kiddie corps.... Iowans don't want to be told by kids from out of state how to vote."[22] And as anti–Iraq War as the Democrats were, it was not the Democrats' only issue, yet it seemed it was Howard Dean's.

If Dean's failure in the Iowa caucuses was one big strike against his campaign, his speech at a rally of supporters after the election results came in nearly finished him off. It soon became known as the "I Have a Scream" speech. One reporter described the scene:

> He took off his suit jacket, rolled up the sleeves of his blue shirt, and acknowledged, "I'm sure there are some disappointed people here." Then he tried to motivate them to continue the fight. Getting revved up by the crowd's cheers and chants, he promised to take his campaign on to New Hampshire, South Carolina, California, and a string of other states, the names of which he shouted out like a cheerleader at a high school pep rally. His face reddening and his right hand balled into a fist, Dean shouted: "And then we're going to Washington, D.C.—to take back the White House—YEEEEEAAARGH!"[23]

The media captured that moment and played it again and again—as did the late-night comedians. Truth be told, it was unfair how often they played it, making Dean look a madder and angrier man than he was, but it reinforced the major criticism of Dean: that he was a great rally speaker to the youth and to the most anti-Bush crowds, just not very presidential.

The next stop was Massachusetts's and Vermont's neighboring state,

---

* Vermont, in truth, did have a less than 1 percent black population.

New Hampshire. But while Dean ran as the Washington outsider, Kerry was much better known, and Massachusetts and New Hampshire were linked much more than Vermont and New Hampshire. The big question was, who would Al Gore endorse? Antiwar as he was, he did not go with his former running mate, Joe Lieberman. Seizing on his popularity with the youth and "angry" anti-Bush sentiment, he endorsed Dean. In all reality, Lieberman probably did not expect Gore's endorsement, but he was publicly angry about the fact that Gore did not even speak to his former water-carrier before making his public endorsement. The theme that Bush was still an illegitimate president in the mind of the left was resurrected when, with Gore's endorsement, Dean stated how happy he was to receive the endorsement from "the *elected* President of the United States."[24]

It was not enough for Dean. When Kerry finished first in New Hampshire, to Dean's second, Kerry had accomplished a rare feat: winning both Iowa and New Hampshire. And Dean, perched as he was so high in late 2003 and very early 2004, having raised a great deal of money with unique and much-envied Internet usage, had now lost two races in a row. When Dean came in fifth in South Carolina, he was done. John Edwards won the state he was born in, but John Kerry finished second and it soon became a Kerry-Edwards race. The other candidates had not done well and slowly and quietly withdrew as their support waned, going instead to Kerry and Edwards. Most of the Democratic primary drama would soon end as Kerry wrapped up March's Super Tuesday primaries with Edwards winning, still, only South Carolina.

Now to the public, Edwards was youthful and had a somewhat moderate feel to him, perhaps in part because of his boyish charm. His theme of "two Americas," one doing well, one doing not so well, had become a popular stump speech for him. And in part to show geographic diversity, as well as capture some of these other benefits John Edwards brought with him, Kerry would soon choose him as his running mate.

President Bush realized he would have a tough campaign. Despite the capture of Saddam Hussein, more and more people doubted the wisdom of going into Iraq, especially with no WMDs to be found. As early as January, shortly after Saddam Hussein's capture, about 50 percent of those polled were saying that the president might have been too quick to go into Iraq and that the effort was not worth the cost.[25]

III. "Your Government Failed You": Bush in Doubt

By March, close to six hundred U.S. soldiers had been killed in Iraq.[26] Meanwhile, on national television, the congressionally mandated 9/11 Commission hearings were investigating what had gone wrong in the government and our national security apparatus that led to the attacks of 11 September, and those hearings were creating their own political bombshells.

Toward the end of March, a former National Security Agency counter-terrorism officer, Richard Clarke, had delivered a tough assessment of the pre-9/11 intelligence failures, and though having served most of his time in the Clinton administration, he trained his sights on the Bush administration. He had a new book out, and the television show *60 Minutes* had given it and him a lot of attention. Most knew that throughout the 1990s, America was hit again and again by terrorists and had not responded very strongly. But Richard Clarke was now making the case that the Bush administration (in office when 9/11 happened, after all) was little better. He opened his testimony by turning to some of the victims' families in the audience and telling them, "Your government failed you." He went on to testify that he did not think the Bush administration had treated terrorism in its first months in office as an "urgent issue."[27]

Clarke had his supporters and his detractors, and given all he had said over the years, it was hard to understand fully why he was giving a pass to the Clinton administration, which had been in office for years and did little, while strongly criticizing the Bush administration, which had been in office for less than nine months. Perhaps, several had thought, there were some sour grapes; he had expected to be taken more seriously by the Bush administration than by the Clinton administration when, in fact, the Bush administration had actually demoted Clarke upon taking office. But Clarke was seen as an expert's expert, and his testimony played far and wide. Especially in conjunction with what came next.

When Condoleezza Rice testified, Democratic Commissioner Richard

Ben-Veniste had his sights trained on her and would make great hay of a presidential daily brief (PDB) the president had received a month prior to the attacks:

MR. BEN-VENISTE: Isn't it a fact, Dr. Rice, that the August 6th PDB warned against possible attacks in this country? And I ask you whether you recall the title of that PDB.

MS. RICE: I believe the title was "Bin Laden Determined to Attack Inside the United States." Now, the PDB—

MR. BEN-VENISTE: Thank you.

MS. RICE: No, Mr. Ben-Veniste, you—

MR. BEN-VENISTE: I will get into the—

MS. RICE: I would like to finish my point here.

MR. BEN-VENISTE: I didn't know that there was a point.

MS. RICE: Given that you asked me whether or not it warned of attacks—

MR. BEN-VENISTE: I asked you what the title was.

MS. RICE: You said, did it not warn of attacks? It did not warn of attacks inside the United States. It was historical information based on old reporting. There was no new threat information, and it did not, in fact, warn of any coming attacks inside the United States.[28]

Perhaps these commission hearings should have not been held in front of cameras so that political scores could not be made, but the headline from Rice's hearings was that there was an August memo titled "Bin Laden Determined to Attack Inside the United States." Rice's explanation that it had no new or specific information in it was less important, as was her further statement that "had we thought that there was an attack coming in Washington or New York, we would have moved heaven and earth to try and stop it," which made common sense to most people but was not a headline.

Rice also was correct that the briefing had identified previous information on bin Laden's efforts, information that had taken place when President Clinton was in office. And it had speculated that bin Laden was interested in "hijack[ing] . . . a US aircraft" in order to release the Blind Sheikh and other captives.[29] But the briefing also stated, "We have not been able to corroborate" such reporting, and in any event, "The FBI is conducting approximately 70 full field investigations throughout the US that it considers bin-Laden related."[30] A reasonable reader of such a brief *could* conclude that the case was being well handled and that, short of, say, a *preemptive* strike in Afghanistan or assassination of bin Laden, not much more could be done.

Richard Clarke in his *60 Minutes* interview had stated, "I find it outrageous that the president is running for reelection on the grounds that he's done such great things about terrorism. He ignored it. He ignored terrorism for months, when maybe we could have done something to stop 9/11. Maybe. We'll never know."[31]

He had also said, "I think he's done a terrible job on the war against terrorism." And for these statements, much of the public was not sure what to believe. On the one hand, there were the charges that the administration "maybe" could have prevented 9/11. On the other, the administration was in office only a short period when 9/11 took place. On the one hand, the Clinton administration was not being blamed for doing little. On the other, the Bush administration was. And as for doing "a terrible job," yes, Iraq was still bloody, but it had an interim new government. More significant, there were other successes to be proud of. For example, Americans had not been attacked again on their homeland; al Qaeda had been radically disrupted with two-thirds of its leaders killed or taken into custody at that point; the Taliban controlled nothing; Afghanistan was attempting a constitutional government; and Osama bin Laden and Ayman al-Zawahiri were living a troglodyte existence on the run.

But then came other news in April, which was indeed turning out to be "the cruelest month." Abu Ghraib prison in Iraq had been a hellhole under Saddam Hussein, where torture took place regularly. American troops had taken it over once they had liberated Iraq, and in March 2004 there were reports that Iraqi prisoners, captured and imprisoned by U.S. soldiers, were being tortured there. The U.S. Army had announced that it was relieving seventeen soldiers from duty who were involved in that abuse and that several of them would face court-martial. But by the end of April, *60 Minutes*

II had obtained some photographs of the abuse, and they were reproduced and spread throughout the nation and the world.[32] While most Americans, despite their political views about the mission in Iraq, were supportive of the troops in Iraq (a common mantra on the left was, "I support the troops, not the mission"), these photographs were enough to turn anyone's stomach.

What is important to point out was that of the tens of thousands of U.S. soldiers in Iraq, this abuse took place at the hands of seventeen. And the U.S. military was disciplining those soldiers—those involved were punished with prison sentences, relieved of duty, and demoted.

The problem was, the pictures were graphic and spoke more loudly than any overall defense of the larger mission and larger efforts of the military there. That the overwhelming majority of soldiers in Iraq were also astonished by their colleagues' behavior at Abu Ghraib did not matter. Here were officials in uniform acting as if they were sadistic gang members.

Support for the efforts in Iraq and the president was dropping. By May, the president's approval rating was 41 percent (the lowest of his presidency), and his approval rating for the handling of Iraq was even lower, 34 percent.[33] More people disapproved of President Bush and his handling of the situation in Iraq than had approved. And the election was looming.

IV. Dishonest and Demagogic

The Democrats now thought they could make the upcoming election about war, and they had a big assist. Michael Moore was a left-wing documentary producer who had made a name for himself attempting to expose in a bad light what he deemed to be conservative causes. In June 2004 he released the biggest film production of his career: *Fahrenheit 9/11*. The movie was heavily advertised as a documentary that would expose the administration's carelessness, if not ignorant complicity, leading up to the slaughter of 11 September. And for many George Bush haters, it looked like exactly the lift and indictment they would need to finish him off politically.

For a $6 million production, the movie packed a punch, as well as the theaters, earning more than $100 million.[34] It also earned the respectability of a good many Democratic Party officials. At its premiere in Washington, D.C., attendees included Senate Minority Leader Tom Daschle, Florida Senator Bob Graham, Democratic National Committee Chairman Terry McAuliffe, and several members of Congress, among others.[35] And after they saw the movie, McAuliffe was quoted as saying, "I think anyone who sees this movie will come out en masse to make sure John Kerry is elected president this November. . . . Credit to Michael Moore for taking the time to put this together."[36]

The problem was, much of the movie was dubious, full of half-truths and questionable allegations. "To describe this film as dishonest and demagogic," Christopher Hitchens wrote, "would almost be to promote those terms to the level of respectability."[37] Never mind the multiplicities of distortions in the film (a great many of which were detailed in the blogosphere), Moore had become a hero to the left and to the Democratic Party—and the efforts to show the president as indifferent to and incompetent at his job, at best, were planted going into the summer election season.

V. A New Voice on the Scene

By settling on John Kerry as the Democratic frontrunner, the party had selected one of the most liberal members of the Senate, but they had also selected a Vietnam veteran who had wartime service credentials. They had done one other thing too: they selected a Vietnam veteran who had turned against the war in a very prominent way and who, during the course of the campaign, would tear open—again—the healed wounds from Vietnam. Many people, especially other Vietnam veterans, well recalled John Kerry's testimony to the Senate in 1971 when he charged that other U.S. soldiers in Vietnam had, among other things, "raped, cut off ears, cut off heads, taped wires from portable telephones to human genitals and turned up the power, cut off limbs, blown up bodies, randomly shot at civilians, razed villages in fashion reminiscent of Genghis Khan."[38]

John Kerry made no bones about his wartime service and intended to show it and make it an issue in the election. While he also wanted to show he could understand when a war needed to end, he was not as excited to have his previous Senate testimony brought up. But bring up his service he did—right out of the box in Boston at the Democratic Convention in 2004. He came into the Boston harbor with several of his Swift Boat friends from Vietnam. And in his opening line to the convention he stated, "I'm John Kerry, and I'm reporting for duty," at which point he gave a military salute to the crowd. He would go on to say, "To all who serve in our armed forces today, help is on the way" and that he would work to "bring our troops home." In one other reference that would have pleased the Michael Moore fans, he promised, "I will be a commander in chief who will never mislead us into war."[39]

But Kerry's speech turned out *not* to be the most important speech of the convention. The most important was the keynote address delivered two days before John Kerry would deliver his. The speech was aired on all three networks—and cable—and delivered by Illinois State Senator Barack Obama, who was then running for U.S. Senate in Illinois. Obama's campaign team had to do a little convincing with the John Kerry staff that this relatively unknown man would deliver a great speech and be good for the convention, but the Kerry staff consented. State Senator Obama worked hard on this speech, knowing it would be an important one, and he had said to his friends he'd hoped this trip to this Democratic Convention "goes a whole lot better."[40] For he had gone to the Democratic Convention in 2000 in Los Angeles, nearly broke, could not rent a car because his credit card was denied, and could not secure a floor pass—ultimately watching most of the convention from the outside on a Jumbotron.[41]

His seventeen-minute speech in 2004 was, by all accounts, a knockout, praised by left and right alike. He opened with his autobiography—an "only in America" story about how he was given birth by a white mother and an African father, and how his grandfather had served under General Patton in Europe. He spoke of the meaning of his name, Barack, meaning "blessed," and how his parents had given him that name because they believed, though they were not wealthy, in "America you don't have to be rich to achieve your potential."[42] Here was the beginning of a story not resentful of those who made it in America despite their struggles, here was the beginning of a first-person story not complaining about his station in life or the prejudices in America but, rather, a story about how nothing can stop any American. Conservatives and Republicans were taking note, approvingly.

He then cited the Declaration of Independence and spoke of the greatness of America, how it provided the greatest freedoms and safety in the world, how it was the best country in the world. It was not a "blame America" first speech that so many had come to expect at Democratic Conventions; it was not a recitation of grievances that many had come to expect at Democratic Conventions; it was a statement and testament to the exact opposite. To be sure, he delivered some partisan shots about the war and spoke up on behalf of John Kerry, but those were not the most memorable lines of his speech—every convention speaker had said much the same. The most memorable lines were to come:

> The pundits like to slice-and-dice our country into Red States and Blue States; Red States for Republicans, Blue States for Democrats. But I've got news for them, too. We worship an "awesome God" in the Blue States, and we don't like federal agents poking around in our libraries in the Red States. We coach Little League in the Blue States and yes, we've got some gay friends in the Red States. There are patriots who opposed the war in Iraq and there are patriots who supported the war in Iraq. We are one people, all of us pledging allegiance to the stars and stripes, all of us defending the United States of America.[43]

This not only brought the house down as he led to his concluding lines on behalf of John Kerry, but also woke up a great many analysts and citizens who knew what he said to be true and who, themselves, were tiring of the strict dividing lines in which too many had been engaged in categorizing people's political beliefs. Here, people thought and analysts discussed in the following days, was the future of true political leadership and politics: a politics that recognized the greatness of America from the perspective of both parties.

And more: this young and athletic-looking man with an unusual name and dark complexion—truly, given his father's birth country of Kenya, an African American—made only two references to race beyond the description of his father's birth country: (1) by stating what many race-neutral theorists had been saying for years ("there is not a Black America, there is not a White America") and (2) in giving a message to fellow African Americans:

Go into any inner city neighborhood, and folks will tell you that government alone can't teach our kids to learn; they know that parents have to teach, that children can't achieve unless we raise their expectations and turn off the television sets and eradicate the slander that says a black youth with a book is acting white.

The days of Al Sharpton and Jesse Jackson dominating the podium as Democratic Party spokesmen for black Americans ended that July night in Boston.

President Bush, in his convention speech, did not cede any credibility on the war or with the military fighting it, nor did he back away from his decision to go into Iraq. He addressed the charges of misleading our nation into war in Iraq by saying he made the tough choice after countless UN resolutions and labor and rhetorically asked, "Do I forget the lessons of September 11th and take the word of a madman or do I take action to defend our country? Faced with the choice, I will defend America every time."[44] He recited the progress that America was making in Iraq and our nation's actions in liberating 50 million Muslims in Afghanistan and Iraq. He quoted a soldier in Iraq:

> Our troops know the historic importance of our work. One Army specialist wrote home, "We are transforming a once-sick society into a hopeful place. The various terrorist enemies we are facing in Iraq," he continued, "are really aiming at you back in the United States. This is a test of will for our country. We soldiers of yours are doing great and scoring victories in confronting the evil terrorists."[45]

And he saluted his and his colleagues' efforts: "That young man is right. Our men and women in uniform are doing a superb job for America."[46]

For his coup de grace against Senator Kerry, he brought out the one quote that John Kerry, to this day, probably wishes he had never uttered, one quote that would haunt Kerry the rest of the campaign. In October 2003, there was an $87 billion supplemental war funding bill in Congress. When John Kerry was asked earlier in the campaign why he would vote against sending additional money to the troops abroad, he answered, "I actually did vote for the $87 billion before I voted against it."[47] Kerry and John Edwards were two of only twelve U.S. senators who had voted against that supplemental funding. But his quote fueled the anti-Kerry theme of being a "flip-flopper" throughout the campaign. When President Bush reminded the audience of this quote, the crowd chanted, "Flip-flop . . . flip-flop . . . flip-flop." For a senator who had voted to authorize the war, not voted to fund the troops fighting it, and then given several conflicting explanations for his vote, the charge began to stick.

But the issue of being a veteran did not end there—for either candidate.

VI. Of Swift Boats and Service Records

John O'Neill was also a Vietnam veteran and had few regrets about his service in that war. He had known Kerry for some years—but as an antagonist. When Kerry was opposing the Vietnam War in the 1970s, O'Neill had debated him on television. And when it became clear that Kerry would be the nominee for president on the Democratic ticket, O'Neill and a group of other veterans formed Swift Boat Veterans for Truth to challenge not only John Kerry's claims as having the best interests of our soldiers at heart but also much of Kerry's military service in Vietnam. The Swift Boat group ran ads re-airing Kerry's 1971 testimony and also challenging medals, including Purple Hearts, he had received for his service in Vietnam.

In candor, it was not a pretty or happy business, challenging a war veteran's credentials; and many of these accusations were countered by people with whom Kerry had served—including the testimony of Jim Rassman, who spoke and wrote of how John Kerry risked his own life to save Rassman's.[48] But neither were Kerry's words, still haunting so many of his fellow colleagues from 1971, pretty or happy. John O'Neill backed off on none of his group's allegations, and citizens were left to decide for themselves who was telling the whole truth about Kerry's service.

As Bill Kristol would write at the time: "Kerry did say that he and his fellow soldiers had routinely committed war crimes [in 1971]. And it is this that chiefly explains his fellow veterans' disdain for Kerry. Their contempt does not rest primarily on what Kerry did or did not do in 1968 or 1969."[49] Ultimately, Kristol wrote:

> John Kerry has never retracted the charge of war crimes. It is fair to hold him accountable for his testimony—but it is also up to each American to decide how much weight to give this, or any other, three-decade-old event. What was said or done during the Vietnam era may end up being relatively unimportant in determining how people vote in 2004. But the Vietnam war, and the antiwar movement, is relevant to understanding a possible Kerry presidency at least in this sense: It is clear from Kerry's subsequent career that his real band of brothers—his political band of brothers, his ideological band of brothers—are the antiwar activists with whom he marched in 1971.[50]

And that was the point. What Kerry had done or not done when he volunteered to go to Vietnam (a noble thing in itself) was not the crux of the conservative or even nonideological criticism of Kerry; it was what he said about his fellow soldiers when he came home and that he had never retracted such charges. By having the statements about soldiers committing crimes against humanity on his record, was that his view of soldiers today? That was the question on people's minds.

But Kerry's service was not the only service questioned in this heated election season. *60 Minutes*, CBS, and particularly CBS's Dan Rather had taken some strong shots at President Bush and the administration—and drawn some blood from those shots. Now they had a story they thought would really explode. For several years there had been an undercurrent of left-wing chatter and political finger-pointing that many people supportive of military force had never actually served in the military. This charge was mostly absurd on its merits. What military service had their hero Howard Dean achieved? What war did Franklin Roosevelt fight in before he led us through World War II? Or Woodrow Wilson in World War I? What war did Bill Clinton fight in before he was president? And what of those arguing for our founders' taking up arms, like James Madison, Thomas Jefferson, or Benjamin Franklin? Nevertheless, the phrase "chicken-hawk" to describe the pro-Iraq liberation opinion leaders adhered in left-wing circles. Michael Moore had even gone so far as to call President Bush "a deserter" during Vietnam—desertion being an actual crime.

Dan Rather and his lead producer, Mary Mapes, thought they had something to give credence to these charges, and in September, *60 Minutes II*, in a story anchored by Dan Rather, put forward documents they had received along with a story claiming George W. Bush had not fulfilled his National Guard duty and had received preferential treatment in his avoidance of it. The story did not sound right to some; the documents did not look right to others. The next day, one conservative blogger alleged the documents looked forged, and another blogger at the Power Line blog raised similar questions, especially given the odd fonts on the documents and the state of font technology at the time the documents would have been typed.

The blogosphere went wild. Power Line received so many visitors, it crashed; and more and more amateurs familiar with typesets and fonts weighed in on their and others' blogs. Within about twenty-four hours of the blogosphere's criticizing of the documents, ABC News announced its doubts about the story and also speculated that the documents CBS had received and publicized were forged.[51]

CBS was standing by its story, but to those who had been paying attention, there was as much doubt about CBS's story as there was belief in it. CBS—especially Dan Rather—seemed to not know what had hit them. Some were still defending CBS by criticizing bloggers as not having typical media credentials, but the problem was the credentials of the experts sending in information to the bloggers seemed to be better than anything CBS could produce. And at least in the case of Power Line, the three authors/publishers of that blog were highly credentialed and experienced attorneys.

Soon enough, the evidence against the CBS story became overwhelming: the *Dallas Morning News* piled on with an interview of Lt. Col. Jerry Killian's secretary (the documents were alleged to have been written by the deceased Killian),* who said that her boss had never typed and that she didn't type the memos in question. That night ABC News ran a story with

---

* Killian was one of George Bush's commanding officers in the Texas Air National Guard.

interviews of two document experts who had been consulted by CBS. Both of them claimed to have told CBS that they could not authenticate the documents. One of them, Emily Will, said that she sent CBS

> an email message about her concerns and strongly urged the network the night before the broadcast not to use the documents. "I told them that all the questions I was asking them on Tuesday night, they were going to be asked by hundreds of other document examiners on Thursday if they ran that story."[52]

Meanwhile, Dan Rather told *Washington Post* media critic Howard Kurtz, "If the documents are not what we were led to believe, I'd like to break that story." To this, one prominent writer had written: "Earth to Dan, the story is broken." Indeed, it was. Internal investigations revealed the documents were just as the bloggers had alleged: forgeries. CBS News President Andrew Heyward issued a public apology: "Based on what we now know, CBS News cannot prove that the documents are authentic, which is the only acceptable journalistic standard to justify using them in the report. . . . We should not have used them."[53] CBS put together an outside panel to investigate what had happened, and the panel concluded, among other things, in CBS CEO Les Moonves's words: "The fact is that basic journalistic steps were not carried out in a manner consistent with accurate and fair reporting, leading to countless misstatements and omissions."[54] By the beginning of 2005, Rather would retire from CBS News as its evening anchor, and by the following year, he would be gone from CBS entirely. The Internet had taken another scalp. A new media dimension to politics in the twenty-first century was established.

VII. The Way the Culture Blows

On top of the growing mistrust of the mainstream media, as well as the charges and countercharges about Kerry's and Bush's military service, there were other cultural trip wires at play as well, and John Kerry seemed to get tangled up in all of them. Kerry could not seem to connect with the so-called average American. He was married to Teresa Heinz, the wealthy heiress to the food and ketchup brand of the same name, and had sporting tastes that spoke more to the elite class than to the common man. To show he was an athlete in the John Kennedy sense, he did not release pictures of himself playing football with his family; rather, they were pictures of him dressed in a colorful water suit windsurfing off the cape of Nantucket. The Bush campaign used this picture to great political spin in an ad featuring it that said: "Kerry voted for the Iraq War, opposed it, supported it, and now opposes it again. . . . He bragged about voting for the $87 billion to support our troops before he voted against it. . . ." All the while the image was flipped one way, then the next. "John Kerry," the ad concluded, "whichever way the wind blows."[55]

And then there was the Hollywood–New York problem. At a fund-raiser for the Kerry-Edwards ticket at Radio City Music Hall in New York that raised more than $7 million for the ticket, the star-studded entertainment roster of comedians and musicians lashed out at the president in front of a laughing and appreciative John Kerry and John Edwards. Several comedians called the president "a liar" and made sport of his malapropisms and supposedly poor intellect. John Mellencamp called the president "a cheap thug," but Whoopi Goldberg stole the show.[56]

In a tirade of sexual innuendo she delivered about President Bush that would lead to the Slim-Fast company firing her as a paid spokesperson, Goldberg turned the fund-raiser into a verbal cascade of profanity. And to make matters worse, at the end, John Kerry stated, "Every performer tonight . . . conveyed to you the heart and soul of our country."[57] Between that view of the heart and soul of the country and the kinds of other stories that were emerging about his being out of touch, Kerry had a problem.*

Senator Kerry portrayed himself as more sophisticated than President Bush and attempted to make a strong point of his internationalism and ability to restore what he claimed was a lack of credibility abroad with frayed

---

* One particularly funny story was about a campaign stop at a Wendy's hamburger shop where Mrs. Kerry had to ask what the chili was when she saw it. The lunch they had at Wendy's was truly just a photo-op. What they actually ate back on the campaign bus was a catered meal from the Newburgh Yacht Club consisting of shrimp, scallops, and prosciutto.

relationships with our allies. The truth was, Kerry *was* more of an internationalist. His wife was born of Portuguese parents in Africa, and he had studied in Europe and was fluent in French. But while Kerry had claimed America did not have enough allies, particularly in its efforts in Iraq, he had also said the Iraq War was a "grand diversion," and President Bush scored on him on this in the presidential debates:

> My opponent says we didn't have any allies in this war. What's he say to Tony Blair? What's he say to Alexander Kwasniewski of Poland? You can't expect to build an alliance when you denigrate the contributions of those who are serving side by side with American troops in Iraq. Plus, he says the cornerstone of his plan to succeed in Iraq is to call upon nations to serve. So what's the message going to be: "Please join us in Iraq. We're a grand diversion. Join us for a war that is the wrong war at the wrong place at the wrong time?"[58]

Still, it was looking to be a very close race.* But as Florida was the deciding state in 2000, Ohio was in 2004. And so were "moral issues," as the exit polls had shown, the most prominent being gay marriage.

Amendments opposing gay marriage succeeded in all eleven states where they were on the ballot, even in liberal Oregon. In job-wracked Ohio, which delivered Bush's Electoral College victory, the amendment succeeded by more than 60 percent; and Phil Burress, a family values activist in Ohio who organized the initiative there, registered 54,000 new voters on the strength of that issue alone. Black churches were an important part of this initiative and in Ohio, the black community voted for President Bush by a greater percentage than their national average, giving him 16 percent compared to 11 percent nationwide. As a result, Ohio, which might have lost more jobs than any other state in 2004, delivered a 118,000 vote majority to Bush because of something more important, apparently, than jobs.[59]

To say Kerry couldn't connect and George Bush could was told by the

---

* I recall one airplane ride during the campaign on which several of us in the commentary business were on the same plane, and one well-known political commentator yelled, "Will somebody please tell me who is going to win this thing?"

numbers: George Bush increased his support from almost every sector imaginable from four years before. He increased with black voters (although only a little, by about 3 percentage points), Hispanic voters (13 points), Jewish voters (5 points), and Catholic voters (about 5 points, which translated, however, into at least 1.5 million votes, half of his margin of victory). He even won Florida by five points. While the Senate Republicans picked up four seats, Democratic Senate Minority Leader Tom Daschle from South Dakota became the first party leader in the Senate to be ousted in more than fifty years.[60] In the House, Republicans picked up three seats.

In the middle of a war, even one of questionable popularity, Americans do not like changing horses, especially when the direction the new horse would run is unclear.

Six

Peril and Promise in War,
Two Great American Stories,
A New Direction for America

The battlefield engagements and missions had become highly conten-
tious, and our nation would rend itself over them. Meanwhile, the
Republicans would lose the Congress they had taken back in 1994 after
forty years of exile from leadership. And throughout the country, citi-
zens would take more and more responsibility for their news and infor-
mation through the ever-expanding Internet—actually breaking stories
before the traditional media. We would endure a historically horrible
natural disaster and a financial collapse that would bring back memo-
ries of the 1930s. Amidst all this, the nation, long struggling to overcome
its mixed past on race relations, would close a complicated chapter on its
original sin of slavery—electing its first black president in history.

I. Grand Goals and an Uneasy Coalition

It has been said that in modern history, second terms are a mixed blessing
at best. Richard Nixon scandalized himself out of office in his second term.
Ronald Reagan had a time of it overcoming the Iran-Contra affair. And Bill
Clinton was impeached. The next four years for President Bush and the
country were met with great promise, but also great peril.

In his 2004 victory, George Bush decisively, and without any question,
won reelection. Bush beat Kerry by more than three million votes. President
Bush stated that he had "earned capital in the campaign, political capital,

and now I intend to spend it." He identified his proposed second-term agenda: "Social Security and tax reform, moving this economy forward, education, fighting and winning the war on terror."[1] Any one of those issues would be hard enough to take on—especially what had long been considered "the third rail" of politics, Social Security reform. Many had viewed Bush as a wartime president and wished to see the war on terror prosecuted vigorously and brought to an end so that—then—the other issues could be addressed.

In his 2005 Inaugural, the president spoke to what was becoming his view of his mission abroad: to help build democratic institutions throughout the Middle East and to foster democracy throughout the world. To Bush, it was clear that in not finding WMDs in Iraq, this would now be the ancillary benefit of what America had begun to seriously accomplish in Afghanistan and Iraq, the building of two democracies, including (in the case of Iraq) the first Arab democracy in history.*

President Bush had been reading former Soviet dissident Natan Sharansky's recently published book, *The Case for Democracy*, and had told an interviewer: "If you want a glimpse of how I think about foreign policy read Natan Sharansky's book."[2] President Bush was not telling just reporters that; he was telling his White House staff to read it as well. *The Case for Democracy*'s thesis is partially described in the subtitle: *The Power of Freedom to Overcome Tyranny and Terror.*

Sharansky's book detailed and maintained the argument that democracies rarely start wars with democracies and that free societies are more peaceful than oppressed societies. The book and its thesis were perfectly pitched to what President Bush was thinking. His conviction for staying the course in Iraq was based on his desire to build a foothold of democracy in a region whose policies had primarily been based on authoritarianism and tyranny, that in turn had been the cause of so much war and terrorism from within and without.

---

* Where were or what had become of the WMDs remains an unanswered question to this day. Most recently, reports have surfaced that Saddam Hussein was deliberately misleading about his weapons, wanting perceived and actual enemies to think he had them. To have blamed those who took him seriously when he was lying rather than to blame Hussein for lying is an interesting turn of logical standard deduction.

The president's view was that the U.S. had gone to war with Iraq for the purpose of protecting our national security, but the president had also spoken of Hussein's human rights abuses and the sponsoring and coddling of terrorists. In the entire indictment of Hussein, WMDs were a pre-eminent but not exclusive part. And as others had pointed out, had not other wars changed emphases in medias res? Lincoln scholar (and, politically, a Bush critic) Harold Holzer had written: "Just as Bush widened (diluted?) the war against terrorism by invading Iraq, Lincoln broadened American goals mid-conflict. The war to save the Union became a war to end slavery."[3] Of course most fair readings of Lincoln—or Bush—would argue that ending slavery would protect the Union just as instilling a democracy in Iraq would make America safer. The ends, however they were emphasized, were not wholly divorced from the beginnings. But in his case, Bush's critics were not appeased by such comparisons or shifting.

President Bush made these full-throated cases in his Inaugural Address:

We have seen our vulnerability, and we have seen its deepest source. For as long as whole regions of the world simmer in resentment and tyranny—prone to ideologies that feed hatred and excuse murder— violence will gather, and multiply in destructive power, and cross the most defended borders and raise a mortal threat.

There is only one force of history that can break the reign of hatred and resentment and expose the pretensions of tyrants and reward the hopes of the decent and tolerant. And that is the force of human freedom.[4]

After detailing our nation's birth of freedom, the president invoked Abraham Lincoln: "No one is fit to be a master, and no one deserves to be a slave." He then went on to say:

The imperative of self government . . . is the honorable achievement of our fathers. Now it is the urgent requirement of our nation's security and the calling of our time. So it is the policy of the United States to seek and support the growth of democratic movements and institutions in every nation and culture, with the ultimate goal of ending tyranny in our world.[5]

While the president did go on to say that this would not primarily be the "task of arms" and that such work would take generations, he also said, "All who live in tyranny and hopelessness can know: The United States will not ignore your oppression, or excuse your oppressors. When you stand for your liberty, we will stand with you."[6] That was quite a guarantee, especially if heard and taken seriously by the oppressed in all of the oppressed nations of the world.

The United States had promised to help others in the past, and sometimes it was able to, but other times not. The uprisings in Hungary in 1956, Poland in 1968, and even more recently Tiananmen Square in China in 1989 come to mind as times when the U.S. was unable or unavailable to help dissidents. And by this point in America's recent history, the country had done much to help liberate millions of Muslims from their oppressors, from Afghanistan to Kuwait to Iraq to the former Yugoslavia. Still—from Iran to the Sudan, where "genocide," as Secretary of State Powell had labeled it, was taking place—it was a big question as to what the U.S. could or would do. And what of America's uneasy allies in Egypt and Saudi Arabia, where human rights were regularly ignored?

Many had applauded this speech and this grand testimony to freedom, human rights, and democracy. But many on the left, and not a few on the right, were made quite nervous by it. First, would it mean more military intervention abroad, even as the country's hands were full in Iraq and Afghanistan? Second, while America's hands were full there—and other nations from Europe to Asia were still being targeted by Islamic terrorism—was the war on terror over? It was the signature issue of the Bush administration since 11 September, and it was the basis for the president's national reelection (as a wartime commander and leader), yet the words *terror*, *terrorism*, and *war* appeared nowhere in his Inaugural Address.

Conservative columnist and author Peggy Noonan was perhaps the most critical from the right. "George W. Bush's second inaugural will no doubt prove historic because it carried a punch," she wrote, "asserting an agenda so sweeping that an observer quipped that by the end he would not have been surprised if the president had announced we were going to colonize Mars."[7] She wasn't finished. The speech was "dreamy and disturbing," she said, and while short on specifics, "it seemed a document produced by a White House on a mission. The United States, the speech said, has put the world on notice: Good governments that are just to their people are our friends, and those that are not are, essentially, not."[8] This would, of course, please human rights activists, one would have thought, but as a general statement of policy, it would be impossible to fulfill. She concluded by arguing the speech, filled as it was with theological references, confused heaven and earth: "The most moving speeches summon us to the cause of what is actually possible. Perfection in the life of man on earth is not."[9]

The truth was, the conservatives had rallied around the president for the election, but they were increasingly nervous—and even disturbed with him—on various fronts. First, there were the spending increases on several domestic programs. The president was increasing the budget at a rate that many on the right had been critical of, and that was winning him no support from the Democrats in any event. For example, his 2003 prescription drug benefit created a federal entitlement in Medicare reform for elderly patients, but came with a cost higher than the White House had promoted—hundreds of billions of dollars over a ten-year period.[10] And take just one department, the Department of Education: all the spending sought for No Child Left Behind certainly did not keep Ted Kennedy or other Democrats supportive of the program for very long. They would, ever after, criticize it for not being funded enough. In the meantime, between the 2001 and the proposed 2005 budget, government spending on education increased more than 35 percent.[11] The budget for the Department of Education, alone, was more than $60 billion.*[12] Quite a change in direction for a department that conservatives had long thought should be eliminated.

On economic matters, the administration had placed tariffs on steel imports, upsetting the notions and doctrines of free trade. And the

---

* To provide a sense of proportion, when I was secretary of education in the 1980s, my highest budgets remained below $20 billion.

administration had been slow to act on the growing concern of illegal immigration, which most had thought included more than ten million illegal immigrants living in the country at the time—and causing budgetary, as well as social, problems. On foreign policy, most conservatives were foursquare with the president in fighting terrorism and maintaining the course in Iraq, but many had thought the U.S. was too appeasing of countries like China, where religion was anathema, and Saudi Arabia, from where more poisonous indoctrination was flowing than from perhaps any other country.

But President Bush seemed to have no shortage of political courage, and if the Inaugural was light on domestic issues, his State of the Union address was not. He unveiled one of the two most far-reaching domestic policy reforms of his second term: Social Security reform. Reform of Social Security had been a longtime passion among economic conservatives, but was rarely touched because, equally, it had become a favorite program of Democrats, a symbol of the centerpiece of Franklin Delano Roosevelt's presidency—and the elderly population in America certainly had one of the strongest, if not the strongest, lobbies in the country.

Nevertheless, in his State of the Union, the president pointed out what many economic analysts had agreed upon: the Social Security system could not go on unreformed forever, and it was "headed toward bankruptcy."[13] As the president noted, when Social Security was created by Franklin Roosevelt in 1935, the economy was in far worse shape (it was the Great Depression, after all), people were living shorter lives, and at that time, given the population, about sixteen workers were paying into the system for every person who was drawing benefits from it.[14] But a massive demographic shift now meant that each beneficiary was supported by a mere three workers, a number that would shrink to two in the coming decades. By "2018, Social Security will be paying out more than it takes in."[15]

What did the president propose? Not taxing more income and making life harder on workers; not raising the retirement age; not means-testing Social Security, which some had suggested over the years. While promising he would not do anything that would affect anyone ten or so years away from retirement, he offered voluntary personal retirement accounts for younger workers who would like an alternate system whereby they could invest their retirement in the stock market and, theoretically, in greater rates of growth.

This proposal, what President Bush called part of creating "an ownership society," set the nation on a several-months-long national debate. The Democrats and the retirees' political lobbying community (for which Social Security was sacrosanct) pushed back against such a reform even harder than those in favor of it pushed for it. Indeed, the Democratic leadership on Capitol Hill would stand so firmly by the program of Franklin Roosevelt that they even held one press conference from his Washington, D.C., memorial statue. President Bush, for his part, would hold town hall meetings on the issue but, in the end, could not overcome the opposition that, taking a page from Al Gore's 2000 presidential campaign talking points, labeled such an alternate investment idea "a risky scheme." This would be one of the last times conservatives would unite to rally strongly behind the president on domestic policy proposals.

II. The Storms Hit

The war in Iraq was still ongoing, and although there had been several good news stories from Iraq, including the turning over of authority to a transitional government made up of Iraqis, the writing of a new constitution for Iraq, and the training of more and more police and security forces there, there was still a great deal of violence—striking at both America and its allies as well as at allied Iraqis. By the end of 2004, the U.S. death toll in Iraq had reached more than one thousand, and it would reach more than two thousand by the end of 2005.[16] The master terrorist in Iraq—heading a group called al Qaeda in Iraq and leading much of the violence—was Abu Musab al-Zarqawi.

The antiwar left argued that the U.S. had drawn terrorists into Iraq and increased terrorism there. While it was true many supporting the terrorists there rallied to the war and entered Iraq to fight, it was also true master terrorists were living in Iraq before America ever entered, including Abu Musab al-Zarqawi. Meanwhile, the damage done from the images and abuse from the previous year's Abu Ghraib story could not be discounted. They served as propaganda for the terrorists and other Muslim sympathizers, strengthened the hands of those opposed to the mission and back home in America.

If all this was not bad enough news for the Republican party in America, more would soon come. For years, one of the most well-known and prominent Republican lobbyists in Washington was a man named Jack Abramoff. He had worked with several conservative groups and done favors for any number of conservative leaders, officials, and causes. Most of his lucrative lobbying career had been, of late, working with Indian tribes involved in the gaming industry. He lived lavishly, spent lavishly, and bragged to many about his purchase-for-power abilities and connections to elected representatives and members of the administration. In the meantime, he had earned tens of millions of dollars in lobbying fees from Indian tribes.

The *Washington Post* had begun an investigation into his activities, as had the Senate Commerce Committee in 2004. When e-mails he had sent were released from those hearings, he looked to be strong-arming officials on behalf of his clients and playing both sides in one particularly distasteful case: working against one tribe only to offer his services to that same tribe later in an effort to undo his previous work, all for a casino license—and fee.[17] He was seen in his e-mails to be making fun of his clients behind their backs and, in sum, illustrating the worst possible caricature of the worst possible image of a fat cat lobbyist making a lot of money off people and trading favors to government officials.

But beyond the imagery, Abramoff was also violating the law, and in August 2005 he was indicted on fraud and conspiracy charges.[18] As the Abramoff scandals played out in the press, including the wrongdoing of at least one Republican congressman (who would later plead guilty to crimes associated with Abramoff), several of Abramoff's associates with Republican Party and administration ties would also be reported on—and plead guilty to white-collar crimes as well. Although some Democrats had been the recipients of Abramoff's largesse, this was a Republican scandal—no getting around it—and ultimately Jack Abramoff would be sentenced to several years in prison, but not without first tainting many elected Republicans by their association with him.

If some in the GOP looked to be drunk with, or insensitive to, power over time, the Abramoff scandal may very well be the genesis of that imagery. While a couple of former subcabinet-level officials were implicated in the Abramoff dragnet, what may have hurt most was that he was known as a close friend to a good many White House advisors and a longtime associate of White House political director Karl Rove.

But that was just the beginning of the headaches for George Bush and the Republicans related to power in 2005.

Off the Gulf Coast of Louisiana, a huge storm was brewing in August. It was labeled Hurricane Katrina. By the time the hurricane had come and gone, it had left in its wake more physical, human, and even political damage than almost any natural disaster anyone could remember.* To this day, people associate Katrina with both human and natural disaster of untold proportions. It physically drained the city of New Orleans of its citizens, and—fairly or unfairly—it drained President George Bush of lasting political credibility beyond his base of support. It may very well have been the biggest story, causing the most damage, of the year.

The day before Category 4 Hurricane Katrina hit Louisiana, on 29 August, New Orleans Mayor Ray Nagin issued a mandatory evacuation of the city, and tens of thousands of Louisiana residents started to leave their homes.[19] Governors Kathleen Blanco of Louisiana, Haley Barbour of Mississippi, and Jeb Bush of Florida (the president's brother) had declared states of emergency for their respective states a few days prior and asked the president to do the same, thus putting federal monies and efforts into play. Still, a great many residents had not left New Orleans as ordered, and for many, there was a question about how they could leave. Aside from the worry about the wind and rain, the bigger worry, particularly for New Orleans—sitting as a bowl below water levees—was that the levees could break or overflow with water

---

* It was one of the worst natural disasters that most anyone could recall. In financial damage, Katrina probably was the worst. But, in the human death toll, Americans had suffered worse before—for example, the Galveston hurricane of 1900 had killed up to 10,000 people; the Florida Okeechobee hurricane of 1928 had killed as many as 2,500. Katrina's death toll is still imprecise but fixed in most estimates at over 1,500 people. See, for example: http://hnn.us/articles/17193.html.

and flood the city in a deluge. That was precisely what happened, and by 9:00 a.m. on the twenty-ninth, the Ninth Ward of New Orleans was flooded with as much as eight feet of water.[20]

As timing goes, the politics of it all was disastrous. President Bush had been on vacation in Texas and on the twenty-ninth was traveling in Arizona and California to speak about Medicare legislation.[21] The president's director of the Federal Emergency Management Agency (FEMA, tasked with disaster preparedness, response, and recovery), Michael Brown, had briefed the president by videoconference. The president had spoken of the Katrina storm in his comments in California but awaited further briefing from Brown and Homeland Security Secretary Michael Chertoff before taking further action. In the meantime, the Coast Guard began to send in helicopters to help with further evacuation and relief.

By the thirtieth, some 80 percent of New Orleans was under water, and reports surfaced of looting of homes and businesses there.[22] All of what happened after the flooding would become the center of a great deal of finger-pointing and accusation among the media, state, city, and federal officials—with any number of allegations (including racism) spread on talk radio and the Internet.

What is known is that on the third day of the crisis, the thirty-first, President Bush left Texas and flew back to Washington to help coordinate the federal response. His flight path took him over Louisiana where a picture of him looking down at the wreckage was soon disseminated. National Guard troops from other states were arriving to help with the situation, and Army Lieutenant General Russel Honoré began leading the military help and response on the ground in Louisiana. Meanwhile the head of the Red Cross asked to enter the city with relief supplies but was denied permission by state officials; and the Louisiana Superdome, where thousands of evacuees had gone for refuge, began flooding at the same time it was becoming a site of squalor and overcrowding. In short order, additional rumors about the nature of the chaos and mayhem at the Superdome circulated—creating more of a media sensation, even as many of the rumors proved untrue.[23]

Shortly thereafter, President Bush left the White House to tour the damaged areas from Katrina and, in Alabama, stated at a news conference,

"Brownie [to Michael Brown], you're doing a heck of a job . . . my attitude is, if it's not going exactly right, we're going to make it go exactly right. If there's problems, we're going to address the problems."[24]

Two pictures and then a sound bite summed up the elected officials' culpability here more than any number of reports and rumors would. They were lasting images and audio that will be remembered for a long time. The first was a picture about how the opening part of the tragedy could happen, with so many people not evacuating the city as ordered. The picture showed some two hundred school buses, sitting in a lot, available for emergency transportation, but unused by the city and now underwater. When confronted about this picture and the idle, never deployed buses ordered by Federal authorities to be used, Mayor Nagin had no comment.[25]

The other picture was that of President Bush flying over Louisiana, gazing down at the damage, not stopping in Louisiana but heading back to the White House. The problem was the picture, not the action. The White House released the picture in an effort to show President Bush's concern; instead it became a symbol to people that the president was just flying by. President Bush would later explain that if he had landed in New Orleans or any other Louisiana city that day, it would have been irresponsible. In the midst of all that was going on, a presidential visit would have taken too many law enforcement and rescue officials off their immediate duty.

But the sound bite that summed up for many the near entirety of the problem was, "Brownie, you're doing a heck of a job." The truth was, Michael Brown was ill-equipped for his job, with little experience in emergency response and evacuation, and when he spoke, he seemed to have little command of the facts on the ground or what was happening. When e-mails surfaced between him and a staffer showing, in the midst of the crisis, he was concerned about the clothes he was wearing and whether they would show him as a man in control of a crisis or not, the lie was fully put to his judgment, whatever else he might have done right or wrong.

The ultimate credit for the good news from New Orleans—the rescue and recovery—belongs to the military and the Coast Guard who, from the moment they arrived, worked hard and valiantly where other government agencies had failed (the Coast Guard, alone, rescued more than thirty thousand people).

Pictures of helicopters and other rescues tell only part of the story. But on the side of the failures, only part of the story was told there as well—depending on what one wanted to believe: Was this the federal government's or the local officials' fault? Louisiana Congressman and now Governor Bobby Jindal was ultimately right: "There is enough blame to go around at every level of government."[26] And that would include FEMA and other federal agencies, Mayor Nagin and his charges, and Governor Blanco and hers.

Nagin fed a lot of undue hysteria during the crisis—and, in retrospect, did so with the least amount of credibility. As historian Doug Brinkley would later point out, in the lead-up to the hurricane's landfall, "instead of marshaling the personnel and deploying the resources necessary for confronting the storm, Ray Nagin stalled," and during the crisis, he "showboat[ed]" and "cloister[ed] himself in the Hyatt hotel" where— unlike other mayors on the ground in their cities—he had a comfortable room and received his news by radio.[27] Nagin also ginned up hysterical stories about tragedies taking place at the Superdome.[28] Communication systems were down, feeding much of the rumor mill about what was taking place, but the rumors circulated throughout the country and on the blogosphere like wildfire—rumors such as an infant's body being found in a trash can, sharks swimming through the business district, and bodies being stacked in the Superdome basement.[29] That there was local misfeasance, at best, in Louisiana was testified to the way that the state of Mississippi handled itself during the hurricane, with far more orderly evacuations and far, far less drama.

Katrina was a disaster—with the ultimate death toll reaching more than 1,500 people. And while the country went through a media blitz of truths and untruths about the tragedies from Katrina, and Washington debated the best way to repair the city of New Orleans, the underreported story was the tremendous generosity and humanity of the rest of America that opened its homes and schools and churches and wallets and hearts to the hurricane's victims and evacuees. Literally billions of dollars were raised to help the victims as all kinds of private and public individuals, from Hollywood actors and actresses to businessmen and women to churches and congregations and Americans at every station in life, organized en masse to donate time, money, food, clothing, and even their own homes. To this day, many are still involved in helping restore the city of New Orleans.

The political fallout for the president lasted as well. Even his closest political advisors would later admit that after Katrina, the president had lost much credibility with the public: "He no longer had the capacity to talk to the American public. State of the Union addresses? It didn't matter. Legislative initiatives? It didn't matter. Travel? It didn't matter."*[30] Many blamed the administration, many blamed state and local officials, but Katrina was a natural disaster that is better thought of in terms of what in contract law is known as a *force majeure*—a superior force, an act of God. That should have tempered some of the finger-pointing and rush to blame. Some.**

The news on other fronts seemed to not improve much either, and toward the end of the year, three big stories were reported that took further steam from the president on his and America's key success story: the war on terror.

III. Questions of Legality

To say that President Bush had a rocky relationship with the mainstream media or press (fast becoming known as the MSM) would be more than fair. Indeed, study after study has shown press bias toward Democrats and liberal politics, but beyond that, many in the press thought that they had not done a good enough job of investigating the lead-up to the liberation of

---

* Shortly after the Katrina hurricane, I asked a friend of mine, one of the most respected conservative analysts in the country, if Clinton could have handled Katrina better. My friend said to me, unequivocably: "Yes." I asked why, and he said, "First, he would have related to the people, he was always very good in a tragedy that way, but moreover, he had a better FEMA director." I asked, "Really? James Witt [Clinton's director of FEMA] would have done better?" My friend said, "Oh, sure. First, he had experience; second, President Clinton understood how important that job was, and I'm not sure President Bush, before Katrina, did—it just wasn't on his radar screen. But Clinton usually had a good sense for those kinds of positions." Maybe so.

** Some of the criticism of President Bush was simply beyond the pale, but it was an undercurrent of the more legitimate criticism. Some cultural and political spokesmen, who never gave Bush any credit for his associations with and historic appointments of minority Americans, would say he showed New Orleans (a city with a majority of black residents) a racial benign neglect at best and a racial animus of neglect at worst. The famous, award-winning rap artist Kanye West, for example, said, "George Bush doesn't care about black people" on a nationally televised fund-raiser for Katrina relief efforts. This was grossly unfair.

Iraq and that if they had done a better job of investigating, perhaps they could have helped persuade the nation that expanding the war into Iraq was not a good idea.

The second Bush administration would garner a stronger reaction from the mainstream media. And the left had now in earnest created its own alternative media—from bigger and better news and opinion Web sites to new think tanks to its own radio network. And many of those on the left were making no bones about their actual "hatred" for George W. Bush.* There was a new left and a new vigor in the left in America in 2004 and 2005.

President Bush had his fair detractors, to be sure. His policies from cutting taxes, to ending late-term abortions, to circumscribing the full-bore federal funding of embryonic stem cell experimentation that some wanted, to the war in Iraq and its basis were all fair political game—and the merits of those policies could, obviously, be argued back and forth. On the other hand what was not arguable was that President Bush and his administration's policies had kept the country safe since 11 September 2001, even after so many predicted a second wave, or more, of attacks. On this issue, it seemed, the administration could stand tall.

The mainstream media started to investigate this issue too, and three stories soon spread like wildfire, casting their own doubts on how the administration was going about keeping the U.S. safe. In early November 2005 the *Washington Post* splashed across its front page a story whose headline read: "CIA Holds Terror Suspects in Secret Prisons—Debate Is Growing within Agency about Legality and Morality of Overseas System Set Up After 9/11."[31] The story opened thusly:

> The CIA has been hiding and interrogating some of its most important al Qaeda captives at a Soviet-era compound in Eastern Europe, according to U.S. and foreign officials familiar with the arrangement.
>
> The secret facility is part of a covert prison system set up by the CIA nearly four years ago that at various times has included sites in

---

* As early as 2003, one of the senior editors of the very credible liberal-left magazine in America, the *New Republic*, went so far as to open an essay by writing: "I hate President George W. Bush. There, I said it." That was the moderate and respectable left.

Wall Street Journal reporter Daniel Pearl, kidnapped and later beheaded.

The damaged port side of the USS Cole after the terrorist bombing.

Hijacked United Airlines flight 175 flies into the South T_____ of the World

Rescue personnel respond to the attack on the Pentagon just minutes after
American Airlines flight 77 struck it.

Smoke rises behind investigators as
they comb the crater left by the crash
of United Airlines flight 93 near

Osama bin Laden, Al Qaeda leader
and mastermind of the 9/11 attacks.

British Prime Minister Tony Blair (L) listens as President George W. Bush speaks to the media about the war in Iraq.

The "Shock and Awe" campaign lights up Baghdad on the second day of war.

Former Iraqi leader Saddam Hussein just moments after his capture by U.S. forces at a farm outside Tikrit, Iraq.

Major Mark Bieger carries an Iraqi child wounded by a car bomb, as captured by journalist Michael Yon.

Vice President Dick Cheney meeting with General David Petraeus during a surprise visit to Baghdad.

President George W. Bush peers out the window of Air Force One as he surveys the damage caused by hurricane Katrina.

President George W. Bush at Camp Arifjan, Kuwait.

Illinois Senatorial candidate and keynote speaker Barack Obama speaks during the 2004 Democratic National Convention.

President-elect Barack Obama, his daughters Sasha, 7, and Malia, 10, and his

t Ground Zero

eight countries, including Thailand, Afghanistan and several democracies in Eastern Europe, as well as a small center at the Guantanamo
Bay prison in Cuba, according to current and former intelligence officials and diplomats from three continents.[32]

One would have to read an online discussion hosted by the *Washington
Post* a day later to find out from this reporter that "[the program was] not
illegal under U.S. law, which allows for the CIA to undertake covert actions
abroad."[33] This seemed odd. The administration had been criticized by Joe
Wilson and his supporters on the left about how sacrosanct a covert person
or operation at the CIA should be held. Yet here was a report—leaked from
within the CIA to the national news media—exposing a covert program that,
in turn, exposed our allies in the war on terrorism and was, in fact, legal; and
the left jumped to condemn the program and praise the press for exposing it.

To be sure, the *Post* did not reveal the actual names of the countries
cooperating with the U.S., but it was not hard to surmise which countries
were involved, given the descriptions within the stories. In any event, the
U.S.—through this press exposure—had now made those allies subject to
targeting by terrorist acts. Already, our allies from Spain to the UK had been
subject to immense Islamic terrorist attacks against their people.

Within a day of the *Post* story, the Arabic news channel Al Jazeera was
running it throughout the Middle East, and the *Washington Post* reporter
was bragging, "The article [I wrote] is bommeranging [*sic*] around Europe,
especially Eastern Europe."[34] Who were the detainees in these prisons?
Some would legitimately call them "the worst of the worst," as they included
Khalid Sheikh Mohammed and several of his colleagues. And so a legal CIA
covert operation was disclosed—and soon ended.*

A little more than a month later, the *New York Times* exposed another
program. On 16 December, the paper's headline, in an article by James Risen

---

* I had made a very big deal of the impropriety of disclosing this program on my radio show and
in the blogosphere and, in short order, was invited on *Meet the Press* to discuss the ethics of such
reporting. Aside from Dana Priest (the *Washington Post* reporter on the secret sites story) as a
sparring partner they had booked me with, they also had three other members of the
mainstream media taking her side on our panel. Perhaps the name of the show was never more
true. To the best of my knowledge, I have not been invited back on since then.

and Eric Lichtblau, read: "Bush Lets U.S. Spy on Callers without Courts." The article reported:

> President Bush secretly authorized the National Security Agency (NSA) to eavesdrop on Americans and others inside the United States to search for evidence of terrorist activity without the court-approved warrants ordinarily required for domestic spying, according to government officials.[35]

What was surprising about the lead sentence was that it was generally understood that agencies such as the NSA could intercept only communications abroad. One had to read a bit further in the article to understand that this was a program used to intercept phone calls not exclusively originating and taking place within the United States but calls to and from abroad where one party was in the United States. One also learned from the story that the New York Times had had the story for about a year, was sitting on it, and was asked specifically not to disclose it lest it damage a highly successful terrorist-monitoring program. On its own time frame, the New York Times decided to run the story anyway.

Another covert, wartime, national security program had been leaked to the press, and the press—this time with the explicit request from the administration to *not* run the story—disclosed it. Was such a program illegal? Were warrants required to intercept and monitor phone calls between Americans and people overseas? And if so, why would the New York Times sit on the story for so long—even if not, what had given the newspaper of record in America the right to hold back a story it thought deserved airing for the declared purpose of "the public right to know"? These questions dominated the end of 2005 and beginning of 2006 in America.

Of course any good lawyer can argue for the illegality or legality of any vague law. And the laws about the NSA and Fourth Amendment were, indeed, hard to understand. It was all a complicated area of law. But before that discussion could take place, the Democratic National Committee sent out a release "condemning the program as 'illegal surveillance' constituting an 'explosive scandal.'"[36]

As people began to take seriously the issues involved, however, the debate came down between civil libertarians, who would argue that the 1978 Foreign Intelligence Surveillance Act (FISA) required a judicially approved warrant before any U.S. "person" could be monitored, and constitutionalists, who saw other precedent—especially in wartime. For example, a 2002 decision by the FISA Court had, in fact, said, "We take for granted that the President does have that authority [to engage in warrantless searches 'to obtain foreign intelligence information'] and, assuming that is so, FISA could not encroach on the President's constitutional power."[37]

Notwithstanding the contemporaneous debate about all this in early 2006, or the very legitimate question of whether the *New York Times* and the *Washington Post* had violated the law by disclosing these covert programs, yet another program would soon be disclosed. Known as the SWIFT program (Society for Worldwide Interbank Financial Telecommunication), the Treasury Department had been monitoring financial transactions "of people suspected of having ties to al Qaeda by reviewing records from the nerve center of the Belgian global banking industry."[38] The *New York Times*, again, broke the story and the covert nature of the program—putting an end to what 9/11 Commission Co-Chairman Tom Kean had called "a good program, one that was legal, one that was not violating anybody's civil liberties . . . and something the U.S. government should be doing to make us safer."[39] In fact, it was one program that the 9/11 Commission had identified as doing great work—and again, the government had asked the *Times* not to run the story.

Very little was done in trying to find out who had been leaking information to the newspapers, and less was done to commence legal investigations into the newspapers.* But programs had been disrupted with impunity, and some regarded this whole period as the beginning of "the war against the war" back home in the United States. Because of public sentiment, the administration had a problem doing much about any of this. Lincoln had argued that "public sentiment is everything. With public sentiment, nothing

---

* Several of us had urged the administration to go after the press here and open up a legal investigation, but the administration was uninterested in picking such a fight. It's been said, "Never pick a fight with someone who buys ink by the barrel," but I've never subscribed to that advice.

can fail; without it nothing can succeed."[40] And the president—after Katrina, and during an increasingly unpopular war in Iraq—didn't have it.

By the summer of 2006, American forces had tracked down and killed the leader of al Qaeda in Iraq, Abu Musab al-Zarqawi. Nevertheless, the war, with its increasing toll on America and its allies (America had lost more than two thousand soldiers by 2006), was highly unpopular—some 55 percent thought the war was going badly, and the president had an approval rating of just 33 percent.[41] And the president was not shoring up a good deal of his base.

IV. Losing the Base

In the super bowl of judicial appointments, the Supreme Court, it was one step backward, two steps forward for the president and his base. The president had caused concern with conservatives the year before upon the retirement of Justice Sandra Day O'Connor. President Bush put forward his friend and White House counsel Harriet Miers as her replacement. Many in the conservative movement thought she was not up to the job, was too inexperienced, and was not sufficiently steeped in an understanding of constitutional law that would lead her to "originalist" judgments and conclusions. Few in the conservative base wanted another "surprise" like David Souter, a judge who they were told was conservative but with little evidence to back that up and little to prove their skepticism incorrect later.

President Bush won back his supporters with his selection of Samuel Alito for the Supreme Court instead of Miers after she withdrew her candidacy. His earlier nomination of John Roberts as Chief Justice of the Supreme Court was also considered a home run by conservatives. In looking to a lasting, overriding conservative legacy of George Bush, these two appointments—Roberts and Alito—could have been it.

But the president had alienated much of his base, particularly around two issues: (1) a port management proposal that would have a subsidiary of the United Arab Emirates manage ports in the United States; and (2) an illegal immigration reform plan that, in most conservatives' minds, amounted to little more than amnesty for those who had entered this country illegally.

The Dubai Ports World issue lost the president a great many supporters who had backed him on his tough stance against terrorism and his pledge toward transforming the Middle East as he had spoken about in his second Inaugural. But the United Arab Emirates had a shady background when it came to its commitment to fight terrorists, and its human rights record was wholly antithetical to everything President Bush had said about freedom and human rights in his Second Inaugural. Now they were going to manage our ports? A vulnerable place of cargo entry for the U.S.? Congress ginned up a resolution to oppose such a deal, and the president went so far as to threaten to veto such legislation—putting him at odds with both Democrats and Republicans. Ultimately, Dubai Ports World withdrew its bid in an effort for everyone to save face and sold off its American assets to the American International Group.[42] But it was a fight the president did not need from his base.*

There was no question the president had strong feelings about immigration. He spoke Spanish and had earned high numbers of votes from the American Hispanic community. But while generous, the American people by and large had grown tired of the flood of illegal immigrants coming into the country. The sentiments of many could be summarized as: legal immigration, yes; illegal immigration, no. But the president was adamant that the only way to solve the problem was to show mercy to those who had traveled and settled here illegally, put them on "a path to citizenship," and then address future illegal immigration. Those opposed to such a plan had little doubt our government could even process the illegal immigrants here and "bring them out of the shadows," as the argument went. One report revealed that the system was so broken, the U.S. Citizenship and Immigration Services "had lost track of 111,000 files in 14 of the agency's busiest district offices and processed as many as 30,000 citizenship applications [in one year] without the required files."[43]

The president had some support for his plans among conservative and

---

* I remember stating on CNN early on that that program "would not stand" and urged the president to find a way to back off it, and fast.

in Republican circles, but most of the conservative base, blogosphere, and talk radio were overwhelmingly against any amnesty plan. In the Senate, the president had one vociferous ally in the Republican Party—John McCain of Arizona. But McCain himself, while a hawk on Iraq—like the president—was not a favorite with much of the base either, having voted against the president's first tax cut and supported campaign finance laws that many had thought unconstitutional abridgements of their political speech.*

The president would try twice to reform our immigration laws (once in 2006, once again in 2007), and both times he failed miserably. By the midterm elections of 2006, his "political capital" was pretty much expired, and Republicans were thumped. "Iraq, Iraq, Iraq," was the reason Democrats took back the Senate and the House for the first time since 1994 as NBC's Washington Bureau Chief Tim Russert had said on election night—and he was mostly right.

Even hawkish Democrats, like Jack Murtha of Pennsylvania, had become outspoken opponents of our efforts in Iraq.** Americans were tiring of a war they had thought would be a "cakewalk."*** CBS asked Congressman Murtha and me to deliver our views, side by side, one Sunday morning, summarizing the case for staying and the case for getting out. Murtha put it this way:

> To say that the United States should stay in Iraq to avoid a full-blown civil war is a disservice to our American troops. Our military has completed its mission in Iraq. I said nearly two years ago, and most

---

* Curbs on political contributions to candidates were deemed by many as curbs on speech, as it was money that could buy commercial airtime, campaign literature, and the like. Just as no newspaper would allow Congress to curb how much money it could spend on promoting a point of view or candidate on its editorial page, many thought it unconstitutional to curb what individuals could spend supporting a candidate of their choice.

** And even Murtha—long respected on Capitol Hill as a Democrat that many pro-defense and national security Republicans could do business with—would go on to use extreme, harsh language, saying at one point that our soldiers had "killed innocent civilians in cold blood," when he had learned of a massacre that had taken place in Iraq. Eight U.S. Marines were charged with crimes related to the Iraqi deaths; as of this writing, all but one has been cleared.

*** Nobody in the administration had said Iraq would be a "cakewalk." The phrase belonged to former Reagan administration official Ken Adelman, who used it in an op-ed leading up to the war in Iraq. This was, perhaps, the most ill-advised pro-war word offered about Iraq.

military leaders now agree, Iraq cannot be won militarily. It's time to redeploy our troops from Iraq. Nearly $300 billion will be spent by the end of this year. More than 30,000 Iraqis have lost their lives. Over 800 lives were lost in Iraq in January alone.

There have been nearly 20,000 US casualties since the start of the war. More than 2,300 US service members have died and 17,000 have been wounded. Iraq is not a "we" thing anymore, it's a "they" thing. The Iraqis had their elections, they elected their parliament, now let's allow the Iraqis to govern themselves, provide for their own common defense and promote their own general welfare.[44]

That was the essence of the call for withdrawal in 2006: too many lives had been lost, too much money was being spent, and the U.S. should withdraw from a "civil war" it had no business policing. I had argued on the same CBS broadcast that those numbers, astounding to the modern mind unused to major wars as it was, were not the whole story.

Almost 7,000 American soldiers died in one month at Iwo Jima. In the Battle of Okinawa, we lost more than 12,000 men in two months. In Europe, on D-Day, we lost 2,500 of our brave men in just twenty-four hours. Those numbers are exceedingly high, but they were not the whole story in World War II either. The whole story was the ultimate success born of our resolve, from not quitting when the going got tough—and by sticking with it, we freed Europe and Japan from tyranny.

Too many have forgotten what Iraq was before we went in. It was a place led by a ruthless barbarian who, thanks to our work, was in jail and by the end of 2006 would be hanged to death after an Iraqi court found him guilty of crimes against humanity. In three years, Iraq had gone from an entrenched tyranny to a fledgling democracy, but it can not yet stand alone.

Bin Laden has called on the U.S. to leave Iraq, and for Muslim fighters to join the struggle to push us out. We do not want to give him a victory there. And while Iraq is fledgling, with lots of fits and starts, no country can be expected to go from barbarism to democracy on a theoretical deadline. Terrorists who behead civilians are not to be left alone to destroy our new ally, the first democracy in the Arab world.

But, it seemed, this was not an argument enough of the country wanted to hear. The president was compromised, and in late September his party had yet another scandal on its hands. ABC News was reporting that a former male House page had been having an inappropriate relationship with Republican Congressman Mark Foley of Florida. ABC News confirmed their sources for the story and soon had access to excerpts of instant messages Foley had been sending to that page and other underage male pages. The instant messages were at once sexually graphic and juvenile—as if written in the vernacular of a teenager. Within hours Foley announced his resignation from Congress. But the matter was far from over.

Soon after, reports came in from a former Mark Foley staffer that Speaker of the House Denny Hastert's staff had been warned about Foley's behavior some years earlier and seemingly had done little about it other than verbally warn Foley.[45] To make matters worse, Foley was the cochairman of the House Missing and Exploited Children Caucus.*

As media critic Howard Kurtz would put it, the Foley scandal "was a godsend for the news casts," feeding "their love of scandal, sleaze, and an unraveling mystery."[46] That was exactly what the Republicans did not need going into midterm elections in November.

Meanwhile, little good was being reported from Iraq—also deemed "the Republicans' war." The media were framing the situation in Iraq as "an unmitigated mess" and "shaping public sentiment" with that message, as Kurtz put it.[47] The nightly newscast anchors "looked for ways to dramatize the grim statistics."[48] Most pollsters were showing November 2006 to be a loss for Republicans—and it was.

The Republicans lost thirty seats in the House and six seats in the Senate.[49] The most interesting race of the year was Democrat Joe Lieberman's

---

* To be sure, the Democrats had their scandals, and two years earlier the governor of New Jersey, James McGreevey, had resigned from office over the admission of an extramarital affair with a man. But the GOP had been the party that most strenuously went after Bill Clinton; it was the party that had won its elections two years before on the issue of "moral values." And so it was special trouble for them.

Senate reelection in Connecticut. The left of the Democratic Party wanted to punish him for his staunch support of the Iraq War—in truth, few were as articulate and supportive as he was, even throughout the election—and they supported a primary challenger against him and defeated him in the primary. Lieberman ran in the general election as an independent and held off his Democratic and Republican challengers—but not without a few scars. Democratic National Committee Chairman Howard Dean had publicly called for Lieberman to leave the race and respect the Democratic primary, and Lieberman found himself in the general election without many other prominent national Democrats campaigning for or supporting him.

Democratic Congresswoman Nancy Pelosi from California would become the new Speaker of the House—the first female to ever hold that position—and a new year would soon begin, with Democrats in charge on Capitol Hill. And charged with the mission by their votaries to get the U.S. out of Iraq.

V. The Surge

The day after the election, President Bush announced that Secretary of Defense Donald Rumsfeld had submitted his resignation and that Bush had accepted it. Rumsfeld, one of the most popular men in public life shortly after the 11 September attacks, had become one of the most unpopular representatives of the war in Iraq.

Secretary Rumsfeld had been resolute in staying the course in Iraq while not increasing troops as many had suggested he should, but he was not the commander in chief—those ultimate calls would always have to be made by the president. Secretary Rumsfeld had offered his resignation at least twice prior to 2006, and the president did not accept those offers. But with a new direction planned for Iraq and an increased drubbing from the media and the party that would now run Capitol Hill, the president had accepted this resignation.*

Indeed, a new plan for Iraq had been in the works—from both outside

---

* High-level resignations can be odd things in Washington—sometimes they are offered; sometimes they are solicited. By most accounts, this last resignation offer from Rumsfeld—unlike his previous ones—was solicited.

and inside the administration. In January 2007, the president announced a new commander in Iraq and a new strategy: the commander, General David Petraeus; the strategy, "a surge." Far from withdrawing from Iraq, the administration was going to ramp up and send more troops into Iraq with a counterinsurgency plan developed by General Petraeus. The plan was detailed but it could be broadly summed up as increasing the troop levels, clearing and holding enemy territory, and staying after the enemy once he fled. This, in brief, was the surge. Petraeus was known in the military as "a warrior-scholar," having graduated from West Point, but also having received a master's and doctorate from Princeton University. If previous generals heading the multinational forces in Iraq had become symbols of the problems and the violence there, David Petraeus and the surge would, in short order, be given one last chance to turn it all around—or fail once and for all in Iraq.

But that was only half of the American story in early 2007; the other half was the new Democratic Congress and an antiwar Democratic Congress at that. Nancy Pelosi assumed her role with a great many expectations, both as the first female Speaker of the House and as a liberal Democrat taking the helm of the House for the first time in twelve years. The Democrats had promised to, and been expected to, end the war in Iraq, and Speaker Pelosi did not shrink from that expectation. In an early interview after the election, she said,

> The American people and the Congress support those troops. We will not abandon them. But if the president wants to add to this mission, he is going to have to justify it and this is new for him because up until now the Republican Congress has given him a blank check with no oversight, no standards, no conditions.[50]

The new Senate Majority Leader, Harry Reid of Nevada, was more negative about the surge: "Based on the advice of current and former military leaders, we believe this tactic would be a serious mistake."[51]

But the Democrats knew they had to walk a careful line here, as the Republicans and others in favor of prosecuting the war to the end, and successfully, had been reminding the public: if America left Iraq too early, it could very well be a repeat of Vietnam with a precipitous withdrawal—very much begun with Congress cutting off aid—leading not just to the loss of American credibility abroad (including with allies who had depended on us) but to the huge loss of human life.

Before January was out, the Senate Foreign Relations Committee had passed a nonbinding resolution opposing the surge. Committee Chairman Joe Biden said, "This is not designed to say, 'Mr. President, ah-ha, you're wrong. . . . This is designed to say, 'Mr. President, please don't go do this.'"[52] Vice President Dick Cheney had become a whipping boy for the antiwar crowd, given his strong support for the war as well as his often terse dismissals of the opposition. When asked by a reporter about the vote, he replied: "It won't stop us."[53] And it did not.

The Congress had budget authority, but the president had veto power—and he was still the commander in chief. He knew time was running out on his administration, and it was his last chance to turn Iraq around. Who knew what the 2008 elections would bring? But the Democrats knew, too, why they were elected and what they stood for and what they stood against, and they passed a war-financing budget that demanded the beginning of troop withdrawals by October 2007. President Bush vetoed it, saying, "It makes no sense to tell the enemy when you plan to start withdrawing. All the terrorists would have to do is mark their calendars. . . . Setting a deadline for withdrawal is setting a date for failure, and that would be irresponsible."[54] But that would not be the most famous statement about Iraq in 2007.

The most far-reaching thing said about Iraq in 2007 belonged to Senate Majority Leader Harry Reid. At an April news conference discussing why timelines for withdrawal should be imposed and why the surge of troops to Iraq was the opposite direction he thought America should take, he said, "I believe myself that the secretary of state, secretary of defense and—you have to make your own decisions as to what the president knows—that this war is lost and the surge is not accomplishing anything as indicated by the extreme violence in Iraq."[55]

"This war is lost" was the statement that would shoot across the world. America was in the midst of a war and a new plan for winning the war, with increased troops in and on the field of battle, and the leader of the U.S. Senate pronounced the war "lost." He was criticized far and wide within the country, and by the troops, who did not want to hear and did not believe they were fighting for a lost cause or for a war that had ended. As perhaps the leading Republican in the Senate arguing for the surge and for sticking it out in Iraq, John McCain had said, "If the war is lost, who won?" But such was the state of heated rhetoric in 2007.

As the debate on Capitol Hill was brewing and boiling, another story south of the capital would soon seize the nation's attention. On 16 April, a disturbed young college student had seized and bound entry and exit doors at Virginia Polytechnic Institute and State University (Virginia Tech, as it is known) and shot thirty-two students and professors to death, wounding many others. It was one of the largest shooting rampages in American history and the deadliest shooting on any school campus in America. In the shooting aftermath, the media descended on the scene, Katrina-like, and covered the story from nearly every angle, interviewing victims, family members, associates, other students, anyone they could—and another national debate and discussion on school violence, gun laws, and security commenced.

It was the darkest day of the year on the American home front, but it—as with almost any tragedy or disaster in America—was not without its heroes. Seventy-six-year-old Liviu Librescu, a Romanian-born citizen of Israel—and a Holocaust survivor—had been teaching at Virginia Tech for years. One of the more popular professors, he was holding his mechanics class on 16 April when he heard gunshots down the hall. Several students in Librescu's classroom hid behind tables or under their desks, recalled Alec Calhoun, a student in the class, while others leaped from the windows. Professor Librescu ran to the door and blocked it shut with his body as he ordered the rest of his students to flee through the windows. One student remembered, "Before I jumped from the window, I turned around and looked at the professor, who stayed behind."[56] Librescu was shot through the door of his classroom, holding off the shooter, giving his life for his students so they would have time to escape. "All the students [in that room] lived—because of him," another of his students would say.[57]

While many were focused on what wire had been crossed in the brain of the student-murderer, and endless discussions tried to psychoanalyze him and discuss the depredating lives of too many in our country, one commentator got the sense of the story—which unfolded the day after Holocaust Remembrance Day—just right:

> Shouldn't [Dr. Librescu's] bravery do more to steady our faith in the possibility of human goodness than the crimes of death-dealers like [the student] do to destroy it?
>
> To answer Yes is to see in [Dr. Librescu] a kindred spirit with the most famous Romanian-Jewish survivor [of the Holocaust], Elie Wiesel. In his 1986 Nobel lecture, Wiesel said, "A destruction, an annihilation that only man can provoke, only man can prevent." Wiesel, as a defender of human rights, has dedicated his life to this proposition. Librescu gave his life for it. I believe we can justly presume that their common experience led them to this common wisdom. . . . Their sensitivity to the suffering of others, their perseverance, and, as with Prof. Librescu, their heroism, is a tribute to the triumph of light.[58]

Back on Capitol Hill, the House and Senate worked to put together a financing budget that could save Democratic face, showing opposition to the war, but not denying all funding for the war—thus undercutting the troops and being seen as responsible for a Saigon-type fall of Iraq. Ultimately, the Democrats signed off on legislation that would seek timetables from the Iraqi government as benchmarks for success, timetables that would make future funding of the war effort contingent on the benchmarks being met.[59]

When General Petraeus (along with U.S. Ambassador to Iraq Ryan Crocker) came to Capitol Hill to deliver his much-anticipated assessment of the surge in Iraq in September, he was greeted rather unfortunately. The left-wing advocacy group Moveon.org had taken out a full-page ad in the *New York Times*—in bold, at the top, the ad read: "General Petraeus or General Betray Us?"[60] The ad had cited statements of General Petraeus—and a three-year-old op-ed—that were in conflict with some facts about Iraq that Moveon and the antiwar left had cited. But those facts were not the issue, disputed as they were. The issue was the headline Moveon had written. It had long been stated by the left that even if they did not support the military policy in

Iraq, they had (or most of them anyway) supported the troops themselves. This ad questioned that sentiment to its core: General Petraeus was the commander of the troops in Iraq, and now he was being called a betrayer.

Even a good many Democrats on the Hill thought the ad went too far— although they pulled their punches against a group they relied on to turn out numbers for them at rallies, at protests, and during voting season. "Not helpful," was what one Democratic staffer had said.[61]

But there were only two sitting senators on the Democratic side of the aisle whom people were watching and listening to, to hear what they had to say about the ad: Hillary Clinton of New York and Barack Obama of Illinois. Neither would condemn the ad or Moveon. When a sense of the Senate resolution was put forward to condemn the ad by a literal vote of the members, Clinton voted against it, and Obama did not vote at all.[62] Asked about all this two weeks later on *Meet the Press*, Senator Clinton sounded a different note: "I don't condone anything like that [ad], and I have voted against those who would impugn the patriotism and the service of the people who wear the uniform of our country. I don't believe that that should be said about General Petraeus, and I condemn that."[63]

Petraeus and Crocker testified about slow but steady and "fragile" and "reversible" progress in Iraq: "The situation in Iraq remains complex, difficult and sometimes downright frustrating. . . . I also believe that it is possible to achieve our objectives in Iraq over time, although doing so will be neither quick nor easy."[64] It was no rosy scenario they were painting, but they did object to any withdrawal that would reverse the course they were on. Democrats were still having little of it. Senator Reid said, "U.S. national security requires that we truly and immediately change course in Iraq."[65]

As important as all of this was in the eyes of much of the public, it was still a sideshow compared to the presidential election that would take place in 2008.

VI. The 2008 Presidential Race Begins

The reason the only two Democratic senators being watched were Clinton and Obama was that they were the two major Senate Democrats questioning

Petraeus and the war, promising to do their best to end it, and they had already entered the field for president.

Senator Barack Obama—the one who had given an antiwar speech as a state senator in 2002, the one who had dazzled the Democratic Convention in 2004, the one who had been elected that year and seated in the U.S. Senate just two years prior—had become a serious candidate for president. Senator Obama and his advisors had read the mood of the country and their party and thought it needed something different, something substantially different—a change. Obama was young (forty-six years old in 2007), a newcomer to Washington, against the Iraq War from the beginning, articulate, and a black American. His middle name was Hussein. He was different; he was change. And in February 2007 on a frigid day in Springfield, Illinois, to a crowd of thousands, he had announced he was running for president.

In his announcement, Obama did not shy from speaking of the perceived "presumptuousness" of running for president with so little experience. He embraced it and folded it into his message of change: "I recognize there is a certain presumptuousness—a certain audacity to this announcement. I know I haven't spent a lot of time learning the ways of Washington. But I've been there long enough to know that the ways of Washington must change."[66] He rattled off the problems he saw, from "a war with no end" to domestic failures, and offered himself up as a new kind of political leader who could fix them. While crowd estimates varied, it was a massive event. One person who was not there, however, was Barack Obama's pastor, Rev. Jeremiah Wright.

Senator Hillary Rodham Clinton had already announced her candidacy in January. Hers was no less an interesting candidacy. Never elected to office until she ran for Senate from New York in 2000, she had been a divisive figure in politics during her husband's tenure in office and was much watched as a senator. She had made great strides in the Senate by her diligence and discipline. She knew she was a newcomer to elected office; she knew her every step and word would be monitored; she knew the Clinton brand had had an uneasy relationship with the press. But she also, by 2007, knew something else: there was no bigger name or draw in Democratic Party politics than "Clinton." She was a hero to many Democratic women, her husband was still a great party fund-raiser and political mind, and together they could gin up their political machine of advisors and friends and people for whom they had done favors over their long years in public service. On the Democratic side were the first truly plausible black candidate and female candidate for president.

Others entered the Democratic ring as well, including Senator John Edwards and then Senator Joe Biden, but none was as interesting as Obama and Clinton, with the possible exception of the still young and, to many, charming former vice presidential candidate John Edwards.*

Aside from Joe Lieberman, who was caucusing with the Democrats even though he called himself an independent-Democrat, the strongest and most ardent supporter of the surge and the campaign in Iraq was Republican John McCain.** And never one to revel in the conventional wisdom of his party or a poll, McCain had justifiably earned the nickname of "Maverick." He had announced he would run for president for 2008, and his announcement was marked by not a few raised eyebrows. He was a war hero like few others, having had bones and teeth crushed in a Vietnam prison camp after his plane was shot down, and he took that beating for more than five years. But he was also a Republican like few others. He had opposed President Bush's initial tax cuts and had disappointed much of the Republican base on other initiatives he had taken on over the years—from campaign finance reform legislation to antitorture legislation, which many had deemed was too vague and would hamstring intelligence and military efforts. He had a solid voting record on most right-to-life issues, but was in favor of federal funding of embryonic stem cell research (which the right-to-life community strenuously opposed). And he was not a frequent speaker on or to social issues. Still, he thought his long service in the party and his dedication to the troops and military put him in the right place and right time to run for

---

* After many denials and after his campaign had ended, John Edwards would finally admit that he had carried on an adulterous affair in 2006 with a campaign staffer. Edwards had concealed the affair leading up to his run for president. He had held himself out as a strong family man and, moreover, his wife, Elizabeth, had earned a great deal of national sympathy as both a survivor and victim of life-threatening cancer. These and other factors that came to light later made his actions unusually unconscionable.

** I recall sharing an airplane ride with McCain around this time, and I asked him if he thought we could really pull out of Iraq before the country was truly pacified. He slammed his fist on the table and said, "We cannot, we cannot, we cannot do that. I never want to see another helicopters-fleeing-Saigon situation again."

president in 2008—even if much of the country was opposed to his position on the Iraq War. About that, he would say, "I'd rather lose an election than lose a war." A maverick, indeed.

Outside of political office, Rudy Giuliani, the famous former mayor of New York City—who had been seen as a hero on 9/11 and during the following weeks—had formed a consulting firm and had been traveling the country, delivering motivational and crisis management speeches. He was also a strong proponent of the war in Iraq and not withdrawing before the job was done, and he had announced his candidacy as well. Giuliani's candidacy also raised eyebrows. As articulate as anyone on the war against radical Islam (or what he called "radical Islam's war against us"), he was known as a social liberal, pro-choice and pro-gay rights; a tough if not seemingly impossible sell in the conservative national Republican Party.

Former Massachusetts Governor Mitt Romney was also not known as a Republican standard-bearer when he announced his candidacy. He was declaring himself staunchly pro-life, even on embryonic stem cells, and had written op-eds opposing gay marriage as he was debating its legalization in Massachusetts when he was governor. But he was not always pro-life or tough on the social issues. When he had run for governor of Massachusetts in 2002 and prevailed in that race, he ran as a socially liberal, pro-choice Republican. He had had a change of mind, he would say, when he began studying the stem cell issue in 2004. Romney had good friends at conservative think tanks, had become extremely wealthy, and had a hugely winning personality. (People who had suffered from the occasional sharp elbows of McCain and Giuliani never had that problem with Romney.)

There were two other things about Mitt Romney. Before he became a one-term governor of Massachusetts, he had built for himself the reputation as a whip-smart businessman and turnaround expert, someone who turned around failing companies. Many recalled that he had turned around a scandal-plagued Olympics a few years earlier. The other thing about Mitt Romney, however, was his religion. He was a member of the Church of Jesus Christ of Latter Day Saints, a Mormon, and many religious conservatives had very mixed feelings about that church's theology, or their perceptions of it.

Former Arkansas Governor Mike Huckabee had also thrown his hat in the ring. A former Baptist preacher, he had been known as a cultural crusader on social issues and had lately made an even more interesting name for himself as an amateur health expert, having dropped more than one hundred pounds from his large frame; he had even run in a marathon. Few at the beginning of 2007 gave much thought to his candidacy, and he had not been known for saying much about the issue of the day—the war against terrorism.

Still, among a lot of conservative troops, this field left many cold. Each candidate seemed to be missing a big something they had wanted—and throughout the year, there would be talk of another big candidate entering the race, perhaps Newt Gingrich or the former actor and Senator Fred Thompson.

Meanwhile, what 2008 would bring remained a mystery. The economy had been steadily picking up, unemployment was low again, and the Dow Jones stock market indicator was hitting record highs in 2007.[67] By the end of the year, those who had supported the surge in Iraq were given some good news, as was the rest of the country. Michael O'Hanlon and his colleagues at the liberal Brookings Institute—who had been reporting on Iraqi benchmarks, successes, and failures—were able to report at least a glass-half-full report on Iraq in the *New York Times*:

> As 2007 comes to close, how should we understand the situation in Iraq? Are we witnessing the greatest American military comeback late in a war since Sherman's march to the sea in 1864? Or is Iraq still a weakly governed and very violent place where sectarian reconciliation is starkly absent?
>
> The problem for American policymakers, troops and voters is that both these situations are simultaneously real. Iraq's security environment is considerably improved, with security at its best levels since early 2004. This is largely thanks to the surge-based strategy of Gen. David Petraeus and the heroic efforts—and sacrifice—of so many American and Iraqi troops and police officers (more Americans have died in Iraq in 2007 than in any previous year, though death

rates have dropped greatly in the last few months). But Iraq's political environment and its economy are only marginally better than a year ago.[68]

Security was improving to a record level, and deaths were on the decline. Good news in any war. The politics and economy of Iraq were important—but for the military and security situation, order was beginning to be restored, something many (including those who declared the war "lost") were not sure could happen. Indeed, by the end of General Petraeus's tenure in Iraq the following year, the surge would turn out to be one of the great military achievements in recent memory, so much so that the news operations closed down bureaus in Iraq and called back their correspondents, and Iraq became less and less of a headline.

VII. The Audacity of Barack Obama

The opening of President Bush's final year in office seemed to secure him his place as a lame duck. Aside from it being his last year in office, his approval ratings had not improved, and he began the year at a record low—with 32 percent of Americans approving of the job he was doing, and 66 percent disapproving.[69] He was, simply put, "beset by growing economic concerns on top of the long unpopular war in Iraq."[70] If Bill Clinton was morally compromised in his last year in office, George Bush was politically compromised in his. Yes, Iraq was turning around, but the war was so very unpopular in most of the country (some 64 percent were saying it was not worth fighting)[71] and so was almost everything else (with 77 percent saying the country was heading in the wrong direction).[72] With those numbers it was difficult to get a message out that was good news about anything and equally hard to be believed. The country was ready for a big change and was listening to the candidates for president more than anybody else.

Senator Barack Obama, a junior senator with only two years in the Senate, was taking on the strongest Democratic political machine recent history had known, the Clintons—a former president and a powerful senator. He was the opposite of their establishment machine and had attracted the youth as Howard Dean had, but in greater numbers and without any of the temper—he was a gifted speaker and seemingly never broke a sweat. He was cool, young, and athletic. For the antiwar activists, he was on the right side from the beginning, and for the liberals on other issues, he was that and more (some ratings had him the most liberal member of the Senate). For the lifelong dream of so many, putting a black man into the White House, this was their chance. If "change" was what the Democrats or country wanted, this man was it. This dream was given purchase when Senator Obama won the Iowa caucuses in early January. It was a remarkable feat and an explicit response to those who would worry that the country was not ready to elect a black man to the presidency; Iowa, after all, was almost 95 percent white—a good test for the proposition.[73]

Could Obama carry the momentum with him, or would the Clintons be able to stop him in New Hampshire and beyond? Senator Clinton knew she had to win New Hampshire to remain viable; she could not lose two in a row. And while the polling was uncertain, even showing an Obama lead, Clinton squeaked out a victory there, beating Obama by just two points.[74] Bill Clinton had been campaigning hard for his wife, and the Obama team had been campaigning equally hard. And at the staff level and among their mutual supporters, the contest was getting very hot. Change versus experience, first black man versus first woman. The other candidates soon dropped out.

Back and forth Obama and Clinton went—with the famous Bill Clinton temper flaring in a few places along the way. It looked to be like an interminable primary season for the Democrats with each candidate winning big and small states along the way. Politics was supposed to be fun; for the Democratic insiders this was not. It would come down to superdelegates (Democratic Party insiders who could also vote generally for their primary candidate of choice) and a very narrow margin of primary and caucus voters. And in the end, Barack Obama clinched it, a remarkable first—a black man would lead the ticket for a major party for president. The *New York Times* reported the historic race and victory this way:

A last-minute rush of Democratic superdelegates, as well as the results from the final primaries in Montana and South Dakota, pushed

Obama over the threshold of winning the 2,118 delegates needed to be nominated at the party's convention in Denver in August. It was an improbable triumph for Obama, the son of a black Kenyan father and white Kansan mother, who served as an Illinois state senator just four years ago. In giving Obama the victory, his party broke a racial barrier.[75]

And the country had broken one too. Obama proved to be a hugely able campaigner, and during the primary campaign there was only one moment when things looked as though they could spell really big trouble for him—a human hurricane named Jeremiah Wright.

For years, Jeremiah Wright had been Barack Obama's pastor, mentor, and friend, leading the black Trinity United Church of Christ in Chicago. Obama had even titled one of his books, *The Audacity of Hope*, after one of Wright's sermons. For some time, several talk radio hosts and Fox News Channel hosts, most prominently the hugely popular Sean Hannity, had been airing YouTube audio and video of several fiery rants Jeremiah Wright had delivered from his pulpit. And by March 2008, the rest of the media had picked up on the story. The rants showed him whipping himself up into a lather and saying things such as "God Bless America? No, no, no, God damn America. . . . God damn America for treating our citizens as less than human. God damn America for as long as she acts like she is God and she is supreme."[76]

Barack Obama would maintain he had never been in church when Wright had said such things and had not earlier heard him say things like that. To many, that was hard to believe, especially after it was noted Obama had asked Wright to not lead the invocation at his presidential campaign kickoff event in 2007, telling Wright, "You can get kind of rough in the sermons."[77] At first, Obama had dismissed the critiques of Wright, saying he was "like an old uncle who says things I don't always agree with."[78] But with so many questions circulating about Wright's indefensible preaching, Obama decided to go to Philadelphia and give a talk on race and the church.

In that speech, Obama said he found Wright's statements to be offensive, but he covered for Wright and their relationship: "Did I strongly disagree with many of his political views? Absolutely—just as I'm sure many of you have heard remarks from your pastors, priests, or rabbis with which you strongly disagreed."[79] He went on to defend Wright as a man, as someone more than those sermons that appalled so many, saying, those sermons were not "all that I know of the man. The man I met more than twenty years ago is a man who helped introduce me to my Christian faith, a man who spoke to me about our obligations to love one another; to care for the sick and lift up the poor," and he spoke of Wright's other virtues.[80]

It was not enough distancing for many, and it was too much attention for Jeremiah Wright, who then went on a speaking tour and tried to justify much of his fiery rhetoric with racial stereotypes and the kinds of statements about blacks and whites that would be described as nothing short of vile even from Obama's supporters. Finally, Obama divorced his pastor, saying that Wright had become not the person he had come to know "20 years ago," and that "whatever relationship I had with Reverend Wright has changed, as a consequence of this." Obama would quit his membership in Wright's church.[81]

On the Republican side, things were surely less interesting, but not without surprises. Former Senator Fred Thompson did enter the race—late. And he made his announcement on the *Tonight Show* of all places, at the very time his Republican colleagues were debating in New Hampshire.[82] Former Governor Mitt Romney found himself having to answer more and more questions about his recent switch on abortion policy and about his Mormon faith. When Mike Huckabee hired Republican campaign veteran Ed Rollins to run his campaign, Rollins heated things up in Iowa, and Huckabee made an all-out effort there, thinking if he could win Iowa (where he would have a good shot given his sincere and long-held affiliation with the evangelical community) he could pick up more and more momentum. Huckabee had become quite the sleeper candidate, written off by many as an also-ran when he had announced but then showing great debating skills, humor, and an easygoing, if not charming, public personality. Romney had also staked out Iowa as his hoped-for first-place finish. Romney's campaign had a lot of money and hired help; Huckabee's was run on a shoestring but had a mass of volunteers. And Huckabee won by nine points.[83] That win took a lot of air out of the Romney campaign, but they knew they would do well and make a comeback in New Hampshire, where Romney had a second home and which was flooded with Massachusetts media. McCain's campaign had a staff shakeup before Iowa but found its grounding—and he had decided to stake his first claim on New Hampshire as well, where he had won the primary in 2000.

McCain was right, and Romney wasn't: McCain won, and Romney, again, came in second. Rudy Giuliani was waiting for the big Florida primary and was spending most of his efforts there. Fred Thompson seemed to not be connecting, playing the elder statesman, relaxed—perhaps too relaxed—with southern charm. And he showed little fire in his belly during the debates, to boot. Voters rewarded that effort in kind, and soon Fred Thompson would withdraw. If there was an elder statesman, it was surely McCain (at age seventy-one), and he was campaigning for every vote he could, hard.

Romney won Michigan—where he was born and where his father, George, had been a well-known automobile executive and governor—and campaigned hard. But he could not pick up another first-place win in a big noncaucus early state. After Super Tuesday in February, Romney saw the writing on the wall, and bitter though the campaigning was between McCain and Romney, Romney pulled out of the race and gave a generous endorsement to John McCain. Rudy Giuliani, having staked so much on Florida but giving away the earlier primaries without much campaigning there, came in third there, and it was also over for him.[84] The race was between McCain and Huckabee, who at times, it appeared, had been quite close and colluded to work against Romney. Huckabee had done well in some big southern states like Georgia and Tennessee, but McCain had him almost everywhere else. Republicans, it has been said, often nominate the guy whose turn it is. McCain had been in Congress since 1983, served valiantly in Vietnam ("he suffered greatly for his country" is how one friend of mine succinctly put it, and arguably he suffered more than any other serious contender for the presidency in history), and it was his turn.*

---

* At various times throughout the campaign, I had given solicited and unsolicited advice to the various candidates—some they took; some they did not. I had also donated money to both the Romney and the McCain campaigns. And all of the leading candidates (and some of the also-rans, like Congressman Duncan Hunter of California) were fairly regular guests on my radio show.

But there was something else about McCain too. He had staked almost his whole political career on standing up for the U.S. not standing down in Iraq—and he was being proved right. The Brookings team reported continuing successes of the surge: in March 2008 they would write, "Iraq's security turnaround has continued through the winter";[85] and in June, "It would be too much to talk of imminent victory in Iraq. But we may at least be able to avert strategic defeat with a careful plan for gradual handoff of more responsibility to the Iraqi government over the coming years."[86] By the end of July, Michael O'Hanlon and former Clinton NSA official Kenneth Pollack would write:

> We are finally getting somewhere in Iraq, at least in military terms. As two analysts who have harshly criticized the Bush administration's miserable handling of Iraq, we were surprised by the gains we saw and the potential to produce not necessarily "victory" but a sustainable stability that both we and the Iraqis could live with.[87]

As the year moved on, the violence in Iraq would continue to abate; "victory" seemed not so far. What General Petraeus and the military had done in Iraq was nothing short of miraculous—they were the true turnaround experts of the year.

This fact did not make the war much more popular than it had been—most in America had tuned out to the good news, and Senator Obama would continue on his theme that Iraq was the "wrong war" that took our focus off the "right war" in Afghanistan. If elected, he said, he would get us out. In contrast, McCain would not back down from Iraq and made every effort to show his credibility and experience on foreign and defense affairs as compared to Obama's experience, which was little to none.

The polling going into the election showed a pretty tight race. It was still a center-right country in many respects, McCain was a very well-known entity, and Obama (despite his huge and enthusiastic crowds of supporters) was, simply, not. And Americans like stability, even if at times they desire change. It was neck and neck through September, with McCain ahead of or behind Obama by only a few points.[88]

VIII. End Game

When it was to time to pick running mates, Obama went for experience and confidence building, if not inspiration and exuberance—someone who would show the country that, though he was young and not very experienced on the international scene, his vice president would be. Obama chose Senate Foreign Relations Committee Chairman Joe Biden. Biden was nothing if not experienced; he'd been in the Senate since 1973.

McCain, ever the maverick, knew he needed to go the other way: experience he had; exuberance and an electrification of the base he needed. He chose the then little-known first-term governor of Alaska: Sarah Palin. And did she ever electrify! A young governor, with an informal way of speaking, attractive, the mother of five with her youngest (who had Down syndrome) born that year. Her eldest son had enlisted in the army and was off to Iraq. She was pro-life, she was pro-Iraqi victory, she was energetic and unabashed in her conservatism, and she was unknown to most. But for many conservatives, she was what was needed for them to get behind McCain (who had an uneasy relationship with the base).

The media went after Palin intensely, and she did not fare well in her nationally televised interviews. Some on the left despised her—and started all forms of false rumors about her and her family on the Internet. Some of the fodder Palin handed to the press when it was announced at the Republican Convention that one of her daughters was then pregnant, while in high school. Governor Palin said the teens would wed and handled the story as well as could be expected from a family going through such news—and under the international spotlight at the same time, never mind a national political campaign. Senator Obama, upon hearing the reports, had stated to the press, "I think people's families are off limits and people's children are especially off limits," but the press was not listening—and to Alaska they went, digging into every possible story line they could about Palin. (Not much more negative turned up, or turned out to be true.)[89]

Palin and her family would become much of the story of the second half of 2008. In the single vice presidential debate, she acquitted herself well against Senator Biden, even if her casual manner of speaking and lack of media-preferred experience was nonstop sport for the media and late-night comedians (especially *Saturday Night Live* where actress Tina Fey perfectly played her character and caricature). Palin was a good sport about much of this, even appearing on *Saturday Night Live* with the same Tina Fey, but ongoing reports (some leaked from the McCain campaigners who did not like her) continually fed the story line that Palin was not up for the job. That Obama was a first-term senator running at the top of the ticket and Palin a first-term governor on the bottom of the ticket did not seem to bother the media in their continual questioning of her, not his, abilities.

There was plenty the media, and for that matter, John McCain, could examine and hammer regarding Obama's past—but with few exceptions, they remained, in the media's case, uninterested, and in McCain's, unwilling. Conservatives were troubled by a good deal of Obama's pre-U.S. Senate career, especially his friendships with questionable associates. Perhaps none was as problematic as Bill Ayers, the former leader of the Weather Underground, a radical left-wing organization that had resorted to violent action—including the use of bombs—to protest the Vietnam War. Once on the FBI's most-wanted list, Ayers had been a friend of Obama and had even thrown a fund-raiser for him in his home. Obama was also to the left of many liberals on abortion policy, but again, with few exceptions, the media did not report much on this (especially his state senate career, where he voted against legislation that would protect babies slated for abortion once the procedure had failed and they were actually born).

John McCain had created some of his own problems—and was the victim of others. When the economy collapsed in late September, he—ever the maverick—suspended his campaign (putting in doubt whether he would attend the first presidential debate scheduled that week) and, in an effort to appear presidential, flew back to Washington to discuss bailout plans . . . and then did very little. (What could he do? The administration was negotiating with Congress on the legislation.) As if President Bush or the country needed one more catastrophe, it got it in the economic collapse of September 2008.

It had been a year of increased job losses, and there were worries of a coming recession—few, but some, predicted how bad it would be. The

Dow Jones dropped more than 1,800 points in the first week of October.[90] The month prior, the financial house and financial services firm Lehman Brothers had declared bankruptcy, the largest bankruptcy in the history of the United States.[91] The worst financial crisis to hit the United States since the Great Depression was upon the country as it began to realize how deep the problems of the subprime mortgage crisis had become. The administration was proposing and the Congress would pass a $700 billion bailout that allowed the U.S. Treasury to purchase troubled assets from financial firms to help ease the credit crisis that had struck.[92] The country was in a recession, and McCain's polls would show no more leads.[93]

McCain was not the greatest debater, and he was uneasy talking about core Republican issues such as social policy or tax cuts. He was much more comfortable speaking about government spending and waste—not the issues that had typically been known to create a charge up a hill on domestic policy. On foreign policy, when Russia invaded the country of Georgia, McCain spoke tough against Russia while Obama held his counsel. And on the issue of the ever-more-worrisome Iran, McCain would strongly criticize Obama's calls to openly negotiate with the regime that had been at war with America for close to thirty years. But Obama did as well as or better than McCain in the debates—the man with little experience showed he could stand head to head with the man of experience, and he made no grave errors.

Much can, has, and will be written about the 2008 election. In the end, it was two great American stories. One was about a boy born to a white woman from Kansas and a black man from Kenya who had abandoned the boy and his mother. This young boy's mother and grandmother raised him, sent him to the best of schools, and he worked hard to become a lawyer, community organizer, state senator, and U.S. senator. The other was the story of a boy born of a navy admiral and a mother who raised him when the father was away serving the nation. He would join the navy, become a fighter pilot in Vietnam, and become a prisoner of the enemy there, bearing more than five years of immense brutality and suffering. He came home, worked hard, and became a congressman and senator.

One would make a name for himself as an author and liberal activist. The other, as a politician never at ease with the status quo in his own party.

Come 2008, one would argue and campaign on the themes of hope and change for America; the other, on the themes of experience and strength. The political journalist and scholar Michael Barone has described a "hard America" and a "soft America." "Soft America coddles"; "Hard America plays for keeps."[94] America had been governed for the past eight years by a Texan, and an evangelical Christian, who deployed military force to destroy terrorists and liberate the immiserated. His party's successor would have been an Arizonan who had served in that military and defended its actions in its antiterrorist and liberating missions. But another America was speaking in 2008. It was an America that had grown tired of military force and tired of seeing the world in terms of *good* and *evil*. It was an America raised on ideas of acceptance and diversity and conflict resolution.

On 4 November 2008, that other America, in the form of its unique gift to the world—peaceful, democratic elections—gave more than sixty-six million votes to Barack Obama and elected him the forty-fourth president of the United States, and the first black president of the United States.

There was a deep recession in the land. There were unfinished wars in Afghanistan and Iraq. Osama bin Laden and Ayman al-Zawahiri were still alive. Iran was on track to becoming a nuclearized nation. North Korea was testing missiles. Russia was flexing its muscles. And a new president, with a new approach to the country and the world, would take the reins of power with new hopes and new fears on many sides of him and the country he was charged to lead.

Epilogue

In the introduction to my second volume of *America: The Last Best Hope*, I quoted G. K. Chesterton on what he saw in America when he visited this country in the 1920s. He wrote that in America, "In truth it is inequality that is the illusion. The extreme disproportion between men, that we seem to see in life, is a thing of changing lights and lengthening shadows, a twilight full of fancies and distortions. . . . It is the experience of men that always returns to the equality of men."

As I write this, we are nine months into the administration of the first elected black man as president of the United States. I still marvel at the arc of American history and the wonder of its ability to live up to its best hopes and aspirations. In my lifetime, I can recall seeing restaurants and restrooms that blacks and whites could not share. I recall parts of the country where illegal stumbling blocks were placed in front of a black person's right to vote. Appealing to our Declaration of Independence, we as a country shattered those practices and policies. And so in my lifetime I've lived to see a black man elected to the highest office in the land by a majority of Americans.

Barack Hussein Obama was both the most improbable of candidates and the most representative man of a new America. "Improbable" because he was a relatively unknown state senator in Illinois when he was asked to deliver the keynote address to the Democratic National Convention in 2004. "Improbable" in that he was a first-term U.S. senator who then ran for president after very little time in national office. "Improbable" because his middle name was Hussein and we were recently at war with a man of the same name. But "representative," given his dedication to hard work and education: still the two best ways to succeed at anything in America.

Four years before he delivered the keynote at the Democratic National Convention in Boston, eight years before he was the nominee of the Democratic Party at the convention in Denver, he was unable to obtain credentials to enter the Democratic Convention in Los Angeles. This, too, is representative of "changing lights," and testimony to the greatness of America: from practically nothing to leader of the free world in eight years—and a racial minority at that. "It is the experience of men that always returns to the equality of men," in America.

Upon President Obama's inauguration, I had written a plea:

> What our founders envisioned, what Lincoln fought for, what Martin Luther King, Jr., marched, spoke, and died for, we as a nation have achieved. In the most fundamental manner and meaning, the hour has come for us to put the politics of race behind us. The politics of America is before us, so let us not talk of Barack Obama as a black man but as a man, as "our American president," representing all of America, the one I always knew was possible.

Today, the weight of the world—perhaps the balance of the world—is on the president's shoulders. It almost always is.

But today, more than ever, the hopes, fears, challenges, and dangers within and around us seem greater than ever. Unemployment is at 10 percent. The chief sponsor of terrorism in the Middle East—Iran—is working to become a nuclear power. North Korea is a nuclear power, testing more and more missiles by the month. And our national debt is growing toward unsustainable levels of our gross domestic product. Still, in all of this—and so many other dangers I have not mentioned—one thing has come true: in all the statements, speeches, and press conferences the president has given and held, one almost never hears anything about his race, and few think of the president as a member of a minority race.

The election of President Barack Obama has achieved that one, great dream of Martin Luther King Jr.: this man is judged not by anything more or less than the content of his character and his presidency, by the wisdom of policies. His skin color is the least thought of, least spoken of, and least important thing about him. What a great distance we have traveled in so short a time. Very American.

This is not to say that I, and many others, agree with the positions he has staked out. In candor, I am compelled to admit I disagree with the president on most things, in fact I strongly disagree. I disagree with the unprecedented billions of dollars he is spending. I disagree with the president on his reorganization of American life where the government, and not self-reliance, seems to be the preferred forcefield of energy for our future. I disagree with the president on his foreign and intelligence policy that begins with the American president expressing regret and apology for the actions of his own country, especially when abroad. And many other things as well. In the end, he may be right, and I and many others may be wrong. But it will all soon play out, and we shall see whether more hopes or more fears come true—perhaps it will be some of both. As the famed jurist Learned Hand once wrote, "The spirit of liberty is the spirit that is not too sure that it is right."

I subtitled this book *New Hopes, New Fears* because of all the hope represented by the person and president of Barack Obama. But the fears are, indeed, great as well.

In 1976, Ronald Reagan delivered impromptu remarks to the Republican National Convention held in Kansas City, Missouri. He spoke of a letter he was writing for a time capsule to be opened one hundred years from then and said:

> I thought to myself . . . those who would read this letter a hundred years from now will know whether . . . missiles were fired. They will know whether we met our challenge. Whether they have the freedoms that we have known up until now will depend on what we do here.
>
> Will they look back with appreciation and say, "Thank God for those people in 1976 who headed off that loss of freedom, who kept us now 100 years later free, who kept our world from nuclear destruction"?
>
> And if we failed, they probably won't get to read the letter at all

because it spoke of individual freedom, and they won't be allowed to talk of that or read of it.

Today, thinking about one hundred years from now, with several autocracies and tyrannies on the march and an economic debt that may take generations of Americans to pay off, I, too, wonder whether we will meet our challenge. There are many who owe their debt of freedom to America. Eastern Europeans like Vaclav Havel and Lech Walesa are not shy about saying so. And I believe someday that our efforts to help build democracies in Afghanistan and Iraq will have untold domino effects throughout the world—but different from the domino theory we worried about during the Cold War; rather, the opposite. I believe other nations under the thumbscrews of dictators and autocrats will want this "foreigner's gift" of freedom and democracy (as the Middle East scholar Fouad Ajami has called our liberation efforts). And someday we will hear words of tribute from those who once lived under our foes in the Middle East and other oppressive societies.

We are not there yet in Afghanistan and Iraq—and there is a long way to go, both there and elsewhere. But tens and tens of millions of Arabs and Muslims were freed by our efforts there, and it is now increasingly up to them to secure it. Of course, with our help. Always with our help. That is one of our missions.

President John F. Kennedy said, "We shall pay any price, bear any burden, meet any hardship, support any friend, oppose any foe, in order to assure the survival and the success of liberty."[1] This is not a Democratic Party or Republican Party concept. George W. Bush spoke of the same idea in his Second Inaugural. It is an American concept. Abraham Lincoln wrote of our Declaration of Independence as "an abstract truth, applicable to all men and all times," saying, "it shall be a rebuke and a stumbling-block to the very harbingers of re-appearing tyranny and oppression."

How we help make real the promises and principles of the Declaration in this country, and other countries, will vary. But it is those promises and principles we mean to speak of whenever we speak of such things as "American exceptionalism." We do not think there is anything better about any given race in America. We do not think there is anything better about any given first, middle, or last name in America. We do not think there is anything better about any particular bloodline in America. What we do think are better than anything else in the world are the promises and principles of America. When we stand up for them, when we fight for them, when we defend them, we are standing and fighting and defending a cause greater than any self-interest. And when we decline to stand, fight, and defend those promises and principles, we become aliens to our very founding, our very nation, our very best history.

In no part of America, in no time in America, has there ever been an absence of hope. And because we have never known a utopian society of any kind—though many forms of government have promised that and failed—there has never been an absence of fear either. Today, the levels of both hope and fear are at a high point. Whether or not we can expand the former and reduce the latter, continuing to "have the freedoms that we have known up until now," will depend precisely on what we do with the challenges before us today. Will people one hundred years from now say, "Thank God for those people in 2009"?

As an American, as an optimist, as a true believer in the uniquely American capacity for self-renewal, I hope and believe the answer is "Yes."

Acknowledgments

As with my previous editions of *America: The Last Best Hope,* and most of my efforts, I am blessed by great friends and colleagues. *A Century Turns* is no exception.

Deep gratitude is owed to Bob Morrison, one of the great men of Washington who helps this city and country in innumerable ways, and who helped nurture these history volumes to fruition from the very beginning.

Also, to Seth Leibsohn—my good friend and counsel who was critically important at every stage.

And, to Noreen Burns—without whom almost nothing in this office can get done.

I also wish to thank my friends Bill Schulz, Max Schulz, and Tevi Troy for their thoughts and edits all along the way.

Joel Miller is one of the best editors I have ever worked with and I continue to owe him my thanks and gratitude for this and other books.

Team HOPE (History Opens Eyes) is an award-winning group of teachers and administrators led by Jane Foley and Rex Bolinger who saw the usefulness for these editions in our nation's classrooms, and saw to getting them to those classrooms. Thanks, too, goes to Jeff Gall and Mark Ingerson of Team HOPE—for their edits and work on the supplemental education resources.

My attorney Bob Barnett is always at the ready for assistance and wise counsel, and so, too, was he here.

I am also grateful to Brian Kennedy, Lawrence Kadish, and the Claremont Institute for their continued support of my and my staff's efforts—they believe, more than anyone, that we truly do live in the greatest country in the world.

Most important: To my wife, Elayne, and my sons John and Joe: They make both this country and my life better. Their continued interest and enthusiasm is second to none and I thank them for everything I have. They are my first and best love.

Notes

Chapter 1

1. "Biography of George Herbert Walker Bush," George Bush Presidential Library and Museum, http://bushlibrary.tamu.edu/research/bio_ghwbush.php.
2. Laurence I. Barrett, William R. Doerner, and Christopher Ogden, "Setting Out to Whomp 'Em," *Time*, 3 September 1984.
3. E. J. Dionne Jr., "Robertson's Victory in Ballot Shakes Rivals in G.O.P. Race," *New York Times*, 14 September 1987, http://www.nytimes.com/1987/09/14/us/robertson-s-victory-in-ballot-shakes-rivals-in-gop-race.html?scp=3&sq=robertson%20ames%20straw%20poll%201987&st=cse.
4. Public Broadcasting System, "George H. W. Bush: The Election of 1988," American Experience, http://www.pbs.org/wgbh/amex/bush41/more/1988.html.
5. Timothy Naftali, *George H. W. Bush* (New York: Macmillan, 2007), 51.
6. Ibid.
7. "1988: Thank You, New Hampshire," Union Leader, 1 November 2004, http://www.unionleader.com/article.aspx?articleId=79cd006a-04a7-4520-a2f4-e702dcd3af89.
8. "Dukakis Lead Widens, According to New Poll," *New York Times,* 26 July 1988, http://www.nytimes.com/1988/07/26/us/dukakis-lead-widensaccording-to-new-poll.html.
9. "The Republicans in New Orleans: Ex-lawmaker Denies Scandal," *New York Times,* 18 August 1988, http://www.nytimes.com/1988/08/18/us/the-republicans-in-new-orleans-ex-lawmaker-denies-scandal.html?scp=1&sq=quayle%20paula%20parkinson&st=cse.
10. Richard L. Berke, "Bush and Bentsen Each Have Son Who Served in the National Guard," *New York Times,* 22 August 1988, http://www.nytimes.com/1988/08/22/us/bush-and-bentsen-each-have-son-who-served-in-the-national-guard.html.
11. James Hebert, "Lee Atwater's sorrow for the road taken," *The San Diego Union-Tribune,* 19 May 2006, http://www.signonsandiego.com/uniontrib/20060519/news_1c19fixin.html.

12. Steven V. Roberts, "Bush Intensifies Debate on Pledge Asking, Why It So Upsets Dukakis," *New York Times,* 25 August 1988, http://www.nytimes.com/1988/08/25/us/bush-intensifies-debate-on-pledge-asking-why-it-so-upsets-dukakis.html.

13. Robin Toner, "Prison Furloughs in Massachusetts Threaten Dukakis Record on Crime," *New York Times,* 5 July 1988, http://www.nytimes.com/1988/07/05/us/prison-furloughs-in-massachusetts-threaten-dukakis-record-on-crime.html.

14. Karen S. Johnson-Cartee and Gary A. Copeland, *Negative Political Advertising: Coming of Age* (Hillsdale, NJ: Lawrence Erlbaum Associates, 1991), 133.

15. Michael Dukakis, second presidential debate with George H. W. Bush, 13 October 1988, quoted in Commission on Presidential Debates, http://www.debates.org/pages/trans88b.html.

16. Ibid.

17. George Bush, second presidential debate with Michael Dukakis, 13 October 1988, quoted in Commission on Presidential Debates, http://www.debates.org/pages/trans88b.html.

18. Jack W. Germond, *Fat Man in a Middle Seat: Forty Years of Covering Politics* (New York: Random House, 1999), 247.

19. Leonard Bernstein, "I'm a Liberal, and Proud of It," *New York Times,* 30 October 1988, http://www.leonardbernstein.com/newsletter_past.htm.

20. Tom Wolfe, "Radical Chic: That Party at Lenny's," *New York,* 8 June 1970, http://nymag.com/news/features/46170/.

21. Lloyd Bentsen, vice presidential debate with Dan Quayle, quoted in Commission on Presidential Debates, 5 October 1988, http://www.debates.org/pages/trans88c.html.

22. Ibid.

23. "U.S. Misery Index—1948-2008," Misery Index, http://www.miseryindex.us/customindexbyyear.asp.

24. "1988 Presidential General Election Results," Dave Leip's Atlas of U.S. Presidential Elections, http://www.uselectionatlas.org/RESULTS/national.php?f=0&year=1988.

25. Philip Shenon, "After the Debate: A.C.L.U. Reports Rise in Membership Calls in Wake of Bush's Attacks," *New York Times,* 27 September 1988, http://www.nytimes.com/1988/09/27/us/after-the-debate-aclu-reports-rise-in-membership-calls-in-wake-of-bush-s-attacks.html.

26. Garry Wills, "The Power Populist," *Time,* 21 November, 1988, http://www.time.com/time/magazine/article/0,9171,968978,00.html.

27. Ibid.

28. John Kerry, quoted in "The Gaffes of John Kerry: His most embarrassing quotes, in context," by Timothy Noah, William Saletan, and Chris Sullentrop, *Slate,* 2 October 2003, http://slate.msn.com/id/2089125/.

29. "Timeline: the Bombing of Pan-Am Flight 103," WashingtonPost.com, http://www.washingtonpost.com/wp-srv/inatl/longterm/panam103/timeline.htm.

30. George Bush, inaugural address, 20 January 1989, quoted in "Inaugural Addresses of the Presidents of the United States," Bartleby.com, http://www.bartleby.com/124/pres63.html.

31. Ibid.

32. Ibid.

33. Ibid.

34. "Cities in Crisis: Drug Abuse Spans the Nation," *Washington Post*, 27 December 1988, Z-18.

35. Michael Isikoff, "'Two-Tier' Drug Culture Seen Emerging; Studies Show Cocaine Use Declining Among Middle Class, Concentrating Among Urban Poor," *Washington Post*, 3 January 1989, A-3.

36. George Bush, "Address on Administration Goals before a Joint Session of Congress," quoted in The American Presidency Project, http://www.presidency.ucsb.edu/ws/index.php?pid=16660.

37. William J. Bennett, *The De-Valuing of America* (New York: Simon and Schuster, 1992), 149.

38. National Security Archive, "Tiananmen Square, 1989: The Declassified History," *Electronic Briefing Book No. 16*, http://www.gwu.edu/~nsarchiv/NSAEBB/NSAEBB16/documents/index.html#1-6.

39. Joseph Kahn, "China to Give Memorial Rite to Hu Yaobang, Purged Reformer," *New York Times,* 15 November 2005, http://www.nytimes.com/2005/11/15/international/asia/15china.html.

40. "We can Develop a Market Economy under Socialism," *People's Daily*, 26 November 1979, http://english.peopledaily.com.cn/dengxp/vol2/text/b1370.html.

41. National Security Archive, "Tiananmen Square, 1989: The Declassified History," *Electronic Briefing Book No. 16*, http://www.gwu.edu/~nsarchiv/NSAEBB/NSAEBB16/documents/index.html#1-6.

42. Nicholas D. Kristof, "Chinese Students, in About-Face, Will Continue Occupying Square," *New York Times*, 30 May1989, http://www.nytimes.com/1989/05/30/world/chinese-students-in-about-face-will-contine-occupying-square.html.

43. David C. Wright, *The History of China* (Westport, CT: Greenwood Press, 2001), 180.

44. Ibid.

45. Steven Erlanger, "Top Aides to Bush Are Visiting China to Mend Relations," *New York Times,* 10 December 1989, http://www.nytimes.com/1989/12/10/world/top-aides-to-bush-are-visiting-china-to-mend-relations.html.

46. Dick Kirschten, "Chinese Students Lobby on Bush Veto," *National Journal*, 30 December 1989, 52.

47. Pat Wingert and Douglas Waller, "For Now, Chinese Students Can Stay," *Newsweek*, 11 December 1989, 98.

48. Center for History and New Media, "Warsaw Embassy Cable, Poland Looks to President Bush," Making the History of 1989, http://chnm.gmu.edu/1989/items/show/379.

49. George Bush and Brent Scowcroft, *A World Restored* (New York: Knopf, 1998), 122.

50. Gregory F. Domber, ed., "Solidarity's Coming Victory: Big or Too Big? Poland's Revolution as Seen from the U.S. Embassy," The National Security Archive, http://www.gwu.edu/~nsarchiv/NSAEBB/NSAEBB42/.

51. Robert J. McCartney, "Reform in East Germany: How Much, How Soon?" *Washington Post*, 19 October 1989, A-29.

52. Ibid.

53. British Broadcasting Corporation, "1989: Berliners Celebrate the fall of the Wall," *On this Day: 9 November*, See http://news.bbc.co.uk/onthisday/hi/dates/stories/november/9/newsid_2515000/2515869.stm (visited 7 April 2009).

54. Ibid.

55. Ronald Reagan, quoted in Public Broadcasting System, "Reagan Quotes," American Experience, http://www.pbs.org/wgbh/amex/reagan/sfeature/quotes.html.

56. George Bush, quoted in Marlin Fitzwater, *Call the Briefing!* (New York: Random House, 1995), 262.

57. Fitzwater, *Call the Briefing!* 262.

58. Robert Schlesinger, *White House Ghosts* (New York: Simon & Schuster, 2008), 375.

59. Ibid.

60. Helmut Kohl, quoted in Schlesinger, *White House Ghosts*, 376.

61. George Bush, Thanksgiving address, 22 November 1989, quoted in "Public Papers," George Bush Presidential Library and Museum, http://bushlibrary.tamu.edu/research/public_papers.php?id=1259&year=1989&month=11.

62. Ibid.

63. William Horsley, "Romania's Bloody Revolution," BBC News, 22 December 1999, http://news.bbc.co.uk/2/hi/europe/574200.stm.

64. British Broadcasting Corporation, "1989: Malta Summit Ends Cold War," *On this Day: 3 December*, http://news.bbc.co.uk/onthisday/hi/dates/stories/december/3/newsid_4119000/4119950.stm.

65. Bush and Scowcroft, *A World Restored*, 115.

66. BBC, "1989: Malta Summit Ends Cold War."

67. Mikhail Gorbachev, quoted in BBC, "1989: Malta Summit Ends Cold War."

68. Bush and Scowcroft, *A World Restored*, 187.

69. History.com, "February 26, 1990: Sandinistas Are Defeated in Nicaraguan Elections," *This Day in History*, http://www.history.com/this-day-in-history.do?action=Article&id=2589.

70. In 2006, Daniel Ortega would come back to power in Nicaragua after winning a plurality of the vote there—still a leftist, he did temper much of his rhetoric from the 1980s during the campaign. Without the Soviet Union, however, his leadership of Nicaragua would become less of a threat to the United States. Yet for Nicaraguans and the region, what becomes of his tenure remains to be fully seen; already his vice president is opposing Ortega in his effort to change the Nicaraguan Constitution so that he can extend his presidency. See Blake Schmitt, "Nicaragua's Morales Opposes Ortega Re-election Bid," Bloomberg.com, 9 September 2009, http://www.bloomberg.com/apps/news?pid=20601086&sid=a2yzXzhod6qQ.

71. "Timeline: America's War on Drugs," National Public Radio, http://www.npr.org/templates/story/story.php?storyId=9252490.

72. Senate Committee on Foreign Relations, Subcommittee on Terrorism, Narcotics, and International Operations, *Drugs, Law Enforcement, and Foreign Policy*, report

by Clairborne Pell, chairman, 100th Cong., 2nd sess., December 1988, Committee Print 100-165, http://www.gwu.edu/~nsarchiv/NSAEBB/NSAEBB113/north06.pdf.

73. Philip Shenon, "Noriega Indicted by U.S. for Links to Illegal Drugs," *New York Times,* 6 February 1988, http://www.nytimes.com/1988/02/06/world/noriega-indicted-by-us-for-links-to-illegal-drugs.html.

74. "Fighting in Panama: A New Government; the 3 Panamanians Who'll Lead Where Noriega Held Sway," *New York Times,* 21 December 1898, http://www.nytimes.com/1989/12/21/world/fighting-panama-newgovernment-3-panamanians-who-ll-lead-where-noriega-held-sway.html.

75. "Operation Just Cause," Global Security.org, http://www.globalsecurity.org/military/ops/just_cause.htm.

76. Bernard Weinraub, "Denouncing Fraud, Bush Bolsters Force in Panama," *New York Times,* 12 May 1989, http://www.nytimes.com/1989/05/12/world/denouncing-fraud-bush-bolsters-force-in-panama.html.

77. Walter V. Robinson, "Every Other Avenue Was Closed," *Boston Globe*, 20 December 1989, 1.

78. George Bush, quoted in "Noriega's Surrender; Panama in Disorder: the 1980s," *New York Times,* 5 January 1990, http://www.nytimes.com/1990/01/05/world/noriega-s-surrender-panama-in-disorder-the-1980-s.html.

79. Fred Kaplan, "Military Mission an Intricate One," *Boston Globe*, 21 December 1989, 1.

80. "Operation Just Cause."

81. William J. Bennett, interview, *MacNeil/Lehrer NewsHour*, PBS, 22 December 1989.

82. "Panama, No Place to Run," *Time,* 8 January 1990, http://www.time.com/time/magazine/article/0,9171,969132,00.html.

83. Ibid.

84. Francis Fukuyama, "The End of History?" *National Interest,* Summer 1989, http://www.wesjones.com/eoh.htm.

85. Miller Center of Public Affairs, "George Herbert Walker Bush: Domestic Affairs," *American President*, http://millercenter.org/academic/americanpresident/bush/essays/biography/4.

86. Ibid.

87. George Bush, "Statement on Federal Budget Negotiations," quoted in The American Presidency Project, See http://www.presidency.ucsb.edu/ws/index.php?pid=18635&st=&st1=.

88. "Bennett's New Deal: William J. Bennett's Selection as Head of Republican National Convention, *National Review,* 17 December 1990, http://findarticles.com/p/articles/mi_m1282/is_n24_v42/ai_9254660/.

89. Richard L. Burke, "Senate Confirms Souter, 90 to 9, as Supreme Court's 105th Justice," *New York Times,* 3 October 1990, http://www.nytimes.com/1990/10/03/us/senate-confirms-souter-90-to-9-as-supreme-court-s-105th-justice.html.

90. British Broadcasting Corporation, "1990: Iraq Invades Kuwait," *On this Day: 2 August*, http://news.bbc.co.uk/onthisday/hi/dates/stories/august/2/newsid_2526000/2526937.stm.

91. Steven F. Hayward, *The Real Jimmy Carter* (Washington, D.C.: Regnery, 2004), 10.

92. Bob Woodward, *The Commanders* (New York: Simon & Schuster, 2002), 315.

93. Qassim Abdul-Zahara, "Iraqi lawmakers vote to change flag," *USA Today,* 22 January 2008, http://www.usatoday.com/news/world/2008-01-22-3463034374_x.htm.

94. British Broadcasting Corporation, "1991: Iraqi Scud missiles hit Israel," *On this Day: 18 January,* http://news.bbc.co.uk/onthisday/hi/dates/stories/january/18/ newsid_4588000/4588486.stm.

95. Ryan Chilcote, "Kuwait still recovering from Gulf War fires," CNN.com, 3 January 2003, http://www.cnn.com/2003/WORLD/meast/01/03/sproject.irq.kuwait. oil.fires/index.html.

96. Ibid.

97. "Bush rejects peace 'hoax'," Guardian, 16 February 1990, http://www.guardian. co.uk/world/1991/feb/16/iraq.davidfairhall; Charles Krauthammer, "A Fight for Shiites," *WashingtonPost,* 26 Nov. 2004, A-39.

98. David Bauder, "America's Fighting Spirit Fills Airwaves on Home Front," *Deseret News,* 17 February 1991, http://archive.deseretnews.com/archive/147570/ AMERICASFIGHTING-SPIRIT-FILLS-AIRWAVES-ON-HOME-FRONT.html.

99. Pat Buchanan, quoted in Anti-Defamation League, "On American Jews and the Pro-Israel Lobby," Pat Buchanan: In His Own Words, http://www.adl.org/special_ reports/buchanan_own_words/print.asp.

100. Ibid.

101. "L.A. Riots Timeline: Looking Back 15 Years," ABC News, 29 April 2007, http:// abcnews.go.com/WN/story?id=3098746.

102. Doug Linder, "The Trials of Los Angeles Police Officers in Connection with the Beating of Rodney King," Famous American Trials, http://www.law.umkc.edu/ faculty/projects/ftrials/lapd/lapdaccount.html.

103. Hector Tobar and Lee Colvin, "Witnesses Depict Relentless Beating," *Los Angeles Times*, 7 March 1991, B-1.

104. Ibid.

105. Sally Ann Stewart and Haya El Nasser, "Chief Wants L.A. Police Prosecuted," *Los Angeles Times*, 8 March 1991, 1A.

106. Ken Rudin, "Waiting for a Court Vacancy," National Public Radio, 29 June 2005, http://www.npr.org/templates/story/story.php?storyId=4723460.

107. Pearl Bailey, commercial, "1976: Carter vs. Ford," on The Living Room Candidate: Presidential Campaign Commercials 1952-2008, http://www. livingroomcandidate.org/commercials/1976/pearl-bailey.

108. Leon Daniel, "Ralph Abernathy Defends His Support of Reagan," *St. Petersburg Times,* 20 December 1980, http://news.google.com/newspapers?nid=888&dat=19801 220&id=OfALAAAAIBAJ&sjid=P1oDAAAAIBAJ&pg=5192,3864016.

109. See http://news.google.com/newspapers?nid=757&dat=19720211&id=xRYKAA AAIBAJ&sjid=LEcDAAAAIBAJ&pg=5766,2782801 (visited 10 April 2009).

110. Elizabeth Kaston, "House Trims NEA Budget as Reprimand; Drastic Cuts Rejected in Arts Funding Bill," *The Washington Post,* 13 July 1989, http://www. encyclopedia.com/doc/1P2-1200992.html.

111. George F. Will, "The Helms Bludgeon," *Washington Post*, 3 Aug. 1989, A-27.

112. Ibid.

113. Irving Kristol, "Pornography, Obscenity, and the Case for Censorship," quoted in The English Composition Board, http://www-personal.umich.edu/~wbutler/kristol.html.

114. Will, "The Helms Bludgeon."

115. British Broadcasting Corporation, "1991: Gorbachev Resigns as Soviet Union Breaks Up," *On this Day: 25 December*, http://news.bbc.co.uk/onthisday/hi/dates/stories/december/25/newsid_2542000/2542749.stm.

116. Ibid.

Chapter 2

1. Robin Toner, "Casting Doubts: Economy Stinging Bush," *New York Times,* 26 November 1991, http://www.nytimes.com/1991/11/26/us/casting-doubts-economy-stinging-bush.html.

2. "Ross Perot: The Billionaire Boy Scout," *Entrepreneur,* http://www.entrepreneur.com/growyourbusiness/radicalsandvisionaries/article197682.html.

3. "The Political Fray," All Politics, http://www.cnn.com/ALLPOLITICS/1996/conventions/long.beach/perot/political.fray.shtml.

4. James B. Stewart, "Common Sense: Lessons from the 1990-1991 Recession," Smart Money, http://www.smartmoney.com/investing/stocks/lessons-from-the-1990-1991-recession-22807/.

5. U.S. Department of Labor, Bureau of Labor Statistics, "Civilian Unemployment Rate: 1948-2009," 6 November 2009, http://research.stlouisfed.org/fred2/data/UNRATE.txt.

6. "U.S. Misery Index—1948-2008," Misery Index, http://www.miseryindex.us/customindexbymonth.asp. There were one or two months of lower Misery Index numbers in 1991, but they were exceptions.

7. Michael Kranish, "Candidates' Stances Vary with Audience," *Boston Globe*, 22 April 1999, http://graphics.boston.com/news/politics/campaign2000/news/Candidates_stances_vary_with_audience.shtml.

8. Michael Wines, "The 1992 Campaign: White House; Concerned about Buchanan, Bush Makes Final Appeal in Georgia," *New York Times,* 1 March 1992, http://www.nytimes.com/1992/03/01/us/1992-campaign-white-house-concerned-about-buchanan-bush-makes-final-appeal.html.

9. Robin Toner, "The 1992 Campaign: New Hampshire; Bush Jarred in First Primary; Tsongas Wins Democratic Vote," *New York Times*, 19 February 1992, http://www.nytimes.com/1992/02/19/us/1992-campaign-new-hampshire-bush-jarred-first-primary-tsongas-wins-democratic.html.

10. George Bush, quoted in "The 1991 Election: Louisiana; Bush Denounces Duke as Racist and Charlatan," *New York Times,* 7 November 1991, http://www.nytimes.com/1991/11/07/us/the-1991-election-louisiana-bush-denounces-duke-as-racist-and-charlatan.html.

11. Epictetus, quoted in "Epictetus Quotes," Essential Life Skills, http://www.essentiallifeskills.net/epictetusquotes.html.

12. "Obama to troops: I won't hesitate to use force…but," *Los Angeles Times,* 26 October 2009, http://latimesblogs.latimes.com/washington/veterans/.

13. Robin Toner, "Under the Big Top—The Overview; Perot Quits Race, Leaving Two-Man Field; Clinton Vows Change and 'New Covenant' as He and Bush Court Abandoned Voters," *New York Times,* 17 July 1992, http://www.nytimes. com/1992/07/17/news/under-big-top-overview-perot-quits-race-leaving-two-man-field-clinton-vows.html.

14. Ross Perot, quoted in Robin Toner, "The 1992 Campaign: The Overview; Perot Re-enters Campaign Saying Bush Clinton Fail Address Government 'Mess'," *New York Times*, 2 October 1992, http://www.nytimes.com/1992/10/02/us/1992-campaign-overview-perot-re-enters-campaign-saying-bush-clinton-fail-address.html.

15. Richard L. Berke, "The 1992 Campaign: The Overview; Perot Says He Quit in July to Thwart G.O.P. 'Dirty Tricks,'" *New York Times,* 26 October 1992, http://www.nytimes.com/1992/10/26/us/1992-campaign-overview-perot-says-he-quit-july-thwart-gop-dirty-tricks.html.

16. Marlin Fitzwater, quoted in Berke, "The 1992 Campaign."

17. "L.A. Riots Timeline: Looking Back 15 Years," ABC News, 29 April, 2007, http://abcnews.go.com/WN/story?id=3098746.

18. Ibid.

19. Rodney King, quoted in Ralph Keyes, *The Quote Verifier* (New York: Macmillan, 2006), xii.

20. George Bush, "Address to the Nation on the Civil Disturbances in Los Angeles, California," 1 May 1992, quoted in The American Presidency Project, http://www.presidency.ucsb.edu/ws/index.php?pid=20910.

21. Bill Clinton, quoted in Michael Kranish, "Bush Orders 4,500 Troops to LA; Denounces Riot, Vows New Investigation of Beating Case," *Boston Globe*, 2 May 1992, 10.

22. Bill Clinton and Ross Perot, quoted in "Clinton Calls for Healing, While Perot Blasts Bush," *Seattle Post Intelligencer*, 4 May 1992, A-8.

23. "L.A. Riots Timeline," ABC News.

24. History.com, "1992: South Central Riots," *Black History Milestones,* http://www.history.com/genericContent.do?id=61726&milestoneid=37.

25. Sister Souljah and Bill Clinton, quoted in Joan Vennochi, "Sister Souljah Moments," *Boston Globe,* 16 September 2007, http://www.boston.com/news/nation/articles/2007/09/16/sister_souljah_moments/.

26. George Bush, quoted in Hunt, 492.

27. Richard Brookhiser, "Quayle Is Serious. Why Aren't We?" *New York Times,* 18 June 1992, http://www.nytimes.com/1992/06/18/opinion/quayle-is-serious-why-aren-t-we.html.

28. Barbara Dafoe Whitehead, "Dan Quayle Was Right," *The Atlantic Online,* April 1993, http://www.theatlantic.com/politics/family/danquayl.htm.

29. Michael Isikoff, "Clinton Team Works to Deflect Allegations on Nominee's Private Life," *Washington Post*, 26 June 1992, A18.

30. Bill Clinton to Eugene Holmes, 3 December 1969, in Public Broadcasting System, "Clinton Years: Bill Clinton's Draft Letter," Frontline, http://www.pbs.org/wgbh/pages/frontline/shows/clinton/etc/draftletter.html.

NOTES

31. Gwen Ifill, "The 1992 Campaign: New Hampshire; Clinton Thanked Colonel in '69 for 'Saving Me from the Draft,'" *New York Times,* 13 February 1992, http://www.nytimes.com/1992/02/13/us/1992-campaign-new-hampshire-clinton-thanked-colonel-69-for-saving-me-draft.html.

32. Bill Clinton, quoted in Gwen Ifill, "The 1992 Campaign: New York; Clinton Admits Experiment with Marijuana in 1960s," *New York Times*, 30 March 1992, http://www.nytimes.com/1992/03/30/us/the-1992-campaign-new-york-clinton-admits-experiment-with-marijuana-in-1960-s.html.

33. "Bill Clinton Jokes," Funny Jokes, http://www.jokes-funblog.com/categories/20-Bill-Clinton-Jokes.

34. George Bush, first Clinton-Bush-Perot presidential debate, 11 October 1992, quoted in Commission on Presidential Debates, http://www.debates.org/pages/trans92a1.html.

35. Bill Clinton, third Clinton-Bush-Perot presidential debate, 19 October 1992, quoted in Commission on Presidential Debates, http://www.debates.org/pages/trans92c.html.

36. "1992 Presidential General Election Results," Dave Leip's Atlas of U.S. Presidential Elections, http://uselectionatlas.org/RESULTS/index.html.

37. "U.S. Misery Index—1948-2008," Misery Index, http://www.miseryindex.us/URbymonth.asp.

38. George H. W. Bush, "Forrestal Lecture," U.S. Naval Academy, March 2004.

39. Jonathan Rauch, "Father Superior: Our Greatest Modern President," JonathanRauch.com, http://www.jonathanrauch.com/jrauch_articles/bush_41_father_superior/.

40. Bill Clinton, first inaugural address, 21 January 1993, quoted in "Inaugural Addresses of the Presidents of the United States," Bartleby.com, http://www.bartleby.com/124/pres64.html.

41. Richard L. Berke, "Clinton Picks Miami Woman, Veteran State Prosecutor, to be His Attorney General," *New York Times,* 12 February 1993, http://www.nytimes.com/1993/02/12/us/clinton-picks-miami-woman-veteran-state-prosecutor-to-be-his-attorney-general.html.

42. Public Broadcasting System, "Clinton Years: Chronology from Hope, Arkansas, to the White House," Frontline, http://www.pbs.org/wgbh/pages/frontline/shows/clinton/cron/.

43. Colin Powell, quoted in Eric Schmitt, "The Inauguration; Clinton Set to End Ban on Gay Troops," *New York Times,* 21 January 1993, http://www.nytimes.com/1993/01/21/us/the-inauguration-clinton-set-to-end-ban-on-gay-troops.html.

44. Colin Powell, quoted in Elizabeth Drew, *On the Edge* (New York: Simon & Schuster, 1995), 44.

45. Drew, *On the Edge*, 48.

46. Jamie Reno, "Beginning the Conversation," *Newsweek*, 21 July 2008, http://www.newsweek.com/id/147961.

47. Mark Thompson, "'Don't Ask, Don't Tell' Turns 15," *Time*, 28 January 2008, http://www.time.com/time/nation/article/0,8599,1707545,00.html.

48. Paul F. Horvitz, "Clinton Now Says: The 'Big Things' Never Included His Tax-cut Vow," *New York Times*, 15 January 1993, http://www.nytimes.com/1993/01/15/news/15iht-cut1.html; Michael Kelly, "Clinton's Economic Plan: The Campaign; Gambling that a Tax-cut Promise Was Not Taken Seriously," *New York Times,* 18 February 1993, http://www.nytimes.com/1993/02/18/us/clinton-s-economic-plan-campaign-gambling-that-tax-cut-promise-was-not-taken.html.

49. George F. Will, *The Leveling Wind: Politics, the Culture & Other News, 1990–1994* (New York: Viking, 1994), 255.

50. Ibid., 256.

51. "Former Cult Members Claim Leader Abuses Children, Stockpiles Weaponry," AP, 27 February 1993.

52. Ibid.

53. Ibid.

54. "At Least Five Dead, 15 Injured in Two Shootouts at Cult Compound," UPI, 28 February 1993.

55. Ibid.

56. See http://tlc.discovery.com/tv/specials/children-of-waco/timeline_print.html (visited 30 May 2009).

57. Ibid.

58. See http://encarta.msn.com/encyclopedia_761580496/branch_davidians.html (visited 30 May 2009).

59. Steve Higgins, "The Waco Dispute—Why the ATF Had to Act," *Washington Post*, 2 July 1995, http://www.rickross.com/reference/waco/waco5.html.

60. John Conyers, quoted in "Tear Gas Only Way to End Siege: Reno," *Courier-Mail*, 30 April 1993.

61. Janet Reno, quoted in "Lawmaker, Reno Spar about Role of U.S. in Siege," *St. Louis Post-Dispatch*, 29 April 1993, 1A.

62. Public Broadcasting System, "Waco: The Inside Story; Chronology of the Seige," Frontline, http://www.pbs.org/wgbh/pages/frontline/waco/timeline.html.

63. Andrew C. McCarthy, *Willful Blindness* (New York: Encounter Books, 2008), 8.

64. Ibid.

65. "First Strike: Global Terror in America," Federal Bureau of Investigation, 26 February 2008, http://www.fbi.gov/page2/feb08/tradebom_022608.html.

66. Ibid.

67. McCarthy, *Willful Blindness*, 3.

68. Mark Mooney, "40 Years Later: Sirhan Sirhan's Latest Mug Shot," ABC News, 10 June 2008, http://abcnews.go.com/TheLaw/story?id=5037471.

69. Alan M. Dershowitz, *Why Terrorism Works* (New Haven: Yale University Press, 2002), 58–75.

70. Lawrence Wright, *The Looming Tower* (New York: Vintage Books, 2007), 65–66.

71. Omar Abdel-Rahman, quoted in Wright, *The Looming Tower*, 66.

72. Richard Bernstein, "Trail of the Sheik—A Special Report; On Trial: An Islamic Cleric Battles Secularistm," *New York Times,* 8 January 1995, http://www.nytimes.com/1995/01/08/nyregion/trail-sheik-special-report-trial-islamic-cleric-battles-secularism.html.

73. Wright, *The Looming Tower*, 201.

74. Richard Engel, "Inside Al-Qaeda: a window into the world of militant Islam and the Afghani alumni," *Jane's*, 28 September 2001, http://www.janes.com/security/international_security/news/misc/janes010928_1_n.shtml.

75. Wright, *The Looming Tower*, 201.

76. Public Broadcasting System, "Timeline: Al Qaeda's Global Context," Frontline, http://www.pbs.org/wgbh/pages/frontline/shows/knew/etc/cron.html.

77. Wright, *The Looming Tower*, 204.

78. "Whitewater Timeline," *Washington Post*, http://www.washingtonpost.com/wp-srv/politics/special/whitewater/timeline.htm.

79. Brit Hume and Bill Clinton, quoted in Hedrick Smith, "The Unelected: The Media and The Lobbies," The People and the Power Game, http://www.hedricksmith.com/site_powergame/files/uneltrans.html.

80. Byron York, "Advice and Consent? How Clinton Chose Ginsberg," *NRO Weekend,* 5 July 2005, http://article.nationalreview.com/?q=NzdlNTFmNjNmOTBlZDJiNTZhYTM3YmEwNzEzOWYyZmU=.

81. See http://articles.latimes.com/1993-08-04/news/mn-20339_1_supremecourt (visited 2 June 2009).

82. "What led to the founding of the Palestinian Liberation Organization (PLO) in 1964?" Palestine Facts, http://www.palestinefacts.org/pf_1948to1967_plo_backgd.php.

83. Tom Bullock, "Q&A: Hamas and Faith," National Public Radio, 19 June 2007, http://www.npr.org/templates/story/story.php?storyId=10390803.

84. "Mideast Accord: Three Letters That Sealed the Diplomatic Bargain," *New York Times,* 10 September 1993, http://www.nytimes.com/1993/09/10/world/mideast-accord-three-letters-that-sealed-the-diplomatic-bargain.html.

85. Douglas Jehl, "Iraqi Tells F.B.I. He Led Attempt to Kill Bush, U.S. Official Says," *New York Times,* 20 May 1993, http://www.nytimes.com/1993/05/20/world/iraqi-tells-fbi-he-led-attempt-to-kill-bush-us-officials-say.html.

86. Public Broadcasting System, "Clinton Years: Chronology."

87. Madeleine K. Albright, quoted in "Raid on Baghdad; Excerpts from the U.N. Speech: The Case for Clinton's Strike," *New York Times,* 28 June 1993, http://www.nytimes.com/1993/06/28/world/raid-on-baghdad-excerpts-from-un-speech-the-case-for-clinton-s-strike.html.

88. "Whitewater Timeline," *Washington Post*.

89. "Whitewater Scandal," *Encyclopedia of Arkansas History and Culture,* http://www.encyclopediaofarkansas.net/encyclopedia/entry-detail.aspx?entryID=4061.

90. U.S. Army Center of Military History, "The United States Army in Somalia, 1992-1994," http://www.history.army.mil/brochures/Somalia/Somalia.htm.

91. Ibid.

92. Ibid.

93. Wright, *The Looming Tower*, 214–15; Peter Bergen and Rachel Klayman, *Holy War, Inc.* (New York: Simon & Schuster, 2001), 82.

94. Byron York, "The Life and Death of *The American Spectator*," *The Atlantic,* November 2001, http://www.theatlantic.com/doc/200111/york.

95. Bruce Lindsey, quoted in William C. Rempel and Douglas Frantz, "Troopers Say Clinton Sought Silence on Personal Affairs," *Los Angeles Times*, 21 Dec. 1993, A1.

96. Rupert Cornwell, "Gore Trounces Perot in NAFTA debate: Vice-President's triumphant TV performance boosts White House hopes of congressional approval for pact," *The Independent,* 11 November 1993, http://www.independent.co.uk/news/world/gore-trounces-perot-innafta-debate-vicepresidents-triumphant-tv-performance-boosts-white-house-hopes-of-congressional-approval-for-pact-1503459.html.

97. Adam Clymer, "Senate Approves Brady Legislation and Trade Accord," *New York Times,* 21 November 1993, http://www.nytimes.com/1993/11/21/us/senate-approves-brady-legislation-and-trade-accord.html.

98. Bill Clinton, quoted in Serge Schmemann, "Clinton in Europe; On Russian TV, Clinton Backs Reforms, *New York Times,* 15 January 1994, http://www.nytimes.com/1994/01/15/world/clinton-in-europe-on-russian-tv-clinton-backs-reforms.html.

99. Schmemann, "Clinton in Europe."

100. Bill Clinton, state of the union address, 25 January 1994, quoted in "1994 State of the Union Address," *Washington Post,* http://www.washingtonpost.com/wp-srv/politics/special/states/docs/sou94.htm.

101. Ibid.

102. Herman Cain, *They Think You're Stupid* (Macon: Stroud & Hall, 2005), 86.

103. Bill Kristol, quoted in "The Health Care Debate: In Their Own Words; Why Health Care Fizzled: Too Little Time and Too Much Politics," *New York Times,* 27 September 1994, http://www.nytimes.com/1994/09/27/us/health-care-debate-their-own-words-why-health-care-fizzled-too-little-time-too.html.

104. See http://articles.latimes.com/1994-02-12/news/mn-21924_1_arkansasstate-trooper.

105. Ibid.

106. *Jones v. Clinton and Ferguson,* quoted in "Paula Jones Complaint Against President Clinton and Danny Ferguson," *'Lectric Law Library,* http://www.lectlaw.com/files/cas03.htm.

107. "Chronology of the O. J. Simpson Trials," *Famous American Trials: O. J. Simpson,* http://www.law.umkc.edu/faculty/projects/ftrials/simpson/simpsonchron.html.

108. Mark Maske, "After the Strike, Baseball's Disgusted Fans Decide to Strike Back," *Washington Post*, 29 April 1995, p. A1.

109. Richard Sandomir, "Baseball; Why Baseball Faces Strike: A Primer on the Salary Cap," *New York Times,* 10 August 1994, http://www.nytimes.com/1994/08/10/sports/baseball-why-baseball-faces-strike-a-primer-on-the-salary-cap.html.

110. "Republican Contract with America," *United States House of Representatives,* http://www.house.gov/house/Contract/CONTRACT.html.

111. Jackie Koszczik, "Rostenkowski Hopes to Set Forth on the Road to Redemption," *CQ News,* 24 January 1998, http://www.cnn.com/ALLPOLITICS/1998/01/26/cq/koszczuk.html.

112. "The Oklahoma City Bombing: Timothy McVeigh Was Executed June 11, 2001 for his role in the April 19, 1995 bombing in Oklahoma City which Killed 168

People," *Indianapolis Star,* 9 August 2004, http://www2.indystar.com/library/factfiles/crime/national/1995/oklahoma_city_bombing/ok.html

113. William Jefferson Clinton, Oklahoma Bombing Memorial Prayer Service Address, 23 April 1995, quoted in *American Rhetoric: Top 100 Speeches,* http://www.americanrhetoric.com/speeches/wjcoklahomabombingspeech.htm.

114. Ibid.

115. Bill Clinton, quoted in Todd S. Purdum, "Terror in Oklahoma: The President; Shifting Debate to the Political Climate, Clinton Condemns 'Promoters of Paranoia,'" *New York Times,* 25 April 1995, http://www.nytimes.com/1995/04/25/us/terror-oklahoma-president-shifting-debate-political-climate-clinton-condemns.html.

116. Abraham Lincoln to James C. Conkling, Washington DC, 26 August 1863, in "Letter to James C. Conkling," TeachingAmericanHistory.org, http://teachingamericanhistory.org/library/index.asp?document=1066.

117. "Unabomber," Biographia e Historia, 20 January 2009, http://cunday.blogspot.com/2009/01/unabomber.html.

118. David Johnston, "On the Unabomber Track: The Overview; Ex-professor Is Seized in Montana As Suspect in the Unabomb Attacks," *New York Times,* 4 April 1996, http://www.nytimes.com/1996/04/04/us/unabomber-track-overview-ex-professor-seized-montana-suspect-unabom-attacks.html.

119. CNN, "Gloves," *O. J. Simpson,* http://www.cnn.com/US/OJ/evidence/glove/index.html.

120. Johnnie Cochran, quoted in "Closing Argument of Johnnie C. Cochran (Excerpts)," *Famous American Trials: O. J. Simpson,* http://www.law.umkc.edu/faculty/projects/ftrials/Simpson/cochranclose.html.

121. See http://www.latimes.com/entertainment/news/la-oj-annivverdict,3,5813618.story?page=1 (visited 11 June 2009).

122. Darryl Fears, "Black Opinion on Simpson Shifts: African Americans Now More Likely to Say He Murdered Ex-wife, Her Friend," *Washington Post,* 27 September 2007, http://www.washingtonpost.com/wp-dyn/content/article/2007/09/26/AR2007092602351.html.

123. Ibid.

124. Cited in Irving Kristol, *Neoconservatism: The Autobiography of an Idea* (New York: Free Press, 1995), 68.

125. Ibid., 67.

126. Henry Louis Gates Jr. and Cornel West, *The African-American Century: How Black Americans Have Shaped Our Country* (New York: Free Press, 2000), 372.

127. William Goldschlag, "Bitter Blast at Music Biz: Lyrics Dirty, Violent as Ever Despite Promise, Critics Say," *New York Daily News,* 11 December 1996, http://www.nydailynews.com/archives/news/1996/12/11/1996-12-11_bitter_blast_at_music_biz__l.html.

128. Joe Lieberman, quoted in Goldschlag, "Bitter Blast."

129. Bernard Weinraub, "Films and Recordings Threaten Nation's Character, Dole Says," *New York Times,* 6 January 1995, http://www.nytimes.com/1995/06/01/us/films-and-recordings-threaten-nation-s-character-dole-says.html.

130. Richard L. Berke, "Politics: The Overview; Buchanan a Narrow Victor over Dole in New Hampshire," *New York Times,* 21 February 1996, http://www.nytimes.com/1996/02/21/us/politics-the-overview-buchanan-a-narrow-victor-over-dole-in-new-hampshire.html.

131. Patrick J. Buchanan, speech, Manchester, New Hampshire, 20 February 1996, quoted in "1996 Victory Speech," *Patrick J. Buchanan, Right from the Beginning,* http://buchanan.org/blog/1996-victory-speech-manchester-nh-183.

132. Francis X. Clines, "Clinton Signs Bill Cutting Welfare; States in New Role," *New York Times,* 23 August 1996, http://www.nytimes.com/1996/08/23/us/clinton-signs-bill-cutting-welfare-states-in-new-role.html.

133. Robert Rector, "Really Stand for Children: Fix Welfare," *Heritage Foundation,* 6 June 1996, http://www.heritage.org/Press/Commentary/ED060696b.cfm.

134. Daniel P. Moynihan, "When Principle Is at Issue," *Washington Post,* 4 August 1996, C07, http://www.washingtonpost.com/wp-srv/politics/special/welfare/stories/op080496.htm.

135. William J. Bennett, "A Welfare Test," *Washington Post,* 18 August 1996, C07, http://www.washingtonpost.com/wp-srv/politics/special/welfare/stories/op081896.htm.

136. *The Cox Report: The Unanimous and Bipartisan Report of the House Select Committee on U.S. National Security and Military Commercial Concerns with the People's Republic of China* (Washington, D.C.: Regnery, 1999), 57.

137. Mark Helprin, "The threat that blows from China—China as economic and military threat," *National Review,* 20 March 2000, http://www.findarticles.com/p/articles/mi_m1282/is_2000_March_20/ai_59705345/pg_4.

138. Rich Lowry, *Legacy: Paying the Price for the Clinton Years* (Washington, D.C.: Regnery, 2003), 22. Will, *With a Happy Eye, But . . . America and the World: 1997–2002* (New York: Free Press, 2002), 238.

139. "1996 Presidential General Election Results," Dave Leip's Atlas of U.S. Presidential Elections, http://www.uselectionatlas.org/RESULTS/national.php?f=0&year=1996.

140. Osama bin Laden to King Fahd, open letter, 3 August 1995, in "Open Letter to King Fahd from bin Laden," *Answers.com,* http://www.answers.com/topic/open-letter-to-king-fahd-from-bin-laden.

141. National Commission on Terrorist Attacks upon the United States "The Foundation of New Terrorism," *9/11 Commission Report,* 17 October 2004, http://govinfo.library.unt.edu/911/report/911Report_Ch2.htm.

142. Osama bin Laden, *Declaration of War Against the American Occupying the Land of the Two Holy Places,* August 1996, in Public Broadcasting System, *Online Newshour,* http://www.pbs.org/newshour/terrorism/international/fatwa_1996.html.

143. Doug Struck, Howard Schneider, Karl Vick, and Peter Baker, "Borderless Network of Terror," *Washington Post,* 22 September 2001, http://www.washingtonpost.com/ac2/wp-dyn?pagename=article&node=&contentId=A10543-2001Sep22.

144. National Commission on Terrorist Attacks upon the United States "Counterterrorism Evolves," *9/11 Commission Report,* 17 October 2004, http://www.9-11commission.gov/report/911Report_Ch3.htm.

145. PBS, "Timeline: Al Qaeda's Global Context."
146. Douglas Brinkley, quoted in Hayward, *The Real Jimmy Carter*, 221.
147. Will, *With a Happy Eye*, 174.
148. Marvin Kalb, *One Scandalous Story: Clinton, Lewinsky, and Thirteen Days That Tarnished American Journalism* (New York: Free Press, 2001), 11.
149. Ibid.

Chapter 3

1. Dick Morris, quoted in "Double Trouble for Two-Termers," *New York Daily News,* 4 January 1998, http://www.nydailynews.com/archives/opinions/1998/01/04/1998-01-04_double_trouble_for_two-terme.html.
2. Mother Teresa, address, National Prayer Breakfast, 5 February 1994, quoted in "Mother Teresa Goes to Washington," Catholic Education Resource Center, http://www.catholiceducation.org/articles/abortion/ab0039.html.
3. Mike Barnickle, quoted on Public Broadcasting Service, "Regional Reactions," *NewsHour,* 5 September 1997, http://www.pbs.org/newshour/bb/media/july-dec97/princess_9-5.html.
4. Peter Johnson, "Late on Di Story, CBS to Unveil a New Crisis Plan," *USA Today*, 10 Sept. 1997, 3D.
5. Susan Schmidt, Peter Baker, and Toni Locy, "Clinton Accused of Urging Aide to Lie," *Washington Post,* 21 January 1998, http://www.washingtonpost.com/wp-srv/politics/special/clinton/stories/clinton012198.htm.
6. Marvin Kalb, *One Scandalous Story: Clinton, Lewinsky, and Thirteen Days That Tarnished American Journalism* (New York: Free Press, 2001), 161.
7. Bob Bartley, quoted in Kalb, *One Scandalous Story,* 161.
8. "A Chronology: Key Moments in the Clinton-Lewinsky Scandal," All Politics, http://www.cnn.com/ALLPOLITICS/1998/resources/lewinsky/timeline/.
9. Hillary Clinton, quoted in Associated Press, "Excerpts of Mrs. Clinton Interview," *Washington Post,* 27 January 1998, http://www.washingtonpost.com/wp-srv/politics/special/clinton/stories/excerpts012798.htm.
10. Bill Clinton, quoted in Joe Klein, *The Natural* (New York: Doubleday, 2002), 19.
11. Bill Clinton, state of the union address, 27 January 1998, quoted in "Text of President Clinton's 1998 State of the Union Address," *Washington Post*, http://www.washingtonpost.com/wp-srv/politics/special/states/docs/sou98.htm.
12. "Clinton Demands Total Access for UN Arms Inspectors," CNN Interactive,17 February 1998, http://www.cnn.com/WORLD/9802/17/iraq.clinton/.
13. "U.S. Policy on Iraq Draws Fire in Ohio," CNN Interactive,18 February 1998 http://www.cnn.com/WORLD/9802/18/town.meeting.folo/.
14. Madeleine Albright, quoted in "The Clinton Administration's Public Case Against Saddam Hussein," Project for the New American Century, http://www.newamericancentury.org/iraq-20040623.htm#30.
15. World Islamic Front, "Jihad Against Jews and Crusaders," 23 February 1998, http://www.fas.org/irp/world/para/docs/980223-fatwa.htm.
16. Ibid.

17. Bill Clinton, statement, 31 October 1998, in "Discours de M. William Clinton," *Le Monde,* http://www.monde-diplomatique.fr/cahier/irak/iraqliberationact.

18. Public Broadcasting System, "Timeline: Al Qaeda's Global Context," Frontline, http://www.pbs.org/wgbh/pages/frontline/shows/knew/etc/cron.html.

19. Ibid.

20. Ibid.

21. Jack W. Germond, *Fat Man in a Middle Seat: Forty Years of Covering Politics* (New York: Random House, 1999), 253.

22. "A Chronology: Key Moments in the Clinton-Lewinsky Scandal," All Politics.

23. Bill Clinton, statement, 18 August 1998, in "Text of Clinton's Statement," *Washington Post,* http://www.washingtonpost.com/wp-srv/politics/special/clinton/stories/text081898.htm.

24. "Clinton Admits to 'Wrong' Relationship with Lewinsky: President reverses earlier denial; asks the matter be ended," All Politics, 17 August 1998, http://www.cnn.com/ALLPOLITICS/1998/08/17/speech/.

25. "Key Events in the Clinton Investigation," *New York Times,* 13 February 1999, http://partners.nytimes.com/library/politics/impeach-timeline.html.

26. Ted Koppel, commencement address, Stanford University, June 14, 1998, quoted in "Koppel: 'Aspire to decency; practice civility,'" *Stanford Report,* 17 June 1998, http://news.stanford.edu/news/1998/june17/koppel98.html.

27. Jennifer Senior, "The End of the Trench Coat Mafia," *New York Times,* 16 April 2009, review of *Columbine,* by Dave Cullen (New York: Hachette Book Group, 2009), http://www.nytimes.com/2009/04/19/books/review/Senior-t.html.

28. Kevin Simpson and Jason Blevins, "Klebold Came from Jewish Background," *Denver Post,* 24 April 1999, http://extras.denverpost.com/news/shot0424e.htm.

29. Greg Toppo, "10 years later, the real story behind Columbine," *USA Today*, 14 April 2009, http://www.usatoday.com/news/nation/2009-04-13-columbine-myths_N.htm.

30. Steve Forbes, quoted in Associated Press, "Candidates ruminate on a time capsule," *Boston Globe,* 11 January 2000, http://graphics.boston.com/news/politics/campaign2000/news/Candidates_ruminate_on_a_time_capsule+.shtml.

31. "Summary of Findings," Pew Internet and American Life Project, http://www.pewinternet.org/Reports/2008/Networked-Families.aspx?r=1.

32. James Redin, "A Tale of Two Brains," http://www.xnumber.com/xnumber/kilby.htm.

33. *Wikipedia,* s.v. "Andrew Grove," http://en.wikipedia.org/wiki/Andrew_Grove.

34. Walter Isaacson, "Person of the Year: Andrew S. Grove," *Time,* 29 December 1997, http://www.time.com/time/subscriber/personoftheyear/archive/stories/1997.html.

35. Luisa Kroll, Matthew Miller, and Tatiana Serafin, eds., "The World's Billionaires," *Forbes Magazine,* 11 March 2009, http://www.forbes.com/2009/03/11/worlds-richest-people-billionaires-2009-billionaires_land.html.

36. "The Wealthiest Americans Ever," *New York Times,* 15 July 2007, http://www.nytimes.com/ref/business/20070715_GILDED_GRAPHIC.html.

37. "Michael Dell: Dell, Inc.," *eCorner,* http://ecorner.stanford.edu/authorMaterialInfo.html?author=248.

38. See http://www.internet-story.com/amazon.htm (visited 1 Sept. 2009).

39. Joshua Cooper Ramo, "Person of the Year: Jeffery P. Bezos," *Time,* 1999, http://www.time.com/time/subscriber/personoftheyear/archive/stories/1999.html.

40. Helen Leggatt, "U.S. Online Retail Sales May Break $200 Billion Barrier," *BizReport,* 1 August 2007, http://www.bizreport.com/2007/08/us_online_retail_sales_may_break_200_billion_barrier.html.

41. See http://pages.ebay.com/aboutebay/community.html (visited 6 Sept. 2009).

42. "Americans Going Online…Explosive Growth, Uncertain Destination," Pew Research Center for the People and the Press, 16 October 1995, http://people-press.org/report/136/.

43. U. S. Department of Commerce, "National Economic Accounts: Gross Domestic Product, Third Quarter 2009 (Advance Report)," Bureau of Economic Analysis, 29 October 2009, http://www.bea.gov/newsreleases/national/gdp/gdpnewsrelease.htm.

44. John Steele Gordon, "The 50 Biggest Changes of the Last 50 Years," *American Heritage,* June/July 2004, 55, no. 3, http://www.americanheritage.com/articles/magazine/ah/2004/3/2004_3_22.shtml.

45. Bill Platt, "Learning the Lessons of the Dot-Bomb Era," *Ezine,* http://ezinearticles.com/?Learning-the-Lessons-of-the-Dot-Bomb-Era&id=111568; "Will dotcom bubble burst again?" *Los Angeles Times,* 16 July 2006, http://www.qctimes.com/business/article_114ea0f5-677a-5487-8f16-de1faca2dddd.html?mode=story.

46. Public Broadcasting Service, "A Chronology of Elian Gonzalez Saga," *Frontline,* http://www.pbs.org/wgbh/pages/frontline/shows/elian/etc/eliancron.html.

47. Mike Carter, "Clarke book has errors about arrest of Ahmed Ressam," *Seattle Times,* 12 April 2004, http://community.seattletimes.nwsource.com/archive/?date=20040412&slug=ressam12m.

48. Public Broadcasting Service, "Ahmed Ressam's Millennium Plot," *Frontline* http://www.pbs.org/wgbh/pages/frontline/shows/trail/inside/cron.html.

49. Carter, "Clarke book has errors."

50. British Broadcasting Corporation, "2000: Suicide Bombers Attack USS Cole," *On this Day: 12 October,* http://news.bbc.co.uk/onthisday/hi/dates/stories/october/12/newsid_4252000/4252400.stm.

51. Jane Novak, "Yemen's Truce with Al Qaeda: Who Will Be the Next Victims?" *Weekly Standard,* 31 October 2007, http://www.weeklystandard.com/Content/Public/Articles/000/000/014/290rbfed.asp.

52. National Commission on Terrorist Attacks upon the United States "From Threat to Threat," *9/11 Commission Report,* 17 October 2004, http://govinfo.library.unt.edu/911/report/911Report_Ch6.htm.

53. Lawrence Wright, *The Looming Tower* (New York: Vintage Books, 2007), 374.

54. Nation Commission on Terrorist Attacks upon the United States "From Threat to Threat."

55. Public Broadcasting System, "The Impeachment Trial: President Clinton Responds," *NewsHour,* http://www.pbs.org/newshour/impeachment/hearings/clinton_12-19.html.

56. Chuck Schumer, quoted in Klein, *The Natural,* 16.

57. Al Gore, quoted in Public Broadcasting System, "Al Gore: Part 4," *NewsHour,* 17 August 2000, http://www.pbs.org/newshour/election2000/demconvention/gore4.html.

58. Joe Lieberman, remarks, Democratic National Convention, Los Angeles, CA, 16 August 2000, http://www.gwu.edu/~action/lieb081600.html.

59. George Bush, acceptance speech, Republican National Convention, Philadelphia, 4 August 2000, in "Text of Bush Acceptance Speech," http://www.usatoday.com/news/conv/118.htm.

60. Katharine Q. Seelye, "Boy's Case Could Sway Bush-Gore Contest," *New York Times,* 30 March 2000, http://www.nytimes.com/2000/03/30/us/boy-s-case-could-sway-bush-gore-contest.html.

61. Gail Collins, "Public Interests; While You Were Sleeping…" *New York Times,* 18 April 2000, http://www.nytimes.com/2000/04/18/opinion/public-interests-while-you-were-sleeping.html.

62. Katharine Q. Seelye, "Gore Supporting Residency Status for Cuban Child," *New York Times,* 31 March 2000 http://www.nytimes.com/2000/03/31/us/gore-supporting-residency-status-for-cuban-child.html.

63. Rick Bragg, "The Elian Gonzalez Case: The Overview; Cuban Boy Seized by U.S. Agents and Reunited with His Father," 23 April 2000, http://www.nytimes.com/2000/04/23/us/elian-gonzalez-case-overview-cuban-boy-seized-us-agents-reunited-with-his-father.html.

64. "Elian 'Joins Cuba's Communists,'" BBC News, 16 June 2008, http://news.bbc.co.uk/2/hi/americas/7455748.stm.

65. Jeffrey Toobin, *Too Close to Call: The Thirty-Six Day Battle to Decide the 2000 Election* (New York: Random House, 2001), 24.

66. Peter Marks, "The 2000 Elections: The Media; A Flawed Call Adds to High Drama," *New York Times,* 8 November 2000, http://www.nytimes.com/2000/11/08/us/the-2000-elections-the-media-a-flawed-call-adds-to-high-drama.html.

67. Toobin, *Too Close to Call,* 25.

68. Thomas C. Tobin, "10 Reasons Why Al Gore Lost Florida," *St. Petersburg Times,* 14 December 2000, http://www.sptimes.com/News/121400/Election2000/10_reasons_why_Al_Gor.shtml.

69. Ibid.

70. Sam Smith, "Poll Analysis: Nader Not Responsible for Gore's Loss," http://www.prorev.com/green2000.htm.

71. Toobin, *Too Close to Call,* 278.

72. Al Gore and George Bush, third Gore-Bush presidential debate, 17 October 2000, quoted in Commission on Presidential Debates, http://www.debates.org/pages/trans2000c.html.

73. Dennis Ross on *Fox News Sunday,* Fox News Channel, 21 April 2002, http://www.foxnews.com/story/0,2933,50830,00.html.

74. Ibid.

75. Steven Emerson, "Get Ready for 20 World Trade Center Bombings," *Middle East Quarterly,* June 1997, 4, no. 2, http://www.meforum.org/353/steven-emerson-get-ready-for-twentyworld-trade.

76. Bill Gertz, "Remember Rick Rescorla," The Rick Rescorla Memorial Webpage, 20 September 2002, http://www.rickrescorla.com/Remember%20Rick%20Rescorla%20 --%20%20Bill%20Gertz.htm.

77. Ibid.

Chapter 4

1. George W. Bush, inaugural address, 20 January 2001, quoted in "Inaugural Addresses of the Presidents of the United States," Bartleby.com, http://www.bartleby. com/124/pres66.html.

2. Jack Kemp, "The Bush Tax Agenda," *Townhall.com,* 24 January 2001, http:// townhall.com/columnists/JackKemp/2001/01/24/the_bush_tax_agenda.

3. David Leonhardt, "Economy Grew at the Slowest Rate in 5 Years in 4th Quarter," *New York Times,* 1 February 2001, http://www.nytimes.com/2001/02/01/business/ economy-grew-at-slowest-rate-in-5-years-in-4th-quarter.html.

4. George W. Bush, quoted in http://articles.latimes.com/1999/jul/23/news/ mn-58823.

5. Joseph Loconte, "God's Warden," *Heritage Foundation,* 13 October 2005, http:// www.heritage.org/press/commentary/ed101305b.cfm.

6. *Americans United for Separation of Church and State v. Prison Fellowship Ministries and InnerChange Freedom Initiative,* http://74.125.95.132/ search?q=cache:UxmPZ3LYzfwJ:www.becketfund.org/files/22267.pdf+prison+fellow ship+recidivism+rate&cd=44&hl=en&ct=clnk&gl=us.

7. George W. Bush, state of the union address, 27 February 2001, quoted in "Address of the President to Joint Session of Congress, " *C-Span,* http://www.c-span. org/executive/transcript.asp?cat=current_event&code=bush_admin&year=2001.

8. David Cay Johnston, "The Tax Bill Up Close: Some Facts, Some Tips," *New York Times,* 3 June 2001, http://www.nytimes.com/2001/06/03/business/the-tax-bill-up- close-some-facts-some-tips.html.

9. Frank Bruni, "The 2000 Campaign: The Texas Governor; Bush Tempers His Remarks on Abortion," *New York Times,* 1 October 2000, http://www.nytimes. com/2000/10/01/us/the-2000-campaign-the-texas-governor-bush-tempers-his- remarks-on-abortion.html.

10. George W. Bush, address, 9 August 2001, quoted in "President George W. Bush's Address on Stem Cell Research," All Politics, http://archives.cnn.com/2001/ ALLPOLITICS/08/09/bush.transcript/.

11. Ibid.

12. Dinitia Smith, "No Regrets for a Love of Explosives; In a Memoir of Sorts, a War Protester Talks of Life with the Weathermen," *New York Times,* 11 September 2001, http://www.nytimes.com/2001/09/11/books/no-regrets-for-love-explosives-memoir- sorts-war-protester-talks-life-with.html.

13. Barry Bearak with James Risen, "Reports Disagree on Fate of Anti-Taliban Rebel Chief," *New York Times,* 11 September 2001, http://www.nytimes.com/2001/09/11/ world/reports-disagree-on-fate-of-anti-taliban-rebel-chief.html.

14. Transcript, NBC, *Today Show*, 11 September 2001.

15. Nicholas Wapshott, "Firemen seeking sainthood for 9/11 priest," *The Times,* 22 February 2003, http://www.timesonline.co.uk/tol/news/world/article1071522.ece.

16. Mychal Judge, quoted in George W. Bush, address at National Prayer Breakfast, 1 February 2007, http://www.gpo.gov/fdsys/pkg/WCPD-2007-02-05/html/WCPD-2007-02-05-Pg107.htm.

17. Gerry J. Gilmore, "Pentagon 9/11 Families Remember Lost Loved Ones," *Department of Defense News,* 11 September 2009, http://www.defenselink.mil/news/newsarticle.aspx?id=55809.

18. Don van Natta and Lizette Alvarez, "A Hijacked Boeing 757 Slams into the Pentagon," *New York Times,* 12 September 2001, http://www.americanmemorials.com/memorial/tribute.asp?idMemorial=1316&idContributor=7466. Video—aired on CNN—shows Secretary Rumsfeld aiding a victim on a stretcher shortly after the attack on the Pentagon.

19. William J. Bennett, "Never again, again: the Holocaust Museum and 9/11," *National Review,* 8 December 2003, http://findarticles.com/p/articles/mi_m1282/is_23_55/ai_n13610363/.

20. Greyhawk, "911 Remember: Rick Rescorla was a soldier," *Mudville Gazette,* September 2003, http://www.mudvillegazette.com/archives/000307.html.

21. Rebecca Liss, "Oliver Stone's *World Trade Center* Fiction: How the 9/11 Rescue Really Happened," *Slate,* 9 August 2006, http://www.slate.com/id/2147350/.

22. "'Let's Roll,' Flight 93 Victim Heard to Say Before Crash," *The Pittsburgh Channel,* 16 September 2001, http://www.thepittsburghchannel.com/news/962011/detail.html.

23. Rudy Giuliani, quoted in "It's More than Any of Us Can Bear," CBS News, 11 September 2001, http://www.cbsnews.com/stories/2001/09/11/archive/main310811.shtml.

24. Steve Johnson, "San Francisco paper puts visceral reaction on page 1," *Chicago Tribune,* 13 September 2001, http://www.chicagotribune.com/features/chi-0109130346sep13,0,4728655.story.

25. George Bush, quoted in "Bush: U.S. Muslims Should Feel Safe," CNN.com, 17 September 2001, http://archives.cnn.com/2001/US/09/17/gen.bush.muslim.trans/.

26. Steven Emerson, "Radical Outreach," *National Review,* 28 June 2007, http://www.investigativeproject.org/207/radical-outreach.

27. George W. Bush, address, 20 September 2001, quoted in "Transcript of President Bush's Address," CNN.com, http://archives.cnn.com/2001/US/09/20/gen.bush.transcript/.

28. Ibid.

29. William J. Bennett, *Why We Fight: Moral Clarity and the War on Terrorism* (New York: Doubleday, 2002), 40–41.

30. Ibid., 46.

31. *Washington Post,* https://listserv.temple.edu/cgi-bin/wa?A2=ind0110c&L=gethic&D=1&P=1460 (visited 7 July 2009).

32. Barbara Lee, statement in opposition to H.R. Res. 64, 14 September 2001, quoted in American Rhetoric Online Speech Bank, http://www.americanrhetoric.com/speeches/barbaraleeagainstinvasion.htm.

33. "Open Letter to Congress on the Patriot Act," 23 September 2004, The Claremont Institute, http://www.claremont.org/projects/pageID.2496/default.asp.

34. Ibid.

35. Ibid.

36. Robert E. Pierre, "Wisconsin Senator Emerges As a Maverick," *Washington Post,* 27 October 2001, http://www.encyclopedia.com/doc/1P2-477705.html.

37. Alan Jackson, "Where were you (when the world stopped turning)?" in CowboyLyrics.com http://www.cowboylyrics.com/lyrics/jackson-alan/where-were-you-when-the-world-stopped-turning-1787.html.

38. Toby Keith, "Courtesy of the Red, White, and Blue," in MusicSongLyrics.com, http://www.musicsonglyrics.com/T/tobykeithlyrics/tobykeithcourtesyoftheredwhiteandbluetheangryamericanlyrics.htm.

39. George Tenet, quoted in Christopher Hitchens, "A Loser's History: George Tenet's Sniveling, Self-justifying New Book Is Disgusting," *Slate,* 30 April 2007, http://www.slate.com/id/2165269/fr/flyout.

40. National Commission on Terrorist Attacks upon the United States "Wartime," *9/11 Commission Report,* 17 October 2004, http://govinfo.library.unt.edu/911/report/911Report_Ch10.htm.

41. Maria Ressa, "Sources: Reid Is al Qaeda Operative," CNN.com, 6 December 2003, http://www.cnn.com/2003/WORLD/asiapcf/southeast/01/30/reid.alqaeda/.

42. Michael Elliott, "The Shoe Bomber's World," *Time,* 16 February 2002, http://www.time.com/time/world/article/0,8599,203478,00.html.

43. "From Collapse to Conviction: A Timeline," CBC News, 23 October 2006, http://www.cbc.ca/news/background/enron/.

44. Paul M. Healy and Krishna G. Palepu, *The Fall of Enron,* http://www-personal.umich.edu/~kathrynd/JEP.FallofEnron.pdf.

45. "From Collapse to Conviction: A Timeline," CBC News.

46. Ibid.

47. "Portfolio's Worst American CEOs of All Time: Bernie Ebbers," CNBC.com, http://www.cnbc.com/id/30502091?slide=17.

48. Grace Wong, "Kozlowski Gets up to 25 Years," CNNMoney.com, http://money.cnn.com/2005/09/19/news/newsmakers/kozlowski_sentence/index.htm.

49. William J. Bennett, "Capitalism and Moral Education," *Chicago Tribune*, 28 July 2002, C-9.

50. George W. Bush, state of the union address, 29 January 2002, quoted in "Bush State of the Union Address," CNN.com, http://archives.cnn.com/2002/ALLPOLITICS/01/29/bush.speech.txt/.

51. Ibid.

52. Ibid.

53. Wright, *Looming Tower,* 335.

54. Ibid.

55. Michael R. Gordon and David E. Sanger, "Powell Says U.S. Is Weighing Ways to Topple Hussein," *New York Times,* 13 February 2002, http://www.nytimes.com/2002/02/13/international/13IRAQ.html.

56. John Miller, "Greetings, America, My Name Is Osama bin Laden...," 1999, in Public Broadcasting System, *Frontline,* http://www.pbs.org/wgbh/pages/frontline/shows/binladen/who/miller.html.

57. Osama bin Laden, in "Transcript of the Osama bin Laden Video," *Telegraph,* 13 December 2001, http://www.telegraph.co.uk/news/1365202/Transcript-of-Osama-bin-Laden-video.html.

58. Peter H. Wehner, "The Connection Continued," *Frontpage Magazine,* 30 June 2005, http://www.frontpagemag.com/Printable.aspx?ArtId=8094.

59. Colin Powell, quoted in David E. Sanger, "Allies Hear Sour Notes in 'Axis of Evil' Chorus," *New York Times,* 17 February 2002, http://www.nytimes.com/2002/02/17/international/asia/17ALLI.html.

60. William Hamilton, "Bush Began to Plan War Three Months After 9/11," *Washington Post,* 17 April 2004, http://www.washingtonpost.com/wp-dyn/articles/A17347-2004Apr16.html.

61. Bennett, *Why We Fight,* 192.

62. Ibid., 192–93.

63. Ann Clwyd, "See men shredded, then say you don't back war," *The Times,* 18 March 2003, http://www.timesonline.co.uk/tol/comment/thunderer/article1120757.ece.

64. Tony Blair, quoted in Sarah Lyall, "Blair Defends U.S. on Iraq, Reaffirming His Support," *New York Times,* 4 September 2002, http://www.nytimes.com/2002/09/04/world/blair-defends-us-on-iraq-reaffirming-his-support.html.

65. Tony Blair, quoted in David E. Sanger, "Threats and Responses: Camp David; Blair, Meeting with Bush, Fully Endorses U.S. Plans for Ending Iraqi Threat," *New York Times,* 8 September 2002, http://www.nytimes.com/2002/09/08/world/threats-responses-camp-david-blair-meeting-with-bush-fully-endorses-us-plans-for.html.

66. George W. Bush, address, 12 September 2002, in "President Bush's Address to the United Nations," CNN.com, http://archives.cnn.com/2002/US/09/12/bush.transcript/.

67. Ibid.

68. Todd S. Purdum and Elisabeth Bumiller, "Bush Seeks Power to Use 'All Means' to Oust Hussein," *New York Times,* 20 September 2002, http://www.nytimes.com/2002/09/20/international/20PREX.html?todaysheadlines.

69. Ibid.

70. Lizette Alvarez, "Man in the News—James Merrill Jeffords; A Longtime Maverick," *New York Times,* 25 May 2001, http://www.nytimes.com/2001/05/25/us/man-in-the-news-james-merrill-jeffords-a-longtime-maverick.html.

71. Al Gore, speech, Commonwealth Club, San Francisco," 23 September 2002, http://www.commonwealthclub.org/archive/02/02-09gore-speech.html.

72. Ibid.

73. Ibid.

74. "Tone of Wellstone Memorial Generates Anger," CNN.com, 31 October 2002, http://archives.cnn.com/2002/ALLPOLITICS/10/30/elec02.fallout.memorial/.

75. Ibid.

76. William Saletan, "No Contest: Paul Wellstone's Memorial Turns into Pep Rally," *Slate,* 30 October 2002, http://www.slate.com/id/2073324/.

77. Ibid.

78. "Threats and Responses: House Vote on Iraq Resolution," *New York Times,* 12 October 2002, http://www.nytimes.com/2002/10/12/us/threats-and-responses-house-vote-on-iraq-resolution.html.

79. Alison Mitchell and Carl Hulse, "Threats and Responses: the Vote; Congress Authorizes Bush to Use Force Against Iraq, Creating a Broad Mandate," *New York Times,* 11 October 2002, http://www.nytimes.com/2002/10/11/us/threats-responses-vote-congress-authorizes-bush-use-force-against-iraq-creating.html.

80. "Senate Vote on Passage: H. J. Res. 114: Authorization for Use of Military Force Against...," Govtrack.us, 11 October 2002, http://www.govtrack.us/congress/vote. xpd?vote=s2002-237.

81. John Kerry, quoted in "The Democrats' Greatest Hits: The WMD Collections," PowerLine, 22 December 2003, http://www.powerlineblog.com/archives/2003/12/005426.php.

82. Hillary Clinton, quoted in "Democrats' Greatest Hits."

83. Jay Rockefeller, quoted in "Democrats' Greatest Hits."

84. Frank James, "Obama's 'big' anti-war speech wasn't big then," *The Swamp,* 25 March 2008, http://www.swamppolitics.com/news/politics/blog/2008/03/obamas_big_2002_antiwar_speech.html.

85. Barack Obama, "Remarks Against Going to War with Iraq," 2 October 2002, Organizing for America, http://www.barackobama.com/2002/10/02/remarks_of_illinois_state_sen.php.

86. Open Letter to Bill Clinton, 26 January 1998, in Project for the New American Century, http://www.newamericancentury.org/iraqclintonletter.htm.

87. "Elections 2002," WashingtonPost.com, http://www.washingtonpost.com/wp-dyn/politics/elections/2002/.

88. Matthew Cooper, "Fallout from a Memorial," *Time,* 9 November 2002, http://www.time.com/time/nation/article/0,8599,388903,00.html.

89. Trent Lott, quoted in John Mercurio, "Lott Apologizes for Thurmond Comment," CNN.com, 10 December 2002, http://archives.cnn.com/2002/ALLPOLITICS/12/09/lott.comment/.

90. John Podhoretz, quoted in Jay Rosen, "The Legend of Trent Lott and the Weblogs," PressThink, http://journalism.nyu.edu/pubzone/weblogs/pressthink/2004/03/15/lott_case.html.

91. Michael Paulson, "Scandal Eclipses a Far-reaching Record," *Boston Globe,* 14 December 2002, http://www.boston.com/globe/spotlight/abuse/stories3/121402_record.htm.

92. Thomas Farragher, "Partners of Abuse Found Nationwide," *Boston Globe,* 14 December 2002, http://www.boston.com/globe/spotlight/abuse/stories3/121402_impact.htm.

93. George W. Bush, state of the union address, 29 January 2003, quoted in "Bush State of the Union Address," CNN.com, http://www.cnn.com/2003/ALLPOLITICS/01/28/sotu.transcript/.

94. Ibid.

95. Ibid.

96. Ibid.

97. Hamilton, "Bush Began to Plan."

98. Ibid.

99. Hans Blix, quoted in Julia Preston, "Threats and Responses: Report to Council; U.N. Inspector Says Iraq Falls Short on Cooperation," *New York Times,* 28 January 2003, http://www.nytimes.com/2003/01/28/world/threats-responses-report-council-un-inspector-says-iraq-falls-short-cooperation.html.

100. Colin Powell, quoted in Preston, "Threats and Responses."

101. U.S. Department of State, "Weapons of Mass Destruction," GlobalSecurity.org, http://www.globalsecurity.org/wmd/library/news/iraq/2003/iraq-030205-powell-un-17300pf.htm.

102. Ibid.

103. Ibid.

104. Ibid.

105. Ibid.

106. Anne-Marie Slaughter, "Good Reasons for Going Around the UN," *New York Times,* 18 March 2003, http://www.nytimes.com/2003/03/18/opinion/good-reasons-for-going-around-the-un.html.

107. Natalie Maines, quoted in Jarrett Murphy, "Dixie Chicks Slammed for Bush Jibe," CBSNews.com, 14 March 2003, http://www.cbsnews.com/stories/2003/03/15/entertainment/main544132.shtml.

108. Faye Bowers and Scott Baldauf, "Major Score for Anit-war Terror," *Christian Science Monitor,* 3 March 2003, http://www.csmonitor.com/2003/0303/p01s04-wosc.html.

109. "Military: Khalid Sheikh Mohammed," GlobalSecurity.org, http://www.globalsecurity.org/military/world/para/ksm.htm; Marc A. Thiessen, "The CIA's Questioning Worked," *Washington Post,* 20 April 2009, http://www.washingtonpost.com/wp-dyn/content/article/2009/04/20/AR2009042002818.html.

110. George W. Bush, address, 17 March 2003, in "President Bush Addresses the Nation," *NewsHour,* http://www.pbs.org/newshour/bb/white_house/jan-june03/bush_3-17.html.

111. Michael E. O'Hanlon, "Operation Iraqi Freedom and the Future of the Military," Brookings, 19 June 2003, http://www.brookings.edu/papers/2003/0619iraq_ohanlon.aspx.

112. "Threats and Responses: Congress; Both Parties Close Ranks Behind the President," *New York Times,* 18 March 2003, http://www.nytimes.com/2003/03/18/us/threats-and-responses-congress-both-parties-close-ranks-behind-the-president.html.

113. "Quotes from the Iraqi Information Minister," Military Quotes, http://www.military-quotes.com/information-minister.htm.

114. "Saddam statue toppled in central Baghdad," CNN.com, 9 April 2003, http://www.cnn.com/2003/WORLD/meast/04/09/sprj.irq.statue/.

115. "Commander in Chief Lands on USS Lincoln," CNN.com, 2 May 2003, http://www.cnn.com/2003/ALLPOLITICS/05/01/bush.carrier.landing/.

Chapter 5

1. "Commander in Chief Lands on USS Lincoln," CNN.com, 2 May 2003, http://www.cnn.com/2003/ALLPOLITICS/05/01/bush.carrier.landing/.

2. Tony Blair, "Transcript of Blair's Speech to Congress," CNN.com, 17 July 2003, http://www.cnn.com/2003/US/07/17/blair.transcript/.

3. Bob Schieffer, quoted in Bootie Cosgrove-Mather, "Are More Troops Needed in Iraq?" CBS News, 3 August 2003, http://www.cbsnews.com/stories/2003/08/04/opinion/schieffer/main566537.shtml.

4. Walid Phares and Robert G. Rabil, "De-Baathification Went Too Far," History News Network, 5 March 2004, http://hnn.us/articles/4624.html.

5. Joseph C. Wilson 4th, "What I Didn't Find in Africa," *New York Times,* 6 July 2003, http://www.nytimes.com/2003/07/06/opinion/what-i-didn-t-find-in-africa.html.

6. Ibid.

7. Ibid.

8. Ibid.

9. Ibid.

10. Robert D. Novak, "Mission to Niger," *Washington Post,* 14 July 2003, http://www.washingtonpost.com/wp-dyn/content/article/2005/10/20/AR2005102000874.html.

11. Eric Lichtblau and Richard W. Stevenson, "White House Denies a Top Aide Identified and Officer of the C.I.A.," *New York Times,* 30 September 2003, http://www.nytimes.com/2003/09/30/politics/30LEAK.html?pagewanted=print.

12. Ibid.

13. John Hughes, "Some vindication of claims Iraq was Uranium shopping," *Christian Science Monitor,* 21 July 2004, http://www.csmonitor.com/2004/0721/p09s01-cojh.html.

14. "Cheney's Top Aide Indicted; CIA Leak Probe Continues," CNN.com, 29 October 2005, http://www.cnn.com/2005/POLITICS/10/28/leak.probe/.

15. Timothy J. Burger, "Qadhafi's 9/11 fears," *Time,* 4 April 2006, http://www.time.com/time/nation/article/0,8599,1179975,00.html.

16. Elisabeth Bumiller and Richard W. Stevenson, "Aide Says Bush Is Already Absorbed in 2004 Race," *New York Times,* 11 January 2004, http://www.nytimes.com/2004/01/11/politics/campaigns/11ELEC.html?pagewanted=2.

17. Ibid.

18. Osama bin Laden, quoted in "Alleged bin Laden tape a call to arms," CNN.com, 14 February 2003, http://www.cnn.com/2003/WORLD/meast/02/11/sprj.irq.wrap/.

19. Wesley Clark, quoted in Edward Wyatt, "The 2004 Campaign: The Retired General; Tape Show General Clark Linking Iraq and al Qaeda," *New York Times,* 12 January 2004, http://www.nytimes.com/2004/01/12/us/2004-campaign-retired-general-tape-shows-general-clark-linking-iraq-al-qaeda.html.

20. *Authorization for Use of Military Force Against Iraq Resolution of 2002,* Public Law 107-243, 107th Congress, (October 16, 2003), http://www.c-span.org/Content/PDF/hjres114.pdf.

21. Howard Dean, quoted in "Dems Battle over Confederate Flag," CNN.com, 2 November 2003, http://www.cnn.com/2003/ALLPOLITICS/11/01/elec04.prez.dean.confederate.flag/.

22. Katharine Q. Seelye and Marjorie Connelly, "The 2004 Campaign: Iowa; Dean's New-Voter Strategy Seemed to Work, For Others," *New York Times,* 21 January 2004, http://www.nytimes.com/2004/01/21/us/the-2004-campaign-iowa-dean-s-new-voter-strategy-seemed-to-work-for-others.html.

23. Kenneth T. Walsh, "The Battle Cry That Backfired on Howard 'The Scream' Dean," *U.S. News and World Report,* 17 January 2008, http://www.usnews.com/articles/news/politics/2008/01/17/the-battle-cry-that-backfired.html.

24. "Gore Endorses Dean As Dems Ready for NH Debate," WCVB Boston, 9 December 2003, http://www.thebostonchannel.com/politics/2694385/detail.html.

25. Robin Toner and Janet Elder, "Poll Bolsters Bush on Terrorism but Finds Doubt on Economy," *New York Times,* 18 January 2004, http://www.nytimes.com/2004/01/18/politics/campaigns/18POLL.html?pagewanted=2&pagewanted=print.

26. "Operation Iraqi Freedom U.S. Casualty Status," 31 March 2004, GlobalSecurity. org, http://www.globalsecurity.org/military/library/news/2004/03/d20040331cas1.pdf.

27. Kyra Phillips, "Richard Clarke Testifies before 9/11 Commission," CNN.com, 24 March 2004, http://transcripts.cnn.com/TRANSCRIPTS/0403/24/bn.00.html.

28. National Commission on Terrorist Attacks upon the United States, ninth public hearing, 8 April 2004, http://govinfo.library.unt.edu/911/archive/hearing9/9-11Commission_Hearing_2004-04-08.htm.

29. National Security Administration, "Bin Laden Determined to Strike U.S.," 6 August 2001, declassified 10 April 2004, http://www.gwu.edu/~nsarchiv/NSAEBB/NSAEBB116/pdb8-6-2001.pdf.

30. Ibid.

31. Richard Clarke, quoted in Rebecca Leung, "Clarke's Take on Terror," *60 Minutes,* CBS News, 21 March 2004, http://www.cbsnews.com/stories/2004/03/19/60minutes/main607356.shtml.

32. Rebecca Leung, "Abuse of Iraqi POWs by GIs Probed," CBS News, 28 April 2004, http://www.cbsnews.com/stories/2004/04/27/60II/main614063.shtml.

33. John Esterbrook, "Poll: Iraq Taking Toll on Bush," CBS News, 24 May 2004, http://www.cbsnews.com/stories/2004/05/24/opinion/polls/main619122.shtml.

34. *Fahrenheit 9/11,* BoxOfficeMojo.com, http://www.boxofficemojo.com/movies/?id=fahrenheit911.htm.

35. Bootie Cosgrove-Mather, "Michael Moore: Establishment Pol?" CBS News, 24 June 2004, http://www.cbsnews.com/stories/2004/06/24/opinion/main625985.shtml.

36. Terry McAuliffe, quoted in Cosgrove-Mather, "Michael Moore."

37. Christopher Hitchens, "Unfairenheit 9/11," *Slate,* 21 June 2004, http://www.slate.com/id/2102723/.

38. Senate Foreign Relations Committee, "Vietnam War Veteran John Kerry's Testimony," April 22, 1971, in The War at Home: The Anti-war Movement, https://facultystaff.richmond.edu/~ebolt/history398/JohnKerryTestimony.html.

39. John Kerry, acceptance speech, Democratic National Convention, Boston, MA, 29 July 2004, in "Text of John Kerry's Acceptance Speech at the DNC," *Washington Post,* http://www.washingtonpost.com/wp-dyn/articles/A25678-2004Jul29.html.

40. Eli Saslow, "The 17 Minutes That Launched a Political Star," *Washington Post,* 25 August 2008, http://www.washingtonpost.com/wp-dyn/content/article/2008/08/24/AR2008082401671.html.

41. Ibid.

42. Barack Obama, keynote address, Democratic National Convention, Boston, MA, 27 July 2004, in American Rhetoric: Online Speech Bank, http://www.americanrhetoric.com/speeches/convention2004/barackobama2004dnc.htm.

43. Ibid.

44. George W. Bush, acceptance speech, Republican National Convention, 2 September 2004, in "Text: President Bush's Acceptance Speech to RNC," *Washington Post,* http://www.washingtonpost.com/wp-dyn/articles/A57466-2004Sep2.html.

45. Ibid.

46. Ibid.

47. Joel Roberts, "Kerry's Top Ten Flip-Flops," CBS News, 29 September 2004, http://www.cbsnews.com/stories/2004/09/29/politics/main646435.shtml.

48. "Republican-funded Group Attacks Kerry's War Record," *FactCheck.org,* 6 August 2004, http://www.factcheck.org/republican-funded_group_attacks_kerrys_war_record.html.

49. William Kristol, "Kerry's Band of Brothers," *Weekly Standard,* 30 August 2004, 9 no. 47, http://www.weeklystandard.com/Content/Public/Articles/000/000/004/480rttrq.asp.

50. Ibid.

51. Jonathan V. Last, "What Blogs Have Wrought," *Weekly Standard,* 27 September 2004, 10, no. 3, http://www.weeklystandard.com/Content/Public/Articles/000/000/004/640pgolk.asp?pg=2.

52. Ibid.

53. Andrew Heyward, quoted in http://www.redorbit.com/news/general/87545/cbs_apologizes_over_bush_guard_duty_memos/ (visited 12 July 2009).

54. Les Moonves, quoted in http://www.poynter.org/content/content_view.asp?id=76700 (visited 12 July 2009).

55. Anne E. Kornblut, "Bush Ad Plays on Kerry Windsurfing," *Boston Globe,* 23 September 2004, http://www.boston.com/news/nation/articles/2004/09/23/bush_ad_plays_on_kerry_windsurfing/.

56. "Celebs Turn Out for Kerry-Edwards," FoxNews.com, 10 July 2004, http://www.foxnews.com/story/0,2933,125141,00.html.

57. Ibid.

58. President Bush, first Bush-Kerry presidential debate, 30 September 2004, quoted in Commission on Presidential Debates, http://www.debates.org/pages/trans2004a.html.

59. William J. Bennett, "Bush's Mandate," Claremont Institute, Winter 2004, http://www.claremont.org/publications/crb/id.1208/article_detail.asp#.

60. Office of the Clerk, U.S. House of Representatives, "Election Statistics," Election Information, http://clerk.house.gov/member_info/electionInfo/index.html.

Chapter 6

1. Dan Froomkin, "Bush Agenda: Bold but Blurry," *Washington Post,* 5 November 2004, http://www.washingtonpost.com/wp-dyn/articles/A27833-2004Nov5.html.

2. Chris Suellentrop, "My Sharansky: Bush's favorite book doesn't always endorse his policies," *Slate,* 26 January 2005, http://www.slate.com/id/2112699/.

3. Harold Holzer, http://www.latimes.com/news/opinion/commentary/la-oeholzer29dec29,0,7290977.story?coll=la-news-comment-opinions (visited 12 July 2009).

4. George W. Bush, inaugural address, 20 January 2005, in "'No Justice Without Freedom,'" CNN.com, 20 January 2005, http://www.cnn.com/2005/ALLPOLITICS/01/20/bush.transcript/index.html.

5. Ibid.

6. Ibid.

7. Peggy Noonan, "Way Too Much God," *Wall Street Journal,* 21 January 2005, http://www.opinionjournal.com/columnists/pnoonan/?id=110006184.

8. Ibid.

9. Ibid.

10. Ceci Connolly and Mike Allen, "Medicare Drug Benefit May Cost $1.2 Trillion," *Washington Post,* 9 February 2005, http://www.washingtonpost.com/wp-dyn/articles/A9328-2005Feb8.html.

11. Diane Jean Schimo and Lynette Clemeton, "The President's Budget Proposal: Domestic Spending; Education Gets Large Increase, Especially for New U.S. Law, *New York Times,* 3 February 2004, http://www.nytimes.com/2004/02/03/us/president-s-budget-proposal-domestic-spending-education-gets-large-increase.html.

12. U.S. Department of Education, "President's FY 2004 Budget Request for the U.S. Department of Education," http://www.ed.gov/about/overview/budget/budget04/index.html.

13. George W. Bush, state of the union address, 3 February 2005, quoted in "Transcript of the State of the Union," CNN.com, http://www.cnn.com/2005/ALLPOLITICS/02/02/sotu.transcript.3/index.html.

14. Ibid.

15. Ibid.

16. Richard Sisk and Bill Hutchinson, "Roadside Bomb in Iraq Kills 4 U.S. Soldiers, Bringing Death Toll to 4,000," *New York Daily News,* 24 March 2008, http://www.nydailynews.com/news/us_world/2008/03/23/2008-03-23_roadside_bomb_in_iraq_kills_4_us_soldier-1.html.

17. "The Abramoff Affair: Timeline," *Washington Post,* http://www.washingtonpost.com/wp-dyn/content/custom/2005/12/28/CU2005122801176.html.

18. Ibid.

19. Willie Drye, "Hurricane Katrina: The Essential Timeline," National Geographic News, 14 September 2005, http://news.nationalgeographic.com/news/pf/47001822.html.

20. Ibid.

21. See http://articles.latimes.com/2008/dec/31/nation/na-katrina31 (visited 13 July 2009).

22. "Katrina: What Happened When?" FactCheck.org, 16 September 2005, http://uspolitics.about.com/gi/dynamic/offsite.htm?site=http://factcheck.org/article348.html.

23. Ibid.; Matt Welch, "They Shoot Helicopters, Don't They?" Reason.com, December 2005, http://www.reason.com/news/show/36327.html.

24. Welch, "Helicopters."

25. Lisa Meyers, "What Went Wrong in Katrina's Wake?" MSNBC.com, 6 September 2005, http://www.msnbc.msn.com/id/9231926/.

26. Bob Warren, "President Bush concedes mistakes during Katrina, but says Fed action not slow," *New Orleans Metro,* 12 January 2009, http://www.nola.com/news/index.ssf/2009/01/bush_concedes_mistakes_during.html.

27. Douglas Brinkley, "How New Orleans Drowned," *Vanity Fair* (June 2006), http://www.vanityfair.com/politics/features/2006/06/brinkley_excerpt200606.

28. See http://articles.latimes.com/2005/sep/27/nation/na-rumors27 (visited 13 July 2009).

29. Ibid.

30. See http://articles.latimes.com/2008/dec/31/nation/na-katrina31 (visited 13 July 2009).

31. "CIA Holds Terror Suspects in Secret Prisons—Debate Is Growing Within Agency about Legality and Morality of Overseas System Set Up After 9/11, *Washington Post,* http://www.washingtonpost.com/wp-dyn/content/article/2005/11/01/AR2005110101644_pf.html.

32. Ibid.

33. Dana Priest, "National Security and Intelligence," *Washington Post,* 3 November 2003, http://www.washingtonpost.com/wp-dyn/content/discussion/2005/10/28/DI2005102800907.html.

34. Ibid.

35. James Risen and Eric Lichtblau, "Bush Lets U.S. Spy on Callers Without Courts," *New York Times,* 16 December 2005, http://www.nytimes.com/2005/12/16/politics/16program.html?_r=1&pagewanted=print.

36. "On the Legality of the NSA Electronic Intercept Program," PowerLine, 22 December 2005, http://www.powerlineblog.com/archives/2005/12/012438.php.

37. Ibid.

38. Eric Lichtblau and James Risen, "Bank Data Is Sifted by U.S. in Secret Terror Block," *New York Times,* 23 June 2006, http://www.nytimes.com/2006/06/23/washington/23intel.html.

39. Tom Kean, quoted in Byron York, "A Good Program…To Make Us Safer…Is Over," *National Review,* 28 June 2006, http://article.nationalreview.com/?q=MDZmOGQyNmVlNTQxNjk4ZmE5NmE5NjliNzY3MzNhMDI=.

40. Abraham Lincoln, quoted in Lucas E. Morel, "Abraham Lincoln: The Better Angel of Our Nature," Journal of the Abraham Lincoln Association, (Winter 2008) 26, no. 1, http://www.historycooperative.org/journals/jala/29.1/morel.html.

41. Joel Roberts, "Poll: Bush's Numbers Remain Low," CBS News, 12 June 2006, http://www.cbsnews.com/stories/2006/06/12/opinion/polls/main1703346.shtml.

42. Neil King Jr., and Greg Hitt, "Dubai Port World Sells U.S. Assets," *Wall Street Journal,* 12 December 2006, http://online.wsj.com/article/SB116584567567746444.html?mg=comwsj.

43. Seth Leibsohn, "Practical Compromise," *National Review,* 23 May 2007, http://article.nationalreview.com/?q=YjY5Y2Q3ZmZmMGEwYzYxZjRjODc0MGIwMDAyZWRlMGQ=.

44. CBS News, transcripts, 19 March 2006.

45. Howard Kurtz, *Reality Show* (New York: Free Press, 2007), 308.

46. Ibid., 309.

47. Ibid., 310.

48. Ibid.

49. CNN.com "U.S. Senate," America Votes, http://www.cnn.com/ELECTION/2006/pages/results/senate/.

50. Nancy Pelosi, quoted in James M. Klatell, "Pelosi: No Blank Check for Bush in Iraq," CBS News, 7 January 2007, http://www.cbsnews.com/stories/2007/01/07/ftn/main2335193.shtml.

51. Ibid.

52. Joe Biden, quoted in http://www.nytimes.com/2007/01/25/world/americas/25iht web.0125capital.4335212.html (visited 15 July 2009).

53. Dick Cheney, quoted in Ibid.

54. "Bush Vetoes War-funding Bill with Withdrawl Timetable," CNN.com, 2 May 2007, http://www.cnn.com/2007/POLITICS/05/01/congress.iraq/index.html.

55. Harry Reid, quoted in Jeff Zeleny, "Leading Democrat in Senate Tells Reporters, 'This War Is Lost'," *New York Times,* 20 April 2007, http://www.nytimes.com/2007/04/20/washington/20cong.html.

56. Joseph Tartakovski, "Tribute to Professor Librescu, Claremont Institute, 19 April 2007, http://www.claremont.org/publications/pubid.710/pub_detail.asp.

57. Ibid.

58. Ibid.

59. Mark Silva, "Bush signs war bill," *The Swamp,* 25 May 2007, http://www.swamppolitics.com/news/politics/blog/2007/05/bush_signs_war_bill.html.

60. Jake Tapper, "Moveon.org Ad Takes Aim at Petraus," ABC News.com, 10 September 2007, http://abcnews.go.com/Politics/Decision2008/story?id=3581727.

61. Ibid.

62. Lauren Pratapas, "Public opinion gets support from Hollywood actress," CNN Political Ticker, 21 October 2009, http://politicalticker.blogs.cnn.com/category/moveonorg/.

63. Hillary Clinton, on *Meet the Press,* NBC, 23 September 2007, http://www.msnbc.msn.com/id/20941413/.

64. David S. Cloud and Thom Shanker, "Petraus Warns Against Quick Pullback in Iraq," *New York Times,* 11 September 2007, http://www.nytimes.com/2007/09/11/washington/11policy.html?_r=1&scp=2&sq=petraeus%20testimony%20september%202007&st=cse.

65. Ibid.

66. Barack Obama, announcement of presidential candidacy, Springfield, IL, 10 February 2007, http://www.barackobama.com/2007/02/10/remarks_of_senator_barack_obam_11.php.

67. "Dow Jones Industrial Average History," *New York Stock Exchange,* http://www. nyse.tv/dow-jones-industrial-average-history-djia.htm.

68. Jason H. Campbell and Michael E. O'Hanlon, "The State of Iraq: An Update," Brookings, 22 December 2007, http://www.brookings.edu/opinions/2007/1222_iraq_ ohanlon.aspx?p=1.

69. Gary Langer, "Poll: A New Low in Approval Starts Bush's Year," ABC News.com, 15 January 2008, http://abcnews.go.com/PollingUnit/Vote2008/ story?id=4133095&page=1.

70. Ibid.

71. Ibid.

72. Ibid.

73. U.S. Census Burean, "State and County Quick Facts," http://quickfacts.census. gov/qfd/states/19000.html.

74. "Clinton Wins Back Women, Narrowly Takes New Hampshire," CNN.com, 9 January 2008, http://www.cnn.com/2008/POLITICS/01/08/democrat.results/index.html.

75. See http://www.nytimes.com/2008/06/04/world/americas/04iht-ht-04elect.13446784.html (visited 15 July 2009).

76. Brian Ross and Rehab El-Buri, "Obama's Pastor: God Damn America, U.S. to Blame for 9/11," ABC News, 13 March 2008, http://abcnews.go.com/Blotter/ DemocraticDebate/story?id=4443788&page=1

77. Jodi Kantor, "Disinvitation by Obama Criticized," *New York Times,* 6 March 2007, http://www.nytimes.com/2007/03/06/us/politics/06obama.html.

78. Ross and El-Buri, "Obama's Pastor."

79. Barack Obama, address, Philadelphia, PA, 18 March 2008, http:// my.barackobama.com/page/content/hisownwords.

80. Ibid.

81. Barack Obama, press conference on Jeremiah Wright, 29 April 2008, http://www. foxnews.com/politics/elections/2008/04/29/transcript-obama-press-conference-on-jeremiah-wright/.

82. Susan Saulny, "Thompson Reenters Race from 'Tonight Show' Couch," *New York Times,* 6 September 2009, http://www.nytimes.com/2007/09/06/us/ politics/06thompson.html.

83. "Obama Turns Back Clinton to Win Iowa Caucuses," MSNBC.com, 4 January 2008, http://www.msnbc.msn.com/id/22484066/.

84. "Election Center 2008," CNN.com, 20 August 2008, http://www.cnn.com/ ELECTION/2008/primaries/results/candidates/#val=32884.

85. H. Campbell and Michael E. O'Hanlon, "The State of Iraq: An Update," *New York Times,* 9 March 2008, http://www.nytimes.com/2008/03/09/opinion/09ohanlon.html.

86. H. Campbell and Michael E. O'Hanlon, "The State of Iraq: An Update," *New York Times,* 22 June 2008, http://www.nytimes.com/2008/06/22/opinion/22ohanlon.html.

87. Michael E. O'Hanlon and Kenneth M. Pollack, "A War We Just Might Win," *New York Times,* 30 July 2007, http://www.nytimes.com/2007/07/30/opinion/30pollack. html?_r=2&pagewanted=1&oref=slogin.

88. "White House 2008: General Election Trial Heats Up," Polling Report, http:// www.pollingreport.com/wh08gen.htm.

89. Maria Gavrilovic, "Obama: People's Families Are Off Limits," CBS News, 1 September 2008, http://www.cbsnews.com/blogs/2008/09/01/politics/fromtheroad/entry4404967.shtml.

90. "Dow Jones Industrial Average History," *New York Stock Exchange,* http://www.nyse.tv/dow-jones-industrial-average-history-djia.htm.

91. Sam Mamudi, "Lehman Folds with Record $613 Billion Debt, Wall Street Journal Market Watch, 15 September 2008, http://www.marketwatch.com/story/lehman-folds-with-record-613-billion-debt?siteid=rss.

92. "Bailout Plan Wins Approval; Democrats Vow Tighter Rules, " *New York Times*, 4 October 2008, http://www.nytimes.com/2008/10/04/business/economy/04bailout.html?pagewanted=2.

93. "White House 2008," Polling Report.

94. Albert Mohler, "Hard America, Soft America: The Battle for America's Future," The Albert Mohler Show, 1 November 2004, http://www.albertmohler.com/commentary_read.php?cdate=2004-11-01.

Epilogue

1. John F. Kennedy, inaugural address, 20 January 1961, quoted in "Inaugural Addresses of the Presidents of the United States," Bartleby.com, http://www.bartleby.com/124/pres56.html.

Index

INDEX

Fairness Doctrine, and Federal Communications Commission, 17
faith-based initiative, 145–146, 159
Faith-Based Initiatives, Office of, 155–157
Falwell, Jerry, McCain attack on, 142–143
family diversity, 67
Family Research Council, 109
"family values," Gore on, 144
Farris, Mike, 76
fatherlessness, 66, 107–108
fatwas, 83
fear, 275
federal budget
    balancing, 102
    Education Department increase under Bush, 233
    and Iraq war financing, 255
    and troop withdrawals, 253
Federal Bureau of Investigation. *See also* New York Joint Terrorism Task Force
    terrorist investigations, 170
Federal Communications Commission, and Fairness Doctrine, 17
Federal Emergency Management Agency (FEMA), 237
Feingold, Russ, 169
Feinstein, Dianne, 157, 186
Feith, Doug, 178
Felzenberg, Al, 191n
Fey, Tina, 267
Finn, Chester E. Jr., 158n
Fitzgerald, Patrick, 85, 207
Fitzwater, Marlin, 30, 62
"flip-flopper," Kerry portrayed as, 221–222
Florida, in 2000 election, 148
Flowers, Gennifer, 57
Focus on the Family, 76
Foley, Mark, 249–250
Follett, Ken, *On Wings of Eagles*, 54
Forbes, Steve, 109, 110, 132, 141, 143
force majeure, 241
Ford, Gerald, 3
Foreign Intelligence Surveillance Act (FISA), 244
Fortas, Abe, 47
Foster, Vince, 89–90, 92
Fox News Channel, 120, 263
France, opposition to UN authorization of force, 196–197
Frankfurter, Felix, 47
Franks, Tommy, 177
freedom, and health care plan, 77
Frohnmayer, John, 49
Frum, David, 173n
Fukuyama . . . . and the Last Man," 36

furlough for criminals, Dukakis on, 11–12

G

gangsta rap, 49n, 108
Gates, Bill, 133
Gates, Daryl, 46
Gelernter, David, *Drawing Life*, 104n
Gephardt, Dick, 6, 7, 186
German reunification, 32–33
Germond, Jack, 127
Gerson, Michael, 155n, 173n
Gingrich, Newt, 95–96, 101, 122, 124, 260
    resignation, 130
    as Speaker of the House, 102
Ginsburg, Ruth Bader, 85–86
Giuliani, Rudolph, 162, 164
    as presidential candidate, 259, 265
global competition, 55
Goldberg, Arthur, 47
Goldberg, Whoopi, 226
Goldman, Ronald, 100, 105, 107
Goldwater, Barry, 5, 143n
Gonzalez, Elian, 137
    and presidential campaign, 146–147, 149
Google, xiii, 135
Gorbachev, Mikhail, 27, 51
    Bush and, 32, 42
    and East Germany, 29
Gordon, John Steele, 136
Gore, Al, 6, 7, 12, 122
    as Clinton running mate, 60–61
    conceding election, 150, 151
    debate over NAFTA, 93
    election results in 2000, 148
    and Elian Gonzalez case, 146–147
    endorsement of Dean, 212
    in presidential campaign in 2000, 143–144
    as presidential candidate, 140
    presidential nomination, 143
    response to call for force against Iraq, 183–184
Gore, Tipper, 49n
government debate about organization, 36
Graham, Bob, 217
Greenberg, Reuben, 22–23
Greenfield, Meg, 167
Greenspan, Alan, 155
Greenwood, Lee, 44
Grier, Roosevelt, 48
Grove, Andrew, 133
Guantanamo Bay prison, 242–243
Gulag Archipelago (Solzhenitsyn), 51
Gulf War, opposition to, 44–45, 55

H

Haig, Alexander, 3
Hand, Learned, 273
"hanging chad," 149n
Hannity, Sean, 263
Harman, Jane, 198n
Hart, Gary, 6
Hastert, Denny, 250
Havel, Vaclav, 30, 51
health care reform, 76–77
    opposition to, 97–98
    task force on, 73
Heinz, Teresa, 226
Helms, Jesse, 50
Helprin, Mark, 113
Helsinki Final Act, 32
Heyward, Andrew, 225
Higgins, Steve, 79
Hill, Anita, 48–49
Hitchens, Christopher, 127, 170, 189, 218
Holzer, Harold, 230
Home School Legal Defense Association, 76
Homeland Security department, 170
homeschooling, efforts to outlaw, 75–76
homosexuals in military, Clinton and ban on, 73–74
Honoré, Russel, 238
hope, 275
Horton, Willie, 11–12
Hoyer, Steny, 186
Hu Yaobang, 25
Huang, John, 113
Huckabee, Mike, 260, 264, 265
Hume, Brit, 86
Hungary, 28, 232
Hurricane Katrina, 237–241
Hussein, Saddam, 40, 43, 44, 89, 117
    and Al Quaeda, 176
    capture, 208
    need for force against, 178
    record of terror, 179–180
    and UN weapons inspection, 124–125
    views on danger of, 188
    weapons program, 179

I

illegal immigration, 233
    reform plan, 246
    reform plan, Bush and, 247
iMacs, 134
Index of Leading Cultural Indicators, 108
Indian tribes, lobbying fees from, 236
information-based economy, shift to, 55
integrated circuits, 133

INDEX

Top *New York Times* Best-selling Author

WILLIAM J. BENNETT

THE IDEAL GIFT

Two great American books and an exclusive CD celebrating
the great American Ronald Reagan *all in one*

Chronicling the *American Story* from the Age of
Discovery to a World at War and the Triumph of Freedom.

365
Reasons to Love America

THE AMERICAN PATRIOT'S ALMANAC

WILLIAM J. BENNETT & JOHN T. E. CRIBB

Here is America day-by-day. Discover a year's worth of history, heroes, and achievements that sum up what this nation is all about.

* Military heroes such as Nathan Hale and the Navajo Code Talkers
* Medal of Honor winners such as recently honored Lt. Michael Murphy in Afghanistan
* Famous American women, including Abigail Adams, Mary Todd Lincoln, and more
* Patriotic symbols such as Uncle Sam and the Liberty Bell
* Civil rights heroes such as Frederick Douglass and Martin Luther King, Jr.
* Heroes of exploration like Zebulon Pike and Lewis & Clark
* Inventors like Alexander Graham Bell and the Wright brothers
* Famous speeches by our presidents and other historic leaders
* Sports icons such as Jesse Owens and Lou Gehrig
* Famous immigrants such as Bob Hope and Andrew Carnegie
* 50 All-American movies
* Poems, founding documents, songs, and prayers

From the author who brought you
the *New York Times* Bestselling books
America: The Last Best Hope vol I & II.

To learn how to use these volumes in your school by visiting
www.RoadmapToLastBestHope.com

THOMAS NELSON
Since 1798

www.thomasnelson.com
Available wherever books are sold

AMERICA
THE LAST BEST HOPE

Join author William J. Bennett and students and teachers across the country in reading *America: The Last Best Hope*, the story of America written as drama, romance, comedy, mystery, action, yes the tragedies, and yes the triumphs.

Dr. Bennett's partners, a group of nationally recognized educators called Team HOPE (History Opens Eyes), joined together because they believe that *America: The Last Best Hope* and the online companion curriculum materials, called the Roadmap, have the potential to shape the future of history education, improving both attitudes and achievement.

Team HOPE consists of author Dr. William J. Bennett, five recipients of the Milken Educator Award (www.mff.org), and Thomas Nelson Publishing. Their vision is curriculum adoptions, *Last Best Hope* in school libraries, American History teachers reading *Last Best Hope* to inform their instruction, college professors teaching survey courses with *Last Best Hope*, and homeschool parents using *Last Best Hope* for their curriculum. In essence, this generation will be learning American History through *Last Best Hope*, a balanced, comprehensive, narrative about our country's people and events.

Visit **www.roadmaptolastbesthope.com** for more information and ordering options for schools and homeschools. There is no time like the present to get excited and knowledgeable about the past.